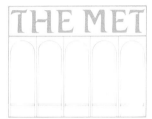

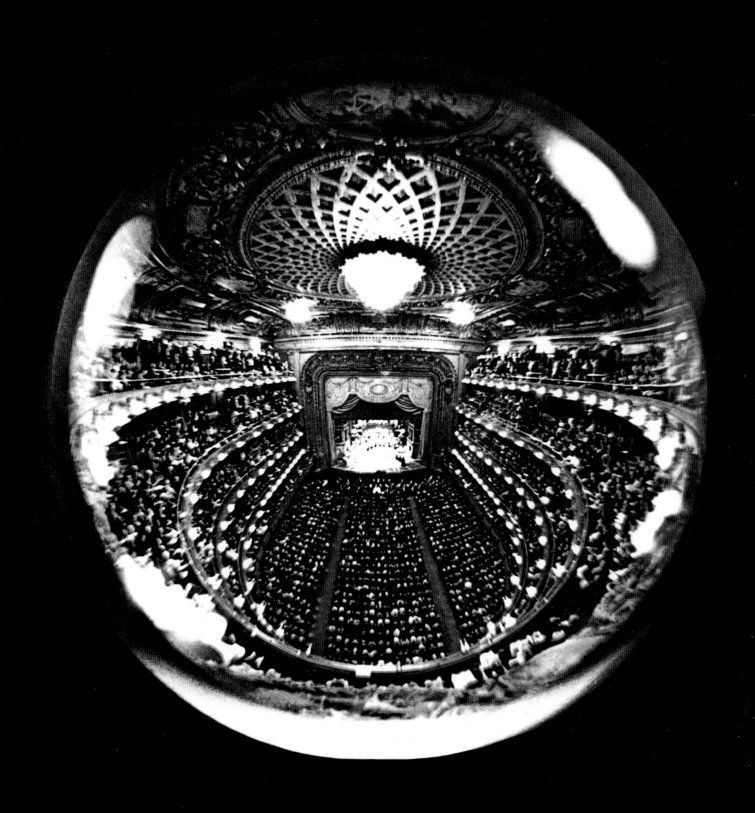

MARTIN MAYER

THE MET

ONE HUNDRED YEARS OF GRAND OPERA

PICTURE EDITOR: GERALD FITZGERALD

WITH 212 ILLUSTRATIONS IN DUOTONE,
AND 41 IN COLOUR

THAMES AND HUDSON

In memory of Eleanor Robson Belmont,
without whose ministrations the Met on so many occasions
would have died or (worse) lost its soul

This publication was conceived and created by
The Metropolitan Opera Guild in collaboration with
Thames and Hudson Ltd

© 1983 Thames and Hudson Ltd, London

Printed and bound in Japan by Dai Nippon

CONTENTS

ACKNOWLEDGMENTS 6

ONE

THE AUDIENCE, ITS THEATER AND ITS OPERA 9

TWO

STAR SEASONS 33

THREE

MILESTONES I: 25TH ANNIVERSARY. THE JOYS AND PAINS,
THE POLITICS AND PERSONALITIES OF A GREAT SEASON 81

FOUR

CARUSO AND THE GATTI MACHINE 115

FIVE

MILESTONES II: THE FIFTIETH ANNIVERSARY.
DELIGHTS AMIDST DESPAIR 165

SIX

KIRSTEN FLAGSTAD AND THE AMERICAN YEARS 195

SEVEN

MILESTONES III: THE SEVENTY-FIFTH ANNIVERSARY SEASON.
MR. BING IN CHARGE 231

EIGHT

VALE ATQUE AVE: THE MOVE TO LINCOLN CENTER 263

NINE

NEW HOUSE, NEW ERA 297

TEN

THE TENTH DECADE, THE SECOND CENTURY 327

NOTES ON THE TEXT 359

SOURCES OF ILLUSTRATIONS 361

INDEX 363

ACKNOWLEDGMENTS

This book draws heavily on the long labors of the late Mary Ellis Peltz, who with the help of many volunteers founded, catalogued, and maintained the archives of the Metropolitan Opera. This astonishing treasure-trove of material, much of which has never before been accessible to a historian of the opera, was made available to me because the Metropolitan Opera Association desired that this volume fairly represent the first hundred years of the company. Robert A. Tuggle, Mrs. Peltz's successor as archivist, has been of immense help in guiding me through the archive's riches.

The extracts in these pages from directors' minutes, committee reports, internal memoranda, and the like are taken from material in the archives, as are most of the letters. Quotations without specific references in the Notes on the Text are from the author's interviews with Sir Rudolf Bing, Anthony A. Bliss, Schuyler G. Chapin, John Gutman, Erich Leinsdorf, James Levine, Max Rudolf, Marilyn Shapiro, Risë Stevens, Frank E. Taplin, and the late Max de Schauensee, and from videotaped interviews by Kirk Browning with George Cehanovsky, Jerome Hines, Leinsdorf, and Miss Stevens. I am grateful to them all and to the (literally) hundreds of artists and others I have interviewed over more than thirty years of musical journalism, to the many who helped while I was working with Rudolf Bing on the first volume of his memoirs, and to Max Rudolf for permission to quote several pages from his own unpublished recollections.

I am obliged also to good friends: to Harold C. Schonberg of the *New York Times* and Martin Feinstein of the Washington Opera, with whom I have had the happy chance of arguing many of these cases over many years; to Edgar Vincent, who has educated so many of us on both sides of the footlights; to Rudolf Bing for the companionship of our time in collaboration; to Julius and Rita Rudel, Maurice Abravanel, Judith Raskin, and Beverly Sills; to Patrick J. Smith and David Hamilton; Frank Merkling, Robert Jacobson, and C. J. Luten of *Opera News*; to Al Hubay; to Dorle and the late Dario Soria, and to others sadly departed—John Coveney, Anne Gordon, Francis Robinson.

The New York Historical Society, the New York Public Library, and the New York Society Library have provided access to printed material both commonplace and rare. Quotations from newspapers subsequent to the 1908–09 season have been taken by the author from the books of press cuttings in the archives or from William H. Seltsam's *Metropolitan Opera Annals*; those from the first season were found at the New York Public Library by Gary Lipton, who also gleaned nuggets from the fashionable publications of the early years and uncovered letters to and from personages of the opera in the library of the Museum of the City of New York, Columbia University, Yale University, and the files of the law firm of Cravath, Swaine, and Moore.

Everyone who works in this field owes a debt to Irving Kolodin, whose pioneering history of the Met, first published in 1936 and periodically revised and updated, remains a vade mecum to all who enter the maze. Gerald Fitzgerald, for over a quarter of a century an editor for *Opera News*, has of course been much more than a picture editor for this volume. He and Robert Tuggle have read and commented very helpfully on the chapters as they emerged from the typewriter. So—necessarily—has the book's instigator and editor, Roland Gelatt, who brought to the task some forty years of operagoing, and experience as a critic as well as an editor. He also wrote the excellent captions. Mrs. Theodor Uppman found and corrected some errors in spellings and dates – and defended some accuracies from challenge.

I am grateful also for many courtesies from David M. Reuben, press director of the Metropolitan Opera and his associate Johanna Fiedler, and from Geoff Peterson, managing director of the Metropolitan Opera Guild, who commissioned this volume and took the risk of letting it be my book.

I first met Mrs. August Belmont, to whose memory this book is dedicated, when she was over 90 years old. We lunched at her club. That evening, when I described the experience to my wife, she said, "I never thought I would be jealous of a woman 90 years old. . . ."

MARTIN MAYER
New York, February 1983

ONE

THE AUDIENCE,
ITS THEATER AND ITS OPERA

Part of the definition of a great city is that it has an opera house. Baron Haussmann set Charles Garnier's opulent Opéra at the center of the grand boulevards he cut through Paris for Louis Napoleon. In Vienna, the Court Opera was implanted on the great Ring that replaced the city's walls. When the Sultan of Turkey decided that the infidels of Europe were there to stay, he erected a wooden "O" of an opera house above the Golden Horn. The exuberant gold miners of the American West and the ambitious settlers of the upper Amazon built their opera houses, the earliest of their public structures, as a necessary statement that there was more to life than making money.

From its beginnings in the palaces of Italian dukes, opera was the princely art form, an occasion for social gatherings. Attendance at the opera was, until very recent years, the preferred way of showing off a woman's jewels and costumes and hair-dos, of demonstrating by the excellence of one's place in the theater the rank one had achieved in society.

But there was always something more than that, for opera was also, uniquely, both a popular and an intellectual art form, a visceral experience for its audience, a collaborative challenge for its authors and performers. "An exotic and irrational entertainment," Dr. Johnson said, expressing an Anglo-Saxon disapproval, and the ledger recording the moneys advanced for the production of opera in the first season at the Metropolitan carried the heading "Amusement Account." Many Americans felt that the emotions roused by operatic performance were dangerously beyond the pale of propriety. *Rigoletto* was banned in Boston and *Traviata* in Brooklyn long before *Salome* created its more famous scandal at the Met; and when the soprano Clara Louise Kellogg appeared in the New York premiere of *Faust* in 1863, her friends were horrified by her participation in so improper a presentation.

Opera singers were the original matinee idols, their comings and goings chronicled on the front pages of the newspapers, with special interest in evidence—sometimes forthcoming—of extraordinary sexual energy. They traveled at the expense of impresarios with retinues of family and servants (it was not unusual for a

Earliest photo of the old Met, looking north up Broadway to Longacre (now Times) Square. "A more unsightly, ungraceful place I never saw," wrote a columnist in the New York *Dramatic Mirror*.

contract at the Metropolitan Opera to provide ocean passage *aller-et-retour* for as many as five members of a prima donna's party); they stayed at the very best suites of the very best hotels (also often at the expense of the impresario); they came to rehearsals dressed by the world's most renowned couturiers (the men, too, formally attired: the critic W. J. Henderson left an account of a *Tristan* rehearsal at which Jean de Reszke wore a morning coat and bowler hat, which he doffed to accept instruction from conductor Anton Seidl); they left the theater after performances through crowds of idolators gathered at the stage door.

But opera was also the center of artistic revolution, as Monteverdi, Lully, Gluck, Mozart, Weber, Berlioz, Wagner, Debussy, and Berg broke with the traditions of their time in the interest of emotional expression. And because opera was deliberately, almost from its beginnings, "spectacular"—an art form where real horses pranced onto the stage—it was the seedbed of new stagecraft, from the hidden mechanical contrivances and muscle power of the Palladian stage to the electronic marvels of today.

Nowhere was opera more popular than in New York, where as early as the 1840s there might be as many as four theaters in use as opera houses, one of them the 1,800-seat Astor Place Theater. In 1852–53, there was opera every month of the year, at the Astor Place, Niblo's Gardens, Castle Garden in the Battery, or the Broadway Theater. On one evening in early 1853, the New York operagoer had a choice between Marietta Alboni's first *Sonnambula* and Henriette Sontag's New York debut in *La Fille du régiment*. New operas that had won audiences in Europe were heard in New York within a year or two of their premieres. It was New York's first Golden Age of Opera. The historian George Odell, whose experience included the 1900–20 years we now consider so resplendent, wrote of the period that "New York had heard Bosio, Salvi, Badiali, Marini, Lind, and the little Patti; and now here was Alboni. We of later decades can but envy auditors so richly blest as those of 1852."

The Academy of Music on 14th Street near Union Square opened in 1854, and remained the city's leading opera house for almost thirty years. Walt Whitman was often in the audience to hear *Ernani*, one of his favorites. "With the rise of the curtain," he wrote of Verdi's early opera, "you are transported afar—such power has music. You behold the mountains of Aragon, and the bandits in their secure retreats, feasting, drinking, gambling, and singing. And such singing, and such an instrumental accompaniment! Their wild, rollicking spirits pour themselves out in that opening chorus. . . ." Replying to a criticism of *Leaves of Grass*, Whitman said that his "method in the construction of his songs is strictly the method of Italian Opera."

But the Academy of Music had other purposes too: it was here that the fledgling New York Philharmonic played; and here that the financier August H. Belmont staged a gala in honor of his father-in-law, Commodore Matthew Perry, and the first

The Academy of Music on 14th Street had only eighteen boxes, nine on either side of the proscenium. Its president was August H. Belmont (*below left*); its great star, Adelina Patti (*below right*, costumed as Rosina in Rossini's *Barbiere*).

party of Japanese visitors to American shores; and here that New York society, ignoring the ongoing election that would produce the Lincoln presidency and the Civil War, organized a grand ball to welcome the eighteen-year-old Prince of Wales.

It was this Belmont who later put the operations of the Academy of Music on a stable footing. He was an aggressively entrepreneurial German (the name was a Frenchification of Schönberg), who walked with a limp from an old duelling wound and represented the Rothschild interests in the United States. Taking over the presidency of the Academy in 1878, he solicited Colonel James Henry Mapleson to lease the house for the performance of opera on a regular, annual basis; in 1880, Mapleson signed a five-year contract to provide four months of opera a year, renting the house for $175 a night with a guarantee against losses by the Academy stockholders should box-office receipts prove insufficient to pay the estimated bills.

An Englishman who had played violin and sung tenor roles under an Italian name before becoming an impresario (the Colonelcy derived from a unit of London militia, and was the British equivalent of Kentucky's), Mapleson became first of all the proprietor of Adelina Patti, a bel canto soprano of warm voice and precise intonation who was the greatest box-office draw since Jenny Lind. Sometimes Mapleson was flush with money, and sometimes he was a step ahead of the sheriff. At the end of the first season in which the Academy faced competition from the new Metropolitan Opera, Belmont and his board had to pick up a $24,000 bank debt Mapleson had left behind, trusting his "honor" to repay the stockholders. A theatrical journal suggested that "perhaps the 'Colonel's' honor is securely locked up in the safe at the Academy, or more likely he has left it at home in England for fear that it might suffer injury at the hands of his ruthless creditors in this country."

Mapleson ran touring companies around the world featuring Patti's services (for which, taught by experience, she insisted on being paid in gold before the curtain rose), but his base was England. "Being the lessee of the Opera in London," Belmont wrote, explaining his choice to his friend Levi P. Morton, former Vice President of the United States, "he has the control of a powerful company with the best talent of Europe . . . Our people will rush and pay liberally for celebrities and good artists."

The new management improved attendance at—and attention to—opera at the Academy. On the nights when Patti appeared, the demand for good seats— particularly for places in the three tiers of boxes in the proscenium, where the occupants were part of the show the audience paid to watch—far exceeded the supply. There were only 18 boxes. It was a subject of great annoyance to some of the wealthiest men in New York that their wives were denied the possibility of display in the Academy's boxes because the old "Knickerbocker" aristocracy of the city had first call on these places. "The world of fashion," as Edith Wharton put it some years later, "was still content to reassemble every winter in the shabby red and gold boxes of the sociable old Academy. Conservatives cherished it for being small and inconvenient, and thus keeping out the 'new people'."

The German soprano Lilli Lehmann, who first came to New York after the demise of the Academy as an opera house, was told that one specific incident had stimulated these "new people" to build their own house. She recounted the story later: "As on a particular evening, one of the beautiful millionairesses did not receive the box in which she intended to shine because another beautiful woman had anticipated her, the husband of the former took prompt action and caused the Metropolitan Opera House to arise, wherein his beloved wife might dazzle." The world is a little more complicated than that, for New York's vanity also wanted what Wharton called "a new Opera House which should compete in costliness and splendor with those of the great European capitals." But it seems likely that some episode involving a Vanderbilt sparked the movement to build a new opera house, for it was George Henry Warren, the Vanderbilt lawyer, who summoned the first meeting for that purpose—and who then negotiated fruitlessly with a concerned Belmont on the Academy's offer to add 26 boxes if the new people would refrain from building a new house. But the added boxes would necessarily be inferior to the old in prominence before the public, so the offer was refused.

The guiding spirits of the new Metropolitan Opera House project were the doers of the city, the Morgans and the Vanderbilts, the people who were changing the face of the nation's finance and industry, but the six incorporators on April 10, 1880, also included representatives of the landed gentry. (Among them were Robert and Ogden Goelet, descended from 17th-century Huguenot pilgrims, who owned much of the midtown East Side of New York and whose descendants a hundred years later still served significantly on the boards of the Metropolitan Opera, the American Museum of Natural History, and other cultural institutions.) Most of the proposed stockholders in the new Metropolitan Opera, in fact, had been stockholders in the Academy, which had ten times as many stockholders as there were boxes.

By April 20, the founding group had 60 commitments to purchase boxes in a new theater, each box representing 100 shares of stock at $100 each. The hope was that the new theater would be self-supporting from rentals of the auditorium and the shops that would be built along the perimeter, so that the boxholders would have no expenses other than their initial investment. Some thought that they would pay an admission charge to the events they wished to attend (as the stockholders did at the Academy and at Covent Garden in London); others expected that by purchasing a box they would be entitled to free entertainment at the new opera house at all times.

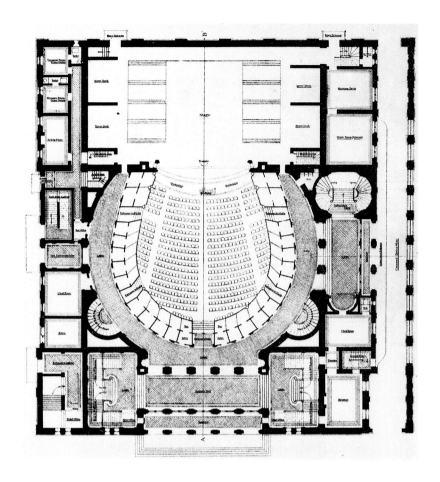

ELEVATION on FORTY THIRD ST

SECTION THROUGH FOYER and LOBBY on LINE C·D

Competitive Design for the

METROPOLITAN OPERA HOUSE.

NEW YORK, N.Y.

The site of the proposed theater was to be across the street from Grand Central Station—not then the imposing structure built in the early years of the 20th century by Carrère & Hastings—on a block 190 × 200 feet fronting what was already called Vanderbilt Avenue. (Later the plot was used for the Biltmore Hotel; still later, for the international headquarters of the Bank of America.) It was owned by William H. Vanderbilt's Harlem Rail Road Company, and would be made available for the new opera house at a bargain price of $300,000. A Committee on Building, chaired by Egisto P. Fabbri, a Morgan partner of Italian birth, was appointed to investigate the likely cost of an opera house on that site. Fabbri reported back within a month on his "preliminary examination":

The Opera Houses in Europe especially those lately built are noted for the perfection of their interior arrangements and of everything affecting acoustics, stage property, comfort, ventilation and safety, and before any plans should be adopted by us they should be carefully examined and reported upon.

Without any positive knowledge as to their actual cost, it is well known that they have been constructed, mostly, at Government expense and at enormous outlay.

There is no Theater or Opera House in this country that can be taken as a model for what we intend to have.

In order, however, to arrive at some idea of the cost of the proposed building, it may answer to take as a basis the Opera House in Philadelphia [The Philadelphia Academy of Music, still very much in use], which is, perhaps, the best building we have of the kind. It was erected in 1855–57 at a cost of nearly $300,000. If we should be satisfied to reproduce such a structure here owing to the increased cost of labor and material besides the greater expense in New York over Philadelphia in building enterprises, its cost would be fully 50% larger, say $450,000, and as that building is not fire proof, the necessary expenditure for this purpose should be added, as we deem it of first importance that the building should be fire proof . . .

Sundry conversations had with people conversant with such kind of undertakings also tend to convince us that we shall find as we proceed unavoidably increased expenditure over the most liberal estimates we may obtain. As Trustees of other people's money, we certainly cannot afford experiments in dealing with so serious an undertaking, and we therefore recommend either that more subscriptions to the Stock be obtained, or that the $600,000 be devoted for the purpose of the erection of the building, and that the cost of the land remain on mortgage.

This report was accepted, and Fabbri's committee was sent off with a maximum budget of $5,000 to get competitive designs for an opera house, with rough cost estimates, from the city's best architects. Four such accepted the offer of $1,000 to pay their expenses in preparing designs, elevations, and sketches, and they presented their results, each under a pseudonym, in September 1880. A lengthy description of one of the losing designs, by the architects themselves, appeared that fall in the *American Architect and Building News*:

The Metropolitan Opera House that never got built. Plans for an auditorium at Vanderbilt Avenue and 43rd Street had to be scrapped because of financial problems over the site.

The plan of the auditorium of La Scala has been pronounced as the most perfect in existence, and it has been upon the proportions of that auditorium that the one shown in the accompanying plans has been designed . . .

In the treatment and arrangement of the boxes, balconies and gallery, the method employed in the new opera house at Paris [the Palais Garnier] has been followed . . . There are eighty-five boxes in all . . . The stalls are arranged for arm-chairs, similar to those used in London . . . A bar and smoking-room is provided under the main entrance hall . . . The grand foyer and the salons in connection with it, which form the suite of assembly rooms, have been placed on a level with the first or middle tier of boxes . . .

The orchestra has been dropped below the floor of the auditorium and partly under the stage, in the manner in which it was arranged in the Bayreuth Theater, built for the production of Wagner's operas . . .

It is rather sad that so clever a sales piece did not win the assignment for its authors, but their proposal, submitted under the name "In Me mea spes omnis," was the first rejected, for six reasons:

First. Cost.
Second. It does not meet the requirements of Mr. William K. Vanderbilt as to height of the building on the side of Vanderbilt Avenue.
Third. The extreme height of the building.
Fourth. The inconvenient location of the Assembly-Rooms and Ante-Rooms.
Fifth. The Bar-room underneath the Assembly Room being situated in the least desirable corner of the building, namely Forty-Fourth Street and Vanderbilt Avenue.
Sixth. The small number of available stores.

What was accepted was a proposal from Josiah Cleaveland Cady, architect of several churches, hospitals, university classroom buildings, and the American Museum of Natural History, who said he could build a house with 117 boxes and a seating capacity of about 3,200, for $430,000. It was Cady's first and last theater. Submitted under the name "Lyre," his design was seen as offering five advantages:

First. The smaller cost.
Second. The more perfectly fire proof character of the building.
Third. The greater number of available stores.
Fourth. The more convenient arrangement of the building for purposes other than that of the Opera House.
Fifth. The more careful and convenient distribution of the space outside of the stage and auditorium for the general purposes of the theater.

Through all the vicissitudes of the succeeding three years, Cady remained the architect of the company, and his design retained its essential form: a long, deep horseshoe, with an orchestra floor of about 600 seats (the "parquet"), three tiers of

Four of the Met's founding fathers: (*l. to r.*) William H. Vanderbilt, Robert Goelet, Ogden Goelet, James A. Roosevelt. Below them, some of the society ladies who attended opening night in 1883, seen in their costumes for the Vanderbilt Ball earlier that year: Mrs. Cornelius Vanderbilt II, Mrs. Luther Kountze, and Mrs. William K. Vanderbilt.

boxes, a balcony and a second balcony (the "Family Circle") rising above, for a grand total of 3,045 seats. Everything except the flooring and the doors to the alcoves of the boxes was to be built of iron inside thick masonry walls, to minimize the danger of fire in what was still (though channels for later wiring were provided) a gas-lit auditorium and stage. Every box would have its own small anteroom where the occupants could hang their cloaks and retire at will from the auditorium. The stage would be shallow—less deep than any of the major theaters in Europe—with a large rectangular apron (directly accessible from backstage through doors at the ends) slashed in a straight line before the proscenium.

Cady's approach to the job was revealed four years after the theater opened, in an article he wrote for *The American Architect*. He noted then that an opera house served three purposes—musical, dramatic, and social. The expense of producing opera was such that subsidy was required. In Europe, that subsidy came from Government; in America, "where the Government is not 'paternal'," it had to come from

the wealthy, fashionable classes, who, even if not caring especially for, nor appreciating deeply the music, find it a peculiar and valuable social feature.

Its boxes afford a rare opportunity for the display of beauty and toilette.

They also give opportunity for the informal exchange of social courtesies, being open to selected callers through the evening; the long waits between the acts especially favoring such interchange.

If at any time the box is not needed, the tender of it to friends is a very handsome compliment . . .

The social feature is so important in a financial way that it naturally is the foundation of any enterprise of this kind, and in no small degree determines the size and character of the house . . .

As the incorporators of Lincoln Center were to learn in their turn over eighty years later, the building of opera houses and music centers is not a task for the faint-hearted. The first difficulty the proprietors of the putative Metropolitan Opera House had to face was the loss of their site. It turned out to be encumbered by covenants with two of the city's churches, whose vestries were not delighted at the idea of a place of entertainment on their land, and in any event wished to be paid. On December 30, 1880, the Board of Directors met at the Morgan offices and approved an anguished letter to William H. Vanderbilt:

The Committee on "Site" of the Board of Directors of the Metropolitan Opera Co. Limited find that the restrictions of the 43rd St. lots can be removed for about $65,000, and beg to ask you whether, under all the circumstances of the offer and purchase, their plans drawn and approved by you and subscriptions taken on your promise of the lot, you will pay the necessary sum (or, if not all, what portion) to clear the title and enable the Managers to proceed to erect the Opera House in accordance with the accepted plans.

Should you refuse to do this, there is but one other available site, and the Committee have thoroughly examined all land offering.

That site is the S.E. corner of Park Avenue and 34th St. [where the Vanderbilt Hotel was later erected] and they would be pleased to have you name your *very lowest* price for that plot, 200 feet on Park Avenue by 225 or 250 feet on 33rd and 34th Sts. . . .

Failing one of these sites the Committee fear the New Opera House will have to be abandoned after all the trouble and expense already incurred, and with every prospect of success if completed.

Trusting your interest in the Opera will cause you to give our suggestions a favorable consideration . . .

But the trust was misplaced: Vanderbilt had given all he felt like giving. Within ten days, the Site Committee had a new site: most of the block from 39th to 40th Streets, Broadway to Seventh Avenue, just south of Longacre Square (which would become Times Square). This site was available for $450,500, and its width of 145 feet was considered just barely adequate, the average depth of the trapezoidal block being 245 feet. Even before the board could meet at Delmonico's Restaurant in January 1881 to consider this proposal, Site Committee chairman James Alfred Roosevelt had made contact with the owners of the rest of the block, and found that the entirety, with an average dimension of 198 × 260 feet, could be purchased for $605,000.

The initial budget had called for expenditures of $910,000—$300,000 for land, $430,000 for structure, $55,000 for taxes and interest during the construction phase, $25,000 for architects' fees, $10,000 for petty expenses, $20,000 for a music library, and a total of $70,000 for costumes and scenery for twenty operas. With land at $605,000, the budget would rise by $305,000 to $1,215,000. After much debate, the board agreed to double their expenditures for the land, leaving a hope that some part of the site not needed for the theater could be sold off, and to notify subscribers to the stock that "the cost of a box in the Opera House will be nearer $15,000 than $10,000, and that they be requested to Communicate their willingness to pay the increased cost through the Secretary, or their desire to withdraw their Subscriptions."

The subscribers came through; indeed, the board was able to sell 70 boxes at $15,000 each, providing an equity base of $1.05 million. On March 4, 1881, the directors gave a go-ahead, with fall 1882 set for opening night. Cady made a tour of European houses to improve his plans, and workmen began to demolish buildings on the site. Some of the storekeepers in the buildings got injunctions against eviction before their one- to three-year leases had expired. The Met had bought the land from a Roger Monoghan, who died, leaving questions about possession in the hands of the Surrogate's Court. Parts of the site could not be excavated until October.

Overleaf: For the architect Josiah Cleaveland Cady (*inset*), "the social feature in no small degree determines the size and character of the house." The prominence accorded the boxes is evident in his floor plan (*right*). Cady's elevations for the Broadway and 40th Street façades (*left*) look somewhat more attractive than their embodiment in yellow brick.

FRONT VIEW, ON BROADWAY.

METROPOLITAN OPERA HOUSE
AND
IMPROVEMENT COMPANY'S BUILDINGS
FORTIETH STREET ELEVATION
J. CLEAVELAND CADY, ARCHITECT.
N.Y.

PARTERRE
36 BOXES

101' 0"

Dressing Room

Dressing Room

Dressing Room

Green Room

Scene Room

Male Chorus

Male Chorus

Balcony Stairs

Auditory Stairs

Office

Office

Upper part of Vestibule

Corridor

Office

Office

Ladies Room

Toilet

Light Well

Hall

Anti Room

Reception Room

Vestibule

Vestibule

Scene Room

Female Chorus

Hall

Toilet

Air Shaft

Female Chorus

Female Chorus

Upper part of Vestibule

Corridor

Balcony Stairs

Auditory Stairs

Light Well

Sewing Room

Case

Hall

Light Well

Ladies Toilet

Ladies Parlor

Passage

Gents Toilet

Closet

Upper part of Hall

Upper part of Restaurant

Vestibule

Upper part of Vestibule

V

METROPOLITAN OPERA HOUSE
AND
IMPROVEMENT COMPANY'S BUILDINGS
INTERMEDIATE STORY
J. CLEAVELAND CADY, ARCHITECT.
N.Y.

"During this interval," the Committee on Building reported in a document printed for distribution to all stockholders in February 1882,

in view of the advance that had taken place in the price of materials and labor (which at the time appeared to the best informed, unreasonable) it was deemed in the interest of the enterprise to go on by day's work, building the foundations only, in the hope that in the Fall when all the specifications could be got ready, prices would have receded to more reasonable limits . . . Later on, when it was found that no decline was likely to occur and that even at heavy extra expense, working nights, etc., the building could not be completed in time for the next Fall Operatic Season, it was decided . . . to continue the work on the foundations as economically as possible until full and reliable estimates and bids for the work to be performed could be obtained. Now that these bids have been received, the total amount so far exceeds the corrected estimates which were made when the site was changed, and is so much in excess of the money still left subject to call . . . that the Committee do not feel justified in proceeding further without definite instructions from the Board . . .

Cady's initial estimate of $430,000 for the structure had risen to a bid estimate of $830,000. The architect offered a Question and Answer section in the pamphlet, on why costs had risen so:

Each part of the building is so varied and so complex, and the whole such a large structure, that plans and specifications involved an immense amount of labor and thought. If it had been merely mechanical, it might have been given to a large corps of assistants, but all had to be carefully laid out and guided, and this of course could be done but by a few.

Take the iron work for instance:

It is estimated that there are nearly three millions of pounds of iron in the building, or over one hundred thousand separate pieces of iron, or, excluding bolts, plates, brackets, etc., about 16,000 beams, channels, rods or other constructional pieces. The greater part of these had to be thought over and designed separately for their respective work and positions, each one forming a distinct calculation by itself . . .

Since last spring labor and materials have advanced from 20 to 50 per cent, and in some cases more. Besides this, the labor market has been so feverish, the trades-unions having obtained entire control, that all contractors not only figure ON *the above rise* in labor and materials, but BEYOND that, they have to allow heavy margins for possible future troubles . . .

An attentive reading of the figures presented in the report reveals, though the text did not highlight it, that $711,000 had already been spent. If the project were abandoned at this point, that money would have to be recovered—which was possible, but by no means certain—from the resale of the real estate or its use for apartment buildings. Having put as good a face as he could on the matter in his report, Fabbri—as chairman of the Committee on Building—gave the board his personal recommendation that the company should quit:

At the meeting at Delmonico's . . . it was . . . acknowledged that no enterprise of this character can prosper if handicapped with a heavy debt, or indeed with any debt at all . . .

Special pains were taken to have shops and accommodation for balls and private entertainments to provide an income towards the payment of taxes, Fire Insurance, Janitors wages, and petty Expenses of repairs.

That provision was not made with a view to secure a dividend to the stockholders but to endeavor to prevent as much as possible the Co. from running in debt even for these comparatively small fixed charges.

The Experience of every Impressario [*sic*] in Europe and in this Country almost uniformly shows that as a rule such business is unprofitable and hazardous, and I know that the Company will find it necessary to offer at least its building free of rent to induce a reliable Impressario to undertake the arduous task of furnishing us and the public with satisfactory operatic performances.

Whence then is the money to come from to pay the interest on such a vast debt as must be incurred to complete the building and to acquire those accessories without which the Institution could not be considered complete?

. . . In view of the fact that in my judgment $15,000 per box is already a very large sum for the privilege that a Stockholder secures thereby, and that more could not be obtained, or reasonably asked for the same, I have reluctantly but deliberately come to the conclusion . . . that the project should be given up.

The stockholders voted by a narrow margin, however, to borrow from the Bowery Savings Bank and finish up, letting the future pay the debts. Fabbri resigned as Treasurer and Chairman of the Building Committee—though he remained a boxholder and paid the additional $2,500 required from each subscriber. When the corner plots proved unsalable at anything like the price the board set on them, the Metropolitan Opera Company itself decided to build apartments for profit, flanking the Broadway front of the theater. In the end, the Treasurer reported the cost of the theater as $1,732,978.71. The 70 boxholders put up $17,500 each for their privileges, and $600,000 was borrowed from Bowery at 5 per cent interest on the security of the land.

☆ ☆ ☆

Few singers were as important to the success of the Metropolitan Opera in its first quarter-century as was one of the boxholders—Caroline Astor, the lady whose annual ball for her 400 defined the high society of the city. Mrs. Astor decreed that appearance at the opera, at precisely 9 o'clock each Monday in season, was the proper thing to do before supper. For the ticket buyers, it was definitely part of the show to watch the lavishly bejeweled Mrs. Astor enter her box wearing the diamond stomacher that reputedly had belonged to Marie Antoinette, the variety and brilliance of her diamonds and emeralds giving her, as her friend Harry Lehr said, the appearance of a walking chandelier.

For two generations, both the boxholders themselves and the New York press placed great emphasis on the social aspect of the Metropolitan Opera. "SOCIETY

HEARS AND APPLAUDS TRISTAN," was the headline of the front-page notice in the New York *Herald* of the incandescent performance by Olive Fremstad, Erik Schmedes, Louise Homer, and Fritz Feinhals that Gustav Mahler, its conductor, considered among the greatest of his life; and more than half the space in the review was given to detailing the occupants of the boxes and what they wore.

The boxes at the Metropolitan Opera, like those of the Academy it displaced, were in the hands of a very exclusive club—especially after the reorganization that followed the fire of 1892, when the number of boxholders (and thus stockholders) was reduced to 35. Though the owners of the boxes did not get their opera free of charge—each box carried an annual assessment that rose from $1,200 in the first season to $4,500 in the 1930s—they were in fact owners, their names on brass plaques on the corridor doors, and other people could sit in their boxes only at their invitation.

While Cady was right in his comment that offering your box to a friend was "a handsome compliment," there was also an element of burden. "The opera comes so often," Alice Duer Miller lamented in *Harper's Bazaar* in 1908. "We should not think of giving a dinner party once, twice, or three times a week during the entire season, yet on a small scale that is what the owner of a box is forced to do . . . If a dinner party begins to go wrong, you can let it go—have a cold, and recall your invitations, but you cannot leave your box empty." To avoid such embarrassments and reduce the expense of annual assessments, the boxes (and the stocks and assessments and publicity associated with them) came increasingly to be shared among friends or members of a family. Each such division was subject to specific approval by the board of directors elected by the boxholders. Other boxholders knew a trick more profitable than sharing: they began renting their boxes for cash, usually on a one-night-per-week basis for the season. To make sure the social value of one box was not demeaned by having unworthy people renting other boxes, these rentals too were controlled by the board, who vetted the suitability of the tenants and fixed the price that could be charged—usually at a level roughly double the assessment allocated pro rata.

Some of the boxholders and some of their guests were unquestionably less interested in the opera than in the social distinction of being in a box at the Met. They cherished long intermissions during which they "received" in their boxes or the anterooms associated with them. Refreshments were available from opening night, when each of the anterooms was supplied with a menu from Mazette on Sixth Avenue, offering what the New York *Mirror* described as "all sorts of ices, creams, punches, wines, etc., etc.," with an order card that could be given to an attendant. Some boxholders liked to see the house lights partly on during a performance so they could examine each other. During an indulgent period of the late 1880s, when the owners of the house were directly in charge of the performances, a bitter laugh from the parquet greeted Florestan's recitative complaining of the dungeon darkness at the beginning of the second act of *Fidelio*. Every season saw moments of scandal when talk or even laughter from the boxes or their anterooms fell painfully on the ears of an audience that cared what it was hearing.

One school of thought held that it was impossible in the conditions of American life in the 19th century to build a cultivated audience for opera. "America," Henry T. Finck of the New York *Evening Post* wrote in 1888,

has plenty of poor loafers but few wealthy *rentiers* who spend their days in bed or in idleness and are therefore insatiable in their appetite for entertainment in the evening. The typical American works hard all day long, whether he is rich or poor, and in the evening his brain is too tired to follow for four hours the complicated orchestra score of a music drama.

And the men who owned the theater were not the producers of the opera: they merely leased the premises to impresarios. The dichotomy between the real estate operation and the opera itself was an invitation to the critics to contrast philistinism in high places against whatever art could be discerned on stage. Moreover, in a city where more than half the population had been born abroad, the audience for specific performances was greatly influenced by the national origins of the opera: the gallery was full of what were considered unwashed Italians on one night, and sausage-stuffed Germans on another, both (but especially the Italians) giving a supercilious press openings for derisive comment.

But the fact was that the great majority of both plutocrats and commoners came to the opera house because they cared about opera—and knew something about it too. Many members of the board of the real estate company were world travelers, linked to Europe by business interests, informed to a degree about what was going on in the opera houses of London, Berlin, Paris, Milan, and even St. Petersburg. And before the arrival of Giulio Gatti-Casazza as general manager in 1908, the impresarios who leased the house were all theater people and operatic amateurs. It is not unreasonable to believe that the board played a significant role in establishing the company's vocal standards as well as its social standards.

They even had views on the operas they wanted to hear. When Belmont offered the Academy to Mapleson, he suggested no fewer than 28 works the impresario might consider for his season, an interesting list that included *Don Giovanni*, *Le Nozze di Figaro* and *Magic Flute*, *Fidelio*, *Lohengrin* and *Der Freischütz*, Rossini's *Barbiere di Siviglia*, *Otello* and *Guillaume Tell*, Donizetti's *La Favorita* and *Don Pasquale* (but not *Lucia di Lammermoor*), Verdi's *Due Foscari*, *Macbeth*, and *Ballo in maschera* (but not *Rigoletto*, *Traviata*, or *Trovatore*). "Of course," he added, "the touchstone of success will always be the material of your troupe and the most popular opera will not draw if it is not well given."

Overleaf: Turn-of-the-century drawings for illustrated magazines convey the flavor of the Metropolitan Opera in an age of elegance: opening-night audience entering under the Broadway marquee (*left, above*), gathering in the Grand Tier restaurant at intermission time (*left, below*), and departing down the main staircase (*right*).

Signing up Henry E. Abbey to deliver opera to the new stage at the Metropolitan (Abbey was a theatrical producer who had seven attractions on the Broadway stage that season of 1883–84), the directors of the new Metropolitan Opera House Company contracted for "first-class opera," which *they* would define. A clause in the contract with Abbey empowered the boxholders to withdraw their lease and take over all his contracts with artists if they felt his plans were inadequate.

The sensational New York debut of the first season was that of the Polish lyric soprano Marcella Sembrich, then only 25 years old, superbly musical, and able to invest passionate intensity in the Lucia-Elvira-Gilda-Rosina repertory. Before her arrival, she was quite unknown to the general public; the box-office take for her first four appearances averaged only $2,300, as against more than $5,000 for the operas in which Christine Nilsson was singing. But the board had known enough about Sembrich to authorize Abbey specifically to guarantee her $25,000 of their money for the season (equivalent of at least $200,000 a century later; Sembrich knew her own worth well enough to make Abbey increase her guarantee to $30,000).

Later, when Leopold Damrosch convinced the boxholders that opera in German could be presented in their theater without serious losses, they confidently gave the task of producing it to the board's secretary, one of their own, Edmund C. Stanton. Lilli Lehmann has left a delicious portrait of "our very elegant young director," who "shook all the wings with his white kid gloves, or ran up and downstairs to try their solidity before the curtain rose." But Stanton knew enough to go to Germany and recruit Wagner's great protégé Anton Seidl as conductor, Lehmann for the major soprano roles, the aging but still magnificent Albert Niemann as leading tenor. And when Abbey was brought back as impresario in 1891, leasing the house for his own productions with a nightly subsidy paid by the board, the new contract required him to submit to the board the names of the six leading singers he had engaged for the season, and gave the board the right to reject any of them and demand a substitute.

The Metropolitan, after all, was not introducing opera to New York; indeed, the first season was very like what the city had been offered by others in the past. Noting the success of the opening-night *Faust*, Mapleson wrote sourly that it offered "a fine cast and perfectly trained since all these artists had played under my direction and did not even require a rehearsal." Of the eighteen operas performed in the first season, only one (Ponchielli's *La Gioconda*) was new to New York. The Metropolitan audience by and large knew what it was coming to hear, and it was susceptible to quality. Nor was it necessarily opposed to novelty, as demonstrated by the great success of Wagner and Goldmark in the 1880s, Puccini and Strauss, Debussy and Montemezzi in later years. Lilli Lehmann wrote movingly about the *Tristan* performances in their premiere year of 1886, "where the audience sat still for minutes, silent and motionless in their places, as though drunk or in a transport, without being conscious that the opera was over."

Twenty-five-year-old Marcella Sembrich, whose brilliant portrayal of Donizetti's Lucia made the Met's second night as memorable as the first.

Aristocratic or ethnic, the New York audience was unquestionably interested first of all in the voices themselves, and aspects of this infatuation were unfortunate. "It is a trite saying," the *Times* critic Richard Aldrich grumbled in 1900,

that the New York public for a century has been spoiled by its constant opportunities for hearing the greatest singers in the world, and that it has little patience with less than the greatest . . . Habitués of the Metropolitan Opera House have been called upon to suffer many things to compensate for the privilege of listening to their great singers—incompetent and inane stage management, miserable and inappropriate scenery and costumes, a chorus wretched in vocal equipment and squalid in appearance . . .

As late as the 1920s, the English critic Ernest Newman, visiting New York for a year, complained that at the Met singers thought nothing of stepping out of their characters to the front of the stage to milk audience reaction to the most popular arias in hopes of earning so great an ovation that the conductor would be forced to grant them a repeat. Enrico Caruso's New York debut as the Duke in *Rigoletto* in 1903 was marked as something less than a triumph (in fact, he was nervous and far from his best) because "La donna è mobile" had to be repeated only once.

And the Metropolitan was—mostly still is—a museum. Though the house inevitably presented the first performance in America of a number of works, some of them more or less contemporary, it did not in its first 25 years create the world premiere of anything. Thereafter, however, until World War II, the Met was about average among the world's opera houses in its receptivity to new music. When something was fashionable—like Korngold's *Die tote Stadt*, or Ravel's *L'Heure espagnole*, or Křenek's *Jonny spielt auf*, or Deems Taylor's *Peter Ibbetson*—society in fact flocked to hear it, begged the Metropolitan management to schedule it for benefits for charities in which the beggar had particular interest. What kept novelty off the Metropolitan stage was not some antiquarian instinct of the *haut monde* but the conservative tastes of a bourgeois public. It was after the boxholders lost control of the theater toward the end of the Great Depression, and especially after Rudolf Bing arrived and saw his future in the expansion of the subscription audience, that the search for (occasional) novelty turned away from the 20th-century composer and toward the lesser or lighter works of the past.

The fury of enthusiasm for great singers, which has always characterized the audiences at the Metropolitan, should not be taken to mean that the members of the audience, aristocrats or plebs, did not care about what they were hearing or, on occasion, seeing. The fundament of a love for opera is susceptibility to that unique communication that comes essentially (conductors help or hinder) from the artists on stage. Music on paper exists to give reason for performance; those who come to the opera house hoping to find some moment of transcendent excitement in the work of a great singer are by no means necessarily barbarians, even if they are rich and should be better educated.

The history of opera in New York is the story of operatic productions. It is not at bottom a tale of social creatures showing off their tiaras, or immigrant communities reveling in ethnic joys from the old country, or intellectuals in the newspaper columns stimulating the city's ambitious autodidacts to rise above themselves—though all these elements at one time or another helped to draw audiences into the theaters. The rich men who planned the Metropolitan Opera House in the early 1880s may have been driven to do so by their exclusion from the inner sanctum of the Academy's boxes, but they knew also that they were providing a service for a large, enthusiastic, and well-informed operatic public, whose purchases of the 2,700 seats *not* in the boxes would support the performances on stage.

A catalogue of names echoes down the corridors of time, of artists whose careers made a quantum jump after their conquest of New York: Sembrich, Lilli Lehmann, Caruso, Fremstad, Farrar, Slezak, Martinelli, Ponselle, Pinza, Pons, Tibbett, Flagstad, Bjoerling, Price, Birgit Nilsson. To be a star at the Met was cherished not for the associated creature comforts (which were nil in the old house, a rabbit warren of cold and comfortless dressing rooms), and not in most years for the money (which was often no better than the money elsewhere), but because New York was the greatest challenge. Simply to stand on that stage and look the astonishing length and height of the horseshoe auditorium—the Family Circle rising up top beyond the back wall, apparently to an infinite depth—was an experience to strike awe in the mind of the casual visitor and terror in the heart of a singer. Nowhere else were vocal cords and resonant cavities expected to fill so large an airspace. The acoustics of the house, the severity of one's colleagues, and the fact that this audience was accustomed to the very best: all these elements added together to make the Metropolitan Opera House, from the day its doors opened on October 22, 1883—certainly from the end of the seven years of German opera in 1891—the most important theater in the world for vocal performance.

Paris was the capital for art, London for theater, Vienna for instrumental music, St. Petersburg for ballet. The best opera, vocally if not dramatically, very nearly year-in and year-out, was to be found in New York. The Met was, as Geraldine Farrar wrote, describing her feelings as she returned to her homeland to make a debut at the Met following her triumphs in Berlin, "the greatest temple of music in the western world." As early as the 1890s, Henry Abbey noted that an invitation to New York boosted the "market value" of a singer by fifty or even one hundred per cent. Alma Mahler would have thought that quite correct: "Americans," she wrote, reflecting on her husband's three triumphant seasons at the Met, ". . . really know something about music."

For the past century, the story of opera world-wide has been inseparable from the story of the Met.

TWO

STAR SEASONS

What got people excited at the Metropolitan Opera House in the 1883–84 season was less the operas or even the artists than the theater itself, the unprecedented lavishness of the all-new sets and costumes, and the continuing tickle of publicized competition between Mapleson at the old Academy and Abbey at the new Met. The impresarios opened their seasons the same night—and the horse show opened that night too, giving Society a terrible problem of priorities. At least one agile lady seems to have gone to all three. There was, indeed, plenty of time to take in some of the Met opening-night *Faust* and do other things. The doors were opened at 6:45 for an 8 o'clock curtain, to give people time to look around, but the crush at the entrances was such that the conductor did not actually start the performance until 8:23. What with four long intermissions for rubbernecking and socializing, the final curtain calls were not completed until after 12:30 the next morning. The opera was sung in Italian; Abbey was offering "Italian Opera," which meant that *everything* was sung in Italian.

Musically, the performance held no surprises. "All the principal artists," Henry H. Krehbiel of the New York *Tribune* wrote some years later, "had been heard in the opera many times, when their powers were greater." Still, Christine Nilsson remained everyone's first choice for Marguerite anywhere in the world (she had created the Grand Opera version of the role in Paris). A rather matronly figure by 1883, Nilsson had been a particular favorite of the New York audience since her debut in 1870, and her services had been the center of a bidding war between Abbey and Mapleson. Abbey won, with a bid of $2,000 per performance. The directors of the Opera House Company were so delighted that she had come to the Met that they arranged to present to her, during the ovation following her Jewel Song, a large and striking piece of jewelry, a sash of hammered gold bay leaves and berries, with medallions in the form of Tragedy and Comedy to serve as clasps. Eighty-three years later, the sash would reappear on the Met stage when countrywoman (but not relative) Birgit Nilsson sang Brünnhilde's Immolation on the night the Metropolitan Opera bade farewell to its old home.

Curtain call at a performance of *Faust* in 1895. The principals here are Edouard de Reszke, Nellie Melba, and Jean de Reszke. Note door in the old (pre-1903) proscenium, used by artists to reach the stage apron when acknowledging applause.

The first-night tenor, Italo Campanini, was, Krehbiel wrote, "the most popular Faust"—though he was well advanced in a process of yelling away his brilliant voice through abuse of the upper register. Later on, he and Nilsson would appear in *Lohengrin* together, as they had at the Academy of Music ten years before—in Italian. Auguste Vianesi, a French-trained Italian well-established at Covent Garden, was the conductor of both operas—indeed, of every performance and concert at the house between October 22 and November 3, when he was spelled by the tenor's younger brother, Cleofonte Campanini, who thereafter led about one performance in six, most of them when his brother was singing.

In any event, the Met premiere was attractive enough to draw nearly $15,000 into the box office—at least $100,000 in 1983 money—an especially remarkable accomplishment when one remembers that 432 of the supposedly best seats, in the owners' boxes, were not included in the figures. The top gallery, the Family Circle, was not full; but everything else was. The evening was deeply festive, men in white tie and opera hat and cape, women in creations ordered, some from Paris, especially for the occasion. There were crowds gathered on Broadway, watching the celebrities arrive.

Of the house itself, there were several views. The prevailing professional opinion, however, was far from positive. One of the most remarkable aspects of the saga of the Metropolitan is that the original opera house survived through almost three generations when most of the rest of 1880s New York was torn down, serving in each era as the most celebrated home of opera in the world, yet with almost no one to say a good word for the theater until just before it was demolished.

Two months before the opening, a columnist for the New York *Dramatic Mirror* went up on the roof of the Casino across Broadway, looked at the completed exterior of the new Met, and wrote that "a more unsightly, ungraceful place I never saw . . . The vast area covered by the building would have allowed of imposing effect, but it has been wholly neglected, and the result is decidedly disappointing . . . The yellow pressed brick of the walls looks like a cheap painted material." Mapleson, who had a gift of invective, referred to his competitor's theater as "the new yellow brewery on Broadway." An essentially admiring article in *Harper's Magazine* written before the opening admitted that "Costly as the building is, it is so very large as to limit the expenditure upon its exterior architecture."

From the outside, the building offered a variety of elevations, pediments, cornices, and window treatments. The vestibule on Broadway occupied less than a third of the frontage, and was dwarfed on either side by a seven-story apartment building. The 39th Street front featured at its eastern end four very high and heavily ornamented windows, behind which lay the grand foyer (later to be divided between Sherry's restaurant and the Metropolitan Opera Club)—and at its western end an array of small rectangular windows behind which were dressing rooms and offices.

The program for opening night, October 22, 1883. Henry E. Abbey (*inset, above*), the Met's first director, was under contract to provide "first-class opera." His soprano for opening night was Christine Nilsson (*inset, below*), already a long-established favorite in New York.

METROPOLITAN
OPERA HOUSE.

MR. HENRY E. ABBEY, - - - - - - Director.
Acting Manager - - - - - MR. MAURICE GRAU.

MONDAY EVENING, OCTOBER 22, 1883,

INAUGURAL NIGHT
AND
First Night of the Subscription,
WHEN GOUNOD'S OPERA OF

"FAUST."

Will be presented with the following Cast :

FAUST, - - - - - -	Sig. ITALO CAMPANINI
MEPHISTOPHELES, - - -	Sig. FRANCO NOVARA
VALENTINO, - - - -	Sig. GIUSEPPE DEL PUENTE
WAGNER, - - - - - -	Sig. CONTINI
SIEBEL, - - - - -	Mme. SOFIA SCALCHI
MARTA, - - - - -	Mlle. LOUISE LABLACHE

(Who has kindly consented to assume the part at short notice.)
AND
MARGHERITA, - - - - Mme. CHRISTINE NILSSON

Musical Director and Conductor, - Sig. VIANESI

WEBER PIANO USED.

Mason & Hamlin's Organ Used.

All the above Operas performed at this House can be had in every form, Vocal and Instrumental
at G. SCHIRMER, No. 35 Union Square, Importer and Publisher of Music.

The Scenery by Messrs. Fox, Schaeffer, Maeder, and Thompson.
The Costumes are entirely new, and were manufactured at Venice by D. Ascoli
The Appointments by Mr. Bradwell.
Machinists, Messrs. Lundy & Gifford.

NIGHTLY PRICES OF ADMISSION:

Boxes, holding six (6) seats....................................	$50
Orchestra Stalls...	6
Balcony Stalls..	3
Family Circle (reserved).......................................	2
Admission to Family Circle.....................................	1

Seats and Boxes can be secured at the Box Office of the Metropolitan Opera House, which
will remain open daily from 8 A. M. to 5 P. M.

Doors open at 7.15. **Performances at 8 precisely**

Gunerius Gabrielson & Son, Florists to the Metropolitan Opera House.

Opera Glasses on Hire in the Lobby.

L. F. Mazette, Caterer.

Parties desiring Ices can be supplied by the Waiter, in Corridor.

Business Manager - - - - - - -	Mr. W. W. TILLOTSON.
Treasurer - - - - - - -	Mr. CHAS. H. MATHEWS.

In the rear, an almost featureless brick wall rose 150 feet, with a narrow doorway 40 feet high to permit the delivery and removal of scenery.

Stage, auditorium, and entrance area had to be set in a straight line. With a deep stage required for operatic spectacle and an auditorium which was to be the largest in the world, the entrance area was necessarily cramped: a vestibule with a rather low ceiling (because the space above was required for an assembly room), and then a double staircase roofed at each level, prohibiting the sort of processional display that other theaters invited. But the parterre boxholders would not use that stairway: they had their own entrances on the side streets. From the side-street vestibules also rose the stairs—separate for the Family Circle—that led to the inexpensive seats up top. The corridors behind the auditorium had low ceilings and there was no exterior ventilation; particularly in the early years, when the hall was lit by gas, they became fearfully hot.

Except for the doors to the anterooms and the floors, which were of allegedly fireproof wood, construction was of iron, brick, and plaster. The most remarkable iron pieces were those that framed the stage: giant pillars supporting a single beam 80 feet long and 15 feet deep that slashed a dramatic straight line atop the 50 × 50 stage opening. Pillars and beam were plastered over and classically ornamented, with small doors cut on both sides for artists to enter and exit the stage apron on curtain calls (the curtain rose and fell, rather than parting in the middle).

The stage itself was built in sections that could be raised or lowered by changing the length of the iron bars that supported them. From apron to the Seventh Avenue wall was 86 feet, and the width was 101 feet, and nothing could ever be done about it because the side walls were structural. Below the stage was a 30-foot pit, which offered some storage capacity. Of machinery, the stage had virtually none—not even a counterweight system for the drops, which had to be raised and lowered by sheer muscle power.

Lilli Lehmann described the backstage scene during her first season in 1885:

The opera-house was not equipped for the newest mechanical demands; no one was accustomed to work rapidly, and so every change turned into a trial of patience . . . It was delayed by requests like, "Please bring me a lath, please let me have another nail here, please fasten these steps, this barrier, this bench, the carpet." Then everything was attended to at a snail's pace . . . I gave my own assistance everywhere, so as not to be put out by a fall, or by being killed, or torn in pieces . . . At last I became mistress also of the incredible confusion behind the scenes, where everybody tramped about, whistled, talked aloud, slammed doors, etc. I declared that I did not wish to sing any further, and that helped matters, for it became as quiet as a mouse, the workmen were given soft shoes, and Mr. Stanton now began to hear and to see.

Though Abbey was more professional than his successor, much the same confusion must have afflicted performances during the first year: everyone noted the

Backstage in the 1880s. John Filmer's wood engravings show the rigging loft over the stage (*above*), the fly gallery (*below left*), and the stage-setters at work. There were no motors; everything depended on muscle power.

length of the intermissions. And the problem of noise from backstage bedeviled the Met through all its years in the old theater. In operas like *Don Giovanni*, where episodes were played before an inner curtain while scenes were shifted behind, the rumbles from the rear were devastating for both singers and audience. Indeed, the baritone George London once physically assaulted a stagehand after such an episode, but by then the worries about whose feelings might be hurt had changed, and management asked London to apologize. He did.

Cady had designed an orchestra pit with some of the features of Wagner's famous hidden orchestra at Bayreuth, a floor sunk below the level of the parquet and a brick-and-plaster umbrella just below stage level to cover about half the area. This was actually built—and described in the *New York Times* after a reporter's visit to the hall nine days before the opening—but when the orchestra and Vianesi came for their rehearsals (one week before opening night), "the Italians and their chief," as Cady's friend M. G. van Rensselaer wrote, "rebelled at any such innovation, and, undaunted by the citation of Wagner, by the dictates of good sense, or the opposition of the architect and building-committee, refused to be heard unless they could also be seen. So the orchestra was floored over and it remains still to be known whether, if sunk, it would not have helped the players as well as relieved the audience from the spectacle they offer." On opening night, then, the orchestra was on a level with the parquet, separated from the audience only by a railing.

Perhaps the most savage criticism of the house appeared the day after opening night on the front page of the *New York Times*, which under the headline "A Grand Temple of Music" had nine days before carried a laudatory preview of "a house without a bad seat in it." The preview had stressed the 700 drawings Cady and his assistants had made to perfect the sight lines from all over the theater. Now the *Times* reported under the more neutral headline "The New Opera House" that:

Much disappointment was caused by the comparative failure of the acoustic properties of the auditorium . . . In the upper rows of the boxes and in the balcony only the high voices were distinctly heard. Nor were the facilities for seeing much better in some portion of the auditorium than the facilities for hearing. In many of the boxes the occupants of the rear seats had to stand and lean over the ladies in front, and from the next row of the balcony and above the only animated thing visible to the occupants of a seat was the expanse of Signor Vianesi's cranium . . .

Van Rensselaer approved the interior decor as "extremely quiet, refined, and even elegant . . . a protest against the tawdriness, the restlessness, the over-elaboration running into distinct vulgarity, of so much decorative work." But even he thought the "yellow tone . . . must be pronounced not the most fortunate that could have been chosen." The *Times* was less charitable: "The upholstery of the boxes is not a good background for an audience in full dress . . . The fabric loses color and design altogether and becomes a pale and rather dirty brown, unattractive in itself and of no

The Met's stars for the first season would mostly have been familiar to habitués of London's Covent Garden, as would their roles and their statuesque poses seen here: Italo Campanini (*above left*) as Don José in *Carmen*, Roberto Stagno (*above right*) as Manrico in *Trovatore*, Giuseppe del Puente (*center*) as Barnaba in *Gioconda*, Zelia Trebelli (*below left*) as Nancy in *Martha*, and Emma Fursch-Madi (*below right*) as Laura in *Gioconda*.

value as a setting for more brilliant colors." This became the accepted view. The "Programme" sold at the theater the next season noted that:

One of the great faults of the Opera House last year, and one which press and public equally decried, was the decoration of the house. The tints of the Silk and paper hangings were not selected with proper judgment . . . All this has been entirely changed this season, and the whole house has been redecorated. The effect produced by the colors on entering this lighter grand house is now very pleasing . . . We wish to express our astonishment and appreciation of the fine quality of the Silk used in the decoration . . . by . . . the large American Silk House, CHENEY BROS.

But if not yellow, it was still ivory: the red background everyone remembers when thinking of the old Met did not come until 1903.

And yet . . . from the beginning there was the glory of that space and shape. Nobody ever entered that auditorium for the first time without a gasp at its grandeur. It was 104 feet long from proscenium to the back of the center box, and more than 80 feet high, and its interior was then outlined by five rising tiers, three of boxes and two of gallery, the line of parterre boxes protruding slightly, all the lines curving gently back from the proscenium and then out again to round off the horseshoe in the center. The house was cruel to poor performances, partly because it took extraordinary voices or extraordinary technique to fill its immense space, but partly also because the level of expectation was raised so high by the experience of entering it. By the same token, it complemented brilliance as only a great architectural statement can.

Many of the defects noted on opening night were curable, and were in fact cured, one way or another, over the years. Van Rensselaer noted that part of the acoustical problem on the first night was the singers' unfamiliarity with the hall: they "evidently overlooked the fact that the stage was very much wider and deeper, and so more difficult to fill, than those to which they had been accustomed, and did not keep as near as they should have done to the footlights." This solution to the acoustics problem, of course, raised another question, because the parade of singers onto the apron was bad for dramatic effect; but eventually a reduction in the size of the apron restored a better, if not ideal, balance.

Because the singers had such desperate trouble projecting their voices over the orchestra in the first *Lohengrin*, Vianesi consented to the removal of the hastily erected floor, and restored Cady's sunken pit (though not the umbrella over it). And when the house was reconstructed in 1893, the soft hangings on the partitions between the boxes—great sound destroyers—were eliminated. There was probably some gain even in the second year, from the elimination of the third tier of boxes and the substitution of a Dress Circle of "stalls". The sight-line difficulties, however, were beyond the wit of man to resolve: for 83 years, 700 seats at the Met offered only a partial view of the stage.

By the second night, when Marcella Sembrich knocked everyone dead with the purity of her intonation and the exactitude and imagination of her roulades as Donizetti's unhappy Lucia, critical commentary on the acoustics was diminished. The fact that the house was rarely full reduced, by rather unfortunate means, the proportion of the audience complaining about sight lines. Commentators then lamented that the theater was too big, because an audience that would have seemed of quite respectable size at the Academy of Music seemed to rattle around at the Met.

Abbey's season proceeded much as a Covent Garden season might, with familiar operas and mostly familiar stars: the dashing Victor Capoul as Wilhelm Meister to Nilsson's Mignon in Thomas's *Mignon* and Alfredo to Sembrich's Violetta in *La Traviata*. A tenor new to New York, Roberto Stagno, stentorian on the high notes but stiff on stage and not always certain of pitch, sang Manrico in *Il Trovatore*, Almaviva to Sembrich's Rosina in *Barbiere*, and the Duke to Sembrich's Gilda in *Rigoletto*. The celebrated mezzo Zelia Trebelli presented her abandoned Azucena in *Il Trovatore* and her heartless Carmen; Emma Fursch-Madi sang Ortrud in *Lohengrin*, Alice in Meyerbeer's *Robert le Diable*, Laura in *La Gioconda*, and Donna Anna in *Don Giovanni*.

A Metropolitan tradition that began in the first year was the Sunday night concert. This had not been part of the prospectus, but at the end of October the Casino across the street (where the house manager was a German actor named Heinrich Conried) began offering concerts of songs by artists who were part of the operetta company run by Abbey's assistant at the Met, Maurice Grau. These did well, and Abbey decided to put on a similar show in the opera house. Obviously, the house profited most from these aria shows when the performers were under weekly contract: Nilsson never sang in a Sunday concert, and Sembrich sang only once. In later years, engagements for the Sunday night concerts became something of a reward for the singers: it was a *cachet* (performance fee) earned for much less work than an opera, before an enthusiastic and very unexclusive audience (prices were about 40 per cent of opera night prices).

Mapleson's troupe at the Academy did not perform on Sunday nights, but during the rest of the week (Monday, Wednesday, and Friday evenings, plus Saturday afternoons) the two opera houses competed head-to-head. What the Academy offered that the Met could not match was, simply, Adelina Patti. Still something of a novelty in New York (she had not appeared there between her 1859 debut and her return as part of Mapleson's company in 1881), Patti could sell out the house at "Patti prices" of $10 for a parquet seat (which Mapleson needed: to keep Patti from Abbey he had been forced to pay her $5,000 a night). People who never went to

42

opera otherwise came to hear the unforced perfection of the diminutive and ever-charming Patti, and she usually obliged with an interpolation of "Home Sweet Home" or the famous waltz "Il bacio" by her conductor Arditi. When she and Etelka Gerster (Mapleson's other great soprano) sang together in *Les Huguenots*, they justified the season.

In one respect, the Metropolitan was judged immensely superior to the Academy: Abbey's sets and costumes were, by universal agreement, nothing short of wonderful. "The mounting which Mr. Abbey bestows upon the productions at the Metropolitan is worthy of the most unstinted praise," a critic wrote, adding:

Never in the annals of American grand opera have such magnificent scenery and dresses been displayed. To turn from the truly regal and scenic appointments of the new Opera House to the drab and nasty daubs which disgrace the Academy produces very much the same effect upon the spectator as a sudden trip from the aristocratic neighborhood of Murray Hill to the unsavory slums of Baxter street.

Lilli Lehmann is the source for the much repeated statement that "every costume, every shoe and stocking was provided . . . by Worth of Paris." This is not true; the costumes were mostly ordered through the London firm that supplied such merchandise to the English opera houses, and were almost without exception manufactured by D'Ascoli in Venice. But they cost $80,000, which was much more than the board had originally budgeted. The sets and properties added another $60,000. Initial estimates prepared for the board had put the cost of all paraphernalia for 20 operas at $70,000. By the time Abbey began his season, that budget had risen to $110,000. Within two weeks, the board was called upon for another $30,000. An accountant hired to go over Abbey's books reported back that the only receipt unavailable (it was later uncovered) was for $14,000 customs duty on the costumes. Abbey had indeed spent the money for the Metropolitan's "Amusement Account," and under the terms of his contract he was entitled to reimbursement, which he received.

He needed the money: Abbey was in financial difficulty from the beginning. Even in a time when little in terms of stage drama or musical polish was expected in an opera house, staging nineteen premieres in a single season in a new theater was an intimidating enterprise. And there were inescapable cash flow problems, because several of the artists had been defaulted on by Mapleson at one time or another, and refused to leave Europe without large cash advances against their contracts. Some $105,000 had been spent that way before the season opened—most of it on the basis that the money could be applied only to the artists' *last* performances of the season. Thus the up-front expenditure could not be written off against the performances of the fall season, when payrolls had to be met in full.

In the Metropolitan's archives there is an odd single sheet of paper listing Mapleson's presumed weekly expenses at the Academy. It shows something more

Leopold Damrosch (*above*; with his son Walter) ran the first of the Met's seven seasons of opera in German. Perhaps the most impressive artist in the first season was the soprano Amalia Materna, seen (*inset, left*) as Elisabeth in *Tannhäuser*. Following the sudden death of the elder Damrosch in February 1885, Edmund C. Stanton (*inset, right*) took over as manager. Young Walter Damrosch replaced his father as a conductor.

than $22,000 a week, or an average of about $5,500 per performance. As $10,000 of that was earmarked for Patti, Abbey's figures should not have been much higher, if at all; and indeed the auditor's report on bills to be paid by Abbey on November 17—included as part of the general study of Abbey's finances commissioned by the board—shows a payroll of $22,390, including three weeks' pay (at $300 a week) for Vianesi. Newspaper advertising, gas, and electricity added about $1,000 a week.

In his first three weeks (leaving out opening night), Abbey had received at the box office an average of $3,670 per performance, counting four operas and a concert every week. Another $400 or so could be allocated pro rata from pre-season subscription sales, and the board had guaranteed Abbey against loss to a maximum of $1,000 per performance. Because of the advance to artists and the over-budget payments for sets and costumes (for which he would be reimbursed), Abbey as of mid-November was about $85,000 out of pocket. On current expenses, however, assuming no payments to himself, he seemed to be breaking even.

Abbey's was a lean operation. The orchestra cost was only about $400 per performance for 65 men; the chorus, less than $300; the ballet, about $100. Scenic artists ran $100 per performance; stagehands, $75; clerical and box-office help, $50; ushers, $25; cleaners, $30. There were only 33 principal singers for 60 performances in a fifteen-week season. The most extravagant estimate of Abbey's costs in the contemporary press was $7,000 per performance, which was probably a little high, and takes the concerts as cost-free.

To pay his bills, Abbey had, rent-free, a house with 50 boxes for sale at $50 each (the 70 stockholders' boxes brought no income), plus 562 parquet seats at $6, plus more than 1,700 seats in the Balcony and Family Circle at $3, $2, and $1. Abbey had scaled the house to yield more than $9,000 at a sell-out—but after the first night, nothing in the first weeks went over $6,000, and only the Nilsson performances went over $5,000. Moreover, those were going to be the best weeks, when sheer curiosity would lead New Yorkers to want to peek at an opera performance. People of no experience in operagoing did come for the glamour of the new theater throughout this first autumn season (in his review of the Christmas Eve *Rigoletto* that ended it, W. J. Henderson sniffed at "an audience which included a great many people who had evidently never attended an operatic performance before and by a few persons—these occupying boxes—who out of consideration for people who care to listen to the singers and band, ought never to attend an operatic performance again"). But there weren't enough of them.

Following the conclusion of the autumn season in the house, Abbey took his troupe on tour; in all, they played 58 performances in Brooklyn, Boston, Philadelphia, Chicago, Cincinnati, St. Louis, Washington, and Baltimore. When he reopened at the Met in March, the *Mirror* estimated that his average loss in the eighteen weeks since October 22 had been $8,000 a week, or about $150,000 all told.

The musical mainstay of the Met's German seasons was Anton Seidl, a protégé of Richard Wagner; his conducting combined meticulous attention to detail with a fiery sense of drama. He is seen here surrounded by laurel wreaths in his New York home.

And the spring season was disastrous, with audiences so poor that the company became demoralized. During the final week, Nilsson, Sembrich, Campanini, and Trebelli (who already had their advance payments, money in the bank for their final performances) all reported sick; a promised *Roméo et Juliette* could not be given, and the last subscription performance had to be canceled.

Everyone was restored to health, probably feeling a little guilty, in time for the benefit concert to honor and reward Abbey, at which Sembrich did a musical magic trick, playing the violin in a performance of De Beriot's Concerto in addition to singing—and then, asked for an encore, delivering a professional performance at the piano of a Chopin Mazurka. Abbey's receipts from the benefit (at which the boxholders paid for their boxes) totaled something like $17,000, which helped a little but not much. The *Tribune*'s Krehbiel, relying on a partner of Abbey's who may have had some *parti pris*, said the losses on the season ran $600,000; Irving Kolodin, being cautious, cut that back to $500,000 in his history of the house. Such figures as remain available in the Metropolitan's archives make both these estimates look high; $250,000, of which more than half was lost on tour, would be more like it. But that was still a lot of money, and it had to come out of Abbey's pocket.

Because of the extravagance of the productions, popular opinion thought that what put Abbey under was lavish expenditure. But the owners of the house had paid for those stagings, and Abbey seems to have forecast his running expenses reasonably well. As late as the auditor's report in mid-November, he thought he was going to come out all right, putting together the box-office receipts, the subvention from the boxholders, and a chunk of ancillary income from renting the house on non-opera nights, selling the libretto rights, etc.

What happened to Abbey was that the box office collapsed, in large part because he had overpriced the house. At a time when a workman might make $2 a day, a price of $3 for a balcony stall and $2 for a seat in the front half of the Family Circle was too high for too many of the potential purchasers, especially among the recent immigrants. And the old Met was, to a degree not generally recognized, a people's opera house: more than half the seats, and more than one-third the revenues from a sell-out at Abbey's prices, were upstairs. At mid-season, Abbey scaled down to a $5 top, but by then attitudes had hardened.

Abbey seems to have offered to undertake a second season of opera on condition that the boxholders absorb his losses resulting from the first, but that would have required an additional assessment of at least $3,000 per box, which the directors were not willing to ask from their friends. The board negotiated with Ernest Gye of Covent Garden, which had a spring season that easily meshed with the Met's calendar, but Gye was not interested in taking a house where he would not have the revenues from the 70 best boxes, and was perhaps concerned that his wife Emma Albani would have to play *seconda donna* to Nilsson. Carl Rosa, who was offering

The first American production of Wagner's *Die Meistersinger*, in 1886, had conductor Anton Seidl's wife, Auguste Seidl-Kraus, and the Bayreuth bass Emil Fischer in the cast. The camera has caught them in the Eva-Sachs scene from Act II.

opera in English in London and the provinces, was also approached, and indicated an interest in 1885–86, but not in 1884–85.

One can imagine the embarrassment of the boxholders, who had by now put $2 million into the house and its accouterments, and were faced with the prospect of leaving it dark in its second season. Mapleson was returning to the Academy, with Patti and some of the artists who had previously appeared for Abbey. Mapleson's backers, the so-called "Knickerbocker aristocracy," having picked up his bad debts the year before, were on the edge of triumph. But in July, providentially, Leopold Damrosch appeared with an offer to manage a season of opera in German at the Met—for a salary of $10,000, the boxholders to run all the financial risks.

The economics of opera in German were entirely different from the economics of Italian opera. Productions in Italian had to be built around stars, who were unbearably expensive. Almost two-fifths of Abbey's payroll had gone to performing fees and hotel bills for Nilsson and Sembrich alone; Patti all by herself, as noted, accounted for 45 per cent of Mapleson's costs. German opera was presented in the court cities of Kaiser Wilhelm's realm by ensembles of artists who were year-round employees, with guaranteed pensions as part of their earnings. Moreover, they were available on short notice through the frugal bureaucrats who managed these theaters, and who were happy to lend artists for a third of their year-round season on the payment of a suitable "forfeit."

Damrosch, a grave and heavily bearded gentleman, was 52, trained in his native Prussia as a medical doctor, with the musical genius to have become a solo violinist in a single year after deciding that music, rather than medicine, was his calling. He had come to New York ten years earlier as the conductor of the Männersingerverein, and had built a symphony orchestra and an oratorio society, from which he would draw instrumentalists and chorus for the opera; he would do all the conducting himself. Presenting the French and Italian repertory (in German), he would have the use of the sets and costumes bought for Abbey; presenting Wagner, he would duplicate the sets and costumes used at Bayreuth, "which must of course be regarded as the model for all time," Krehbiel wrote, "since they were projected and carried out under the eyes of the poet composer." All this could be done, fourteen weeks with 57 performances plus two concerts, at an average cost of $3,000 per evening, and the season could break even at reasonable attendance with the house scaled to a $4 top.

Opposite: Design by E. Prentice Treadwell for the original 1883 proscenium, destroyed in the fire of 1892.

Pages 50, 51: The October 31, 1883, issue of *Puck* Magazine satirized the head-on battle between New York's two rival opera houses—the Academy of Music, led by Colonel James Henry Mapleson, and the Met, led by Henry E. Abbey.

Pages 52, 53: A turn-of-the-century audience in rapt attention at the finale of *Faust*. Gounod's opera was so popular at the Met that the theater was nicknamed the "Faustspielhaus."

THE OPERATIC

IN NEW YORK.

Artists of considerable importance and some celebrity were engaged—among them, Amalia Materna, Bayreuth's imposing Brünnhilde; Marianne Brandt, who sang a tense and impassioned Leonore in *Fidelio*; Auguste Kraus, already married to the conductor Anton Seidl, who moved from Elisabeth in *Tannhäuser* on the opening night to the much lighter Marzelline in *Fidelio* and Ännchen in *Der Freischütz*; the Italian-trained Marie Schröder-Hanfstängl, whose Donna Anna in *Don Giovanni* almost reconciled the critics to a perfomance in German; the big-voiced tenor Anton Schott, who rather displeased the critics with his bellowing and stiff demeanor until he surprised them with a lyrical Siegmund in *Die Walküre*; and the capable baritone Adolf Robinson, who earned the favorite encomium "manly."

But the real star was Wagner. Only three of his operas were given in that first German season—*Tannhäuser*, *Lohengrin*, and *Die Walküre*—but among them they accounted for 25 of the 57 performances, and more were promised in future seasons. The only Verdi in the season was *Rigoletto*; the only Rossini was the uncharacteristic, ambitious *Guillaume Tell*; the French repertory was represented by Meyerbeer's *Les Huguenots* and *Le Prophète*, Halévy's dramatic *La Juive*, and Auber's *La Muette de Portici*.

Performed by an orchestra playing for its own conductor, with artists who knew each other and had worked together in similar stagings (and with real stage direction from the experienced German *régisseur* Wilhelm Hock), the stately opening-night *Tannhäuser* made a great impression on press and public. *Lohengrin* was entirely familiar—it had been in Abbey's repertory and Mapleson's—but now there was a chance to hear it in German. (In the result, some people who believed Wagner could not be presented successfully except in German felt themselves remembering with guilty affection Campanini's lyricism in the title role, which Schott declaimed belligerently and not very musically.) What mattered most was *Die Walküre*, the hinge opera of the *Ring* cycle and the masterwork of Wagner's middle years, never before performed in the United States. Here Damrosch, the fiery Materna (still only 40) as Brünnhilde, Kraus as Sieglinde, the dedicated Brandt as Fricka, Schott as Siegmund, and Josef Staudigl as Wotan all seemed wedded to what they were doing, and held the full house in thrall.

Damrosch had been rehearsing *Die Walküre* all season, and it was perhaps the most polished operatic performance New York had ever seen. It was then done five times in eight days—Friday, Saturday matinee, Monday, Wednesday, and Saturday matinee again). On the second Friday, Schott sang John of Leyden in Meyerbeer's *Le Prophète*, and the following Monday he sang Lohengrin: people had stamina in those days. Damrosch, of course, conducted the other operas too; he was conducting *all* the operas.

Pages 54, 55: A refurbishing by Carrère & Hastings in 1903 provided the maroon-and-gold decor that would remain until the old Met was demolished in 1966. Insets show the view from the Family Circle (*above*), Sherry's bar and restaurant (*center*), and the Grand Tier staircase.

Opposite: Divas of the Golden Age: Nellie Melba (*above left*), Marcella Sembrich (*below left*), and Emma Eames (*right*). Their portraits now grace the walls of Founders' Hall at the Lincoln Center house.

Though the modern world is full of Wagnerites, some of them Perfect, one cannot today quite recapture the feeling of solemn excitement and devotion that Wagner's operas elicited in the 1880s. Opera had begun in late Renaissance Italy as an attempt to restore Greek tragedy, and the 18th-century opera seria had been serious indeed in its exploration of classical myth. Commentators as exalted as Søren Kierkegaard and E. T. A. Hoffmann had found deeper meanings in *Don Giovanni* and insisted on its greatness as a work of art; and enthusiasm for Italian opera had animated such disparate figures as Stendhal and Whitman. But following the ascendancy of the Italian school in the wake of the all-conquering Rossini, the intellectual position of opera had settled into that of entertainment, an excuse for the display of voices. Wagner had revolutionized all that; he wrote not operas but music dramas, in which everything was of a piece, held together by the expressive leitmotifs in the orchestra, making eternal statements of the human condition. A skilled and unscrupulous propagandist for his own work as well as a creator, he had died in 1883 worshipped by his immediate circle and by a large and vocal fraction of those who thought art forms were important in the world.

This fraction did not include any large number of the Metropolitan boxholders (though a Vanderbilt and a Cutting were among the petitioners for a special Wagner season a decade later). They resented the absence of display numbers, the lack of a ballet, the reduced number of intermissions, and the through composition of each act, which left no moments for applause and conviviality. In fairness to them, the boxholders who planned to come the same night every week that first German season may also have felt that they were being bombarded: the Monday night audience heard *Tannhäuser* three times and *Lohengrin* four times in thirteen weeks. The audience on Friday nights, which was then the fashionable night, was spared Wagner most of the season, but had an equally repetitive year, with *Les Huguenots* and *Guillaume Tell* alternating the first five Fridays. Obviously, no one should ever talk during an opera performance, but no man of sensibility can entirely deny his sympathy to the dowager who finds herself chattering with her neighbor when confronted with her third *Guillaume Tell* in four weeks.

Still, the boxholders must have basked in the approbation the German season received. Krehbiel insisted that 5,000 people had crammed into the house for opening night, which cannot be right—but there can be no question that the place was full, and remained nearly full for the Wagner evenings. The city's German community, estimated at 250,000, rallied round the German company—and, meanwhile, nobody rallied round Mapleson, who abandoned the Academy of Music at Christmas and went looking for greener pastures on tour. In January, Damrosch took time off from his *Walküre* rehearsals to sign a contract for the next season. His salary was cut to $8,000, but he would receive a share of what both he and the board anticipated would be profits.

But his second season was not to be: Damrosch at 53 did not have Anton Schott's stamina. Exhausted after the week of *Walküres*, with no rest in sight, he threw himself on a bed for a nap under an open window in the February cold, and woke with pneumonia, from which he died five days later. He spent most of his last two days coaching his son Walter in how to conduct Wagner. The funeral took place on the stage of the Metropolitan, with even the boxes full, and even the boxholders in tears. Walter and chorus master John Lund took over the few remaining performances of the subscription, and led the company on tour.

That summer, the 23-year-old Walter Damrosch and the board's secretary Edmund C. Stanton, who would be business manager of the producing operation for the next six years, went to Europe and returned with the four cornerstones of succeeding seasons—the conductor Anton Seidl, Wagner's personal secretary the last six years of his life; the soprano Lilli Lehmann, beautiful of voice and person, one of Wagner's favorite Rhinemaidens and Valkyries, now grown to full dramatic stature; the bass Emil Fischer, who provided a vocal foundation for the revivals of *Lohengrin*, *Tannhäuser*, and *Die Walküre*, and gave the company a comfortable and appealing Hans Sachs for the first American production of *Die Meistersinger*; and the handsome Max Alvary, a brilliant tenor who sang Don José and Faust in his first New York season and would mature later into a sterling Siegfried. All these artists were still quite young. With Brandt and Kraus (now Seidl-Kraus) and Robinson returned from the previous season, they were the nucleus of a Wagner combination as powerful as any to be found at the Met, or elsewhere, perhaps in any period. The tenor Albert Niemann joined them in the next two seasons, at the end of his career but still the world's premier Tristan. ("His attitudes and gestures," Krehbiel wrote, "are not only instinct with life but instinct with the sublimated life of the hero of the drama . . . The figure is colossal, the head like the front of Jove himself; the eyes large and full of luminous light.") Together, these artists made the supposedly ensemble company of German opera a star company indeed. No explanation for the end of the German seasons need be sought beyond the fact that by 1890–91 only Seidl and Fischer were still at the Met.

Seidl won the respect of his musicians immediately by spotting no fewer than 180 errors in the instrumental parts of the opening-night *Lohengrin*. Meticulous and grave in manner (it was said that he could hold his tongue in seven languages), he also had when necessary a fire traced by the critics to his Hungarian origins, and a lyric gift apparently denied Leopold Damrosch. Seidl brought with him as the season's non-Wagner novelty Goldmark's *The Queen of Sheba*, a work full of Orientalisms and spectacle, perhaps the only opera introduced in the German seasons that was popular with all the boxholders, who called year after year for its return. Goldmark's opera was played fifteen times in its first season. Also new for this year were Wagner's immature, march-time *Rienzi* and a seven-act version of

Overleaf: A group photo from 1890–91 shows the German company at almost full strength. Seated to the left and right of the table are Walter Damrosch and Anton Seidl. The heavy-set man standing seventh from right is Victor Herbert, who played cello in the orchestra. Costumed in roles they sang at the Met are Marianne Brandt as Ortrud, Theodor Reichmann as Wolfram, Max Alvary as Siegfried, and Albert Niemann as Tristan.

H. Rothe — Esser — C. Behrens — Mackhof — Stewart — Dippel
v. Hübbnet — Posch — O. Sachs — Luria — Gould — A. Mielke — Theo Habelmann
Ikenler — Annie Bloch — M. Jahn — W. Damrosch

Th. Reichmann   Fa... ...li   v. Herbert   Russel   E.Smith   Brakwell   Peck   McLennan
...   FK.Tomann...   Schvell   Haag   Fischer   ·Ritter Goetze   Kuhn

Gounod's *Faust* (in German, of course) that went on and on and on, with much work for the ballet.

With this company, year by year, Seidl marched through the Wagner canon, carefully rehearsing each production, modeling its appearance after what he had seen Wagner himself do in Bayreuth. He was tireless in rehearsals, a master of detail both in the music and on the stage. From a later season, Lillian Nordica left a recollection of Seidl accompanying her "to a Broadway store to buy a veil for Isolde in the second act. He asked for samples of various kinds of tulle, and when they came he seized one after another at one end and fluttered the other rapidly through the air, to the great astonishment of the shoppers and shop-girls, who were not quite sure whether he was in his right mind. But he knew just what he wanted." She also remembered a day when "Seidl came to me early one morning to go over my role with me, and he left about two o'clock in the afternoon. I had to rest for two days. Every noise, every sound brought up something from *Tristan und Isolde*."

In 1888–89, Seidl & Co. gave the first *Ring* cycle in America, and took it on tour for two months, Lehmann singing three Brünnhildes every week. All Seidl's Wagner was cut, however, and sometimes rather drastically. Later generations of New Yorkers would place the blame for cut Wagner on Artur Bodanzky, but in 1928 librarian Lionel Mapleson had occasion to write that the parts in use were still those from the Seidl regime; the cuts had been opened once, for Franz Schalk in 1898–99 and Emil Paur the next season, and then Mapleson "with deep pleasure did my job" of restoring them. Time sheets show that Schalk's *Walküre* had been 58 minutes longer than what the Met was offering in the 1920s.

In no season between 1886 and 1890 did Wagner performances represent less than half the total given at the Metropolitan Opera House, and for the critics the change from Italian opera to German opera seemed permanent. "There is no hope," wrote Henry T. Finck, "for the Italianissimi, who sigh for their macaronic arias and the 'Ernani' and 'Gazza Ladra' soup . . . The vastness of the Metropolitan auditorium makes it impossible to hear the weak voices and the thin scores of Italians to advantage." But when the irrepressible Abbey, now running a touring company of opera, gave a crowded week at the Met in spring 1887, his troupe of Patti, Sofia Scalchi, the bass Franco Novara, and the tenor Guille took in $70,000 for six performances—as against a total of $137,000 at the box office for the entire 61 performances of the German subscription season (and the boxholders attended without charge for the Abbey as well as the Seidl performances). Lilli Lehmann reported that in 1889 she warned Stanton and Seidl "about our repertoire that, in my judgment, was made up of too much—indeed, almost exclusively—of Wagner, which would become an excessive amount in the long run . . . It was represented to me that the Wagner operas were the most potent attraction, and I saw that my words of warning were wasted, but the future taught them to know better in the end."

No singer at the Met ever demonstrated greater versatility than the German soprano Lilli Lehmann. Her repertoire included roles as diverse as Brünnhilde and (*inset*) Carmen.

The blow fell in January 1891, when it was announced that the impresario firm of Abbey, John B. Schoeffel, and Maurice Grau had leased the Metropolitan for the next season, and would be presenting opera in French and Italian, with a company including the brothers Jean and Edouard de Reszke, Giulia Ravogli and Emma Albani, the French baritone Jean Lassalle, and the Americans Emma Eames and Lillian Nordica. Anton Seidl would return as a conductor, with Lilli Lehmann and her husband, the tenor Paul Kalisch. There were cries of outrage from the "German audience" and from the critics, and a huge demonstration after the season's final *Meistersinger*, with its closing tribute to German art. But at the end of a season that had showed little vocal quality and promised less—and had offered three hopelessly bad new operas, including the impossible *Diana von Solange* by the Duke of Saxe-Coburg-Gotha (who presumably paid for it)—the end was in any event near.

German opera had been instituted because it was cheap, but in 1890–91 an assessment of $3,200 per box (for 70 boxes) was required to meet the costs. Abbey-Schoeffel-Grau now offered a known quality of opera, with the losses to the Metropolitan limited to the costs of operating the building. Quite apart from any philistinism of the boxholders, it was an offer that could not be refused.

"The most fireproof theater ever built" burned out the morning of August 27, 1892. Cady's primitive sprinkler system had been abandoned because the water in the roof tank froze in the winter; the iron struts for the stage had been replaced by lumber because wood was easier to work when stage levels had to be changed; the asbestos curtain was up because it was August in New York and the ventilating system operated in the auditorium, not on the stage; sets and drops in process littered backstage; and a scene painter dropped a cigarette into a can of paint thinner. The total damage done was estimated at $225,000 in a report to the board on September 9. About $60,000 of that was covered by insurance, and the assessment necessary to refurbish would have been only slightly more than $2,000 per box.

But the board was not prepared to proceed on that basis. A committee headed by James A. Roosevelt argued that the house should not be rebuilt unless the boxholders were prepared to pay off the second mortgage and the "floating debt" of $100,000 accumulated by the German seasons. Together with the usual taxes, interest on the first mortgage, etc., the repair work and repayments would bring the assessment for the year to $10,000 a box. A number of stockholders refused that assessment out of hand, and Roosevelt then proposed that the repairs be undertaken if 36 boxholders could be found who would pledge $18,000 each. A week later it was clear that this plan, too, would fail, and Cornelius Vanderbilt III offered a motion to dissolve the Metropolitan Opera House Company and sell the property at public

"Music's Ruined Temple" proclaimed the caption under a news photo (*above*) of the fire on August 27, 1892. A crowd has gathered on 40th Street, looking across Seventh Avenue to the rear of the house. The damage inside (*left*) was such that the architects designed a new stage-frame (*right*) to replace the burned-out proscenium.

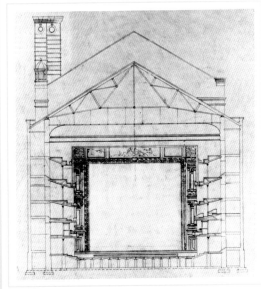

auction. A month later, this procedure was put into effect with a request to the Bowery Savings Bank to foreclose on the mortgage.

The purpose of this procedure, however, was to reconstitute the operation, not to kill it. A new group was being put together to own the rebuilt theater. There would be only 35 in this select circle, and they would occupy only the first tier of boxes. Each would put up $60,000: $30,000 in equity, and $30,000 in the purchase of a bond. The resulting $2.1 million would be enough to pay the 70 existing boxholders $20,000 each—returning their investment of ten years before—and leave $700,000 to pay off the second mortgage and the floating debt, and rebuild the house. For the existing boxholders who continued, of course, the repayment meant that their out-of-pocket cost was only $40,000. Nineteen of the boxholders in the new Metropolitan Opera and Real Estate Company were holdovers from the old Metropolitan Opera House Company, and sixteen were newcomers, several of them from what had been the Academy of Music crowd.

On February 3, Roosevelt bid in the property for $1,425,000. Bowery gave the new owners a new mortgage, and the reconstruction began. Two of the baignoire boxes on the parquet level had been eliminated in the second season to make room for standees; now the others went, yielding to three rows of raised seats facing across the hall, so that people in the "Orchestra Circle" watched with their necks turned. The salon area of the former boxes became standing room. Cady's 3,045 seats became 3,400, with perhaps 600 more foot soldiers. The new decor still eschewed the classic dark red, being essentially cream-colored, but this time there were no criticisms—everything looked different in the gleam of electric light, the "diamonds" glittering on the front of the boxes that gave the name "Diamond Horseshoe."

The construction process saw the start of a Metropolitan institution. Covent Garden had long had its Corridor Club and Paris its Jockey Club, with quarters in the opera house. The foyer areas on the Grand Tier level of the Met had been untouched by the fire, and a group of young bloods came to Roosevelt with the suggestion that they would rent it for private entertainments, retaining the space as an area for recreation during intermissions and after performances. A special large box was built at the side on the Grand Tier level, with 53 (later 63) angled seats, and rented by the year to what was then called the Vaudeville Club; the rental was five to six times the annual assessment on the boxholders for a box.

White tie was *de rigueur* in the Vaudeville Club box, and members spent the intermissions visiting the female boxholders and their daughters (women stayed put during intermissions; men moved about). It was also possible to get a drink, or several, in the club's room across the corridor. "Memberships were high," wrote the Club's historian affectionately in 1949, "and so, at times, were members." Around the turn of the century, the post-performance entertainment in the Club room sometimes verged on burlesque, and that custom was stopped. The name was changed to Metropolitan Opera Club, and with the passage of time the average age of Club members rose very considerably.

Abbey had returned triumphantly the year before the fire, offering on opening night perhaps the most remarkable triple debut in the history of the house: the irresistibly handsome and artistic Polish tenor Jean de Reszke, the first artist men went to hear because their wives insisted; his brother Edouard de Reszke; and the American Emma Eames, 26 years old, Paris-trained, well-bred ("I was brought up," she wrote some years later, "to be fastidious and chaste"), beautiful, and possessed of a silvery, pure voice in the 19th century's favorite style. The opera had been *Roméo et Juliette*, and it had been sung in French, the first time that language had been heard on the Metropolitan stage. Later evenings had presented the debuts of Lillian Nordica, Emma Albani (a mistake: aging and corpulent, she had attempted Gilda), and Jean Lassalle, who later paired with Frère Edouard—as Bernard Shaw liked to call the bass De Reszke—in a Don Giovanni-Leporello combination of elegant French manners. After the subscription season, Abbey had offered a two-week "supplementary season" at advanced prices, with Seidl conducting a *Flying Dutchman* (sung in Italian) and Patti appearing three times in the first of what would be many "farewells." Vianesi did most of the conducting (he directed the first nine performances); and the immigrant Italian orchestra seemed a great comedown from what Damrosch and Seidl had led in the German seasons.

The fire and its timing were, in a sense, providential for the Met. The cadre of boxholders was too large to be sustained, and assessments were going to have to be raised to cover the costs of electrifying the house and restoring some of a hard-used interior. If the fire had come a year later, the house might not have been rebuilt, for 1893 was the year of a great depression, with bankruptcies in Wall Street and the heartland, strikes in the mines and railroads to protest wage reductions, and Coxey's Army forming to march on Washington.

The famous gaiety of the Nineties had a frenetic quality: the rich felt beleaguered on all sides. Charles Parkhurst's crusade against vice, begun in 1892, has become, deservedly, a caricature—but the vice was real, and the running sores of poverty, exposed to the middle-class public by Jacob Riis's *How the Other Half Lives*, were calling for remedy. Theodore Roosevelt was to become police commissioner in 1895, and to bring the city into uproar by enforcing the Sunday closing laws, in the reformer's pious hope of giving the workingman a day of real rest with his family. In 1896, William Jennings Bryan would throw a scare into the entire plutocracy with what John Dos Passos later called the silver tongue in the big mouth, stampeding the Democratic convention with his demand that a community typified by Metropolitan boxholders should not be permitted to crucify mankind upon a cross of gold.

Operatically, the hiatus gave both the new Metropolitan Opera and Real Estate Company and the Abbey forces a chance to regroup and organize on a stable basis. With Jean de Reszke as the great box-office attraction in both houses (he and his brother Edouard were the only singers ever whose contracts with the Met called for a share of the take), the Met and Covent Garden drew together. Abbey, who seems to have been almost as starstruck as his audiences, was quite incapable of businesslike management in opera, but increasingly the conduct of affairs was passing into the hands of his partner Maurice Grau. An Austrian immigrant in his youth, Grau graduated from the Free Academy in New York (later City College) and the Columbia Law School. He was suave, multilingual, apparently conciliatory— and tough as nails, a man who could talk on the phone with his stockbroker while laying out casts and negotiating with artists gathered in his office. It was probably Grau who saw that the company could maximize its receipts by lowering prices, and cut back to $5 for a seat in the parquet, $2.50 and $2 in the Balcony, $1.50 and $1 in the Family Circle. Prices could always be raised—and were—when there was a special attraction.

In 1893, in the rebuilt Met, the De Reszkes were joined by two new sopranos who excited the public as none since Patti: the Australian Nellie Melba, colonial edges rubbed off by the experience of Paris, and the French Emma Calvé. Melba reconciled even the Wagnerians to *Lucia di Lammermoor*; her voice, Krehbiel wrote, "is charmingly fresh, and exquisitely beautiful, and her tone production is more natural, and more spontaneous than that of the marvelous woman who so long upheld the standard of bel canto throughout the world . . . To throw those scintillant bubbles of sound which used to be looked upon as the highest achievement in singing seems to be a perfectly natural mode of emotional expression with her."

Calvé was even more. Making her debut as Santuzza in Mascagni's *Cavalleria rusticana* on the same night that the fine lyric soprano Sigrid Arnoldson and the awesome French bass Pol Plançon appeared on the Met stage for the first time in the first American production of Gounod's *Philémon et Baucis*, Calvé kindled enthusiasm not only for herself but for an opera that had more or less failed in 1891 in the cool hands of Emma Eames. But the revelation was her Carmen, sung in French for the first time in New York, with Jean de Reszke's Don José, Lassalle's Escamillo, and Eames's Micaëla, Luigi Mancinelli conducting. For the first time, a Carmen literally seduced a New York audience with an open display of heedless sexuality that could indeed be redeemed for the Parkhurst contingent only by her death at the end. Nor was it trivial that she was partnered by the achieved innocence of De Reszke, a man whose dominance of the public perception of opera was won more by intelligence in acting and musical phrasing than by any tidal waves of voice. W. J. Henderson noted that the excellence of the principal artists was such "to inspire not only the secondary singers, but to nerve the chorus to a jealous regard for pitch and gradations of light and shade." It was, he thought, a cast that qualified for "the epithet 'ideal'."

Abbey had agreed in his contract that at least two of the six artists he named as his principals would appear in each performance. He did not quite live up to that—but in fact one of the De Reszkes or Melba or Calvé was on stage every evening all season long—and in addition there were Nordica and Eames and Scalchi, Lassalle and Plançon. The novelties were Mascagni's *L'Amico Fritz*, Massenet's *Werther*, and Mozart's *Le Nozze di Figaro*, with Eames and Nordica, the two Americans, giving a lesson in vocal blending in the letter duet.

Except for Calvé, who wanted more money than Grau was prepared to pay, they all returned the next season—together with the stentorian Francesco Tamagno, whom Verdi himself had cast as the first Otello; and the subtle French baritone Victor Maurel, Verdi's choice for Iago and for Falstaff. As a result, the Met staged both the great masterpieces of Verdi's old age, Eames taking the major soprano roles, Mancinelli conducting. *Otello* proved a puzzlement, being not Italian enough for the emerging Italian audience and too Italian for the Germans; nor was it a novelty, Tamagno having performed it with Abbey's touring troupe on this same stage in spring 1890, and De Reszke having sung it once in the subscription series in 1891.

But *Falstaff* was brand new, receiving its first North American performance, and an amazement to all—especially in Maurel's performance, in which the remnants of a knightly delicacy warred with the grossness of the scoundrel's appetites. And Eames was better suited for Alice, a cool customer if ever there was one. The young baritone Giuseppe Campanari, who would still be singing at the Met in 1912, established himself in this *Falstaff* in a single night (as Lawrence Tibbett was to do a generation later) in the role of Ford. Maurel also ornamented the season's *Don Giovanni*, and was one of the seven soloists in the dollar-a-star *Les Huguenots*, when Abbey and Grau raised the price to $7 for Melba, the two De Reszkes, Nordica, Plançon, Scalchi, and Maurel.

Another debut was that of Sybil Sanderson, a light-voiced Californian who had been cutting a swath through the *haut monde* in Paris. Rapturously received by the boxholders, who were entertaining her at their homes, she was nearly inaudible in the upper tiers as Massenet's Manon (and she roused a degree of scorn in the press by wearing her spectacular jewelry—presented by aristocratic French admirers—as she went off to the convent). It was also in this season that Mathilde Bauermeister, already in her third year with the company, universally admired as the ideal *comprimaria*, took over the role of Inez in Meyerbeer's *L'Africaine* after the scheduled protagonist fainted on stage. Inquiring as to how she happened to know it, the press was informed that Bauermeister knew the major female roles in all the operas in which she sang the minor ones.

Overleaf: The Golden Age. Jean and Edouard de Reszke (*left, above*, as Raoul in *Les Huguenots* and Leporello in *Don Giovanni*); Lillian Nordica (*left, below*, as Philine in *Mignon*); Marcel Journet and Nellie Melba (*right, above*, as Colline in *Bohème* and Juliette in Gounod's *Roméo*); Emma Calvé (*right, below*, as Carmen).

Mancinelli conducted the Wagner, all of which was done in Italian—*Die Meistersinger* as *I Maestri Cantori*. Seidl was available—he had become conductor of the New York Philharmonic—but was used only for Sunday night concerts. But the Metropolitan audience got its Wagner straight from an old source that year when a touring company managed and conducted by Walter Damrosch took the house for 21 performances while the regular company was on tour.

Stimulated perhaps by Damrosch's success in that mini-season, Abbey and Grau sought and received permission to add to the 1895–96 season a fifth night of opera every week, a Thursday night series, to be devoted to the German repertory under Seidl's direction. (The year before, they had broken the tradition of Monday-Wednesday-Friday nights and Saturday matinees—Tuesday in Philadelphia—by adding regular Saturday night performances at reduced prices.) The great German event, which appeared in this special series only after its premiere on a previous Wednesday, was Jean de Reszke's first performance as Tristan, in German, with Nordica as Isolde and brother Edouard as King Marke.

This was an astonishing act of conscience by a great matinee idol who had absolutely nothing to gain but artistic satisfaction. Like all Poles of a certain class, the De Reszkes had spoken French from childhood, but never German. In preparation for their entry into Wagner as written, they had been speaking German to each other for two years. They (and Nordica) rehearsed privately as well as publicly with the indefatigable Seidl, and by the time of their appearance they were entirely ready. Germans in the audience were amazed by the quality of their diction; music critics were grateful to the point of worship for their accuracy of pitch: "Never before," Krehbiel wrote, "have we had a Tristan able to sing the declamatory music of the first and last acts with correct intonation, to say nothing of the duet in the second act." In Edouard's hands, King Marke's speech to Tristan was dramatically and vocally anything but a bore. And Nordica, thought of as a known quantity—our Lilli from Maine, who became an opera singer—leapt in her first Isolde to the status of diva, a creature of passion and overwhelming tonal power.

Calvé was back for sold-out *Carmens*, and for several novelties, among them Massenet's *La Navarraise* and Bizet's *Les Pêcheurs de perles*. Her spectacularly staged mad scene as Ophelia in Thomas's *Hamlet* roused special enthusiasm. Krehbiel described it:

Her face was full of simplicity, childish sweetness and wistful wonder, but its simplicity was not that of a happy and intelligent child: it was that of vacancy. Her eyes and her lips had no mind behind them. Her motions seemed to have no guidance. They were sudden, capricious and constantly changing yet always full of grace and prettiness. At the end of her aria she sank in a shapeless heap, and the ushers thought it a fitting time to throw bouquets at her. The members of the chorus brought them to where she lay, but she would have none of them. Then she started up, caught at the bouquets, tore them to pieces and almost buried herself in them. Such an incident with a singer who was less an artist would have destroyed the effect, if she had succeeded in making any. Mme. Calvé made it all a part of her scene, treated it consistently in her own mood and made it contribute to the purpose of all that she had done hitherto.

Melba and Maurel and Scalchi and Plançon also returned, and there was another all-star *Huguenots*, at advanced prices. Melba sang her first Metropolitan Manon in Massenet's opera, and Nordica her first local Aida. Three versions of the Faust story were on the boards—Gounod's, Boito's, and Berlioz's (conducted by Seidl). There were moments of great lavishness in the casting, especially the employment of Melba as Micaëla. But the Thursday night German presentations were mostly second-class, and the audience at the popular-priced Saturday nights did not get to hear either De Reszke, even once.

Something else was happening in this season, though it went unreported in the press and has not been recorded in the histories: the firm of Abbey, Schoeffel, and Grau went broke. The board of the Real Estate Company, rather than hunt for a new tenant, undertook the reorganization itself, placing William Steinway of the piano family in charge. He couldn't just cancel the lease: nobody but Grau could deliver De Reszke. So the board undertook to bail out Grau's company.

What Grau had counted on in his financial analysis, and would later exploit more effectively, was the fact that the impresario producing the operas leased the house for the entire year, and received for his rental payment not merely an annual subsidy for the production of opera (which rose to as much as $16,000 over and above the rent) but also the receipts from any subletting. Grau was forever trying to get more performances into each week of a shorter season, not only to reduce the per-performance cost of his orchestra, chorus, stagehands, and lesser soloists (who worked by the week), but also to earn the Real Estate Company's subvention while opening the house to more rentals. (The directors were by no means enthusiastic about this development, not wishing to go to opera more times each week, but they did eventually agree to up their grant from $4,000 for four performances to $4,500 for five.) After Abbey's death in October 1896, the minutes show increasing concern and sometimes disapproval of the uses to which the house was put. A rental for a presentation ball to Lillian Russell was approved only upon the pledge that the tickets would cost at least $10 each. A few years later an outraged board took unfavorable notice of a Pet Dog Show that had rented the Metropolitan Opera House, and resolved "that hereafter no more dog shows be permitted to be held in the Opera House." Still later, the board rejected Grau's request that the theater be leased for vaudeville, but granted him an extra $10,000 subsidy to make up for the lost income.

Grau's first season without Abbey, but still in the framework of Steinway's reorganized Abbey, Schoeffel, and Grau, was little short of disastrous. The overriding problem, which made newspaper headlines, grew out of the competition among sopranos to appear with Jean de Reszke, whose great event in this season was to be his first Siegfried, in German, in the third of the *Ring* operas. Melba insisted that she must sing the Brünnhildes to the idol's Siegfried, and a deeply offended Nordica, believing (probably correctly) that Grau would never have authorized such a thing without pressure from De Reszke, publicly resigned from the company.

Various conjectures have been floated to explain why De Reszke would want so clearly unsuitable a partner for the final scene of the opera. Perhaps the most convincing comes from Ira Glackens, Nordica's biographer, who picked up a comment by De Reszke later—that he dreaded that final duet, when after singing hard all night he would find himself coupled with a fresh voice rising from a long sleep. Nordica was probably louder than De Reszke, anyway; and that was not what he wanted.

On Monday, December 21, 1896, Melba sang Violetta in *La Traviata*, triumphantly, for the first time in New York; on Saturday the 26th, she sang Lucia; on Wednesday the 30th, she sang Brünnhilde, and very nearly wrecked her voice. She sang only once more the entire season.

The pity of it was that the De Reszkes (as Siegfried and Wanderer) were as greatly admired in this opera as they had been in *Tristan*—and by Krehbiel's account, incidentally, they drew an audience not only from the intellectual and musical community, but from the city's social whirl, though the work is both long and dense, packed with every leitmotif in the entire *Ring*; the performance, though cut in the Seidl manner, ran until well after midnight. Again, Jean de Reszke convinced both in the music and in the character. He had shaved his mustache for the occasion, and what struck all observers was his energetic youthfulness on stage.

One can see, indeed, how Melba might have become confused. If Jean could triumph as all the Massenet and Gounod heroes—as Des Grieux and Roméo and Faust—and move on to greater glory as Lohengrin and Tristan and Siegfried, why should not his Manon and Juliette and Marguerite also reach out for the Wagner roles? But she couldn't, and her attempt cost Grau both his leading dramatic soprano and, after the fiasco, his leading light soprano.

This was also the season of the first death during a Metropolitan performance, when the veteran French bass Armand Castelmary suffered a heart attack (not his first) while attempting energetic stage action. He died in the arms of Jean de Reszke, who was not in the cast, but had come backstage with a premonition of disaster.

☆ ☆ ☆

With Abbey's death, the lease on the opera house had lapsed. During the course of the year, the English firm of Abbey, Schoeffel, and Grau, Ltd., had been formed to take over the lease on Covent Garden, and much of Grau's time would be committed to London. He declined to renew the lease on the Met, either on his own behalf or that of the English firm. He also refused to commit himself to the production of opera in New York the next season. The De Reszke brothers had told him that they would not return to New York for 1897–98, though they hoped to come the year after; Calvé was unavailable; the chastened Melba had put her affairs in the hands of Charles Ellis, manager of the Boston Symphony, who had committed her to the Damrosch touring company (now the Damrosch-Ellis Grand Opera).

What Grau did offer the Met directors was a three-year rental contract, with the option not to produce opera in the first year, leasing the house "at his discretion." Of course, the boxholders (who would have to pay a $2,000 assessment to meet interest and taxes even if the house were dark) would get their admission and boxes free for any event in the theater—and with Damrosch-Ellis around, there would be opera. In fact, though there was no "Met" season in 1897–98, there were five weeks of opera at the house, with Damrosch conducting six Wagner operas, Nordica singing the three Brünnhildes, Melba singing Violetta, Marguerite in *Faust*, Rosina in *Barbiere*—and Aida. Because her first appearance on stage for the previous year's *Siegfried* came after their deadline, the critics had pretty much left Melba's sole Brünnhilde alone. Now they tore into her Aida—but her audience, especially the boxholders, loved her always: one needed no special musicality to enjoy the sound of that voice.

The directors demanded from Grau that he set up a separate corporation—the Maurice Grau Opera Company—insulated from his other theatrical ventures, and that he show a capitalization of $150,000 invested in that company as a cushion for the Met. But when the last chunk of that money proved hard to find, the Real Estate Company itself put up $26,000 for a one-quarter interest in Grau's concern. They had no reason to regret it: Grau showed a profit in every one of the five seasons he produced. In 1899–1900, for example—after paying $80,500 to Calvé, $61,000 to Sembrich, $49,660 to Edouard de Reszke, $39,000 to Nordica, $39,000 to the Wagnerian tenor Ernest Van Dyck, $37,250 to Eames, and $25,700 to Plançon—Grau had split a profit of $103,510 fifty-fifty with his shareholders. This meant that the Real Estate Company received a $12,050 dividend, a 46 per cent return on investment in a single year. What made it possible, of course, was the coolie wages paid to everyone else; the entire orchestra received only $100,000, the chorus $36,000, the ballet $13,000 for the whole season. Each of the seven highest-priced singers was paid more than the entire conducting staff.

The first three of Grau's five years were perhaps the brightest of the Golden Age. Lehmann returned in 1898–99, a matron now but still an artist of power and elegance, sharing the Isoldes with Nordica, singing Sieglinde, Venus, and Valentine. More significantly, for Lehmann was in her last season, Marcella Sembrich returned, now a mature artist of 40, to be a major ornament of the house

Overleaf: The man who presided over the Met's star seasons of the late 1890s was Maurice Grau (*right*), theatrical lawyer and entrepreneur. It was during Grau's years that the Byron Company shot some "candid" views inside the opera house: a rehearsal on stage (*left, above*) and the chorus ladies practicing in one of the assembly rooms (*below*).

for the next decade, sharing the Melba repertory. Lehmann, Sembrich, and Nordica appeared together in a performance of *Don Giovanni*, with Edouard de Reszke as Leporello and Victor Maurel as the Don—another "ideal" cast. Eames and Sembrich began what would be a long partnership as Countess and Susanna in *Le Nozze di Figaro*. The next season, Grau would offer *The Magic Flute* for the first time at the Met (in Italian, unfortunately), with Sembrich as Queen of the Night, Eames as Pamina, and a number of the company's other leading ladies helping out as Ladies or Boys.

Seidl had died in spring 1898, to the horror of all: the city's most influential and revered musician, still under 50. The funeral took place on the stage of the Metropolitan. But Grau found a worthy replacement in Franz Schalk, later to be Intendant and leading conductor at the Vienna State Opera; and Schalk gave New York its first uncut *Ring* cycle—and a *Tristan* with Lehmann and the De Reszkes (Marie Brema, herself an Isolde, as Brangäne; Anton van Rooy, on other evenings a Wotan, as Kurwenal), which Lehmann later told Henderson was the greatest performance of her life.

Of the previous seasons' cast of stars, only Calvé was missing. Among the newcomers were Van Dyck, second only to De Reszke as a Wagnerian tenor; Van Rooy, second to none as a Wagnerian bass-baritone; the tenor Albert Saléza, who had the bad luck in operatic history to be the alternate first for De Reszke and then for Caruso; Johanna Gadski, who later would become the leading dramatic soprano of the company; and the deep-voiced, brilliantly musical Ernestine Schumann-Heink, who would sing her farewell to the Met in 1932.

Jean de Reszke missed 1899–1900, but Calvé returned. And there was again a startling display of new talent: the suave baritone Antonio Scotti, who would sing leading roles for 34 consecutive seasons at the Met, setting a record unsurpassed until Jerome Hines moved into his 35th season in 1980; Milka Ternina, a Yugoslav soprano (later a teacher into whose class wandered the young Zinka Milanov), who soon challenged Nordica for the Isoldes and Brünnhildes; and Antonio Pini-Corsi, for many years the company's trusty *basso buffo*, who could be funny off-stage too. (It was Pini-Corsi who was observed during a rehearsal of Walter Damrosch's *Cyrano de Bergerac* doffing his hat at regular intervals. He was paying tribute, he told an inquirer, to the memories of all the great composers whose music Damrosch had plagiarized.) The presence of Scotti and Pini-Corsi in his company made it a pleasure for Grau to give Sembrich the first Met performance of Donizetti's *Don Pasquale*.

In 1899–1900, the Met had done without Melba; in 1900–01, the board having for the first time exercised its right to disapprove the impresario's list of six leading artists, she was back, at the cost of both Eames and Sembrich, whose roles she would pre-empt. But it was in this season that Melba found the new repertory she had so unwisely sought in Brünnhilde and Aida, when she sang Mimi in the Met's first performance of Puccini's *La Bohème*. Again this year there was a catalogue of important debuts: by the sturdy and handsome American mezzo Louise Homer, the Viennese Fritzi Scheff (a vivacious comedienne who became one of the few sopranos ever to alternate successfully between Broadway operetta and grand opera), and the French basses Marcel Journet and Charles Gilibert.

But the headline material of 1900–01 was the return of Jean de Reszke, who had not sung in almost a year, when he resumed his mastery of Lohengrin on New Year's Eve, before a packed house. There had been rumors that he had lost his voice, and his appearance was greeted with an ovation some observers estimated at half an hour in duration. It was to be De Reszke's last season in New York, and he offered a *tour d'horizon* of his career—Walther in *Die Meistersinger* (with his brother Edouard singing his first German Hans Sachs), Tristan and the two Siegfrieds, Gounod's Faust and Roméo, Roderigo in Massenet's *Le Cid*. The very last hurrah was at a farewell gala to end the season, following the company's spring tour, when the De Reszkes contributed a second act of *Tristan*, Nordica singing Isolde. It was a warm night, the doors to the house were closed, and in the hysteria no fewer than sixteen women in the audience fainted.

After that, for some reason, the Grau regime seemed to run down. The impresario's health turned uncertain—Henderson in the *Times*, in a serio-comic piece, blamed the need to chase around Europe all summer, listening to inadequate singers. The most important debut in Grau's last two seasons was that of the conductor Alfred Hertz. With Edouard de Reszke's voice drying up and Jean gone, the male side of the company seemed far less strong—especially in the tenor category—than the female.

Against a competing application by Walter Damrosch, who had conducted not very interestingly for Grau in 1900–02 and was an experienced manager of touring companies, the lease of the Metropolitan Opera House for the five seasons starting 1903–04 was awarded to Heinrich Conried, a German actor and stage manager who had made money on operettas and with German-language plays in the Irving Place Theater owned by William Steinway. It was written into the contract that no more than 40 per cent of the performances in any season could be in German.

A feeling of malaise spread in the press: the Golden Age was ending. Those glorious creatures who came with their own costumes and jewelry, who scorned rehearsals and drew audiences even if the staging was perfunctory and the orchestra sloppy and the chorus slovenly—they were dying out. Lawrence Reamer expressed the prevailing opinion: "There is no generation of singers in sight to supplant the stars of the present day."

Conried, it was generally agreed, would offer stagecraft, dramatic art, discipline. The kings and queens of opera were fading away: long live ensemble!

The next season opened with Enrico Caruso making his debut in *Rigoletto*.

THREE

MILESTONES I: 25TH ANNIVERSARY. THE JOYS AND PAINS, THE POLITICS AND PERSONALITIES OF A GREAT SEASON

One year in the hundred stands out for the quality of its performances, the drama of the processes by which they came to the Metropolitan's stage, and the strength of its influence on subsequent seasons. The 1908–09 season, the year of the Metropolitan's 25th anniversary (appropriate telegrams of congratulations were sent by various political and cultural leaders), was the year when the opera house acquired the leadership that would guide it for the next quarter of a century.

For New York audiences, it was a year of great conductors and singers at *two* competing opera houses, the Met and the Manhattan Opera of the effervescent Oscar Hammerstein, who eagerly spent the profits of the cigar-making machinery he had invented to prove himself an impresario of genius and a public benefactor. Either of these theaters would have ranked that season as the best in the world, in the absence of the other. The goings-on at the opera received more public attention in 1908–09 than ever before or ever after, as the accumulated sins and glories of the Metropolitan were highlighted by publicized political rivalries and personality clashes within the house. Socially, it was the year that opera was on its own, for Caroline Astor died before the season began, 78 years old and unrelenting, and the Astor box stood empty, even after nine o'clock.

It was a time of immensely lavish construction. McKim, Mead & White were building Pennsylvania Station, Bellevue Hospital, Columbia University, and the First National Bank Building on Wall Street; they had recently completed J. P. Morgan's library and the mansions of Mrs. William K. Vanderbilt, Harry Payne Whitney, and Jasper Innis Kane, all major figures in the Metropolitan constellation. Carrère & Hastings were at work on the New York Public Library, two blocks from the Met, and on the New Theater near Columbus Circle, which was to be run essentially in conjunction with the Met.

The first subway line had been opened in 1904, supplementing the trolleys that ran before the Met's front door and the elevated railway a block away. The hub of the subway system was Times Square, next to the Met; it would increase immensely the catchment area for the larger audience that did not have a carriage and footman

Arturo Toscanini, Giulio Gatti-Casazza, and Geraldine Farrar on stage. Gatti's expression speaks volumes about the relationship between long-suffering impresarios, implacable conductors, and capricious prima donnas.

to wait for their appearance following the completion of the opera. In Detroit, as that season opened, an obscure engineer named Henry Ford was emplacing the machine tools that would build the Model T.

But 1908–09 was not an auspicious year. The Panic of 1907 had hit the economy hard, cut immigration by 40 per cent from its all-time peak in 1907, and doubled the number of emigrants. The recovery was slow and stumbling, with total bank deposits down from the previous year (the New Amsterdam National Bank, which rented space in the Opera House buildings, was among the failures), and with 8 per cent of the labor force unemployed. Nevertheless, thirteen days before the Met season opened, the phlegmatic William Howard Taft had given a final quietus to the Presidential hopes of the ardent William Jennings Bryan. Meanwhile, an American presence had been flung across the Pacific by Theodore Roosevelt, and the Great White Fleet was dithering around the China coast.

For the occupants of the cheap seats at the Metropolitan Opera House, 1908 was going to be a banner year regardless of the performances: the Real Estate Company had for the first time installed an elevator that would spare them the six winding flights of stairs they had been forced to climb in previous years, while the boxholders entering on the other side of the building rode their own elevator one flight up. Yet another important elevator had also been installed—one that would lift or lower the floor of the orchestra pit. The pit itself had been lengthened, and the seats that had formerly run to the stage on either side had been removed.

The company that produced opera at the Met had gone through reorganization that spring under the leadership of the immigrant German-Jewish investment banker Otto Kahn, a small man with a broad forehead and a dark military mustache, who was converting what had been a profit-seeking, dividend-paying venture into a not-for-profit company that would accumulate any earnings from its labors as a rainy-day fund. Kahn had managed to retain the conducting services of Gustav Mahler, who the season before had given New York a blazing *Tristan und Isolde*, but the newcomers were the story. To run his producing company, Kahn had hired La Scala's manager Giulio Gatti-Casazza, the Met's first salaried general manager. And Gatti was bringing with him Arturo Toscanini, already a legend in Italy, never before heard in the United States.

These three were still relatively young men—Kahn and Toscanini were 41; Gatti, 38. Kahn would serve the Met as president of the producing company for 23 years, and Gatti would be general manager for 27, doing business entirely in Italian to the end. Toscanini would conduct at the Met for only seven seasons, but as an orchestral conductor and a conductor of opera in concert form, doing most of his business in highly original English, he would dominate the New York musical scene until the mid-1950s.

☆ ☆ ☆

For Kahn and Gatti and Toscanini, the months before the 1908–09 season were full of alarms and discouragements. Gatti's had been perhaps the most grievous, for Kahn at their one meeting, in Paris the summer of 1907, had not told him much about the conditions he was to encounter. Even the first sight of the building must have been the same sort of jolt to him that it was to his future wife Frances Alda, who encountered it in the same year:

Dirty brown brick. Shabby. Old, weather-stained posters hanging in tatters in the sleety winter wind. The sordid everyday business of Broadway—the hawkers, the actors and actresses out of jobs, the hotel touts, out-of-town sightseers, sandwich men, dope peddlers, gangsters, the thousands who make a living off the weakness and ignorance of other human beings—swirling in a greasy tide around its doors.

Inside, however, Gatti found an elegance very near what Metropolitan audiences would know until the house closed. In the negotiations for a renewed contract with Grau in 1903, before Grau decided to retire, the board had agreed to put $90,000 into a general refurbishing, and had hired Carrère & Hastings to do the job. The fondly remembered maroon-and-gold color scheme was theirs, as was the sunburst chandelier, the baroque shapes on the box fronts, and the softened proscenium, with curved corners up top and the slightly bulging gilded plaques bearing the names Gluck, Mozart, Verdi, Wagner, Gounod, Beethoven. Even the gold curtain was in place when Gatti came, though that had waited until 1906.

Backstage, the renovations of 1903, inspired by Conried, had done some good. The Met now had a counterweighted system of pulleys to control the contents of the fly gallery, and the first trap doors had been cut into the stage. But the resources for the production of opera remained the poorest of any major opera house in the world. There was a single stage that had to be used both for rehearsals and for performances (the orchestra had to rehearse in the pit; the chorus and ballet rehearsed in the Assembly Rooms for lack of other accommodations). Lighting was archaic, with almost nothing available from the auditorium. There was virtually no storage space whatever, in the flies or in the wings: productions had to be carted daily to and from the warehouse. Though some ambitious stage work had been attempted at the Met—Roller's famous sets and costumes for the Vienna *Fidelio* had been duplicated the year before—most productions were shabby and poorly executed.

Gatti toured the 40th Street warehouse, acquired in 1902, and pronounced himself shocked. Later he remembered "a certain set that represented an ugly court and a door in the rear, opening on the sea. 'But what set is this?' I asked. 'It's used interchangeably,' was the reply, 'for the first act of *Mignon* and the first act of *Otello*.'"

Gatti soon discovered that deficiencies in the house could not be remedied by Kahn, who was not even a boxholder and had no vote in the Real Estate Company that controlled the property. Though five of the directors of Kahn's new producing

company were boxholders, they were unable to guarantee to Gatti that the structural revisions he thought essential for the presentation of operas to modern standards would in fact be accomplished. In the end, Gatti did get quick action on a rehearsal stage at roof level: the Real Estate Company at the end of his first season gratefully appropriated $20,000 for the purpose. Little else could be done. Half a century later, the Met chorus was still rehearsing in the crush bar on the Grand Tier level, because there was no other place to work. Kahn told Gatti not to worry about the physical problems of the house: there would be a new theater built for the Met within two or three years . . . "Mr. Kahn," Gatti mused in his memoirs, ". . . was unquestionably a brilliant and gifted man of many qualities. But I cannot attribute to him that of being a good prophet!"

Moreover, Gatti had to contend with competition both outside and inside the opera house. Oscar Hammerstein's Manhattan Opera had enjoyed an astonishing season in 1907–08, its second year of operation. Denied access to Puccini's scores by an exclusive contract between G. Ricordi, their publisher, and the Met (though he had been able to pirate *La Bohème*), Hammerstein had been fishing in French waters, and pulled from them Offenbach's *Contes d'Hoffmann* (which had never been presented at the Met and enjoyed eleven sold-out performances at the Manhattan that season), plus no fewer than three major New York premieres: Massenet's *Thaïs*, Charpentier's *Louise*, and Debussy's *Pelléas et Mélisande*. His prima donna for all three had been Mary Garden, making her New York debut, and he had also brought to New York for the first time the coloratura Luisa Tetrazzini, who had received the kind of hysterical welcome only coloraturas can command.

For 1908–09, Hammerstein would add Nordica and Lina Cavalieri to his list of sopranos, he would have access to the Puccini operas, and he would stage Strauss's *Salome*, prohibited to the Met by J. P. Morgan's fear and loathing. At twenty weeks' duration, his season was the same as the Met's (it opened and closed one week earlier, and the rest overlapped); and he was completing an opera house in Philadelphia, where he would run a separate company in tandem with the Manhattan. His leading conductor, Cleofonte Campanini (who had been the secondary conductor for the opening season at the Met 25 years before and had never been re-engaged), was considered by those who had not yet heard Toscanini to be the world's greatest expositor of Italian opera. Hammerstein's theater on West 34th Street between Seventh and Eighth Avenues was new, well-equipped, and more convenient than the Met to the glories of the Waldorf-Astoria Hotel (then located where the Empire State Building now stands). Though he did not particularly solicit society patronage—his boxes offered little opportunity for display—Hammerstein was beginning to receive it: no less a personage than the Duchess of Marlborough, Consuelo Vanderbilt, had attended his opening night in 1907.

A refurbishing of the interior in 1903 gave the Met the appearance it would have for the next 62 years. This photo, taken during an orchestral rehearsal, shows the new gold proscenium but not the famous gold curtain, which was installed in 1906.

Even more pressing as Gatti looked around was the competition inside the Metropolitan, for he found on his arrival that as "General Director" he was to share the management of the company with an "Administrative Director": Andreas Dippel, an Austrian-born tenor who had been associated with the Met since 1890 (he had, indeed, sung Walther in *Die Meistersinger* in 1891 on the very last afternoon of the seven all-German seasons). An excellent linguist and a quick learner, Dippel had set what is probably an all-time record for versatility in opera: in one season, he had sung sixteen different leading roles, once each, in three different languages. In 1907–08, he had appeared (once) as Almaviva in an Italian *Barbiere*, as Faust in a French *Faust*, as Froh in *Das Rheingold* and Walther in *Die Meistersinger*. An easygoing but hard-working artist, he was popular with colleagues, and had performed assorted managerial chores that had put him into personal contact with both boxholders and stockholders in the producing company.

Gatti was not unreceptive to the notion that he might need some help in running a theater that was new to him in a place he didn't know, where people spoke a language he didn't understand. He did doubt that he needed someone who was not his choice, with little managerial experience but obvious managerial ambitions, and with close personal contacts in the company. In fact, Dippel did have visions of running the German end of the Metropolitan while Gatti ran the French and Italian ends. He had convinced Kahn of the necessity of two choruses, one for Italian opera recruited by Gatti in Italy and one for German opera recruited by Dippel in Germany. Dippel had also recommended the hiring of a double orchestra, totaling 130 players, which presumably could also be specialized.

Gatti's (and Toscanini's) control of the Italian repertory had been watered down by the employment for the coming season of Francesco Spetrino, a Sicilian who had been in charge of the Italian repertory for Mahler at the Imperial Opera in Vienna, and who would (for this one season) share the burden of conducting the Italian works at the Met. Dippel had already been empowered by Kahn to negotiate contracts with some of the returning artists, and it had been Dippel who relayed to Mahler Toscanini's desire to conduct the season's first *Tristan und Isolde*, using the La Scala sets and costumes, before the Viennese returned to the company in mid-December.

(Mahler had rejected this idea with considerable dignity:

I expressly stated when the contract was being discussed, as you yourself can witness, that I wanted to keep in my hands for the ensuing season those works which I had already rehearsed and conducted in New York. I was given every assurance that this would be so, and it was only at your request and desire that I abstained from having it put in writing in the contract. If recently—out of consideration for the wishes of my colleague—I have given a free hand to the new Director, it was with the express exception of *Tristan*—I took very special pains with *Tristan* last season and can well maintain that the form in which the work now appears in New York is my spiritual property. If Toscanini, for whom, though unknown to me, I have the greatest respect, and whom I consider it an honor to be able to salute as a colleague, were now to take over *Tristan* before my arrival, the work would obviously be given an entirely new character, and it would be quite out of the question for me to resume my performances in the course of the season . . .

Toscanini withdrew his request.)

Gatti knew that someone in the existing management had been dealing with Mahler, and with Alfred Hertz, Mahler's distinguished partner in conducting the German repertory (he later served fifteen years as conductor of the San Francisco Symphony), and with some of the artists who were to return. But he had never heard of Andreas Dippel, or known that he was going to have an Administrative Director in his management, until his boat docked on May 1, 1908, for a visit of exploration, and Dippel led the welcoming party.

The politics of the situation were more complicated than Gatti could realize. The brief financial panic of 1901 had resulted from the clash of E. H. Harriman and the Morgan interests over the Northern Pacific Railroad, and 1907–08 was the year of what Kahn later called "the Harriman Extermination League," which was headed in effect by Morgan. Harriman's bankers were Kuhn, Loeb & Co.; Kahn, who had married the boss's daughter, was one of the managing partners of Kuhn, Loeb. There is some reason to believe that Morgan advised Kahn to cut his ties with Harriman for his own good, which Kahn scornfully refused to do.

Kahn had first become part of the picture at the Metropolitan as a financial backer and board member for Heinrich Conried when the German actor-impresario won the lease in 1903 and organized what he called the Conried Metropolitan Opera Company. Before responding to Conried's solicitation, he had consulted Harriman, who had no special interest in opera or anything else cultural, but advised Kahn to take it: if he worked seriously at supervising an opera company, Harriman said, he would be a better businessman for the experience. Quite apart from a strongly held and oft-expressed anti-Semitism, then, Morgan had a reason to dislike Kahn.

By 1907 it was becoming evident that Conried would have to be replaced, and sooner rather than later. The strain of running the Met in competition with Hammerstein had begun seriously to affect his health, and his lapses in judgment were growing ever more troubling. It had been Kahn's plan to take over Conried's company, take off Conried's name, and keep the existing artists' contracts and the lease with the boxholders' corporation, which had another three years to run. Morgan, who had opposed giving the contract to Conried from the beginning, also opposed this arrangement; and in fact a new lease had to be negotiated. Meanwhile, it developed that, as part of the campaign to win Conried's resignation from his own company, the textile magnate A. D. Juilliard, a member of the boxholders' executive committee, had promised him the right to name his successor, and Conried had proposed Dippel. Seizing on this revelation, Morgan had demanded a major role for Dippel in the reorganization, and Kahn acceded. Indeed, Kahn now panicked—after all, he knew little about Gatti or Toscanini—and when the secretary of his producing company traveled to Milan to sign up the two Italians for the Met, the three-year contract he carried with him gave either side an option to back off at the end of each season. A similar clause was then added to Dippel's contract as Administrative Director.

Dippel himself returned to New York in late September 1908—some weeks before Gatti's arrival—and began issuing statements to the press. Dippel had recruited the German chorus and arranged for its prior rehearsal by Hans Steiner of the Hoftheater in Munich . . . Dippel had arranged with Felix Weingartner in Vienna to borrow the tenor Erik Schmedes for the first half of the Metropolitan season . . . The *Daily Telegraph* for October 2 wrote of "the new orchestra pit built at Mr. Dippel's suggestion" . . . the *Evening Sun* of October 6 commented that "Andreas Dippel's revolutionary reforms in the Metropolitan Opera House have become the talk of Broadway in advance of the arrival of his Italian colleague and general director, Gatti-Casazza . . . Dippel's greatest innovations will become apparent when the local season begins." Then, on October 11, Gatti himself arrived, an interesting-looking man with a small squared-off beard and pointed mustache, grave and handsome; and for the next two months, all the ink flowed in his direction.

☆　☆　☆

For Kahn, the months before the reorganized company took over the Met were filled with unpleasant surprises on the financial side. He had not in fact followed Harriman's advice to treat his supervisory role in an opera company as a field for the exercise of business judgment. Indeed, his position from the start had been that it was unsuitable for an opera-producing company to seek the enrichment of its stockholders or directors. Though the producing company was called the Conried Metropolitan Opera Company, the manager himself had only a five-year contract to run it, ending in 1908, and as early as 1906, before he projected Conried's departure, Kahn had wanted its terms extensively altered:

"I am certain that many members of the Board," he wrote to James H. Hyde, who had originally invited him to join that board, "would be disinclined to renew [Conried's] contract on the old terms; the prevailing view being that the profit-sharing feature of his contract is fundamentally wrong; that he ought to be paid a *very liberal* salary, have his benefit performance and every other consideration accorded him, but that he ought not to have the incentive to run the opera for profit, which he has under the terms of his present contract."

Kahn knew that Maurice Grau had run the opera at a considerable profit, and he was under the misapprehension that Conried's management, except for two

---

That traffic jams were already a fact of life is apparent from the "Special Notice" inserted in Met programs of 1908. An illustrator for the *Century* Magazine depicted the new carriage-call arrangements in action, as well-accoutered couples in the 39th Street lobby wait for their numbers to appear on the board.

SPECIAL NOTICE

NEW CARRIAGE CALL ARRANGEMENTS

In order that patrons of the Opera House may reach their carriages with the least possible annoyance, arrangements have been made with the General Acoustic Company to install their Carriage Calling device.

In each lobby a number carrying machine will display the numbers of the first fourteen carriages that turn the corner of Seventh Avenue, thereby notifying the patrons that the number announced is approaching the door. The Management kindly asks that the patrons will STAY INSIDE OF THE LOBBY in order that they may see their number when placed on the machine. The carriages will reach the door as the number reaches the top of the machine.

Patrons will facilitate the movement of carriages and increase their own comfort by approaching the door as their number approaches the top of the machine, and in this manner the passage will be kept clear and they can reach their carriages without delay.

IF THE PATRONS WILL AID THE MANAGEMENT IN THIS EFFORT, THE OPERA HOUSE CAN BE EMPTIED IN TWENTY MINUTES.

instances of severe and well-known loss, had been equally successful. For despite all the chatter about the twilight of the stars that had attended Grau's departure, Conried had benefited by the arrival of several of the greatest box-office attractions in the Met's history. He had inherited from Grau's planning the debuts in his first season not only of Caruso but also of the Swedish-American Olive Fremstad, a dramatic soprano whose repertoire of triumphs ran from Isolde to Carmen. In 1906 he had signed the enchantress Lina Cavalieri—and the most widely popular female singer the Metropolitan ever knew, Geraldine Farrar, the beauty from Boston who had conquered *ganz* Berlin, including the Crown Prince.

Moreover, Conried had a gift for creating events. He had, for example, defied Richard Wagner's will and his widow's wrath and lawyers, and in his first season staged the first production of *Parsifal* outside Bayreuth, for which the composer had tried to reserve it. (Bernard Shaw, hearing that Cosima planned to restrict *Parsifal* to Bayreuth through her lifetime, wrote that it reconciled him to the custom of *suttee*.) Because the opera was supposed to have a religious motif, he scheduled it for Christmas Eve, scandalizing the clergy, who knew that whatever religion Wagner might proselytize, it wasn't Christianity. The production was extremely well received by the public (it sold out no fewer than twelve performances, at premium prices) and by the critics: "All that money, thought, care and intelligent labor could do had been lavished upon the production," Richard Aldrich wrote in the *Times*. "The result . . . nobly crowned the work of many months."

Aldrich was wrong in his perception that Conried had done *all* he could for *Parsifal*. Thirty years later in a letter to the *New York Times*, Charles Henry Meltzer revealed that he had done some moonlighting for Conried from his position as critic of the New York *American* (he later became Conried's press agent), visiting Europe in the summer of 1903 to look for singers who might come to the Met. Part of his mission was to visit Jean de Reszke, who had recently gone into retirement on the Riviera, to find out if anything might induce his return. De Reszke, who had never sung Parsifal, knew of Conried's plans, and offered to come to New York for that production. Meltzer enthusiastically cabled Conried, only to discover that "that shortsighted manager killed all hopes of our hearing Jean again in opera." Conried replied that he would be delighted to welcome De Reszke again at the Met, as Parsifal, but unfortunately he had already promised the opening night to Alois Burgstaller, and De Reszke would have to take a later performance. Conried, of course, was not being shortsighted, merely practical, in his own way. He knew he could sell out *Parsifal* without having to pay a De Reszke fee.

In the 1904–05 season, at the annual benefit for himself, Conried had introduced *Die Fledermaus* to the Met, with a party scene involving interpolations by virtually the entire cast of that year's stars (who were, after all, by contract, singing that

Heinrich Conried (*above*) had his share of both triumphs and troubles during the five years he ran the Met, from 1903 to 1908. Among the triumphs was the first performance outside Bayreuth of Wagner's *Parsifal* (*inset, left*); among the troubles, the American premiere of Richard Strauss's *Salome*, with Olive Fremstad in the shocking title role (*below*), which incurred the wrath of J. P. Morgan (*inset, right*).

Metropolitan Opera House

Lessee - CONRIED METROPOLITAN OPERA CO.

GRAND OPERA

SEASON 1903-1904,

UNDER THE DIRECTION OF

MR. HEINRICH CONRIED.

THURSDAY AFTERNOON, DECEMBER 24, 1903,

at 5 o'clock,

First Performance of

RICHARD WAGNER'S

DEDICATIONAL FESTIVAL PLAY

(BÜHNENWEIHFESTSPIEL)

Parsifal

(IN GERMAN.)

KUNDRY.............................MME. TERNINA
PARSIFAL.................MR. ALOIS BURGSTALLER
AMFORTAS...................MR. ANTON VAN ROOY
GURNEMANZ...................MR. ROBERT BLASS
KLINGSOR ...., ... MR. OTTO GORITZ
(His first appearance in this country.)
TITUREL.................MR. MARCEL JOURNET
FIRST ....   } ....MISS MORAN
SECOND.. } ESQUIRES {.........MISS BRAENDLE
THIRD..   }   } ....MR. REISS
FOURTH.   } ....MR. HARDEN
FIRST.... } KNIGHTS OF {........MR. BAYER
SECOND.. } THE GRAIL { MR. ADOLF MÜHLMANN
A VOICE....................MME. LOUISE HOMER

Continued on next page.

evening without fee). The following year saw the importation of Engelbert Humperdinck to supervise the production of *Hänsel und Gretel,* with a musical comedy star from one of Conried's other ventures borrowed to play Hänsel. In 1906–07, in addition to the enthusiastically anticipated debut of Farrar, who was a genius at publicity in her own right, Conried brought Puccini himself to attend a performance of his early *Manon Lescaut* and to supervise the first Metropolitan production of *Madama Butterfly,* in which Farrar was teamed with Caruso for the first time. Puccini was less pleased with this than the public: "The woman was not what she ought to have been," he wrote to a friend. "Also, as regards your *god* [Caruso], entre nous I make you a present of him—he won't learn anything, he's lazy, and he's too pleased with himself—all the same, his voice is magnificent."

That same 1906–07 season, however, had seen a great commercial disaster (though an artistic triumph), in the American premiere of Strauss's *Salome.* The work was sure to be deeply offensive to lingering Victorian sensibilities among the boxholders, especially with Olive Fremstad's passionate fondling of the severed head of John the Baptist (right at the footlights), and Conried went to some trouble to make the impression worse. He scheduled a dress rehearsal open to a thousand invitees for a Sunday morning right after church services, and he made the work his annual benefit (at double prices), preceding the presentation with the sort of gala potpourri that would draw the less serious-minded of his audience—Farrar and Scotti singing "La cì darem la mano" from *Don Giovanni,* Caruso singing "O, Paradiso," and the Barcarolle from *Contes d'Hoffmann* with Louise Homer, two songs by Sembrich, and at the end (as though to make the maximum contrast with what would follow) the religiosity of the final trio from Gounod's *Faust.*

There followed *Salome,* which, Henry Krehbiel wrote in the *Tribune,* "left the listeners staring at each other with starting eyeballs and wrecked nerves." Krehbiel had a "conscience stung into righteous fury by the moral stench with which Salome fills the nostrils of humanity." This critic had found *La Bohème* morally offensive too; but now he had company.

It was all much too much for J. P. Morgan, who summoned a special meeting of the board of the Real Estate Company and positively forbade any further productions of this obscene and profane spectacle in *his* theater, even outside the subscription series. At his best, Morgan was a fair-minded man, and he offered to make good any losses the Conried Metropolitan Opera Company might suffer by the need to scrap one of the most expensive productions it had ever mounted (the costs included guaranteed performance fees to Fremstad and royalties to Strauss for several years of performances). Conried, who at first threatened to take the production to another theater, may have been tempted to take Morgan's money, but his directors, with Kahn in the lead, righteously refused it. In the lease Kahn had to sign to take over from Conried a year later, a new clause was added, permitting cancellation if "the course of conduct of its affairs by the lessee shall, in the opinion of the lessor, be such as to give just and valid cause to believe that such conduct will be seriously detrimental to the artistic interests of the Metropolitan Opera."

This was also the season when Hammerstein opened his Manhattan Opera House, with casts including Melba, the tenor Alessandro Bonci (whom some critics preferred to Caruso, and whom Conried stole the next season), the French tenor Dalmores, the baritone Maurice Renaud, spectacles including an *Aida* with a cast of 400 and an ensemble universally regarded as superior to that at the Met. On January 2, 1907, the combination of Melba with Bonci and Renaud in *Traviata* for Hammerstein and Emma Eames with Caruso and Scotti in *Tosca* at the Metropolitan was reported to have drawn a total audience of 6,720 people to operatic performances in New York. Richard Aldrich in the *Times* wrote that "It seems to be almost beyond question now that there is an operatic public in New York large enough and discriminating enough to support two opera houses of artistic merit."

The fact remained that Conried lost money on the season, and for the first time since Grau had taken over from Henry Abbey no dividend was paid to the stockholders in the Metropolitan's producing company. Hammerstein, incidentally, added to Conried's discomfort over *Salome* by claiming that Strauss had offered the work to him, but he had declined it on moral grounds. Two years later, with Mary Garden available to sing the title role, he opted for a higher morality.

The official explanation of the loss in 1906–07 was the need to recover from Conried's other disaster, which was the destruction of many of the company's sets and costumes in the San Francisco earthquake and fire of 1906, which had occurred while the Met was on tour there. The box office had taken in $120,000 from the Californians, and it was all refunded, much of it without proof that the applicant had purchased the tickets. How much of the loss was covered by insurance is not shown in the records.

Two weeks before the San Francisco debacle, Kahn had written to Hyde that the Conried Metropolitan Opera Company had "$200,000 in bank and no debt, which is a pretty comfortable position to be in." Even after the San Francisco and *Salome* losses, Kahn was sanguine about the condition of the company he and his associates (most notably William K. Vanderbilt) were planning to take over from Conried. The terms of their transaction with Conried, involving a $90,000 payment to the impresario ($15,000 down, the remaining $75,000 over the succeeding four years), were premised upon Conried's representation that there was $130,000 in the bank. In May, the bubble burst, and the board of the new company, over Kahn's signature, coldly informed Conried that "A statement of our accounts made up last week has disclosed the fact, to our utmost surprise, that the entire Bank balances of our Company, over and above existing indebtedness known to you, amount to about $30,000 . . ."

Kahn should have known better. Conried was an Austrian actor who had come to the United States in 1877 for a play backed, oddly enough, by the young Oscar Hammerstein, who developed an antipathy to the actor that lasted all his life. Conried moved on to be a stage director and theater manager, though he gave acting lessons for a fee (some of them at his office in the Metropolitan) until sciatica crippled him in his last year at the Met. The basis of his success was an exclusive contract for the presentation of Viennese operetta in the United States, and during the Grau days he had operated the Irving Place Theater very profitably as a home for musical comedy. This did not mean that he was either a musician or a businessman. What was on the minds of the leaders of the Real Estate Company when they awarded him the lease was almost certainly the thought that as a stage director he would remedy the disorganized mise-en-scène that was universally regarded as the great weakness of the Grau regime.

Conried had arrived talking, as so many of his successors would talk, of presenting ensemble opera rather than star opera, and some of the productions of his first years—notably the *Parsifal*—were widely admired for the care and intensity of their preparation. But within ten days of his arrival, the critics were also noting instances of slipshod staging: "There were some queer mishaps on the stage last night," W. J. Henderson wrote of the season's seventh performance, a *Tosca* presenting Caruso's first Cavaradossi. "The window in Scarpia's chamber was carefully set slanting backwards, so that it would not stay open when Scarpia ordered his men to open it. Men tried to butt through doors the wrong way, and in one instance this almost resulted in disaster. Where are all those rehearsals?"

Moreover, though he spent money on stars and special publicized presentations, Conried saved money in appalling places, cutting the size of the orchestra and chorus and working their members beyond endurance. It was not an accident that the first strike in Metropolitan history occurred in Conried's reign—in January 1906, when the chorus walked out to demand salaries of $25 rather than $15 a week, and sleeping-car accommodations rather than coach seats when the company's tours required overnight travel. The disorganization of the musical planning was remarkable even by opera house standards, the problems compounded by the fact that Conried himself knew little about music. Casts were made up for each week on the preceding Monday morning in Conried's office, with various employees and artists hanging around the desk, in scenes not unlike the Marschallin's morning levée in *Der Rosenkavalier*.

Conried had boorish manners and a taste for vulgar German luxuriousness. He sealed off the entrances from the Met's business department to his office, where he replaced Grau's work table with an enormous roll-top desk and added plush furniture and brocaded hangings. Alma Mahler, recalling the first visit she and her husband paid on Conried at his home, wrote of unmistakable signs of megalomania . . . In Conried's smoking room, for example, there was a suit of armour which could be illuminated from within by red lights. There was a divan in the middle of the room with a baldachino and convoluted pillars, and on it the godlike Conried reclined when he gave audience to the members of the company. All was enveloped in somber, flounced stuffs, illuminated by the glare of colored electric lights. And then, Conried himself, who had "made" Sonnenthal [a popular German actor] and was now going to "make" Mahler . . .

After five years of being on this gentleman's board (having told E. H. Harriman that he would look on that service as a business proposition), Otto Kahn was now reduced to a *cri de coeur*:

You are aware [he wrote to Conried in the board's letter renouncing their contract] that during the past five years the financial and other management of the Company was exclusively under your control and authority; that, in compliance with your views as to the proper maintenance of discipline in the organization, the Board and the individual Directors never held any intercourse with your subordinates; that the office of Treasurer occupied by Mr. Winthrop was purely an honorary one and that Mr. Winthrop never exercised any functions relating to the active financial management of the Company . . . and that we relied and had to rely exclusively upon your official reports to the Board or its representatives . . .

During the five years of your incumbency of the Presidency you have received in salary, benefits and profits more than $300,000. In reviewing the results of your management with every desire to do you full justice, we find as against a number of accomplishments, entitling you to commendation, grievous and irreparable faults, such as your failure, several years ago (Mr. Toscanini not being then available), to engage Mr. Campanini, in spite of the continuous urgings of your Board to do so, and though the latter was more than willing to come to the Metropolitan Opera House on reasonable terms, long before he was engaged by the Manhattan Opera House, an engagement which has proved nothing less than vital to that House; your failure, in spite of similar urgings, to produce modern French Operas at the Metropolitan; your failure, at least, to protect the Metropolitan Opera House in this respect by entering into a contract with the French operatic publishers (for which most favorable propositions were urged upon you by Mr. Astruc in 1906 and 1907, though you never informed your Board thereof) the result being that Mr. Hammerstein was given almost complete possession of this important operatic field, to the exclusion, at least temporarily, and great detriment of the Metropolitan Opera; your gross and most damaging oversight in the matter of the contract for the Puccini operas; certain quite inexplicably burdensome contracts to which, without submitting them to the Board, you have put your name on behalf of our Company; your neglect in the matter of the Tetrazzini contract, which enabled that artist, after your unfortunate quarrel with her, to disregard with impunity the "binding" agreement which you had for years assured us you had with her; the almost uniform failure of late years of whatever novelties you selected and produced, and many other acts of omission and commission (most of them against, or in disregard of the advice and wishes of your Board) harmful to the Metropolitan Opera and of great advantage to the competing house—so much so, that it is within bounds to say that the very existence today of the Manhattan Opera House is, in considerable part, attributable to what you did and failed to do.

Overleaf: The bearded Gatti-Casazza, general manager from 1908 to 1935, on his arrival in New York, May 1, 1908 (*left, above*). Among his greeters was Andreas Dippel (wearing top hat). Both had been engaged by Otto Kahn (*right, above*). Gatti imported an entire chorus from Italy, seen (*below*) rehearsing in the Grand Tier restaurant. The scope of the Met's operations in the Gatti-Kahn era is illustrated in a 1909 playbill.

METROPOLITAN OPERA COMPANY
GRAND OPERA
Season 1909--1910

GIULIO GATTI-CASAZZA...... General Manager
ANDREAS DIPPEL, Administrative Manager

REPERTORY FOR THE SECOND WEEK, NOV. 22nd to 27th, 1909

| METROPOLITAN OPERA HOUSE | OUTSIDE PERFORMANCES: |
| METROPOLITAN OPERA COMPANY LESSEE | |

MONDAY, NOVEMBER 22

EVENING AT 8 O'CLOCK,

PUCCINI'S OPERA

TOSCA
(IN ITALIAN)

Floria Tosca	Geraldine Farrar
Mario Cavaradossi	Riccardo Martin
Il Barone Scarpia	Antonio Scotti
Cesare Angelotti	Paul Ananian
Il Sagrestano	Angelo Bada
Spoletta	Vincenzo Reschiglian
Sciarrone	Edoardo Missiano
Un Carceriere	Lillis Snelling
Un Pastore	
Conductor	Egisto Tango

**EVENING AT 8 O'CLOCK,
at the Academy of Music, Brooklyn**

PUCCINI'S OPERA

MADAMA BUTTERFLY
(IN ITALIAN)
After the work of JOHN LUTHER LONG and DAVID BELASCO

Cio-Cio-San	Emmy Destinn
Suzuki	Rita Fornia
Kate Pinkerton	Florence Wickham
B. F. Pinkerton	Enrico Caruso
Sharpless	Antonio Scotti
Goro	Albert Reiss
Yamadori	Giuseppe Campanari
Lo Zio Bonzo	Giacomo Bourgeois
Yakuside	Giacomo Bourgeois
Il Commissario Imperiale	Bernard Bégué
Conductor	Vittorio Podesti

TUESDAY, NOVEMBER 23

**EVENING AT 8 O'CLOCK, AT THE
Academy of Music, Philadelphia**

VERDI'S OPERA

OTELLO
(IN ITALIAN)

Otello	Leo Slezak
Iago	Pasquale Amato
Cassio	Angelo Bada
Roderigo	Pietro Audisio
Lodovico	Herbert Witherspoon
Montano	Vincenzo Reschiglian
Un Araldo	Bernard Bégué
Desdemona	Frances Alda
Emilia	Florence Wickham
Conductor	Arturo Toscanini

**EVENING AT 8 O'CLOCK, AT THE
LYRIC THEATRE, BALTIMORE**

VERDI'S OPERA

LA TRAVIATA
(IN ITALIAN)

Violetta	Lydia Lipkowska
Flora Bervoise	Niessen-Stone
Annina	Marie Mattfeld
Alfredo	Alessandro Bonci
Giorgio Germont	Henry Dutilloy
Gastone	Edoardo Missiano
Barone Douphol	Giuseppe Tecchi
Marchese D'Obigny	Edoardo Missiano
Dottore Grenvil	Giamoli-Galletti
	Paul Ananian
Divertissement by Gina Torriani and Corps de Ballet.	
Conductor	Vittorio Podesti

WEDNESDAY, NOVEMBER 24

**EVENING AT 8 O'CLOCK,
DOUBLE BILL**

MASCAGNI'S OPERA.

Cavalleria Rusticana
(IN ITALIAN)

Santuzza	Emmy Destinn
Lola	Florence Wickham
Turiddu	Riccardo Martin
Alfio	Dinh Gilly
Lucia	Marie Mattfeld

Followed by

LEONCAVALLO'S OPERA.

PAGLIACCI
(IN ITALIAN)

Nedda	Jane Noria
Canio	Enrico Caruso
Tonio	Antonio Scotti
Peppe	Angelo Bada
Silvio	Dinh Gilly
Conductor	Egis g° Tango

THURSDAY, NOVEMBER 25---THANKSGIVING DAY

Afternoon at 12:45 o'clock, Special Matinee

RICHARD WAGNER'S FESTIVAL PLAY

PARSIFAL
(IN GERMAN)

Amfortas	John Forsell
Titurel	Herbert Witherspoon
Gurnemanz	Carl Burrian
Parsifal	Otto Goritz
Klingsor	Carl Burrian
Kundry	Olive Fremstad
A Voice	Florence Wickham
1st Knight of the Grail	Julius Bayer
2nd Knight of the Grail	Adolf Mühlmann
1st Esquire	Lenora Sparkes
2nd Esquire	Rita Fornia
3rd Esquire	Albert Reiss
4th Esquire	Willy Haupt
Solo Flower Maidens: Bella Alten, Rita Fornia, Marie Mattfeld, Lenora Sparkes, Rosina Van Dyck, Henrietta Wakefield
and 24 other Flower Maidens.
The Brotherhood of the Knights of the Grail, Esquires and Boys
numbering 200 Voices. Orchestra of 135 Men.
Conductor	Alfred Hertz

ACT I will commence at 12.45 o'clock precisely.
ACT II will commence at 3 P. M.
ACT III will commence at 4.50 P. M.
Intermission of 30 minutes between Acts I and II.
Intermission of 40 minutes between Acts II and III.
The Performance will end at 6 P. M.

EVENING AT 8 O'CLOCK,

VERDI'S OPERA

IL TROVATORE
(IN ITALIAN)

Leonora	Johanna Gadski
Azucena	Louise Homer
Inez	Marie Mattfeld
Maurico	Riccardo Martin
Il Conte di Luna	Dinh Gilly
Ferrando	Giulio Rossi
Ruiz	Giuseppe Tecchi
Un Zingaro	Aristide Baracchi
Conductor	Egisto Tango

**AFTERNOON AT 2 O'CLOCK,
AT THE NEW THEATRE**

ROSSINI'S OPERA.

Il Barbiere di Siviglia
(IN ITALIAN)

Il Conte d'Almaviva	Alessandro Bonci
Dr. Bartolo	Pini-Corsi
Rosina	Lydia Lipkowska
Figaro	Pasquale Amato
Basilio	Andrea de Segurola
Fiorello	Vincenzo Reschiglian
Berta	Emma Borniggia
Un Officiale	Pietro Audisio
Conductor	Vittorio Podesti

FRIDAY, NOVEMBER 26

EVENING AT 8 O'CLOCK,

VERDI'S OPERA

OTELLO
(IN ITALIAN)

Otello	Leo Slezak
Iago	Antonio Scotti
Cassio	Angelo Bada
Roderigo	Pietro Audisio
Lodovico	Herbert Witherspoon
Montano	Vincenzo Reschiglian
Un Araldo	Bernard Bégué
Desdemona	Frances Alda
Emilia	Florence Wickham
Conductor	Arturo Toscanini

**EVENING AT 8 O'CLOCK,
AT THE NEW THEATRE**

MASSENET'S OPERA

WERTHER
(IN FRENCH)

Werther	Edmond Clément
Albert	Dinh Gilly
Le Bailli	Andreas de Segurola
Schmidt	Leo Devaux
Johann	Georges Bourgeois
Brühlmann	Walther Koch
Charlotte	Geraldine Farrar
Sophie	Alma Gluck
Kathchen	Elsa Michaelis
Conductor	Egisto Tango

SATURDAY, NOVEMBER 27

AFTERNOON AT 1:45 O'CLOCK,

RICHARD WAGNER'S MUSIC-DRAMA

TRISTAN und ISOLDE
(IN GERMAN)

Tristan	Carl Burrian
König Marke	Robert Blass
Isolde	Johanna Gadski
Kurwenal	Pasquale Amato
Melot	Adolf Mühlmann
Ein Hirt	Albert Reiss
Der Steuermann	Julius Bayer
Stimme des Seemanns	Georges Bourgeois
Conductor	Arturo Toscanini

EVENING AT 8 O'CLOCK,

VERDI'S OPERA

LA TRAVIATA
(IN ITALIAN)

Violetta	Bernice de Pasquali
Flora Bervoise	Niessen-Stone
Annina	Marie Mattfeld
Alfredo	Enrico Caruso
Gastone	Giuseppe Tecchi
Barone Douphol	Pietro Audisio
Marchese d'Obigny	Vincenzo Reschiglian
Dottore Grenvil	Bernard Bégué
	Paul Ananian
Divertissement by Gina Torriani and Corps de Ballet.	
Conductor	Vittorio Podesti

Gatti had been present at the meeting at which this missive was prepared, and doubtless contributed the further comment that "a large part of the scenery [is] so much worn or in such poor taste as not to be of any further use." To the extent that Dippel had been identified with the Conried management, of course, Gatti could feel the Italian equivalent of *Schadenfreude*, but for Kahn the episode was a humiliating experience.

Taking over, Kahn okayed lavish increases in expenditure for the Metropolitan season. The costs for soloists remained roughly the same—indeed, Gatti was down about $15,000 from Conried's $760,000 in 1907–08. But Conried's chorus had cost $52,000; the new double chorus would cost $92,000, plus the salaries of Steiner from Munich and Giulio Setti from La Scala as chorus masters. Orchestra salaries were up from $124,000 to $193,000; conductors' salaries had gone from $40,000 to $64,000 (of which Toscanini and Mahler between them accounted for $50,000).

Gatti had been promised new and refurbished sets, and through September and October the boats disgorged not only the conductors, administrators, and singers whose arrival was noted in the press (GREATEST SINGERS IN THE WORLD REACH NEW YORK, the front-page headline in the *World* trumpeted on November 4), but also painted cloths, props, and costumes. Gatti informed the press that he had the world's best scenic artists working for the Met—Mario Sala, Vittorio Rota, and Angelo Parravicini. For the opening-night *Aida*, improving on their Scala production, they had visited the Egyptian collections at the British Museum in London and at the excellent museum in Turin, and the setting would have an authenticity new to New York. Mahler would note with amazement later in the season that to secure authentic dancing for *The Bartered Bride*, Kahn was willing to put up the money to import four folk-dancing soloists from Prague. Dippel had commissioned from Vienna, via Mahler (who had been Intendant at that house as well as chief conductor), an entirely new setting of *Figaro*, with the first use at the Met of an inner stage, for greater intimacy.

All this took a toll on the budget, without sufficiently increasing the take at the box office. Though Gatti's total receipts were up $250,000 to $1,595,000, much of that came from extended touring (especially a profitable second week in Chicago, and performances in Brooklyn at the newly built Academy of Music). Conried's 1907–08 season had shown average receipts of $8,687 per performance; in 1908–09, largely because of the failure of the season's three modern works (D'Albert's *Tiefland*, Puccini's immature *Le Villi*, and Catalani's *La Wally*), average receipts were down to $8,349.

The gap between income and expenditures in 1908–09 stretched to the point that Kahn appointed a three-man committee, headed by the theatrical producer Charles C. Dillingham, to look into the business management of the opera house and suggest reforms. Though the report itself was not published (and indeed cannot be found in the Metropolitan's magnificent archives), leaks during its preparation revealed to the public that Emma Eames was being paid for performances not sung, that Emil Ledner, an agent in Berlin, was receiving 5 per cent of all fees paid to artists from northern Europe, and that a Viennese costumer held an exclusive contract for the supply of new costumes to the Met, through 1911. "Why is there so much interest in the management of this enterprise?" Gatti complained to a reporter from the *Sun*. "Is this institution subsidized by the State and is it answerable to a minister of finance that its affairs should receive so much publicity?"

☆ ☆ ☆

None of these political or financial problems troubled Toscanini: indeed, he had reacted to the news that their three-year contract had been amended with a one-year cancellation clause by telling Gatti that people like themselves were not in fact "sent away after a year of trial . . . We have the right to feel absolutely sure of our ability." He arrived in New York on October 14, traveling incognito as "Antonio Tascuri," and when the press recognized him on board—Toscanini's dapper grace and elegant mustache were easily recognizable—he refused to give an interview. He did speak with reporters briefly at the opera house, however, announcing that his first rehearsal with the orchestra would be *Götterdämmerung*, though that opera was not on the schedule until the fourth week of the season, because he felt it would require the most work. He also said he had seen Mahler in the Alps during the summer, and had suggested to him that he might wish to take one of the French or Italian works, as Toscanini planned to take some of the German repertory, but Mahler felt he had enough to do already—with *Tristan*, *Figaro*, *Fidelio*, *Bartered Bride*, and *Pique Dame* (which was then scheduled for that season, though in the event it was put off until 1909–10).

Both halves of the Metropolitan's enlarged orchestra were summoned to Toscanini's first rehearsal on October 19, four weeks before opening night. The maestro was sufficiently nervous about his reception to have written out phonetically a statement of anticipation in English, and to have learned some of the English terms for instructing an orchestra, which led the newspapers to report that he had surprised the men by his fluency in English. He conducted the rehearsal standing up (for four hours), which nobody had done at the Met since Anton Seidl in the 1890s. And he rehearsed the first act of *Götterdämmerung* without consulting his score, which caused a sensation in the newspapers. In fact, this feat was by no means beyond the capacity of other conductors: Toscanini himself always played it down, stressing that his only reason for conducting without score was his own execrable vision, which was so bad that he found it impossible to see the notes on paper on a music stand.

What astonished the men, as it would astonish everyone for another 46 years, was the acuity of Toscanini's hearing. It was at this first *Götterdämmerung* rehearsal that he heard the first cellist playing an A instead of a B-flat in a thickly orchestrated, highly chromatic passage, and when the cellist announced that his part showed an A, Toscanini opened the conducting score to show that the player was wrong. "It is simply beyond understanding," one of the musicians told the *Post*, "the way he knows his scores. We have often heard conductors direct without notes, but when it comes to knowing every mark and every instrument, to make every correction in expression as well as in everything else without once referring to the music, it shows an intimacy with the work and a self-confidence as inspiring as it is remarkable." What made the experience flabbergasting for the mostly German orchestra was the rock-bottom facts that their maestro was an Italian, and that the work was *Götterdämmerung*.

Together with the fantastic memory and the incredible ear, there came, perhaps necessarily, a violent impatience with mistakes. "I have never seen Vesuvius in eruption," Geraldine Farrar wrote some years later, "but probably no more inflammable combustion takes place in its venerable interior than in the person of this musical Napoleon, when the wild mood is upon him." These moments of fury were expressed in Italian, which few of the players understood (and those few were at the start anxious to support their fellow-countryman). But the singers understood, and it was the singers who were most likely to depart from the notes imprinted on Toscanini's memory.

Among Gatti's few expressions of nervousness before the season began was a comment on the poor relations between Toscanini and the easygoing Caruso—a minor thing, he said, relating to a rehearsal Caruso had missed at the Teatro Colón in Buenos Aires five years before. It would work out, he told Charles Meltzer of the *American*: "Artists always defer to Toscanini, because they know that he is always right." But there was less time to work out problems between Toscanini and the singers in these first weeks, because the Met traditions which Toscanini and Mahler would soon change provided for few vocal rehearsals. Emmy Destinn, who was to make her debut with Toscanini in the opening-night *Aida* on November 16, did not arrive in New York until November 10.

With two singers, relations instantly deteriorated. One of them was Emma Eames, the first performing artist ever invited to Mrs. Astor's banquets. Eames alone at the Met had a contract requiring that she be paid in gold, and permitting her to keep all the proceeds of private engagements during the period of her contract. She had been re-engaged before Gatti's arrival, and Gatti did not especially wish her services, because everything she sang could be assigned to Destinn or Farrar with no loss of quality and considerable saving of money. And she was a willful artist—it was not only Toscanini who had trouble. Reviewing *Figaro* later in the season, the *Press*

Geraldine Farrar as Puccini's Butterfly. All the stars were not in heaven.

noted that "Emma Eames tried hard to make Mahler conduct in accord with her ideas, but did not succeed." She had not succeeded with Toscanini either, though there was probably an element of melodrama in the newspaper reports that after she refused to follow his beat at a rehearsal the conductor simply ignored her, allowing her to be out of phase with the orchestra. In her memoirs nine years later, she complained that "His conducting was not an accompaniment but a stone wall of resistance to any personality but his own."

The fight with Farrar was more serious, for though she was only in her third season she already stood second only to Caruso as a box-office draw. Before her return for 1908–09, newspaper headlines had (falsely) announced her marriage to the baritone Antonio Scotti, who was traveling on the same ship. Arriving, and refuting the marriage rumor, she had appeared in what several newspapers called the largest hat ever seen in New York, with a brim 32 inches in diameter and a full coarse-weave veil down to her chin. The Farrar fan club—the Gerryflappers—still lay in the future, as did her career as a movie star (in silent films); but clearly that was the direction in which she was moving.

Farrar came to her first rehearsal with Toscanini from a series of triumphs in Berlin in the role she was to sing with him: Cio-Cio-San in *Madama Butterfly*. It is likely that her phrasing was influenced by the fact that she had been singing the role in German, equally likely that she had mannerisms and vocal tricks not indicated in the score. (Puccini, one recalls, had disliked her Butterfly two years before; and to her fury he would not offer her the creation of Minnie in *The Girl of the Golden West* two years later.) Toscanini was having none of her mannerisms, and his contract gave him complete authority—"right of use," it read in the awkward English translation, "of all that concerns the performing of the art." In one of the most famous contretemps in opera she halted his rehearsal to tell him that he would have to follow her lead in *Butterfly*, because she was the star. In the earliest printed version of Toscanini's reply, which appeared on the front page of the *American* on December 7, the maestro says, "The stars are all in the heavens, mademoiselle. You are but a plain artist, and you must obey my direction." This provoked a demonstration that Miss Farrar had a temper too, and an appeal by the soprano to Gatti-Casazza, who dealt with her disturbance as he would later deal with nearly all artists' complaints: by hearing her out and grunting a noncommittal comment at the end. Farrar then took further appeal to Kahn, requesting to be released from her contract, which of course Kahn refused. Miss Farrar thereupon sang Cio-Cio-San as Toscanini wanted.

The first performance of the season was on Saturday, November 14, in Brooklyn, where Farrar and Caruso inaugurated the new Academy of Music with what must have been a relatively scratch performance of *Faust*, which did not appear on the bills of the main house until December 5. Opening night at the Met itself was the following Monday, and a huge crowd gathered on Broadway, some to see the sights as the year's outstanding fashion parade passed by (it was not only the ladies in the boxes who wore their newest finery and flashiest jewels: *everybody* dressed), some to make the sort of instant judgment every audience makes of the new soprano, the new conductor, the new management of the opera house. Success on all counts was total.

"Incense stealing subtly from the stage of the Metropolitan Opera in the temple scene of *Aida* last night," Max Smith wrote lyrically on the front page of the *Press*, bore to the great audience the spirit of the new regime begun with the season's opening in New York's historic house of opera. Softly as if unfolded from a papyrus coil long hidden in a Pharaoh's tomb, the compelling fragrance spread over the auditorium the message of the aesthetic attention to detail to be expected from the art consciences of Giulio Gatti-Casazza and Andreas Dippel. It was freighted with the clear soprano notes of Emmy Destinn, the new prima donna, and it thrilled with the magnetism of Arturo Toscanini, the conductor, who made his first American appearance. As the significance of this perfumed music, an artistic achievement of the first rank, dawned on the thousands of Paris-frocked women and black-clad men in the big building, the audience forgot social interests, feminine attractiveness, its own wealth, fashion and position, all save that on the stage before them . . .

The cast for that *Aida* included Emmy Destinn in her debut, Caruso as Radames, Louise Homer as Amneris, Scotti as Amonasro, and Didur as Ramfis. The lavish sets and costumes clearly displaced Hammerstein's accomplishments of the previous year. And the musical foundation was rock solid. "Seldom," wrote Richard Aldrich in the *Times*, "has the orchestra sounded of greater richness and fullness." "Of the new conductor," wrote Henry Krehbiel in the *Tribune*, "it must be said that he is a boon to Italian opera as great as and as welcome as anything that has come out of Italy since Verdi laid down his pen." W. J. Henderson in the *Sun* thought the new conductor might even do something about the fundamental problems of this theater: "The Metropolitan Opera House," he wrote in a weekend roundup, "is much berated for its bad acoustics, but . . . shouting will not cure an auditorium of bad resonance. If Mr. Toscanini can drive this truth home among his leading singers, we shall hear less strident and unmusical tones from the Metropolitan stage in the future."

The next night the company was in Philadelphia, with Spetrino conducting Sembrich and Caruso in *La Bohème*, then back in New York for *Die Walküre*, conducted by Alfred Hertz, with Johanna Gadski as Brünnhilde, Fremstad as Sieglinde, Homer as Fricka, Schmedes as Siegmund, and Fritz Feinhals as Wotan. Dippel had supervised this production, and had recruited Schmedes and Feinhals. "Neither Munich at its annual repast of Wagner nor Bayreuth at its festival," Henderson proclaimed, "could now produce such a cast as last night." *Die Walküre* was universally praised for care in execution, though the sets and costumes were unchanged from previous seasons. "No one need fear," wrote the *Evening Post*, "that the artistic scandals of preceding seasons will be repeated."

The amazing first week continued with Toscanini's *Butterfly*, the cast including Farrar, Caruso, and Scotti; with a *Traviata* conducted by Spetrino and sung by Sembrich, Caruso, and the baritone Pasquale Amato in his Metropolitan debut. At the Saturday matinee, *Tosca* was presented with Eames, Caruso, and Scotti; in the evening, Farrar, Amato, and Didur sang *La Bohème*. By then, presumably, Caruso was tired: volunteering to substitute in the opening week's performances for Alessandro Bonci, who had missed a boat from Chile, he had sung six times in eight days.

The second week began with an American premiere, D'Albert's *Tiefland*, staged essentially by Dippel, and included a Thanksgiving Day matinee *Parsifal*, again in Dippel's domain. Bonci finally arrived, took over from Caruso as Rodolfo in *La Bohème* and Alfredo in *La Traviata*, while Caruso rehearsed for the next week's *Carmen*, with Toscanini conducting and Maria Gay making her Metropolitan Opera debut. Spetrino fell off the podium in the pit, and Toscanini took over *Tosca*, handling the unrepentant Eames without a rehearsal.

Early in the second week, it seems to have occurred to Kahn and his board that the bilateral right of cancellation after one year now made Gatti's and Toscanini's contracts riskier for the Met than for the newcomers, and steps were taken to assure that the Italians would remain for at least the initially agreed three years. Dippel apparently got wind that this was afoot, and in what turned out to be a wrongly calculated effort at self-protection solicited a letter on his behalf from some of the leading artists, and passed it along with his own covering note to Otto Kahn . . . and to J. P. Morgan. This vaguely menacing missive, which appeared on the front pages of the newspapers ten days later, read as follows:

We, the undersigned artists of the Metropolitan Opera Company, hearing of a movement to grant Mr. Gatti-Casazza, the General Manager, and Mr. Toscanini, Conductor, a three years' binding contract, do hereby express our desire, in the protection of our artistic interests and the welfare of the Metropolitan Opera House, that Mr. Dippel be granted the same privileges under contract that may be accorded to the above-named gentlemen. Our confidence in the managerial and artistic capabilities of Mr. Dippel gives us sufficient reason to associate ourselves firmly with his ideas, which have been, always will be, and are for the best of the Metropolitan Opera House.

Therefore, we heartily endorse Mr. Dippel in whatever measures he may be obliged to take.

ENRICO CARUSO
EMMA EAMES
GERALDINE FARRAR
MARCELLA SEMBRICH
ANTONIO SCOTTI

On receiving this piece of mail, Kahn called a meeting of his executive committee, who drafted a reply and then asked for a meeting with Morgan's Real Estate Company board to clear it. The timing, from Dippel's point of view, could scarcely have been worse. The boxholders too, after all, had been witness to Toscanini's triumphs. The *Daily Telegraph* expressed the view that "Mr. Pierpont Morgan, who is in all Metropolitan matters the final court of appeal, will stand by Mr. Dippel to the last." But that was already wishful thinking by the Dippel adherents, for Morgan had raised no objection to Kahn's letter of reply, which read in part:

... While we know well that, to accomplish the best results, it is necessary that you be happy in your work and contented and that you have the assured feeling that your great accomplishments are recognized and respected, as they deserve—on the other hand we are entirely convinced that your own experience and intelligent appreciation of the facts must lead you to realize that, however great the individual artists, the greatest artistic successes can only be accomplished if there exists a spirit of willing cooperation with, and submission to the Management, and a recognition of the necessity of centralized authority, together with mutual confidence and good will. It is not possible to administer an organization like the Metropolitan Opera under two heads, and it was never intended that it be so administered ... While there remains a large and important field for Mr. Dippel's valuable capacities, his functions are and must be subordinate to those of the General Manager, Mr. Gatti-Casazza, who is the supreme executive head of the organization ...

Dippel understood what had happened to him, of course, and solicited another favor from the artists—that they send Kahn a letter, and release it to the press, stating that he had had nothing to do with their original message. As Kahn knew perfectly well that the first letter had been an enclosure in a Dippel letter, this was convincing evidence that the Morgan faction was in retreat. A more conclusive public sign was given when Dippel canceled a testimonial banquet to himself—a clear reply to a banquet Walter Damrosch had given for Gatti and Toscanini the Sunday night of the first week—on the grounds that the speeches might inflame the situation.

Max Smith of the *Press*, who spoke Italian and would develop a personal relationship with Toscanini, gave his readers a quick statement of the problem:

Toscanini is a strict disciplinarian. He insists that his orders as conductor be obeyed, and so he not only has made enemies in the orchestra, but has hurt the gentle feelings of some of the Metropolitan's most luminous "stars." Whether a singer gets $50 a week or $2,000 a night is of no consequence to Toscanini in enforcing discipline. Mmes. Eames and Farrar, Messrs. Caruso and Scotti are expected to appear at rehearsals just as punctually as their little sisters and brothers of the chorus. Prima donnas and tenors in New York are not accustomed to obeying orders; they are used to acting according to their own sweet will. That's why they don't like Toscanini at all.

Eames's hostility to a management that didn't want her—and had in effect forced her to announce her retirement at the close of this season—was reciprocated by

Gatti; nobody cared a great deal what she said. Sembrich, too, was retiring, on her own motion. She had not sung under Toscanini in the house and was not scheduled to do so; her signature on the letter was explicable as a gesture for Dippel, who had been her partner in a number of performances and was friendly with her German husband (who probably drafted the letter). She said nothing further, and the house proceeded with a gala Farewell Appearance for her, which in a sense commemorated its own as well as her 25th anniversary in this building—for she was the sole survivor of the company that had opened the house in 1883.

Caruso and Scotti were easily squared, Scotti giving it out that Farrar—whom he had not married but who was a very good friend—had persuaded him to sign against his better judgment. Farrar herself, probably advised by her mother, "assumed all responsibility for the letter" and then shut up. She made her peace with Toscanini in her way, which was also his way, sometimes, when his antagonist was a beautiful woman.

Mid-season, Destinn had replaced Farrar in *Butterfly*, and one day Destinn called in sick. "Gatti phoned," Farrar recalled in her memoirs,

with a certain constraint—would I take over the Butterfly that evening, at such short notice, with Toscanini conducting? . . . It happened to be a popular Saturday night performance. [In point of fact, there was no popular-priced Saturday *Butterfly* in 1908–09.] The house was half-full; and while I never gloat, this circumstance was an obvious reminder to both Gatti and Toscanini of what I had said at the moment of our earlier arguments. There are indeed stars in Heaven . . . but there was also a human constellation that trod the Metropolitan's boards to the renown of that institution and the gratification of the public; not to mention the box office . . .

Toscanini allowed himself the shadow of a smile as he took up the baton. He conducted with every delicate consideration, so that it was a joy. As I had no interpretation to offer different from the earlier one that incurred his withering disapproval, I gathered that his periodic upheavals were without peril to a truly artistic association.

On tour, matters went a step further, and Toscanini for the first time came on stage to share a curtain call with Farrar. "I knew by this and his warm hand-clasp," Farrar wrote, "that our sad differences were at an end . . ." One assumes that their affair, which of course was soon an open secret at the house, began with what Farrar elsewhere called "the very unexpected and friendly overtures" of "one memorable evening of 'Madame Butterfly' in Chicago."

Toscanini's biographer Harvey Sachs argues that it was this relationship with Farrar that weighed most heavily in his decision not to return to New York after the 1914–15 season:

Toscanini's great New York crisis . . . came in the form of an ultimatum from Farrar, who told him that if he loved her, he must leave his family for her. But the family, for him, was something that went beyond his most intense—and intensely egotistic—desires. He broke with her, whether verbally or simply by leaving New York is impossible to say at this time.

A high point of the early Gatti years: Verdi's *Otello*, revived in 1910, with Leo Slezak as the Moor (*above left*), Antonio Scotti as Iago (*below left*), and Frances Alda as Desdemona (*below right*), under the baton of Toscanini (*above right*).

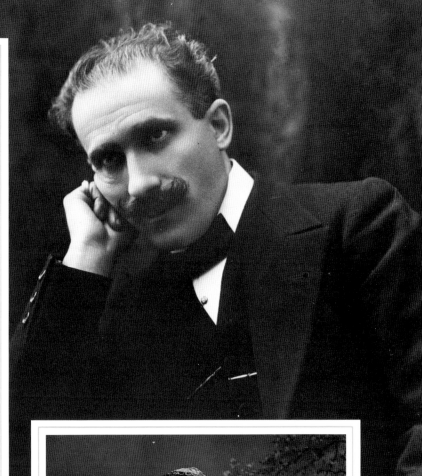

Obviously, he could not face the prospect of having to see her again, day after day, in a working relationship, with everything else changed; and this as much as anything was responsible for his finding the idea of a return to New York unbearable.

Another love affair of that season would cast shadows forward: between Gatti and the redheaded, strikingly buxom New Zealand soprano Frances Alda, who made her debut—very poorly received by the press—as Gilda in *Rigoletto* in the fourth week. (She had sung for Gatti at La Scala too, following an audition at which Toscanini inquired, not very politely, what language she thought she was singing.) They were married in the spring of 1910, and Alda did not sing at the Met the next season. Gatti arranged engagements for her at the Boston Opera.

In 1911–12, Toscanini requested that Mme. Alda be engaged to sing Desdemona in his *Otello* "toward the end of the season." Kahn's lawyer Paul Cravath, who would succeed him in the 1930s as president of the company, vigorously opposed, offering a motion "that the previous decision of the Board that it is inadvisable that the wife of a director should take part in the performances of the Opera Company precludes the engagement of Mme. Alda even in the limited number of performances proposed." With Kahn supporting Toscanini and Gatti, the motion failed by six votes to three, and Mme. Alda continued at the house, to the increasing approval of both the critics and the public, until she divorced Gatti in 1929.

The anniversary season remained in high gear. Toscanini's *Götterdämmerung* went far to soothe the troubled spirits who had feared that the accession of an Italian management would mean second-class Wagner. Quite apart from the impressiveness of the musical preparation, the *Götterdämmerung* also showed the benefits the company would derive in the ensuing years from Toscanini's belligerent control over the stage action, which had been written into his contract.

Mahler returned for the renewal of his overwhelming *Tristan*, and in mid-January, after an unprecedented twenty rehearsals, conducted *Figaro* with Eames as the Countess, Sembrich as Susanna, Farrar as Cherubino, Scotti as Almaviva, and Didur as Figaro. "Such a performance," Aldrich wrote in the *Times*, "shows the dominating influence of a master mind filled with the spirit of Mozart's music, as Mahler's is, with an opportunity to achieve the results he wishes." By request of the artists from the stage, Mahler permitted an encore of the letter duet in the third act, sung by Eames and Sembrich, both appearing in their last new production at the Metropolitan Opera House.

At the January 21 performance of *Figaro*, Farrar left after the third act to change into concert clothes and go to the home of Mrs. Emma Gary, where she was engaged to sing at a private party. These arrangements had been made by the Metropolitan itself, which took a commission on her private engagements; the pay book shows $1,000 to Farrar for "Beginning of Opera" and another $1,000 for the appearance at Mrs. Gary's. Leonora Sparkes donned a Cherubino costume for the darkness of the

The true star of the 1908–09 *Figaro* was the conductor Gustav Mahler (*above*), who demanded and got twenty rehearsals. Geraldine Farrar (*below left*) sang Cherubino; Emma Eames (*below right*), in her last season at the Met, was a stately Countess.

fourth act, in which Cherubino has little (but not nothing) to do. One wonders whether Mahler knew in advance—or noticed.

More triumphs followed in February, with the American premiere of *The Bartered Bride*, Mahler conducting and Destinn (who was Czech) as Marie. Then Toscanini performed the Verdi Requiem (Destinn and Homer among the soloists) in a low-priced Sunday concert. The demand for the Requiem was so great that it was repeated the following Sunday, again in March, and again on Good Friday.

In March, Toscanini restaged Verdi's *Falstaff*, presented at the Met for the first time since 1896, offering Antonio Scotti as the fat knight in what came to be regarded as one of the classic characterizations of the musical theater. Also that month, Hertz performed what was advertised as (but apparently was not) a complete *Tristan* for the first time in the history of the Met, and also what was advertised as (and probably was) an uncut *Die Meistersinger*. The annual benefit to which the artists contributed their services was no longer for the private gain of the general manager, but for "The Metropolitan Opera Company Pension Fund and Endowment."

End-of-season comments in the newspapers were almost uniformly ecstatic. W. J. Henderson in the *Sun* grew concerned that an opera-happy town was neglecting other and higher musical forms. ("Opera," he wrote, "is a form of musical entertainment made easy by pictures.") Financially, the results were less cheerful: the producing company lost more than $200,000. Hammerstein claimed to have made money at the Manhattan Opera, but it was noted approvingly by the Met board that his operation was under considerable financial strain from the costs of building and operating an opera house in Philadelphia. With an expansion of the Met's French repertory at the New Theater on Central Park West, which would open under Kahn's sponsorship in autumn 1909, and with an increase in the number of the company's appearances in Philadelphia and Baltimore, the Met's management hoped to give the interloping cigar manufacturer a coup de grace.

The expansion would be under the direction of Dippel, a compromise Gatti accepted, perhaps with the thought that Dippel was walking into a bag that would close on him. So far as control of the Met itself was concerned, the other shoe had dropped on February 27, when the board of the producing company announced that Gatti and Toscanini would be back at least for the next two years, and that Gatti, "while preserving the authority inherent in his position as General Manager, has willingly consented to the assignment to Mr. Dippel, besides his administrative functions, of an important share in artistic management." Dippel's friends were still trying for something more. A round-up article in the *Independent* at the end of April noted that "attempts were made to get rid of the too-popular Dippel. But this was found to be impossible; it would have been like discharging a man for doing his work too well, and would have made the directors a butt of ridicule. So peace was patched over and Dippel remains . . . It is owing to Mr. Dippel's rare managerial

Never before or since was the Met to experience such powerful competition as from the Manhattan Opera House under the aegis of Oscar Hammerstein (*inset, right*). Mary Garden's portrayal of Charpentier's Louise at the rival theater was the very incarnation of the emancipated New Woman. Her gorgeous colleague, the soprano Lina Cavalieri (*inset, left*), caused havoc among the more susceptible male members of New York society.

ability that the Wagner operas have again become as profitable as they used to be . . ."

Kahn did in fact have big plans for Dippel, which would get him out of Gatti's hair. He was assigned to work with Henry Russell in the organization and management of the new Boston Opera Company. The Met then bought stock in the new Chicago Grand Opera Company, and the world was given to understand by rumor that Dippel would become manager of that operation. Early in the 1909–10 season, Dippel was used to throw down the challenge direct to Hammerstein in Philadelphia, offering to buy his opera house there—or, failing such a purchase, to buy the existing Academy of Music, refurbish it, and match Hammerstein's four-times-a-week Philadelphia season.

A great deal of this did happen. Through the 1909–10 season, Hammerstein was self-destructing. He had got himself into a meaningless fight with Clarence Mackay, scion of Postal Telegraph and the most musical of the New York millionaires (he would later serve as president of the Philharmonic as well as on the board of the Met). To make certain that Mrs. Mackay and her companions would not be boxholders in his theater any longer, Hammerstein had all the boxes torn out in the summer of 1909. A combination of disgust with Hammerstein's treatment of his friends the Mackays, and annoyance at Hammerstein's refusal to give him the kind of rehearsal time he needed to compete against Toscanini, thereupon led Campanini to resign.

Seeking to carry his New York losses with out-of-town profits—and also, John F. Cone argues in his history of the Manhattan Opera, to tempt the Metropolitan into touring schemes that would be ruinous to that company—Hammerstein stretched his resources impossibly thin. On Christmas Day 1909, Hammerstein companies played *Tosca* and *Contes d'Hoffmann* in New York, *Faust* and *Aida* in Philadelphia, *Le Jongleur de Notre Dame*, *Cavalleria rusticana* and *Pagliacci* in Pittsburgh, and *Mignon* and *Le Caïd du tambour-major* in Montreal. Cigar-manufacturing machines were a profitable business, but not that profitable. A quarter of a century before, Col. James Mapleson had abandoned his lease on the Academy of Music, leaving the New York opera field to the exclusive occupancy of the Metropolitan with the words, "I cannot fight Wall Street." It was a pretext for Mapleson; Hammerstein could have said it in simple truth.

The Metropolitan bought out Hammerstein in April 1910 for $1.2 million, much of it apparently supplied by a boxholder who feared that his son was getting involved with the soprano Lina Cavalieri, a real-life seductress. Cavalieri had been barred from the Met stage early in 1908 after luring one of the Astor clan into marriage and demanding that he sign over all his wealth—and had then returned, to the horror of society, as one of Hammerstein's stars. Dippel now resigned from the Metropolitan to become director of a newly formed Chicago-Philadelphia Opera, presided over by Clarence Mackay, which in addition to seasons in those cities appeared on Tuesday nights at the Metropolitan, complete with Campanini, Mary Garden, John McCormack (who drew an Irish audience to the Family Circle), and Hammerstein's French specialties.

Kahn's other operatic quarrel had also ended, with the death of Heinrich Conried in spring 1909. The Metropolitan Opera Company had prudently kept up the payments on a $150,000 life insurance policy that had been taken out when Conried was manager, to make sure the capital of the company could not be impaired by his death. Having cashed in the policy, the Met kindly settled Mrs. Conried's suit for the $75,000 still owing under the repudiated contract, paying her $58,000.

By picking up the losses of the first two seasons after the departure of Conried—they totaled almost $450,000—Kahn became virtually the sole owner of the Metropolitan Opera Company. With the Metropolitan lacking any competitor in New York, Kahn in total personal control of the producing company, and Gatti-Casazza the unquestioned boss in the theater, the Met emerged from a quarter of a century of turbulence to more than twenty years of the greatest stability this—or perhaps any other—opera house has ever known.

FOUR

CARUSO AND THE GATTI MACHINE

For operagoers, the years 1903–20 were not the years of Heinrich Conried or Giulio Gatti-Casazza or even Arturo Toscanini. They were, overwhelmingly, the years of Enrico Caruso. He was the tenor on all but one of those seventeen opening nights; he sang on the Met stage 607 times, in 37 different operas. He was an attraction like Patti—people who would not think of going to the opera as an ordinary matter would go to a performance when Caruso sang. And they were right. "Caruso's voice," said the Philadelphia critic Max de Schauensee, who heard him many times between 1913 and 1920, "was a slice of nature. It was more than just a voice. He was so vibrant, very benign, very good—a member of humanity. It was the voice of a *man* you heard."

Unlike De Reszke, Caruso was not handsome, and he was a lump as an actor, though he did have a comic gift (revealed worldwide in his performance of Nemorino in Donizetti's *L'Elisir d'amore* and displayed at the Met also as Lionel in *Martha*). From the evidence of recordings, he did not seek to achieve characterization by coloring the voice, which sounds essentially the same, darkening but not shortening with the passage of the years—open, slightly pushed, with a marvelous, well-defined ringing at the top. It is probably fair to say that he put a permanent seal of approval on some of the vulgarities that had crept into Italian style—the glottal sob, the interpolation of high notes the composer never wrote in roles like Manrico in *Il Trovatore* and the Duke in *Rigoletto*. But when Caruso did it, he never seemed vulgar; simply natural.

Opera has never known a more thoroughly amiable leading figure. Humanity bubbled from him: De Schauensee remembered a holiday-season curtain call when Caruso looked into the cheering house and called, "Mairy Kreesmas!" Born into the most fearful poverty in the Neapolitan slums—his mother's seventeenth child, he was the first to survive infancy—he enjoyed his success with an unselfish pleasure that radiated around him. He seems not to have had a jealous bone in his body (professionally: romantically, he was in a classic Neapolitan mode). When Conried won Alessandro Bonci away from Hammerstein, Caruso drew a caricature of the

Enrico Caruso, the Met's greatest star ever, as Radames in *Aida*.

Metropolitan welcoming the new great tenor, with himself among the happy welcomers. He was a superb draughtsman with a crayon, and among his hundreds of caricatures there is not one that seems animated by malice.

With help from his accompanist, who shared living quarters with him and was always on call, Caruso learned a large number of roles, but not quickly. A story from his youth says that he once arranged with his Manon to pin Des Grieux's music to her back, to see him through the last act of Puccini's opera. After a single unhappy Lohengrin in Buenos Aires he never again attempted a Wagner role, though Otto Kahn once said he kept working at the problem in private, hoping that the language and the style would some day be revealed to him. But he did become an effective exponent of French roles—he was to some extent typecast from the start as Don José, and toward the end of his career he triumphed as Saint-Saëns' Samson and as Eléazar in Halévy's *La Juive*. Indeed, in the latter role, Krehbiel wrote, he succeeded "perhaps for the first time in his career . . . in giving perfect verisimilitude to a tragic impersonation."

Caruso sang often at the parties of the high and mighty and loved to wear his many decorations on his dress suit, but he was never entirely domesticated. Like many who repeatedly went hungry in childhood, he ate voraciously, retaining to the end his preference for greasily prepared pasta in the Neapolitan style (Frances Alda remembered that he was forever inviting people to join him at a new restaurant somewhere in the Italian district, "just as good as in Naples"). Having put his hands on a considerable piece of loose money for the first time in his life on a trip to Cairo, when a British military unit traveling to India on the same ship raised a purse of $500 to help the fledgling tenor who had sung at the ship's party, he smoked odoriferous Egyptian cigarettes all his life—even in the presence of Nellie Melba, who would permit no one else to smoke at all. (Herself, she chewed gum, and left a wad of it stuck to a piece of glass backstage when she went on, reaching for it immediately when she came off; on one occasion, Caruso substituted a wad of chewing tobacco, which made some' commotion in the theater.)

And it seems unquestionable that Caruso once pinched a lady in the monkey house of the Central Park Zoo, stimulating a misdemeanor charge on which he was convicted and fined $10. This was thought at the time by Caruso and Conried to have endangered his career, especially with Hammerstein's flacks stimulating a good deal of moral disapproval, but a Met audience who couldn't care whom Caruso pinched gave him an uproarious ovation when the curtain rose on the next *La Bohème* to reveal him in his garret, and he sang his Racconto with tears of gratitude in his eyes.

Caruso was under no illusions about the perspicacity of the audience. On one famous occasion he arranged with Angelo Bada that he rather than the *comprimario* would sing Beppe's little offstage serenade in *Pagliacci*, and noted with satisfaction that the audience did not respond with any special applause. And it probably says something about the extent to which he took operatic drama seriously that he was an incorrigible practical joker backstage, sometimes extending the game to the performance itself. *La Bohème* was his favorite victim. Even before he was a world-famous tenor, he brought a toy mouse to the fourth act in a Monte Carlo performance with Melba, and squeaked it in her ear as she sang her death scene. Once with Alda, he removed two of the casters from the bed, so that it rocked every time she took a breath; on another occasion, he and Scotti and Andrès de Segurola equipped themselves with monocles, which they donned to turn and greet her as she staggered into the garret, provoking a giggle that Gatti did not find in the least amusing (he fined them $100 each after the performance).

Money dribbled easily through Caruso's hands: there was so much of it. His entourage included a secretary, an accompanist, a business manager, and a general factotum; after his marriage (adding a wife, quickly a baby and a nursemaid), the Caruso establishment spread over two floors at the Knickerbocker Hotel. Caruso was a soft touch for almost any Italian down on his luck, and a fairly steady loser at poker, which was the opera company's game; in town, he often played following dinner at a restaurant. Mary Jane Matz reports in her biography of Kahn that the banker sometimes went down to Little Italy and joined the card-players. But Caruso could not spend or give or gamble away all he earned, especially when the record royalties rolled in; his estate was estimated at $9 million for probate, and at least $2 million more came in later from the posthumous sale of recordings.

All this was good copy, exploited by the Met and indeed by Caruso himself, who toward the end of his life hired Edward L. Bernays to handle his public relations. Perhaps most important of all, Caruso was in New York for the entire season, and took the tour every year. His name became synonymous with the Metropolitan's. He could be found at lunch at his corner table at the Knickerbocker Hotel two blocks from the opera, where his friend and fellow Neapolitan Antonio Scotti also kept headquarters, and for several memorable years Gatti and Toscanini and their wives were part of the scene. (Toscanini lived at the Ansonia, on 73rd Street, but the Knickerbocker was much closer to the opera; the stars liked to stay near the Met, because the dressing room accommodations were so spartan.)

Conried had launched Caruso with a typically misleading press conference, playing one of the tenor's recordings and assuring the reporters that he had "discovered" this wonder through the miracle of the phonograph. In fact, Caruso had already enchanted London as well as Monte Carlo, Buenos Aires, St. Petersburg, and Milan; and Grau had negotiated a contract for 40 appearances at $960 each—but had failed to sign it before Conried took over. When Caruso would not cut his price (La Scala was willing to pay him more, but he had already determined to sing opera again in Italy rarely if at all; in Italy, he once told Leo

Overleaf: Probably the most distinguished world premiere in the Met's first century: Puccini's *The Girl of the Golden West.* Amato portrayed the top-hatted sheriff Jack Rance, Emmy Destinn sang Minnie, Caruso was a tubby but glorious-sounding Dick Johnson. The group photo (*right, above*) shows Gatti, David Belasco, Toscanini, and the composer, who came to New York for the occasion.

GIULIO GATTI-CASAZZA   GIACOMO PUCCINI   DAVID BELASCO   ARTURO TOSCANINI

First Performance

on any stage of

Giacomo Puccini's

Opera

The Girl of the Golden West

(La Fanciulla Del West)

Founded on the Drama written by

David Belasco

Metropolitan Opera Company

Giulio Gatti-Casazza, General Manager.

Metropolitan Opera House

NEW YORK

DECEMBER 10TH 1910

John Brown
BUSINESS COMPTROLLER

Slezak, "a singer is a slave"), Conried cut the guarantee, to 25 performances. In each of Conried's five years, Caruso sang more often—51 times in the 122 performances offered by the company in New York in 1907–08. This was the season Bonci came, and sang 27 performances: the Italian influence was strong under Conried, whatever the board had feared in appointing him. Counting the tour, and outside appearances booked by the opera company, Caruso sang for the Met seventy times in 1907–08, for a total fee of $140,000—plus expenses.

As early as 1906, W. J. Henderson had complained in the *Sun* that people now seemed to go to the opera only to hear Caruso: "The invariable request . . . at the box office has been, 'Can you let me have seats for Caruso's next performance?'" In the following decade, the board of the Real Estate Company would hold a solemn inquest over the complaints of some Friday night subscribers that they got less than their share of Caruso's performances—and would find it justified, issuing thereupon suitable instructions to Kahn and Gatti to assure that nobody who bought a subscription would have such a grievance again.

Caruso sang too often and traveled too much (the next to last year of his life he was seduced to Havana in the hot weather by fees of $10,000 per performance); he ate too much, on occasion drank too much (though a youthful experience of coming on stage laughing and not wholly in his own control prevented him from appearing drunk as a mature artist); and he did absolutely nothing to keep himself in shape. Until his first bout of pleurisy, nothing could keep him from smoking several packs of Egyptian cigarettes a day. That he held up into his late forties is more remarkable than his death at 48, from complications following an infected kidney that could not be operated on because he was still weak from the pleurisy that had put him on stage in Brooklyn coughing blood through the first act of *L'Elisir d'amore*. (He wanted to continue the performance, and the damned fool doctor was willing to permit it; the house manager at the Academy of Music then took it upon himself to come before the curtain, tell the audience that Caruso was prepared to continue, and inquire whether they wished him to do so. "He was answered," the British biographer Stanley Jackson reports, "by an explosive 'No' from the patrons, many of them in tears.") Ribs strapped, Caruso sang three times more at the Met, the last time in *La Juive* on Christmas Eve 1920.

The notion that there would be no more Caruso at the Met was almost impossible to grasp. Caruso himself began singing again at his hotel in Sorrento, while he was considered to be recuperating from pneumonia and pleurisy. A nice story says that he grew impatient auditioning a young Neapolitan tenor who was trying "M'appari" from Flotow's *Martha* and suddenly said, "No, no, try it like this"—and his wife in the next room suddenly heard Caruso singing, as he had always sung. Gatti came on July 3, and presently sent an optimistic cable back to New York (see p. 132). Less than a month later, Caruso was dead.

Gatti was lucky that Caruso was never greedy in his dealings with the Met. At a time when his recital fee had risen to $7,000 (even higher in sports arenas), he still sang in the opera house for $2,500—and for many years allowed the theater to keep the difference between that fee and what it could get from the very rich when it peddled his presence at private musicales. Meanwhile, however, the public was becoming a little less lucky because Gatti himself was—if not exactly greedy—a very businesslike general manager.

With Hammerstein's disappearance, Gatti raised prices, to a $6 top; clamped down on singers' fees; dissolved the double orchestra; and began squeezing more performances out of less rehearsal time. By 1914–15, which was, not coincidentally, Toscanini's last year, Gatti's artistic budget was $928,000, $3,000 *less* than Conried had spent seven years before on a season of almost identical length.

Gatti's strength, like that of Rudolf Bing fifty years later, was that he knew how to manage an opera house. Trained as a naval engineer, he had taken over the municipal theater in Ferrara while still in his early twenties, when his father, a senior bureaucrat of the town, was elected to parliament and had to drop that responsibility. He was Sovrintendente at La Scala before he was thirty, helping Toscanini and the House of Ricordi win the war against Milan's Teatro Lirico and the House of Sanzogno. He and Toscanini came to New York as a team, escaping the politicized operatic life of Italy and the reluctance of Milanese audiences to accept their introduction of operas by Wagner, Strauss, and Debussy. They brought with them a great deal of intellectual and dramatic baggage relating to the proper employment of the resources of an opera house, and some of these grandiloquent attitudes Gatti kept through all his 27 seasons.

First, there was the matter of productions. Gatti improved the Met's scenery and costumes beyond recognition. In addition to his Scala artisans, he imported Hans Kautsky from Berlin to do *Carmen*, *The Magic Flute*, *Der Rosenkavalier*, and a new *Ring* for the Wagner centennial. Puvis de Chavannes designed Gluck's *Orfeo* and *Armide* for Toscanini; Willy Pogany prepared *Le Coq d'or* for Monteux, and Rossini's *L'Italiana in Algeri* for Gennaro Papi, the weakest of Toscanini's successors in the Italian repertory. As early as 1917, Gatti found Joseph Urban, an immigrant Austrian architect and painter who would give the Met 51 intelligent and sometimes distinguished designs over the next sixteen years. Urban also undertook general supervision of the Met's lighting plots; his affection for the short end of the spectrum led a generation of operagoers to believe that opera was an entertainment that occurred in a blue haze. Later such young designers as Donald Oenslager (for *Salome*) and Jo Mielziner (for *Emperor Jones*) were given assignments by the aging Gatti.

The ballet was strengthened dramatically—no less than Pavlova serving as prima ballerina in 1909–10 and 1910–11. The next year a ballet company was imported

from Russia, with Mikhail Mordkin and Ekaterina Geltzer as soloists. The balletic effort then languished for two seasons, waiting for Diaghilev. Then Rosina Galli became prima ballerina; soon Gatti's mistress; and eventually his wife. Among the more piquant moments at the Met must have been the attendance of Frances Alda at a performance of *Le Coq d'or* in 1917, in the Fokine staging, part singing and part dance, when the soprano was Maria Barrientos, who had been Gatti's fiancée in Milan, and the dancer was Galli. Even Alda, who had her own affairs, appears to have been unable to work up any great resentment of the accomplished, high-spirited, naive Galli: "Like me," the soprano wrote with cheerful cattiness, "she had a rather pretty face but too fat a figure."

Among Toscanini's crusades at La Scala—before 1908 and after 1920—had been the strengthening of the opera orchestra, and its employment for symphonic purposes. At the Met, the Sunday night concerts remained mostly pops evenings, various singers from the company presenting arias and ensembles, but with the passage of time Gatti increasingly engaged major instrumentalists to play concertos as a centerpiece—Rachmaninoff, Hofmann, Heifetz, Elman, De Pachman, Ysaÿe, Kreisler, Casals, Rubinstein, Godowsky all appeared, many of them year after year, with the Metropolitan Opera Orchestra. At the end of the 1912–13 season, Toscanini made his American debut as a symphonic conductor with this orchestra on the stage of the opera house, in a program that included the Beethoven Ninth. The lines formed for that early in the morning; a passer-by observed with some surprise, "I didn't know Caruso sang on Sundays . . ."

Most important of all was Gatti's insistence that an opera company must create as well as repeat. Prior to Gatti, the Met had never done the world premiere of anything, and had never performed an opera by an American composer. He remedied the second of these deficiencies in his second season, offering Frederick Converse's *The Pipe of Desire*. The next year the Met staged two world premieres by important composers—Puccini's *The Girl of the Golden West* (to give it the title of David Belasco's play on which it was based, Puccini having seen the play and admired it on his previous trip to New York); and Engelbert Humperdinck's *Königskinder*, now remembered mostly as the excuse for the delectable Farrar to shepherd a gaggle of real geese around the Metropolitan stage and take her curtain call with a goose under her arm. The year after, Gatti offered the world premiere of an American opera, *Mona* by Horatio Parker of Yale, winner of a $10,000 prize competition Gatti had organized. (Walter Damrosch was the chief judge.) During the next 23 seasons, Gatti would offer eleven more American operas, most of them (to take a phrase Rudolf Bing liked to use when describing similar occasions) "an outstanding disaster." Two remained briefly in the repertory: Deems Taylor's *Peter Ibbetson* and Louis Gruenberg's *The Emperor Jones*, both of which offered special opportunities for one of the Met's reigning stars, Lawrence Tibbett.

Some Italian rarities from the Gatti years: Leoni's *L'Oracolo* (Antonio Scotti as the sinister Chim-Fen, *above left*), Montemezzi's *L'Amore dei tre re* (Adamo Didur and Lucrezia Bori, *above right*), and Zandonai's *Francesca da Rimini* (Pasquale Amato and Angelo Bada, *below*).

Beyond the premieres, there were every year three, four, five "novelties," works never before played in New York. Some might be antiquities, like Gluck's *Armide*, with which Toscanini opened his third season in 1910–11 (Olive Fremstad kept on her night table until the day of her death a memento of the evening inscribed by Toscanini "To my unforgettable Armida"). Or exotic pieces from far away, like Mussorgsky's *Boris Godunov* (another Toscanini premiere), Borodin's *Prince Igor*, Rimsky's *The Snow Maiden*, Janáček's *Jenufa*, Granados' *Goyescas*, Falla's *La Vida breve*. Or new works that were harmonically conservative, like Ermanno Wolf-Ferrari's happy settings of Molière plays, *Le Donne curiose* and *L'Amore medico* (*L'Ecole des femmes* and *Le Médecin malgré lui*). Or new works that were harmonically daring, like Paul Dukas' *Ariane et Barbe-Bleu* and Korngold's *Die tote Stadt*. There was even a jazz opera—Křenek's *Jonny spielt auf*. And there were a slew of conventional operas—by Mascagni and Leoncavallo, by Massenet and Giordano. Gatti ran the company through the less established Verdi too: *Un Ballo in maschera*, *Luisa Miller*, *La Forza del destino*, *Don Carlo*, *Ernani* (fallen from favor since Whitman's day).

From 1912–13 through 1931–32, Gatti's Met offered 23 or 24 weeks in New York in every season but one, and normally the repertory ran 45 to 50 productions a year. This was not all gravy for the audience, because the new productions stole rehearsal time and refurbishing money from the holdovers, so that the Gatti years eventually were characterized by shabby performances of some of the most popular works. But Gatti's practice, so long as he believed in it, maintained that air of the gamble that contributes so much to theatrical excitement.

Some operas stayed in the repertory because they became staples—*Rosenkavalier*, *Boris*, *L'Amore dei tre re*, *Gianni Schicchi*. Others lasted a while because they offered a role beloved of an important artist—Leoni's *L'Oracolo*, for example, Fu Manchu stuff, with the villainous Chim-Fen for Scotti. Most simply died, after a season or two (Gatti was very good about bringing back last year's flop for another try, just in case). When the hard times came, Gatti insisted on maintaining at least a minimal commitment to new things. In 1931–32, there were Weinberger's *Schwanda*, Montemezzi's *La Notte di Zoraïma*, Von Suppé's *Donna Juanita*, the first American production of Verdi's *Simon Boccanegra*. One cut corners to save money, but some things were a matter of principle for Gatti; and one of them was the responsibility of an opera house to be more than a display of acquired artifacts.

Three-quarters of a century after his arrival in New York, it is all but impossible to get a handle on Gatti. In the early years, his companions were his secretary Luigi Villa, Toscanini, and his wife Frances Alda, who was handsome and sexy and a fine

Until America entered World War I, German repertory thrived at the Met. Destinn and Slezak sang Pamina and Tamino in a new production of *The Magic Flute* (*above left*). The American premiere of Richard Strauss's *Der Rosenkavalier* featured Margarete Ober as Octavian, Frieda Hempel as the Marschallin (*above right*). Geraldine Farrar and her flock of geese (*below*) were the chief attractions of Humperdinck's *Königskinder*.

singer, but fifteen years younger than himself and a self-described extrovert. Later, he spent his time with Villa, his second wife (the ballerina Rosina Galli), and his assistant manager Edward Ziegler, formerly a critic for the New York *Herald*. Kahn had originally employed Ziegler to help out with the Diaghilev and Max Reinhardt troupes the banker was sponsoring on American tours, and recommended him to Gatti in 1916 as an ideal assistant. Ziegler spoke some Italian (better French, still better German); he was very smart; and he knew the value of a dollar—he very cheerfully, for example, took charge of making sure that every time some artist appearing in a movie was advertised as "of the Metropolitan Opera," the company got its $50 fee for the use of its name. (It is not true, however, than on arrival he promptly earned the Met "more than his salary," as one history has it, "by selling the Metropolitan's endorsement of a piano for $15,000." The Met had always sold its endorsement of a piano; when Ziegler came, the price was $6,250. He pushed it to $8,400 five years later, and got it up to $15,000 in 1926.)

With his old-fashioned pince-nez and lacquered hair and vested suit, there was not an ounce of the Bohemian about Ned Ziegler—and having worked for and idolized the critic and essayist James Huneker, he knew what Bohemianism was. Gatti, if not the "introvert" Alda called him, was a grave man, and Ziegler could support that gravity. It says something for all involved that although Ziegler was Kahn's man— the two of them shared picnic suppers at Ziegler's office once or twice a week before performances—Gatti was able to make him not only a confidant but a close friend. After Gatti's departure, Ziegler in effect ran the opera house for Edward Johnson until his final illness began in 1945.

Gatti would arrive in his second-floor office at the Met a little before ten in the morning, glance at the mail, and then wander across to Ziegler's office, where he would throw himself into the assistant manager's one comfortable chair; and (Ziegler's secretary Helen Noble recalled) the top button of his fly would spring open. ("Don't worry," Ziegler told her the first time she was present at this ritual, and showed signs of alarm; "it never goes beyond the top button.") The two men would talk over, usually in Italian, the operatic affairs of the day and perhaps other things (Noble had no Italian or French—the other possible language—and could not testify). Both men were intellectuals, and widely read. Ziegler planned the weeks for Gatti, his office walls hung with charts, including one in code that revealed the menstrual periods of the female artists; and as the 1920s wore on, Gatti turned over to Ziegler much of the management of the prima donnas by the simple device of pretending not to understand their problems when they came to his office.

In the afternoon, Gatti was all over the place. During his first year, he had a loudspeaker installed in his office for a primitive but constantly improving sound system that allowed him to eavesdrop on rehearsals. (The Met under Gatti and Ziegler maintained an interest in the progress of electronic technology: Lee De

Gatti had a weakness for the Russian repertory. One of his favorite operas was *Boris Godunov*, first produced under Toscanini's direction in 1913. The photo shows Adamo Didur as Boris, flanked by Leonora Sparkes (Xenia) and Anna Case (Feodor). Gatti's future wife, Rosina Galli (*inset*), danced the Ballerina in Stravinsky's *Petrushka*.

Forest "broadcast" a performance as early as 1910, and in 1931 Ziegler negotiated a contract with NBC that gave the Met payments for the use of its singers on radio but specifically exempted any rights to "television," so-called.) Gatti personally was the liaison between the 39th Street (business and administrative) and 40th Street (stage, mechanical, and technical) sides of the house, which were on dubious terms, Ziegler distrusting the stage department's expenditures and the technical department chiefs unable to understand why a successful opera company kept falling further behind the state of the art in backstage equipment, or let so many productions go on stage in shabby condition. The testimony of all who worked in the house, on the artistic or technical side, is that Gatti kept "appearing" out of corridors and doors, a gracious but solemn presence, a large man with a square-cut beard and sad eyes, thumbs in vest, walking ponderously, nodding occasionally but rarely speaking. Of course, the great majority of the people to whom he appeared did not speak the language he spoke.

Both Gatti and Ziegler were at the theater almost every night there was a performance, sitting in the Director's Box at the angle on the Grand Tier level on the left side of the auditorium. (George Cehanovsky remembers that when someone was making a debut, Gatti would sit on stage just behind the proscenium, beside the "curtain maestro"—as Cehanovsky calls him—whose job was to raise and lower the curtain.) Kahn was often there too: he subscribed to orchestra seats (and after 1920 he was a boxholder), but he felt more at home consorting with the management. Disconcertingly for the occupants of the Opera Club box next door, Kahn and Gatti sometimes hummed along with the music. Gatti typically went backstage before performances and during intermissions, to visit, congratulate, and encourage the company. Afterward, Gatti and Ziegler would share a cab, and often keep it circling for hours in Central Park while they compared notes on the evening's performance and the day's work, told stories, and generally socialized in one of the strangest male bonding rituals on record.

Both Gatti and Ziegler worked for Kahn, who in 1917 converted to stock, which paid no dividends, the bonds he and William K. Vanderbilt had taken in return for making up $363,000 of the Met's 1908–10 deficits. When Vanderbilt died Kahn bought his stock; and thereafter held 84 per cent of the ownership of the Metropolitan Opera Company. His word, clearly, was law.

The extent to which Kahn imposed an artistic judgment is unclear. It was his decision, over Gatti's objections, to give the Met subscribers a month of Diaghilev's Ballets Russes rather than opera in April 1916 (the Met went up to Boston, not very successfully), and Gatti in his memoirs, written while Kahn was still alive, complained of Kahn's demand that Caruso toward the end of his life sing the Duke in *Rigoletto*, a part both Gatti and Caruso considered too light for a tenor who was then concentrating on roles like Samson and Eléazar in *La Juive*.

Margarete Matzenauer was a prodigious all-rounder who moved easily from Verdi to Wagner and from mezzo to soprano roles. She is pictured here as Kundry in the Magic Garden scene of *Parsifal*. Louise Homer was the Orfeo (*inset*) of the acclaimed 1909 revival of Gluck's opera under Toscanini. The American-born Homer made her Met debut in 1900 as Amneris in *Aida* and was still singing the same role there 28 seasons later.

A curious letter from Ziegler to Kahn in 1929 indicates that the banker also exerted an influence on what was perhaps the most central of a general manager's responsibilities: the choice of conductors. "Complementary to our talk of last Saturday night," Ziegler wrote,

I wonder if you have ever thought about Richard Strauss. I am reasonably certain that he can and would come to us. When he wishes, he can be a very great conductor.

Then there is Franz Schalk, of Vienna, who conducted the "Fidelio" performance you heard in Salzburg. He is far from being a young man, but still does some excellent work. [Ziegler was apparently unaware that Schalk had conducted at the Metropolitan in the 1890s.]

. . . So far as the young men are concerned, there is, first of all, a George Szell, who has been engaged as a concert conductor in St. Louis . . . He is a most excellent musician. I heard him conduct an opera and thought he lacked authority, but that was three years ago and I am told that he has improved very much . . .

Then there is the man about whom you wrote me, Eugen Jochum. He is 27 years old; has conducted at Kiel and Mannheim, and is now engaged to conduct concerts at Duisburg. Bodanzky heard him this summer and was enthusiastic . . .

Then finally there is a young chap at Mainz, who conducted a very bad orchestra, through a worse performance of "Carmen." His name is Paul Breisach. He made a very good impression at the conductor's desk, but the performance was so bad that it was difficult to know whether to blame the conductor, the orchestra, or the singers . . .

Have you ever thought of the Spanish conductor, E. Fernandez Arbos? He has quite a reputation in his own country . . . Speaking of Spaniards, reminds me of Pablo Casals, whom you probably know better as a cellist, but who has done some creditable work as a conductor, I am told . . .

P.S. There is, of course, also Fritz Busch in Dresden, who conducted the New York Symphony here for two years, and whose success, or lack of it here was doubtless influenced by the questionable material with which he had to work. In Germany his reputation as a conductor is of the highest. Personally I have always found him a bit heavy handed . . .

Kahn also recommended singers. Nellie Melba in 1929 sent him a telegram from Paris: JOHN BROWNLEE WONDERFUL BARITONE GREAT SUCCESS GRAND OPERA HERE. STRONGLY ADVISE HIM FOR METROPOLITAN. HOPE POSSIBLE. IS YOUNG GOOD LOOKING EASY TO GET ON WITH. Kahn's secretary forwarded the telegram to Ziegler with a covering letter, concluding, "Mr. Kahn did not say what you were to do with the message." Ziegler forwarded the letter to Gatti with a check mark, but Brownlee was not engaged until after Gatti's departure. Also in 1929, Kahn on a trip to Scandinavia heard the young Norwegian Kirsten Flagstad as Tosca, and proposed that Gatti look into it. In 1928, Kahn probably forced management to sign a singer: Frances Alda, who had told Gatti she was divorcing him and had discovered from backstage contacts that he had declared he would not re-engage her. According to her memoirs, Alda called Kahn, and in due course a one-year renewal was offered her.

Kahn also, like any member of the audience, could send written complaints:

Did you notice Martinelli's antics in the Second Act yesterday, after "Carmen, je t'aime!" As you know, he kneels down after the end of the aria and puts his head in Carmen's lap. Followed great applause, whereupon Martinelli arises, bows, kneels down again; and adjusts his head again in her lap. More applause, followed by the same proceedings. Don't you agree that such Vorstadt antics are really not permissible on the stage of the Metropolitan?

☆ ☆ ☆

There is every reason to believe that Kahn, after the losses of the first two seasons, told Gatti to be sure that it did not happen again, and that Gatti's progressive alienation from Toscanini was one of the results. "Time and again," Alda wrote,

Gatti would come home to the apartment to lunch (he always *did* come home to lunch) a thundercloud.

"What's the matter, Giulio?" I would ask.

Vague murmurings in Italian that could mean only one thing: something had offended him.

I would catechize: Was it the stage hands? Was Farrar having a new excess of "temperament"? Were box-office receipts falling off? Had Mr. Kahn discovered a new Russian dancer he wanted to promote?

Shakes of the head to all of these.

Ah-ha!

Was it Toscanini?

"Ah . . ."

Immediately a torrent was loosed.

That *maestro* . . . couldn't he understand that an opera house had to be run so that it would pay? Couldn't he grasp the significant fact that so many seats sold at so many dollars a seat amounted to so much? And equally, that so many stars at two thousand, and fifteen hundred, and even twenty-five hundred dollars a performance, and so many musicians at so much, not to mention stage hands, carpenters, scene-shifters and the like, would amount to a sum equal to or even in excess of that produced by the sale of seats? And yet he wanted them all. There were never enough singers or those fine enough, to satisfy him.

That was a perpetual quarrel between Gatti and Toscanini . . . They would wrangle about it for hours . . .

The earliest rumors that Toscanini might not return to the Met followed a grand quarrel with Gatti over the Metropolitan's new staging of Verdi's *Un Ballo in maschera* in autumn 1913, as part of the season's tribute to the Verdi centenary. Toscanini demanded a stage band for the ball scene; Gatti refused, and insisted that Toscanini use men from the pit. Even in the next season, when *Ballo* was performed on opening night (with Caruso as Riccardo, Pasquale Amato as Renato, Destinn as Amelia, Margarete Matzenauer as Ulrica, and Frieda Hempel as Oscar—perhaps the

finest cast this opera has ever known), Toscanini still had to do without his stage band.

Kolodin mentions as a precipitating cause of Toscanini's departure a performance of *Carmen* in April 1915 when Farrar was not in voice, Martinelli (who had always sung the role in Italian) was having trouble with his French, an inadequate substitute sang Escamillo, and the overworked orchestra made several careless errors. Toscanini did conduct at the Met once more—but only once more—after that disastrous evening, then canceled his last six appearances in New York and the entire tour. He left without signing a contract for the next season, and announced that he would not return.

Kahn and Gatti found it impossible to believe that Toscanini would really give up the Met: however bad things might be in New York, they were much worse in Italy, and Toscanini knew it. Like Mahler, he had cherished the opportunity to work with casts far superior to those he could hope to command elsewhere. Nor could he hope for a contract much better than the one he had signed at the Met in December 1908, which named him "First Master of Concerts and First Director of Orchestra for the operas, concerts and oratorios which will be executed in the Metropolitan Opera House in New York," in which "The Metropolitan Opera Company reserves to Maestro Toscanini the right of use of all that concerns the performing of the art," which provided moreover that "Maestro Toscanini will come to an understanding with the Manager of the Metropolitan as to the distribution of the repertoire." Leaving the Met was, in fact, immensely costly to him—financially, artistically, and spiritually. "Between the spring of 1915 and that of 1920," writes his biographer Harvey Sachs, "he did less work in total than he had formerly been accustomed to doing in a single year."

What the Met was losing was even more vital: much of the tone and no small part of the self-esteem of the enterprise. For Toscanini—like Seidl, like Mahler, like Beecham, like Karajan—took charge of *everything* on stage. His were the dramatic as well as the musical conceptions, and the stage managers worked to do his bidding. From the time at La Scala in the 1920s when Toscanini was "plenipotentiary director," the soprano Toti dal Monte remembered a rehearsal of the third act of *Rigoletto*, in which "Toscanini taught [Carlo] Galeffi his whole scene . . . transforming himself into Rigoletto, showing him every gesture, every expression, every 'spoken' recitative, every anguished outburst of wrath. How infinite were the sensations that man knew how to present, and how he knew how to get to the bottom of Verdi's creation, through music and words." Giovanni Martinelli, who joined the Met in 1913, recalled that Toscanini's "restudied" *Il Trovatore* for the 1914–15 season went into rehearsal in October for a performance in late February, and that "we had a minimum of fifty rehearsals of two hours and more . . . Toscanini staged the opera himself . . ."

Caruso's last appearance at the Met took place on December 24, 1920, as Eléazar in Halévy's *La Juive* (*above*). The following spring he returned to Italy to recuperate from a debilitating illness. Gatti's optimism in the cable of July 6, 1921, to his assistant Edward Ziegler proved premature. Four weeks later, at the age of 48, Caruso was dead.

So Gatti went to Canossa and did homage, and it did him no good. After a year in which the maestro had created the world premiere of Giordano's *Madame Sans-Gêne* with Farrar and Caruso (an opera he liked well enough to introduce it to Italy when he took over La Scala some years later), and brought Weber's *Euryanthe* back to the Met stage for the first time in 27 years ("The Italian master revealed," Krehbiel wrote gratefully, "what is meant by the studious preparation of an opera"), and had his fifty rehearsals for *Il Trovatore*, and led *Boris Godunov* and *Die Meistersinger*, and Montemezzi's *L'Amore dei tre re* (for the first time in New York) and Mascagni's *Iris* as well as *Aida* and *Butterfly* and *Tosca*—after all that, Toscanini gave Gatti what he described in a letter to Kahn as "the usual refrain that we do not value him as he deserves and that I think only about saving pennies for a Board of Millionaires . . . Not even Job in the Bible," Gatti lamented, "was put to such a test of patience."

Gatti was prepared to offer Toscanini the title of "General Musik [*sic*] Director" under an arrangement by which, he wrote Kahn, the two "Generals" would

choose by mutual agreement—saving always the prerogatives of the Executive Committee—the repertory, the artists and artistic personnel, the scheduling of the season, performances, rehearsals, etc. . . . As, thank God, I am neither a prima donna nor a tenor who suffers from jealousy or a need to put others in the shade, and instead I bow voluntarily before real merit—and as I have great affection and admiration for Toscanini and would see him quit the Metropolitan with many sadnesses—I have no difficulty in making this proposition to you and to him.

Gatti warned Kahn against trying to bring Toscanini around with letters or telegrams, which might provoke an irrevocable no—though he suggested somewhat wistfully that a personal visit from Kahn (with Mrs. Kahn!) might be helpful. Instead, he would return in August to see if he could negotiate at least the second half of the next season with Toscanini, permitting them to plan the future years together. If he turned down this offer, Gatti suggested to Kahn, it would mean that "what we guess is absolutely true—that Toscanini has in his soul special reasons for leaving the Metropolitan that have nothing to do with art, and that we have no way to eliminate." In other words, Farrar.

Five years later, Kahn and the Metropolitan would sponsor an American tour of the 100-piece orchestra Toscanini had put together for the postwar reopening of La Scala, hoping to lure his return. But by then he was thoroughly enmeshed with the Socialist government of Milan, which had promised him an unlimited budget and unlimited authority in the reconstituted "ente autonomo" of the theater, and there was no hope. After Gatti's departure, Edward Johnson sent Herbert Graf, who had been the maestro's stage director in Salzburg, to tell Toscanini "he could have anything he wanted—any cast, rehearsals and other conditions." But Toscanini would never conduct again at the Metropolitan.

There were other losses too. Alfred Hertz departed the same year as Toscanini, to become conductor of the San Francisco Symphony—but he was replaceable, by Artur Bodanzky, a Mahler protégé who imposed his own sense of musical (if not stage) drama, writing recitatives for this opera and interpolations for that one, and cutting, cutting, cutting (he got Mozart's *Figaro* down to three acts with only two hours of music). Until he lost interest, however, his was a powerful personality in the pit. Giorgio Polacco and Roberto Moranzoni picked up some of the slack left by Toscanini; and in 1924 the Met acquired a first-class second-best in Tullio Serafin, who remained until Gatti's next-to-last season, by which time he was the second most highly paid person at the Met, exceeded only by Gatti himself (an interesting contrast to all the pre-Depression years, when singers always earned much more than either conductors or managers).

In 1914, Gatti unwisely sacrificed one of the company's finest and most popular artists—Olive Fremstad, whose ability to project herself into a role gave her a power on stage that far transcended what were always carefully managed vocal resources. She was, Gatti wrote in his memoirs, "a woman with a great sense of responsibility, thoroughly serious in her approach to her tasks, and sensitive to the point of being quixotic . . . rather nervous and difficult to keep happy." Her basic demand, which also irritated the indefatigable Toscanini, was that she not be asked to rehearse the day before or the day after a performance. Her fee was $1,000 a night; she had a real (not just newspaper) feud going with Johanna Gadski, the Met's other Wagner soprano, which made the casting of *Die Walküre* and *Tannhäuser* and *Lohengrin* something of a nuisance; and Melanie Kurt from Berlin, who would sing the same repertory, and sing it well and not make trouble about when she rehearsed, was available at $500 per performance.

Informed that she would not be re-engaged, Fremstad asked to depart in the odor of her greatest triumph, as Isolde. Gatti not only refused this request, he scheduled a *Tristan* for the last night before the tour, with Gadski as Isolde. Fremstad read in the newspapers that her farewell was to be as Elsa in *Lohengrin*, a part that lay high for her and that she had never particularly liked. In an effort to dampen the likely demonstration on her behalf, Gatti instituted a new rule that flowers were to be given to artists in their dressing rooms rather than during curtain calls, an excellent regulation despite its mean origins; but the rule was ignored, and an effort to drive the audience home after the third act by lowering the asbestos curtain was so violently resisted by the house that the curtain had to be raised (a process repeated four times) to permit the tearful favorite more than forty curtain calls.

Not long after, Gatti lost both Johanna Gadski and Melanie Kurt when America's entry into World War I made any German *persona non grata* in New York, and Fremstad was engaged again for 1917–18—only to be dropped when the board prohibited performances of German works on the Met stage. Gatti, who had seen the dimensions of popular rage against Austria in Italy, had warned the board that there would be trouble; among the reasons for Toscanini's relative idleness between 1915 and 1920 was his insistence on conducting Beethoven and Wagner in his concerts.

Kahn refused to heed the warnings. German himself by birth, he thought American attitudes would mimic those in Britain, where Covent Garden continued to offer Wagner. (Kahn was in fact a British subject at this time, having acquired that status en route to New York; he did not become an American citizen until the United States entered the war.) When the directors panicked at the nation's mounting xenophobia, Gatti had all of one week to rearrange the 1917–18 season. He had to cancel the contracts of five German artists—not including Gadski, whose husband was a German military attaché (he had been tried and acquitted on charges of conspiracy to blow up the Welland Canal); she had left with her husband and the German ambassador soon after America's declaration of war in April 1917. For several years after the war, German opera was performed on the Met stage only in English, which was presumed to make the return of the Hun less objectionable.

To a far greater extent than the critics had ever wished to admit, the popularity of the Wagner repertory had been a function of the presence of great artists equipped and trained to sing it, and the return of German opera in the German language to the Met stage in 1921 did not provoke any flood of such artistry. Not until the arrival of Flagstad in the mid-1930s did the Wagner operas regain the pride of place they had enjoyed before World War I.

The great loss to the Met in the early 1920s, second only to that of Caruso, was the departure of Geraldine Farrar, who turned 40 in 1922 and quite suddenly abandoned the opera stage. Farrar was probably the outstanding personality of the Met's hundred years; she sang at the house more than 500 times in sixteen seasons. Daughter of a Philadelphia Phillies outfielder, she was both all-American and more exotic than any of the Europeans. She was, Max de Schauensee recalled,

the most enchanting and enticing person you ever saw, something special. She had wonderful red lips and white teeth, and sapphire blue eyes, and charm—a conquering sort of personality. I thought she was a marvelous and very well put together fake. She could read you a French poem as though she were from the Comédie Française, but she would make mistakes. Frances Alda, who was a terrible rival and disliked her as a person, once said that when Farrar was on stage you couldn't look at anybody else. Madame Nordica's husband said that if Farrar told you something was black and you could see it was white, you believed her. She could be very vivid as Carmen, and then exquisitely fragile as Butterfly.

Opposite: In 1908, *Puck* Magazine was still satirizing New York's operatic feuds. Now the combatants were the Met's new general manager, Giulio Gatti-Casazza, and the irrepressible impresario of the Manhattan Opera House, Oscar Hammerstein.

Pages 138, 139: Joseph Urban designed a large proportion of the Met's new productions from 1917 until his death in 1933. Pictured here are his renderings for *Norma* Act II (*left, above*), *La Vida breve* (*left, below*), *Così fan tutte* Act I (*right, above*), and *Les Contes d'Hoffmann* Act II (*right, below*).

Pages 140, 141: A 1918 production of Rimsky-Korsakov's *Le Coq d'or* lasted well into the 1940s, thanks in large part to the colorful sets designed by Willy Pogany. The singers shown here are Margaret Harshaw (Amelfa) and Norman Cordon (King Dodon).

VOL. LXIV. No. 1654.   PUCK BUILDING, New York, November 11th, 1908.   PRICE TEN CENTS.

"What Fools these Mortals be!"

Puck

Entered at N. Y. P. O. as Second-class Mail Matter.

GRAND OPERA OPENS.

TALES OF HOFFMANN · GIULIETTA · METROPOLITAN OPERA

Farrar was the only singer to have her own personal dressing room, permanently chintzed up to her taste, not to be used by anyone else. (Later, this proved a godsend in operas with two soprano leads, for Ziegler could confidently offer "Farrar's dressing room" to the artist who would not have No. 1.) When she traveled, it was in her own railroad car. She made silent films—fortunately, at a period when a throat operation compelled her to be silent anyway. She had the first and probably still the best and biggest operatic fan club, the "Gerryflappers," ardent young women in the fashionable mid-calf skirts, who mobilized when the news came in January 1922 that their heroine at the age of forty was retiring from the operatic stage.

Each Farrar appearance in the succeeding weeks—a matinee *Butterfly* three days later, *Carmen*, Massenet's *Manon*, Charpentier's *Louise*, Leoncavallo's *Zaza*, Marguerite in *Faust*—became the occasion for a greater demonstration. At the performance of *Butterfly* a month before the farewell, she asked the audience at her curtain call which opera they would prefer to hear as her swan song, and the crowd shouted, "*Tosca*." But Gatti was again disinclined to please a departing artist, and he scheduled a matinee of *Zaza*, which featured a first-act striptease by the soprano (part of her stage business, suggested by David Belasco, was a lift of the skirts to spray perfume on her lace panties). The stagehands were ordered to leave the house as the curtain came down to prevent any rebellious shows of affection—but again, of course, management's plans misfired. Just about everybody who worked in the theater joined Farrar on stage to participate in the ovation from the audience, where the fan club was unfurling banners with Farrar's name. A crowd of thousands formed at the stage door, and dragged Farrar's limousine up Broadway into Times Square; and, rather to Gatti's surprise, that was the end of it. Farrar sang concert tours for another ten years, but she never returned to opera.

Fifteen years later, Risë Stevens was in Berlin as a student and got a call from her teacher, Anna Schoen-René, to meet her for tea at the Hotel Continental: "There's someone you must meet, a very great singer." It was Farrar, amidst the wicker furniture and potted palms. "Those eyes," Stevens recalled more than forty years later, "were unbelievable, china blue, piercing. She was constantly looking toward the door of the hotel as we talked, and suddenly a huge cartwheel of a bouquet arrived. A few minutes passed, and a bellboy took the bouquet up the elevator. Farrar excused herself and went to the same elevator. And Schoen-René said to me, 'Keep watching the door.' I did, and a large man with a beard came in, and went immediately to the elevator. 'Do you recognize who that is?' Schoen-René asked me.

I said, 'Isn't that the Crown Prince?' Schoen-René nodded. 'Still following her,' she said." There were others, too, who never stopped following Farrar.

☆ ☆ ☆

During the early years, Gatti benefited not only from the strong company Conried had left him but also from a spectacular outpouring of new singers from around the world. The list is long and flabbergasting. Samples (the dates refer to seasons at the Met):

——Pasquale Amato (1908–21), a Verdi baritone of both grace and force, who sang more than 300 times in thirteen seasons; he and Scotti and Giuseppe de Luca, all three at the Met throughout the year, sang between them virtually the entire Italian baritone repertory. He was Iago in Toscanini's *Otello*, Di Luna in the maestro's restudied *Trovatore*, Rance in the world premiere of *The Girl of the Golden West*.

——Leo Slezak (1909–13), an amiable giant of a tenor who gave Toscanini an Otello capable of picking up Alda for a dramatic staging of the Act IV murder, and a Walther who could wither even Pogner with a glance; and gave Mahler a dominating Gherman in *Pique Dame*. Slezak was a tenor who could also triumph as Manrico and Radames, Lohengrin and Tannhäuser, and as Tamino in *The Magic Flute*. And he was a joy to have around, a man of great wit and self-possession, and a practical joker of far more elegance than Caruso.

John Briggs tells of a performance of *Armide* in Brooklyn, when Slezak exuberantly dragged the house manager on stage for a curtain call and, asked by the press who *was* that distinguished white-haired man, replied "Gluck. He said that in all his experience, he had never heard a man sing the role as I did." No doubt Slezak enjoyed telling that story, embellished by the detail that Gatti fined him $100 and he got Kahn to rescind the fine, and it loses only a little in plausibility when one checks up and finds that Slezak never sang in *Armide* and the Met never presented the opera in Brooklyn.

——Margarete Matzenauer (1911–30), a mezzo who promptly added soprano roles, moving from Amneris in an opening-night *Aida* through Brangäne in *Tristan*, Orfeo, Erda in *Siegfried*—and then, two days later, Kundry in *Parsifal*, replacing an indisposed Olive Fremstad in a role she had never sung before. Matzenauer would become a Brünnhilde and an Isolde, while continuing to sing the mezzo roles in Verdi—a "cathedral of sound," one critic wrote.

——Lucrezia Bori (1912–36), an elegant and lively light soprano from Spain (the name was really Borja, which was considered a little close to the bone). Three seasons of appealing acting and careful if not outstanding singing made her a welcome addition to the company, but a throat condition then forced her off stage

Geraldine Farrar bade farewell to the Met as Leoncavallo's Zaza on April 22, 1922 (*inset*). Wearing a crown made by her fans, the Gerryflappers, she was carried shoulder-high through a huge throng that had gathered outside the stage door on 40th Street.

for six years. On her return in 1921, she became one of the Met's favorite artists and people. Conscientious, cultivated, and celibate, she was one of few singers to move easily in the boxholders' social set. The Met's first Mélisande, she became the inheritor of much of the Melba repertory: Violetta, Mimi, Massenet's Manon, and Juliette. It is possible that she never had a bad review in New York. When the opera company fell on hard times in the 1930s, it was Bori who was put forward to speak for it to the public and to raise money.

——Frieda Hempel (1912–19), a lyric coloratura of supreme smoothness and accuracy, who offered long-remembered performances as Queen of the Night, Rosina, Violetta, Olympia—and the Marschallin in *Der Rosenkavalier*. A management misjudgment let her go prematurely, when it appeared that the young American coloratura Mabel Garrison, whose recordings were best-sellers for the Victor Talking Machine Co., could sing much of her repertory.

——Giovanni Martinelli (1913–45), who alternated Italian and French tenor roles first with Caruso, then with Gigli, finally with Bjoerling—and continued to be a presence at the house, a little man with a mane of white hair enthusiastically welcomed by the audience as he moved down the aisle, for a generation after his retirement from the stage. Though his voice eventually lost its varied color and its capacity for soft charm, Martinelli retained his ringing top, his immaculate phrasing, and his "nobility" into a fourth decade at the theater.

——Giuseppe de Luca (1915–40), a baritone of immense accomplishment both vocally and dramatically, who could handle the high tessitura of roles such as Carlo in *Ernani* as well as the blithe spirits of Rossini's Figaro and the sour comedy of Puccini's Gianni Schicchi, a role he created at the Metropolitan world premiere of the *Trittico* in 1918. His farewell as Germont in *Traviata* in 1940, at age 64, was considered a lesson in vocalism—"the quality of the legato," Olin Downes wrote, "the perfection of the style, the sentiment which ennobled the melodic phrase . . ." This observer heard him four years later, at a Sunday night benefit, when he and Salvatore Baccaloni, in street clothes before a bare curtain, with only a piano accompaniment, produced a performance of "Cheti, cheti immantinente" from Donizetti's *Don Pasquale* that has made all subsequent hearings of this exquisitely funny duet somehow not quite entirely satisfactory.

——Claudia Muzio (1916–22; 1934), a dramatic soprano whose particular genius lay in vocal coloration rather than vocal display. Only 22 on the occasion of her debut, she was no stranger to the house, having grown up backstage as the daughter of Grau's stage manager. The next season she would sing the opening-night *Aida*, and later create the role of Giorgetta in the world premiere of *Il Tabarro*, and sing the first Metropolitan Tatiana in *Eugene Onegin*.

——Florence Easton (1917–30; 1935–36), an Englishwoman turned Canadian, with a ringing high voice and a mastery of all the styles. Lacking dramatic projection, she was used at first mostly for oddities like the heroine of Liszt's *St. Elizabeth*, but within two years had grown into an artist of sufficient prominence to sing Rezia in Weber's *Oberon* and Nedda opposite Caruso's Canio in the great gala for the Prince of Wales (the future Edward VIII and Duke of Windsor). She created Fiordiligi for the Met's first *Così* amd her farewell was as Brünnhilde.

——Rosa Ponselle (1918–37), the greatest fairy-tale figure in American opera. Possessor of a huge, rich, and beautiful voice, the only one Max de Schauensee would bracket with Caruso's as a force of nature, she sprang from the vaudeville stage, where she had been touring with her sister under the family name Ponzillo (her parents were Italian immigrants to Connecticut). Her first appearance was as Leonora in the Metropolitan's first production of Verdi's *La Forza del destino*, one of the most arduous tests in the soprano repertory. She was the first major artist of whom it could be said that everything she did on the Met stage she did for the first time; and it is probably fair to say that never in her eighteen seasons, however experienced she became, did she step on that stage without a preliminary paroxysm of terror. She was an authentic prima donna whose wish was law, if only because she lived so near the edge. She hated steam heat, and would feel the pipes on stage as she entered the theater before a performance, so everyone shivered in the drafty old house, winter afternoons and evenings, when Ponselle was to sing.

Perhaps the greatest of Ponselle's triumphs was in *Norma*, which she sang from 1927 (the opera had not been done at the Met since Lilli Lehmann's performance in 1891); and before she would attempt it she insisted that the pitch of the house be reduced from A = 440 to A = 435. Norma was her debut role at Covent Garden, and one of the most fascinating documents in the Ziegler files is a set of three carbons, alternate drafts of a letter proposing to Col. Eustace Blois, manager of the London house, that he copy the Met's "experiment" with a lowered pitch. The letter eventually sent did not mention Ponselle's name, though Blois could have had no difficulty understanding what was going on. The drop is physically so inconsequential (only a fifth of a semitone) that the purpose must have been entirely psychological.

Tall, with an interesting round face perfectly framed by 1920s hairstyles, Ponselle was good gossip-column material before falling in love with the son of the mayor of Baltimore and retiring to become the great lady of theater and opera in that city.

——Beniamino Gigli (1920–32; 1939), a little man with perhaps the most beautiful lyric tenor voice of his generation, but an incurable seeker after applause, who would abandon any characterization at any time to milk an audience. He left behind a curious memory of lovely sounds and unlovely vanity.

——Amelita Galli-Curci (1921–30), the greatest coloratura sensation since Tetrazzini. She delighted audiences but not Gatti, who had been pressured into hiring her by board members and always found her voice a little thin for the great expanse of the house and her intonation a little flat. An expensive artist with a full concert career, she sang rarely at the Met, and only in a very restricted repertory—Violetta, Gilda, Lucia, a single Mimi, Rosina, and the Queen in Rimsky-Korsakov's *Le Coq d'or*.

——Maria Jeritza (1921–32; plus an appearance in *Die Fledermaus* in Rudolf Bing's first season), the blonde bombshell of opera. (When she died—in 1982!—her obituary referred to her famous jewelry collection and equally famous remark that "no man would ever dare to give *me* flowers.") Her debut was in the American premiere of Erich Korngold's gloomily decadent *Die tote Stadt*; her triumph was as Tosca, when she performed her unique athletic-dramatic feat of singing "Vissi d'arte" while prone on the dusty stage. For the next decade, she owned this role almost as exclusively as Scotti owned Scarpia; she was the Metropolitan's first and (until Birgit Nilsson) almost only Turandot. (Easton had a single shot at it in 1928.) *The Girl of the Golden West* was revived in large part because she was willing to sing Minnie (not for long). But she also sang Octavian in *Der Rosenkavalier*; Janáček's *Jenufa*; Wagner heroines up to and including Sieglinde; and a collection of the sexy roles—Carmen, Thaïs, Aegyptische Helena.

Robert Tuggle, archivist of the Metropolitan, who has read all the correspondence on the subject, considers it demonstrable that Jeritza's arrival provoked Farrar's retirement. That Farrar resented Jeritza's Tosca is visible in her supremely feline comment on the newcomer's most famous feat: "I obtained no view of any expressive pantomime on her pretty face, while I was surprised by the questionable flaunting of a well-cushioned and obvious posterior."

——Feodor Chaliapin (1921–29), who had sung at the Met in 1907–08, receiving bad notices for his tasteless overacting, but returned in glory (for $3,000 a night, until the late 1960s the highest fees ever paid by the Metropolitan) to place a personal stamp on Boris Godunov, which he sang in Russian, the rest of the cast in Italian. Chaliapin also appeared as Boito's Mefistofele and Massenet's Don Quichotte and Gounod's Mephistopheles, and he was the Met's first Philip II in *Don Carlo*, when he demonstrated that he was still a ham. Though the Met was attempting to enforce a rule against encores, the applause following his Act III Soliloquy brought Chaliapin to the footlights to tell the hapless conductor (Papi) precisely where he wished the aria picked up, so he could be applauded again. Still, his dominance over a performance was real. De Schauensee remembered a Mefistofele in Milan: "It wasn't long before Arturo Toscanini, the whole Scala orchestra simply disappeared from your attention, and you saw nothing but Chaliapin." Already 52 years old when he reappeared at the Met, he was still a force on stage at 60.

——Titta Ruffo (1921–29), a Verdi baritone with enormous power in the upper register, whom Gatti also employed sparingly, in roles where that quality would make its greatest impression: Carlo in *Ernani*, Escamillo, Gérard in *Chénier*, Figaro in

Barbiere, Barnaba in *Gioconda*. "Listening to Ruffo," De Schauensee said, "was like looking up from the bottom of Niagara Falls."

——Elisabeth Rethberg (1922–42), possessor of what Kirsten Flagstad (who first encountered her only toward the end of her career) described as the most beautiful soprano voice she had ever heard. "Silvery" was the adjective most frequently employed. Though German, she made her debut as Aida, and sang more Italian than German roles through most of her Met career. Her rare opportunities to sing Mozart left long memories, as did her Agathe in *Freischütz*. Flagstad heard her as Desdemona and Leonora in *Forza*; and she partnered Rethberg's Sieglinde.

——Lawrence Tibbett (1923–50), a Californian, one of very few Met artists to rise from *comprimario* status to stardom, got his first large chance as Valentin in *Faust* in 1923–24, but was still a minor figure when Gatti cast him as Ford in a *Falstaff* revived for Serafin and Scotti in 1924–25. After the first scene of the second act, an ovation lasting fifteen minutes delayed the continuation of the opera, while the audience insisted on a solo curtain call by Tibbett as reward for his performance of the great aria in praise of jealousy. Frederick T. Burnhall, managing editor of the *Times*, decided it was a front-page story, and thereafter Tibbett was a major box-office draw at the Metropolitan, one of very few baritones of whom that could be said. Cehanovsky remembers especially the delicacy and beauty of his soft singing: "His *pianos* were so delightful that even an Italian conductor like Serafin would just open his eyes and listen; he said, 'It cannot be better than that'." As late as the mid-1930s, Edward Ziegler, writing to the head of the production committee of the board, could sell Gatti's choice of a new American opera with the encomium, "It contains an important role for Tibbett." Affection kept Tibbett on stage for a decade after liquor had cost him his voice.

——Friedrich Schorr (1923–43), for two decades the prince of Wagnerian baritones. His Hans Sachs in the first season was, Lawrence Gilman wrote, "the authentic Sachs of Wagner's drama: a poet, a dreamer, a man of sorrows; but a tragedian who has mastered his grief and does not take too seriously his resignation; who is mellow without softness and noble without offense . . . Mr. Schorr has a voice of exceptional beauty, and he sings like a musician. Some of his mezza-voce and pianissimo singing yesterday was of astonishing delicacy, purity, and finesse." His Wanderer in *Siegfried* twenty years later, Olin Downes wrote, was "an interpretation wholly worthy of his distinguished career. The audience had reason again to realize the nobility and authority of his entire conception of this one of the Wotan roles, the feeling as well as the musicianship which inhabited every moment of it; the significance given the text as well as the melodic line; the variety of color and of illuminative detail which have so often been described . . ."

——Lauritz Melchior (1925–50), the second most important tenor of the century, yielding pride of place only to Caruso. For once, Gatti miscast a debut, placing

Overleaf: Gatti had many other superlative artists to make up for the loss of Caruso and Farrar—among them, Rosa Ponselle and Giovanni Martinelli (*left, below,* in Verdi's *Ernani*), Florence Easton (*left, above,* as Liszt's St. Elizabeth), Feodor Chaliapin (*opposite page, above left,* as Massenet's Don Quichotte), Giuseppe de Luca (*above right,* as Rossini's Figaro), and Amelita Galli-Curci (*below,* as Lucia).

Melchior (who had only recently been a baritone) on the Met stage for the first time as Tannhäuser, a role which lies higher than the other Wagner tenor parts. One of the first "international" singers who gave the Met only part of a season (he cut 1928–29 entirely), Melchior did not become the Met's staple Siegmund-Siegfried-Tristan until the 1930s. By then, the wonderful voice was fully ripened, a rich, heroic voice with the Wagnerian sense of "space" around the tone, used with great lyric sensitivity. As a citizen of an opera company, however, he grew intolerable; he would sit in the audience for his own rehearsals in later years, while a cover marked his role and Melchior at some length shared his insights on the production with the management.

——Ezio Pinza (1926–48), perhaps the greatest entirely natural talent the operatic stage has ever known (he could not read music, and it didn't matter), a former racing cyclist with a bass voice both seductive and powerful. In his autobiography, Bruno Walter tells the story of Pinza's visit to his home to discuss an engagement as Don Giovanni in Salzburg. The maid who answered the door came running flustered to Frau Walter: "Ma'am, there is such a *beautiful* man outside . . ." Pinza's dramatic instincts were so secure that gestures which the critics disliked when they were first introduced became welcomed trademarks of a Pinza performance later on—like his foot on the prompter's box as he drew his audience close around him to complain about the fickleness of women in the fourth act of *Figaro*. He was also a great buffo talent, playing Basilio in *Barbiere*, Dulcamara in *L'Elisir*, Gaudenzio in Rossini's youthful *Il Signor Bruschino*. Meanwhile, he was the Met's post-Chaliapin Boris Godunov. When Pinza left the Met, it was for Broadway, as the brilliantly cast, not-quite-spent volcano of Rodgers' and Hammerstein's *South Pacific*.

——Grace Moore (1927–46), everybody's darling (at least, every male's darling), who came to the Met from musical comedy, moved on to Hollywood, and returned to opera. Her debut was attended by a Tennessee delegation one hundred strong, including both the state's senators. Somewhat surprisingly, the voice *was* big enough for the opera house. Tosca was probably her most common and successful role, because she knew full well what it meant to be a star. She was a memorable Louise, because she knew what it meant to escape into love. The things she did not know well she could not act. And to the end—she died in an air crash while on a Scandinavian tour, the Swedish crown prince beside her—Moore could draw large and noisy audiences to the house.

——And this immense list leaves out as many as it includes of the significant artists Gatti brought to the Met in the 1910s and 1920s. It leaves out the Hammerstein artists like Tetrazzini and Renaud, who resumed their New York careers (but rather briefly) at the Met; the handsome Canadian tenor Edward Johnson, who was later to become general manager of the theater; Elisabeth Schumann, mostly a lieder singer, who gave a few Met performances; the American bass Clarence Whitehill, whose

Hans Sachs displaced Fischer's in the memory of one set of old-timers, and was never displaced from the memory of the next set; the dramatic character bass Michael Bohnen; the Italian tenor Giacomo Lauri-Volpi; the splendid, large-voiced, large-boned Swedish mezzos Sigrid Onegin and Karin Branzell; the French-Canadian mezzo Jeanne Gordon, a dark voice with a brilliant top; tiny Queena Mario, who spelled Bori in the light Italian roles and sang Gretel year after year in Humperdinck's *Hänsel und Gretel*; the versatile Editha Fleischer; the Wagnerian sopranos Maria Müller and Nanny Larsen-Todsen and Gertrude Kappel.

There were also shooting stars. The American tenor Orville Harrold soared briefly on a rather fragile instrument abused by a management that, for example, cast him as Lohengrin on Thursday followed by Almaviva on Saturday. And the outrageously promoted Marion Talley, eighteen years old, daughter of a railroad telegrapher from Kansas City, who made her debut as Gilda in *Rigoletto* before an audience that included a trainload of the home folks, her father installed backstage with a special wire enabling him to tap out word of his daughter's success as it happened. The publicity filled the house with paying customers, if not with vocal sufficiency, whenever Talley appeared—and also deprived her of any incentive to improve her technique, until finally the voice ran out entirely.

☆ ☆ ☆

From the end of the Hammerstein competition to the onslaught of the Depression, the board of the real estate company had little to do. The boxholders continued to a remarkable degree to be the same families that had created the company in 1892, feeling somewhat beleaguered in the world of the 1920s, when the café society that drank illegal booze in illegal places rivaled the old families (who drank their illegal booze at home) in the public prominence accorded their activities. So many people had money in the 1920s: the opera boxes were among the last redoubts of exclusivism, and the board was determined that they should so remain. A number of boxes were left in the hands of estates, because the customers who sought them were unacceptable to the board.

The continuing concerns were monetary. The contract with Kahn's producing company remained unchanged. It provided for the company to pay a rental of $67,000, offset by a subsidy of $1,000 per performance, up to a maximum of 70 performances, on Monday, Wednesday, and Friday nights, and on Saturday matinees. Thus Gatti and Kahn got their opera house rent-free, with all taxes and real property insurance paid by the landlord. Significant renovations and repairs to the building were also the landlord's responsibility. The apartment houses that flanked the entrance were part of Kahn's lease (though not the ground-floor bank, which continued to pay its rent to the real estate company), and the producing

company received all the revenues from the rental of the apartments, of the hall to users other than itself, of space in the building used by purveyors of refreshments, libretti, etc.

In return, the 35 boxholders received free admission, six seats per box, to every attraction in the house—for an assessment that remained at $3,000 per box throughout most of these years. As Gatti lengthened the season, the values delivered increased dramatically. A report to the board by its secretary in 1914 showed an increase in the number of subscription performances from 65 in 1900–01 to 120 in 1914–15, with a rise in the number of "extra" performances from 16 to 31. In the 1920s, the number of performances available to the boxholders free of charge was consistently over 165.

Boxholders could rent their boxes, though an amendment to the by-laws—passed with some difficulty in 1899 after an embarrassing incident of gouging—required that all rentals be made through the secretary of the board at prices set by the directors. The rental schedule in 1915–16 was $10,000 for a season (permitted only to estates), $2,400 for one night in each of the subscription weeks, $125 for a single evening (or Saturday matinee). In the 1920s, the approved rentals rose to $15,000 for a season and $3,500 for a single subscription series.

With the passage of time and the steady increase in the value of the opera house and the city's tax rates, the $3,000 annual assessment fell short of the real estate company's needs. Taxes on the property had been $35,000 in 1901; by 1915 they had risen to $60,000; by 1922 the total real estate and franchise taxes assessed on the opera house and its storage building had reached $111,000—i.e. $6,000 more than the entire proceeds from the assessment. What kept the real estate company afloat in 1922, indeed, was an increase from $12,000 to $25,000 in the annual rental charged for the banking premises in the property. Rather than raise the annual assessment, which was utterly inadequate if interest had to be paid on the indebtedness of the company, the boxholders in 1919 heroically hit themselves with a one-time bill of $30,000 per box, to retire the debt. In fairness to the stockholders of the real estate company, some return on what was now a $60,000 investment for the original boxholders does not seem an unwarranted expectation. In fairness to Kahn and Gatti, their poor-mouthing about the financial condition of the producing company through the profitable years can be seen as a measure to hang onto their rent-free status rather than a deception upon the public. There was indeed a proposal before the real estate company board in 1922 that the terms of the producing company's lease, up for renewal in 1923, be changed to make Kahn's group responsible for taxes and insurance on the house.

Still, as was pointed out in the secretary's message to the board as early as 1915, the underlying value of the property the boxholders owned had risen steadily (from $1.4 million in 1893 to an assessed value of $3.25 million in 1915). "Boxes, which

Backstage in the 1920s: (*above*) Maria Jeritza flanked by (*l. to r.*) chorus master Giulio Setti, conductor Louis Hasselmans, the Canadian tenor Edward Johnson, and stage director Wilhelm von Wymetal at a rehearsal of *Carmen*; (*below*) the principals of Puccini's *La Rondine*: Lucrezia Bori, Beniamino Gigli, Armand Tokatyan, and Editha Fleischer.

originally cost $30,000 to the subscribers and early buyers, have mounted steadily in value until recent sales have been on a basis of $150,000, or even more, per box." In the mid-1920s, the price of a box rose above $200,000.

It was in this context that the board of the real estate company considered what became a drumfire of proposals from Otto Kahn to replace the opera house. The first approach, in 1922, involved a City Art Center to be built "from 48th or 49th Street to 51st or 52nd Street, running through from 7th to 6th Avenue." The City would give the land to the real estate company free and clear, and would pledge to purchase the new opera house from the real estate company at original cost if the boxholders ever wanted out of the opera business. "The City makes no claim to representation or supervision or any voice whatever in the affairs of the M.O. & R.E. Co. or the Metropolitan Opera Company. The M.O. & R.E. Co. will have precisely the same right as it has now to determine who are to be the owners of boxes in the new house." This would have been too good a deal for the real estate company to turn down, but it was also too good a deal to be true.

Following the collapse of this project, Kahn began a series of meetings with George C. Haven, president of the real estate company, to explore what it would take to persuade the boxholders to transfer the Metropolitan Opera to a new house. Then Haven died, and Kahn, despairing that he could persuade his successor R. Fulton Cutting by mere argument, made a pre-emptive strike. Late in 1925, Kahn acquired a plot of land 325 feet long by 200 feet deep, taking up about two-fifths of the block between West 57th Street and West 56th Street, Eighth and Ninth Avenues. Early in 1926, he made a formal submission to the board of the real estate company.

The letter opened with a tribute to "the wisdom and public spirit with which the permanent lines of the fundamental policies of the Metropolitan Opera House were established and have been guarded by its founders. We recognize that the high standing in the community of the gentlemen composing your board has contributed greatly to the success and prestige of Grand Opera."

But the real estate company was running a bad property:

The accommodation for those patrons of the opera who cannot afford to buy the more expensive seats, i.e., the masses of the music loving public, is inadequate as to quantity and wholly unsatisfactory as to quality. Indeed, a considerable number of the lower priced seats are so bad that it is really an act of unfairness to take money for them—especially from people of small means . . .

Everything behind the curtain is antiquated and much of it presents grave inconveniences. The wings are far too narrow, the stage lacks depth, the facilities for scenery, wardrobe and stage effects are wholly uncommensurate. The dressing rooms and other conveniences are deficient and in some respects unsanitary. The ventilation of the House is sadly inadequate.

The traffic problem appears to be an insoluble one in the present location of the House . . .

The cost of giving opera in the style befitting the Metropolitan and called for by its audience, is steadily mounting. On the other hand, the limit of income which can be obtained within the capacity of the present House has been reached. Likewise, the limit of artistic effects which can be produced on the present inadequate stage has been reached.

The new opera house Kahn proposed would have roughly the same interior cubage as the existing Met, but would have a seating capacity of at least 4,000. There would be only 30 boxes ("experience has shown that 35 boxes is rather more than the demand warrants," Kahn noted blithely).

The present system [the letter continued] of boxes being *owned* and then rented out or given away by the owners for such evenings as they do not care to retain, has proven, in the course of time, inconvenient, troublesome, and expensive to the owners, and detrimental to the value of the boxes . . . Therefore, it is suggested that in a new opera house there should be no box *owners*, but only box lessees. There being 5 subscription performances each week, and assuming 30 boxes, it is suggested that there be prepared a list of 150 eligible persons who shall be invited to become box holders for *one evening* (or, if preferred, Saturday matinee) *each week* (or more than one evening, if so desired . . .). The cost of thus renting a box for one evening or matinee each week would be approximately $3,500—being at the rate of about $145 for each performance . . .

Kahn suggested that the costs could be met by 30 investors who would put up $133,000 each; the rest of the money would be supplied by an insurance company taking a mortgage. The 30 investors would receive second mortgage bonds and stock in the company that would own the land and building, and "the first right to subscribe for boxes under the scheme above suggested." The Metropolitan Opera Company—the producing company—would lease the building, paying all taxes and upkeep, and assuming responsibility for the interest on the first mortgage and an appropriate sinking fund, plus an amount sufficient to yield the boxholders 4 per cent a year on their investment. In addition, the opera company would make a profit-sharing deal with the real estate company.

At the end, Kahn graciously offered "to continue our reciprocal relationship, in the new building, on the lines and terms of the present lease." But he was insistent upon the construction of a new building. He listed the directors of his company, who had unanimously approved the letter; the list included George Eastman of Rochester, Marshall Field of Chicago, Robert Goelet, Fred A. Juilliard, Clarence H. Mackay, Edward T. Stotesbury of Philadelphia, Harry Payne Whitney, and Cornelius Vanderbilt Whitney. There was no question that these men, as Kahn wrote, "would be in a position themselves to make the necessary arrangements to finance a new Opera House" if the board of the real estate company declined to go along.

A year of negotiations followed Kahn's initial letter, which was—deliberately, one imagines—highly unsatisfactory to the boxholders. Early in 1927, a detailed

---

Overleaf: Three new operas of the 1920s. Puccini's *Turandot* (*left, below*), with Giacomo Lauri-Volpi and Jeritza, had its first Met production in November 1926, seven months after the Scala premiere. Křenek's "jazz opera" *Jonny spielt auf* (*right*) followed in February 1929; Lawrence Tibbett's star turns took place against an extravagant Urban decor. Weinberger's more traditional *Schwanda* (*left, above*) was given in 1931 with Friedrich Schorr as the bagpiper.

CARLO EDWARDS
NEW YORK

proposal was put before the board. By then the cost of the land was up to $2.93 million (two years' taxes had been paid), and the cost of the building, plans for which had been worked on by both Benjamin Morris (Morgan's house architect) and Joseph Urban, was placed at $4.25 million. Of the total needed, $4.64 million would be raised by the sale of 32 parterre boxes at $145,000 each, with a first mortgage of $3.25 million.

The Monday boxes would go to the owners free of charge in perpetuity; the producing company would lease the others by the year, at $3,000 a season, of which the boxholders would get $750. As at the old Met, the theater would be joined to an apartment house, and the boxholders would receive 60 per cent of the revenue from that. The Metropolitan Opera Company would pay a rent of $162,500 a year, covering the mortgage interest, and would be responsible for the upkeep of the properties; the boxholders would continue to pay the taxes. Assuming that the property at Broadway and 39th Street was worth $7 million, the 32 boxholders joining the plan would be able to take out of the deal $55,000 each—virtually their entire investment in the old Met—*after* buying their boxes in the new theater. Kahn estimated that the boxholders' share of the rentals on other than Monday nights, and of the apartment house profits, would cover the real estate taxes with $500 to spare—and the boxholders would have their Monday night opera free and clear in perpetuity.

In his presentation to the board on January 5, 1927, Kahn raised the threat level a notch. In the words of the secretary's summary, he said that:

Conditions at the present Opera House are such that, whether a new Opera House is built or not, the Metropolitan Opera Company could not see its way clear to undertake opera in the present house for more than five years at the outside. The expense would be too great, and the facilities are too poor, to keep up to the standard of first-class productions such as they aim to produce. The Opera Company would prefer that this Company assume the erection and ownership of the new house . . . [because] this Company is permanently composed of representative prominent men with whom Grand Opera in America should continue to be identified . . . If, however, the Metropolitan Opera and Real Estate Company does not desire to act in accordance with this suggestion, then the Metropolitan Opera Company asks that the Real Estate Company will co-operate in the new plan to the extent of making such recommendations to its stockholders and presenting the plan to them so that as many as possible of the present individual stockholders will decide to become identified with the new project. Should any vacancies in the boxes offered by the new plan remain after present stockholders have been invited to join, the Opera Company will have no difficulty in filling the remaining subscriptions . . .

The real estate company could not reject this proposal out of hand. At a board meeting on February 2, 1927, the Kahn plan was accepted as a recommendation to the stockholders. A preliminary response indicated that 7,350 of the company's 10,500 shares would be deposited for shares in Kahn's venture. But that was the high-water mark. At a meeting on April 12, several stockholders registered objections—Mrs. Cornelius Vanderbilt III, William Fahnestock, Mrs. Ogden Goelet and (most damagingly, because he was also a member of Kahn's board and had signed its original letter) Robert Goelet, who was Mrs. Vanderbilt's nephew. The objectors found an argument Kahn could not refute: a site in the center of a nondescript block lacked dignity. By December 21, 1927, a meeting of the board at the residence of George F. Baker, head of the First National Bank and a major Morgan ally, concluded that "the general feeling that the new Opera should be monumental and an ornament to the city seemed to have gained ground among the stockholders."

Early in 1928, Kahn gave up: his threat to go it alone had always been a bluff. He put his property up for sale; the purchasers built the Parc Vendome apartments on the site. Kahn let it be known that he had lost money on the resale, which probably became true only in the Depression, when Parc Vendome was forced into reorganization and the second mortgage Kahn had kept was wiped out. In any event, Kahn was bitter enough to end his campaign for a new opera house. Following up on his statement that he could not continue producing opera at the old Met for more than five years, he resigned as chairman of the Metropolitan Opera Company shortly before the start of the 1931–32 season. Having accepted Kahn's argument that the old theater was inadequate, the real estate company remained charged with the responsibility of finding its own means for providing a new one; but Kahn was out of the picture.

FIVE

MILESTONES II: THE FIFTIETH
ANNIVERSARY. DELIGHTS AMIDST DESPAIR

The machine Gatti had built for the production of opera at the old Met was complicated beyond the imaginings of people who have never been involved with the affairs of an opera house. The singers on stage and the conductor in the pit are in a sense only the part of the iceberg that shows. Gatti and Kahn and Ziegler, representing the company to the boxholders and the public, were backed by a remarkably stable organization that trudged sturdily on its accustomed rounds, year after year. When Edward Johnson took over as general manager in 1935 (retaining in place the entire Gatti substructure), it became fashionable to say in admiration or annoyance that Gatti had organized the affairs of the opera house on pieces of paper that he stuffed in his pockets, but in fact one can still find in the archives the contracts, the pay books that say who did what where on what day for how much, the time sheets that tell how long each act and each intermission ran, and the cash books that report the take for every performance of every opera.

After the early years, Gatti's new productions were mostly built (and almost without exception painted) in New York. The paint frame on which drops were prepared was in use near the back wall of the theater six days a week and sometimes in the evenings, the painters working unconcernedly through performances on their scaffolds high above the stage. Joseph Novak directed this work and painted some of the more difficult drops himself; in the late 1920s he began to get increasing opportunities to design productions.

The built pieces and general carpentry were supervised by Fred Hosli, master machinist and chief stagehand, a large man of strong views, who had an entrepreneurial sideline: a warehouse in which he stored pieces from defunct Broadway shows, selling them later to producers of other Broadway shows or even to the Met itself. Like the work of property man Philip Crispano, costume master Nicholas Lanzilotti, and chief electrician Jacob Buchter (who had to supervise the packing and unpacking of railroad freight cars full of lamps, electric towers, and electrical effects), Hosli's job was incredibly complicated by the need to take productions on tour every Tuesday to Philadelphia or the Brooklyn Academy of

Gatti-Casazza backstage in the 1930s.

Music, plus two weeks in Atlanta, Cleveland, and Rochester at the close of each season.

Transport for this army was planned by Thomas Hillary, who worked at the Met more than 40 years. The traveling manager when the company left town (Gatti might go once a year to Philadelphia, but otherwise remained in New York) was Jules Judels, an efficient Dutchman who had started at the Met in 1891–92 as a call boy, telling singers when to leave their dressing rooms and get ready to go on stage. Still at the Met in the 1930s, he would look back longingly to the Atlanta trips when De Luca, Didur, and De Segurola would relieve the unwary of their funds in all-night poker games while the orchestra members took over the kitchens in the diners and prepared huge cauldrons of spaghetti.

At the center of an entirely separate spider web sat Lionel Mapleson, the nephew of Abbey's rival of 1883, who served as the Met's librarian for 48 years, from 1889 to his death in 1937 (when his son took over), keeping and distributing the orchestral parts and vocal scores. (He also made the first pirate recordings at the Met, on an Edison machine mounted in the flies; these "Mapleson Cylinders," recorded 1901 to 1903 and largely wrecked over the years by Mapleson's own repeated playings of them, are unique aural documents of what the operatic world was like at the turn of the century.) Chorus parts for revivals often were unavailable, because the Europeans who sang in the Met chorus before the 1920s had sung all the works before and memorized them. ("In former days," Mapleson wrote Ziegler in 1931 apropos of a planned revival of *Lakmé*, "the members of the chorus were venerable individuals and had a big repertoire.") Full orchestral scores might also be unavailable ("in former days the Conductors were satisfied to use a *Piano Score*").

For years, there were two stage directors then called "stage managers"—Jules Speck, who handled the Italian and French operas, and Anton Schertel, who handled the German operas. Wilhelm von Wymetal was added in 1922, and proved adept at getting opera on stage in a few hours of place setting. The director's function, it was generally understood, was to tell people where to stand. When Toscanini personally restaged *Il Trovatore*, Martinelli thought one of his major concerns was making sure the singers could see his beat, because that is what the conductors were forever insisting the stage managers must do. Belasco staged *Girl of the Golden West*, and also Leoncavallo's *Zaza* for Farrar, but it was not until the late 1920s that Gatti decided the Germans had a point in their recent emphasis on the *régisseur* and hired Ernst Lert to upgrade the dramatic probity of the repertory. Lert resigned with a blast at a management that simply threw most of its (48 or 49) productions on stage with no rehearsal at all, and gave him no more than three or four sessions with the singers and chorus for even the most elaborate new presentations; Ziegler replied to the press that Lert's contract wasn't going to be renewed anyway.

Elisabeth Rethberg as Aida, the role in which she made her Met debut in 1922. Gatti's final season of 1934–35 opened with an *Aida* featuring Rethberg, Martinelli, Tibbett, and Pinza.

Fernand de Gueldre
-CHICAGO-

Second only to Ziegler in Gatti's management team was Earle R. Lewis, who started at the Met as a boy behind the ticket window in the Family Circle entrance and worked his way up to mastery of an increasingly complicated sales operation. What was sold by subscription was, simply, an evening or matinee each week for the season—subscribers were not told what operas they would hear, let alone what artists. The basic marketing tool was a 10 per cent discount from single-ticket prices. By the early 1920s, more than two-thirds of the seats for the five weekly subscription performances were sold before the season began. (Saturday night was lower-priced, and not on the subscription series.) As more than a fifth of the seats at the Metropolitan offered only partial or obstructed views, this meant that only a few hundred desirable seats were available for single sale on subscription evenings—in itself a great inducement to subscription.

The press was handled by William J. (always "Billy") Guard, a lanky Irishman with a wispy mustache and a string tie, and the attitudes described by Hecht and MacArthur in their 1920s play *The Front Page*. An amusing companion with a quick answer to a question (when someone from the press inquired whether the Met was planning a gala performance for the visit of Queen Marie of Romania, Guard replied that Gatti thought any Met performance was gala enough for any queen), he manipulated the gift of passes with a sure hand. He had come to Gatti from Hammerstein in 1911, and remained until his death in 1932, rarely sober, keeping the Met and its stars in the news and gossip columns from the beginning of rehearsals to the departure on tour. Though he was at the house for virtually every performance, he rarely entered the auditorium, preferring to remain at his desk behind the box office. Having seen that all was in order backstage and in the hall, Gatti would drop by and sit on the bare wooden bench that was the only accommodation for visitors to Guard's lair, drinking grappa and listening to stories to which he did not have to respond, because Guard and the press spoke English, which Gatti never uttered.

Ziegler rewrote all of Guard's press releases, and some contacts with the press had to be handled by even higher authority. In December 1929, Kahn wrote to William Randolph Hearst about a review in the New York *Evening Journal* by Irving Weil. Giacomo Lauri-Volpi (whom Kahn described as "not only a most brilliant, but a thoroughly serious and sincere artist, and a gentleman") had been grievously offended by a Weil review which commented on "the bawling extravagance of his singing and the strutting puerility of his acting" in a performance of *Luisa Miller*. "Mr. Lauri-Volpi is deeply hurt," Kahn wrote, "and his friends are considering what, if any, steps ought to be taken." For himself, Kahn concluded, "I hope I am not transgressing the bounds of propriety if I venture to point to the spirit, tone, temper and mode of expression which at times characterize the attitude of Mr. Weil toward an organization that aims, within its sphere, to serve the community and which, by that token, is, I submit, entitled to goodwill and respect." There is no way to know whether Hearst showed this missive to Weil; Kahn undoubtedly showed it to Lauri-Volpi.

There were also the doormen and ticket-takers, subject to blasts of winter air from the lobby doors. Head usher Harry Richards died of pneumonia, and was replaced by Thomas Beardine, who expired of similar causes. In the 1920s, the new head usher Thomas Bull, who had been taking tickets at the Met since opening night in 1883, arranged to have choke-collar uniforms substituted for the previous evening dress with brass buttons (to distinguish ticket-takers from the audience, whose evening dress did not have brass buttons). With wool jackets buttoned to the neck, the ticket-takers remained healthy.

The passage of time gradually changed the Met's cohorts and the burdens of managing them. In 1918, under the pressures of war, the first Americans were hired for the full-time chorus, previously recruited in Europe—seven women and two men. By the mid-1920s, most of the chorus were in fact Americans by birth or naturalization, and the chorus, like the orchestra and the stagehands, had been unionized in an American Grand Opera Alliance. As early as 1922, Ziegler was writing to Gatti that the negotiations for the next season were going badly: the chorus "are very obstinate in their demands for an increase . . .". They also demanded two weeks' sick pay. Ziegler wrote to Fortune Gallo, whose San Carlo Opera had received the same demand, that "you can have this entire clause thrown out, because it is definitely against the principles of the American Federation of Labor that an employer pay for services which he does not get." Stagehands under the new contract in 1922 were paid $50 a week for an eight-hour day, plus $7 per performance. Ziegler detailed the added costs: on *Die Walküre*, stagehand expenses would rise from $668.35 to $830.50; on *Butterfly*, from $398.20 to $488; on *Don Carlo*, from $534.05 to $651.75.

Between 1921–22 and 1928–29, the costs of the chorus rose from $172,000 to $232,000; of the orchestra, from $228,000 to $405,000; of the soloists, from $759,000 to $1,035,000. These cost increases were met in part by increased ticket prices (which rose from a $7 top in 1922 to $8.25 in 1927), in part by increased audiences (total box-office and subscription receipts peaked at an average of $13,000 per performance in 1928–29), in part by growing ancillary income, which came from a wide variety of sources.

Revenues from renting out the Met's artists topped out in the early Caruso days ($117,000 in 1910–11); increasingly, the established artists refused to sign contracts that gave the Met a cut when they sang outside engagements. Still, Clause XII in the Metropolitan standard contract, requiring the Met's consent for all outside work in the United States during the Met season, remained a part of most artists' arrangements, which gave the company income from recording companies and broadcasters. By the late 1920s, the Victor Talking Machine Company was paying the Met $30,000 a year for the right to make offers to Met singers, and another $30,000 came first from the advertising firm of Batten, Barton, Durstine & Osborne, then from NBC for the exclusive right to broadcast the artists the Met controlled (which did not include the very biggest names). The contract included a clause prohibiting NBC from advertising its exclusivity.

Almost $100,000 a year came in from the apartment house and the rental of the hall to outsiders (at $1,400 a night, sometimes for serious work: Stravinsky's *Sacre* was danced at the Met for the first time in New York in 1930, with Martha Graham as the unlucky chosen one; Leopold Stokowski brought a staged *Wozzeck* from Philadelphia, with surrealistic sets by Robert Edmond Jones, in 1931). Knabe paid $15,000 a year for the piano endorsement. Emil Katz paid $5,000 a year for the right to serve refreshments at buffets and sell cigarettes and cigars. The right to publish the Met's programs and sell advertising in them went for $20,000, with percentages to be paid to the opera company once advertising revenues passed $75,000 a year (in the late 1920s, this yielded the opera company more than $36,000 a year). Another contract gave the Met its publicity pictures almost for free (the photographer, Mishkin, demanded two seats for one performance a week), in return for the Met's designation of Mishkin as its official photographer.

The Great Depression was, first of all, *bewildering*. The nation had known economic setback before, and the first year after the stock market crash did not in fact see as savage a decline in economic activity as 1919–20, when the bubble of World War I inflation burst in a wave of bankruptcies and a desperate trough of unemployment. The Met season in 1929–30, opening on the eve of the stock market's Black Tuesday, brought the highest revenues the opera company had ever earned—$3,411,000, greatly aided by an increase to $350,000 in the company's non-box-office income. In a year of economic collapse, the box office was down by less than $60,000. *Don Giovanni* with Pinza (Gatti's first *Don*: he didn't like the opera, which he thought suffered from too many scene changes), Rimsky-Korsakov's exotic *Sadko*, and an uncut *Ring* with Bodanzky all sold the house to the rafters, with standees packed behind the orchestra circle and upstairs.

In an end-of-season letter, Kahn congratulated Gatti "on the fact that, in a period of severe economic depression, which did not fail seriously to affect the prosperity of 'Broadway,' the attendance of the public at the Metropolitan Opera this season was but slightly diminished, as compared to the best previous season." As a tangible statement of its appreciation, Kahn's board extended Gatti's contract for an additional two years, until 1935, and raised his salary to $67,000 a year. Then the roof fell in.

In retrospect, it is easy to see that the economy of the Metropolitan, like the economy of the nation, had really peaked in 1927. Artistically, the Met had already begun to run down, just a little. Because everything would have to be redesigned for the proposed new house anyway, there were no restagings of old attractions, and the average success of new attractions was still pitiful. Worse, the flood of new talent seemed to dry up: the next four years would see debuts by only one minor (Gladys Swarthout) and one major (Lily Pons) box-office attraction. (Pons, of course, always *très chic*, was a personality par excellence: single-handed, Risë Stevens recalls, she made the 1930s at the Met "a glamour time, when everyone dressed and was bejeweled. You were expected to be very glamorous. And we were.")

Financially, the 1927–28 season was the certified top, showing a profit of $141,000; subscription revenues, helped by an increase in seat prices, reached a high-water mark of almost $55,000 per week. In 1928–29, the number of subscribers was down from 11,446 to 11,210, and for the next season (before the Crash) it had dropped to 10,883. Moreover, costs had begun to get out of control. Despite the record receipts of 1929–30, the Met showed its first loss in two decades: more than $53,000 (reduced on the books to $14,700 by the sale of U.S. bonds at a profit).

For 1930–31, the number of subscribers fell to 9,599, accounting for $170,000 of the $308,000 decline in the Met's total revenues. Another $100,000 was lost when Atlanta and Richmond, their committees unable to guarantee receipts, dropped off the spring tour. And management was unable to cut expenses: despite a reduction of almost two weeks in the total season, losses rose by almost the full extent of the revenue decline. Looking into a 1931–32 season in the opera house he had tried so hard to replace, with subscriptions down to 8,800 (and not all of those paid for as opening night neared), studying a Wall Street littered with the wreckage of the continuing Depression and a Kuhn, Loeb deprived of its leader by the death of Mortimer Schiff—and perhaps embarrassed by a young Swedish singer who was suing him for breach of the promises with which he had allegedly induced her intimacy—Otto Kahn resigned as president and chairman of the Metropolitan Opera Company board in October 1931. His place was taken by his (and Bethlehem Steel's and Westinghouse's and RCA's) lawyer, Paul D. Cravath.

It can scarcely have been an accident that, within a few weeks of Cravath's accession as chairman of the Met board, his client NBC had signed a contract to broadcast 24 operas live (paying $120,000 for the privilege, on a worse than nonprofit basis for the network, which picked up all broadcasting expenses and contracted to pay to the Met any sponsor revenues in excess of $5,000 per performance). Gatti had always refused to countenance the broadcast of Met operas, partly because he feared the quality would be low (he knew what he heard over his desk loudspeaker during the rehearsals), partly because he thought the availability of free opera on radio might reduce attendance. And he had refused to permit any sub-

Overleaf: Milton Cross, announcer for the Met broadcasts, followed the action from Box 44 (*right*). Intermission commentaries were given in the early years by Geraldine Farrar, seen chatting with Cross (*inset*). The first broadcast, on Christmas Day 1931, was of *Hänsel und Gretel*, with Editha Fleischer and Queena Mario (*left, above*). Listening-in backstage: Rosa Ponselle, flanked by Thiline Falco and Irra Petina in *Cavalleria* costumes (*left, below*).

lessees of the Met to broadcast their doings from his stage because he understood the financial value of such a premiere to the Metropolitan.

Under pressure of the deficit, and after a successful demonstration of what NBC engineers could do (a *Butterfly* via telephone line to the offices of NBC president Merlin Aylesworth), Gatti yielded. On Christmas Day 1931, both the Red and the Blue Networks of NBC carried the Met's *Hänsel und Gretel*, which also went by short wave to the BBC and Australia.

Milton Cross was the announcer—a large man with a wonderfully fat speaking voice, who had wanted to be a tenor and failed at that but became for forty-odd years the voice Americans most closely identified with opera. The critic and composer Deems Taylor was the first commentator (in the first broadcasts, he made the mistake of giving a muttered simultaneous translation through the opera, provoking letters to NBC with the complaint that "some idiot keeps talking" through the broadcast). Geraldine Farrar came out of retirement to do intermission features, illustrating her comments on the tiny piano that had been made for her railroad car and that could be fitted into the anteroom of Box 44 on the Grand Tier level, where the entire NBC operation was housed.

Cravath had been on the board since 1910. He had negotiated the deal by which Oscar Hammerstein was bought out of opera, and had enforced the contract when Hammerstein sought to renege five years later (claiming violation of the antitrust laws!). Because he was Kahn's lawyer, and Kahn had retained his 84 per cent interest in the company, it was generally believed that Kahn would continue to call the shots. But in fact, the two men had often disagreed—Cravath, for example, had led the opposition to permitting Gatti to hire his wife as a singer.

A long-time subscriber to the opera (he was never a boxholder), Cravath made no pretense to musical expertise—charmingly, he undertook "music appreciation" lessons from Olga Samaroff-Stokowski when he became chairman of the Met at the age of 70. His major outside interest was in race relations: he was chairman of the board of Fisk University in Nashville (which his clergyman father had founded in the 19th century), and unpaid general counsel to the National Association for the Advancement of Colored People. Noting the presence of Meyerbeer's *L'Africaine* in the Met's repertory, Cravath once suggested that this might be a suitable occasion for the introduction of a black singer on the Met stage, mentioning Caterina Jarboro. The role of Selika, the captive princess, was being shared by Ponselle and Rethberg, and was no task for newcomers. Ziegler, in whose experience a mention by the chairman of the Met often reflected some involvement with an artist, apparently made a cautious inquiry, which provoked a rather sharp reply from

Cravath: "I have no special interest in Miss Yarborough [*sic*] beyond the fact that I am interested in colored people generally, and it occurred to me that if she happened to be a first-class artist, it might be good policy and result in some publicity if we could give her a chance to sing [in] *L'Africaine*."

Cravath moved rapidly to reorganize the company. Kahn's entity was nonprofit in principle but not in law, and thus subject to federal entertainment taxes. The most painless way to improve the Met's fiscal condition was to eliminate these tax payments, which ran about $25,000 a year, and Cravath moved promptly to organize a membership corporation "for educational purposes" that would sublease the theater from and assume all rights and contracts of the existing Metropolitan Opera Company. The Company still had assets at this time; Cravath's resolution called for these assets to be advanced upon need to the new Association, for repayment (without interest) if the Association ever had any earnings. After June 1, 1932, Kahn's Metropolitan Opera Company was a shell, and all the substance was in the new Association, which had the same officers, but was controlled by its self-perpetuating board, one-man-one-vote, rather than by Kahn as the dominant stockholder.

Cravath also had other objectives in replacing the Company by the Association. In 1919, Augustus D. Juilliard, an early boxholder, had left much of his fortune to a "Musical Foundation," the income from which was to

aid worthy students of music in securing a complete and adequate musical education . . . to arrange for and to give without profit to it musical entertainments, concerts, and recitals . . . and (to such extent as it may be lawfully entitled . . .) to aid by gift of part of such income at such times and to such extent and in such amounts as the Trustees of said Foundation may in their discretion deem proper, the Metropolitan Opera Company in the City of New York, for the purpose of assisting such organization in the production of operas, provided that suitable arrangements can be made with such company so that such gifts in no wise inure to its monetary profit.

For the ten years following Juilliard's death, the Met had in fact shown a profit, and Kahn never asked for any of the money. (It became fashionable later to criticize him for this failure; one wonders what criticisms would have been made if he had taken Juilliard money out of the mouths of poor music students for the benefit of a profitable opera company.) Fred Juilliard, A.D.'s nephew and successor to his box, was one of the trustees of the foundation and was on Cravath's board; and Cravath himself was on the board of the Juilliard School. By forming an Association to replace, in effect, the Company, Cravath was also creating the preconditions for an application to Juilliard.

Some legal rough stuff was going on here too. By late fall 1931 it was clear that the Met was going to suffer horrendous losses in the 1931–32 season. Revenues, in fact, dropped by $506,000, despite an increase of almost $50,000 in non-box-office income (derived from the radio contract, which more than made up losses elsewhere in this category). Among them, the losses for this and the two preceding seasons were perilously close to swallowing the Met's $513,000 paid-in capital (four-fifths of it Kahn's money) as well as the accumulated surplus of the previous decade, which netted out to something less than $450,000. The more opera the Met gave, the more money it lost. Clearly, the next season was going to have to be cut in duration (from 24 weeks to 16), and a number of contracts were going to have to be renegotiated. Those artists who had multi-year contracts probably could enforce them against the new Association, which had assumed the obligations of the Metropolitan Opera Company—probably, but not quite certainly, in that age of expertise in the use of the bankruptcy laws.

Cravath whipped the management to economize. "In closing up the business of the Metropolitan Opera Company for the present season," he wrote in January 1933

it is important to reserve enough funds to cover the cost of storing, insuring, and otherwise protecting the Company's personal property, such as scenery, costumes, etc., for another year—say until May 1934 . . . To provide this fund, you will have to be less generous than you would like to be in your settlements with artists who will not have had their guaranteed number of performances by the close of the active season . . . even though some of the artists feel that the settlements you are making with them are somewhat harsh.

Gatti and Ziegler did not just ask artists and executives and working staffs to take pay cuts. They *ordered* cuts, taking the position that the old contracts with the Company had been voided by the change in legal status. Several important artists were lost to the house, most notably Jeritza and Gigli (who was advised by Fiorello La Guardia and denounced by his colleagues at Gatti's insistence). In fairness all round, it should be noted that the U.S. price level dropped about 20 per cent from 1929–30 to 1931–32, so that people who accepted a pay cut of that dimension were no worse off, provided they didn't have any debts. And moving into 1932–33, the Met reduced its ticket prices by about 15 per cent, from a top of $8.25 to a top of $7. The unions refused to accept wage reductions in mid-season 1931–32, but they had little choice for 1932–33.

Even so, it became apparent in spring 1933 that the remaining surplus would not cover the gap between receipts and disbursements in the next season. A meeting of the Association directors on March 24 left open the question of whether another season would be attempted, but during the next month Cravath put together a group of directors who agreed to buy $150,000 of five-year bonds. (The money was never paid back, and the bonds became worthless.) Another $20,000 was raised by a mortgage on a warehouse owned by the Association.

Ziegler in January 1933 told Cravath that another $60–$80,000 would be required to pay all the bills for the theater's 49th year. Fortunately, his deficit estimate proved to be too high, partly because he and Gatti were able to squeeze another $50,000 off their budgeted expenses, partly because the public spent $100,000 more for tickets than box-office expert Earle Lewis had expected.

Suddenly there were major debuts again—Tito Schipa, the best lyric tenor since Bonci, as Nemorino in *L'Elisir d'amore* on the second night; a week later, the 23-year-old then-mezzo Rose Bampton (later a Sieglinde, an Aida, and a Donna Anna); then Richard Bonelli (born Richard Bunn), one of the long line of "American baritones" especially suited to the high tessitura Verdi favored for that register; the young tenor Richard Crooks, already well known to radio audiences; and the vivid Wagnerians Frida Leider and Maria Olszewska. Except for Bampton and Crooks, all these had been singing in Chicago, but Samuel Insull and most of the rest of Chicago had gone broke, closing down that opera house; and the Midwest's loss was the Metropolitan's gain. Moreover, Gatti presented in this season his only American opera that was truly successful at the box office—Louis Gruenberg's setting of Eugene O'Neill's *The Emperor Jones*, with Lawrence Tibbett stunning the audience with the vitality of his acting in the framework of Jo Mielziner's barbaric sets and costumes. Strauss's *Elektra* was also introduced to the Metropolitan in this season (Hammerstein had presented it more than twenty years before), in a staging nobody liked very much but with an orchestral performance that restored the prestige of both Bodanzky and the Met orchestra.

Nevertheless, every penny had to be scrambled for. The directors of the real estate company were running out of their assets too. They had to pay city taxes of $190,000 a year, which meant that an annual assessment per box of $4,500, the maximum permitted in the by-laws, did not even cover the tax bill. A sixteen-week season greatly reduced the income from renting boxes, and a number of the boxes were in the hands of estates, which were not prepared to pay the assessments unless rentals covered them.

It became clear that winter that a 50th anniversary season could not be planned without a guarantee fund, and that neither the boxholders nor the directors of the Association were prepared to pay the freight. Cravath notified the real estate board formally that the Association could not enter into the next year's rental unless something were done to guarantee its losses. The initiative for a public fund-raising drive probably came from Eleanor Robson Belmont, the former actress, who had left the stage in 1910 on her marriage to August Belmont (son of the patron of the old Academy of Music), but had returned to public life as a remarkably successful fund-raiser for the Red Cross during World War I.

A "Committee for Saving the Metropolitan Opera" was formed with Lucrezia Bori as chairman, Edward Johnson and Lawrence Tibbett from the roster of singers, and various directors of the real estate company and the Association. The fund drive was announced by Johnson during an intermission of the broadcast of Massenet's *Manon* (Bori was in the cast) on February 25, 1933. Two weeks later,

NBC gave the Committee a half-hour on the air to make a fund solicitation—an episode then unique in the annals of American broadcasting. Cravath made the opening statement. Opera at the Met, he said, "can no longer rely, as heretofore, upon a small group of rich men. We must now rely upon the support not only of the audience at the opera house, but also on the vast radio audience that listens to opera through the National Broadcasting Company." Bori then sang a recital of arias and songs, and made a direct appeal:

We need your assistance, and if you wish to join the hundreds of radio listeners who have already responded so generously and will communicate with me at the Metropolitan Opera House, you will receive my personal note of appreciation . . . Are you, my dear radio listeners, going to forsake this national institution, the Metropolitan Opera, in its present crisis, or are you coming to its rescue? I can almost hear you shout: To the rescue! Because I know you want the Metropolitan to carry on—just as we do.

Anthony A. Bliss, later general manager of the Met, remembered that his father Cornelius, who represented the boxholders on the Committee, "virtually lived at the opera house" during the months of the fund drive—as did Bori (who was also working there) and Mrs. Belmont. Bori's speeches were written by Ziegler. She not only acknowledged all contributions with a note on the stationery of the Berkshire Hotel, where she lived; she also sent notes of thanks to all who renewed season subscriptions. A little note from Bori—opera's great lady but not a grande dame, chic and charming and Latin—was a souvenir many people would like.

"I write letters to everybody," Bori told the *New York Times* the next fall. ". . . I make speeches before the curtain at the Opera, over the radio, and at other places like the Colony Club, the Dutch Treat, and the Coffee House. I am so interested I cannot eat. I cannot sleep. But I like it . . . Mrs. Belmont speaks and I weep. Miss Farrar speaks so beautifully, also, so that I am ashamed of the way I speak. But I do not stop . . . It is my bread and butter. But it is more than that."

In two months, the necessary $300,000 was raised—$100,000 of it from the radio audience, $50,000 from the Juilliard Foundation (an inaccurate newspaper story that the Foundation was putting up $150,000 almost sank the drive, to Cravath's horror); about $45,000 from two benefit performances, a ball at the opera house (for which Mrs. Belmont dressed as the Empress Eugénie, and Walter Damrosch as Liszt), and a surprise party (a spoof on stage: in the next year's edition, the diminutive Pons and the giant Melchior did an Apache dance, Pons as the macho Apache, Melchior as her moll). The rest came from individuals. A summary sheet in the Ziegler files indicates that $39,000 came from the boxholders and the directors of the Association—$10,000 from the Chicagoan Louis Eckstein, $5,000 each from Kahn, Cornelius Bliss, and Myron C. Taylor; $1,000 from J. P. Morgan, Jr. In May, Mrs. Belmont became the first woman member of the Metropolitan Opera Association board.

☆ ☆ ☆

The Emperor Jones, alias Lawrence Tibbett, feeling his oats on Jo Mielziner's set.

So the 50th anniversary season of the Metropolitan Opera, at fourteen weeks the shortest since the Grau days, opened officially the night after Christmas 1933. (There had been a matinee *Hänsel und Gretel* on Christmas Day, but that was "pre-season," off the subscription.) It was the first season ever underwritten by gifts from the public, and the first to be launched with an American opera—Deems Taylor's dreamy *Peter Ibbetson*, to an archaic story by Daphne du Maurier, which had starring roles for the three artist members of the Save the Met Committee—Bori, Johnson, and Tibbett. Serafin conducted.

This was the first year that Met broadcasts would be sponsored, by the American Tobacco Company. The Met took a large newspaper ad (doubtless paid for by the cigarette company) "to announce that in collaboration with the proprietor LUCKY STRIKE Cigarettes it has been enabled to utilize the complete facilities of both the Red and the Blue Networks of the National Broadcasting Company, to the end that on Saturday, December 30th, and every Saturday thereafter, from two o'clock Eastern Standard Time, and until such time as each opera is finished the complete Opera presented at the Metropolitan Opera House will be broadcast . . ." The ad, signed by Giulio Gatti-Casazza, also ran in more idiomatic Italian in the Italo-American press; it is hard not to believe that Gatti wrote it, in Italian, himself.

The innovation of sponsorship, incidentally, was not applauded by everyone. Olin Downes in the *New York Times* called the commercial arrangements "perfectly logical but rather disappointing," and noted approvingly that "thus far the Philharmonic-Symphony Orchestra has kept itself independent of any commercial association." Lucky Strike lasted only a year; the next sponsor was Listerine.

The audience on opening night, Downes wrote in his review of the performance, "was in the sense of social distinction and spectacle the most brilliant that has witnessed a Metropolitan opening in ten years. There was, moreover, a return of the atmosphere of festivity which has been somewhat dimmed of late at the Metropolitan." This was also the first season in more than ten years when liquor could be openly sold and served at the Met's bars. The house got into some trouble here, for the state law that replaced federal Prohibition permitted the service of alcoholic drinks only to people who were sitting down, and the newspaper pictures of opening night clearly showed people drinking champagne in a standing position. Commissioner Edward B. Mulrooney of the State Alcoholic Beverage Control Board sent a stern letter, and thereafter the seekers after intermission refreshment had to stumble over chairs and tables.

The first significant debut of the season came that Thursday in a matinee *Rigoletto* for the benefit of Wilfrid Grenfell's Mission to the poor fishermen of northern Newfoundland and Labrador, when the radio star Nino Martini sang the Duke in a voice that was less impressive without microphones than it had been with them. (Samuel Chotzinoff wrote in the *Telegraph* that Martini's problems demonstrated the

Lucrezia Bori, chairman of the Committee for Saving the Metropolitan Opera, broadcasting an appeal for donations in 1933.

desirability of an amplification system in the old theater.) Martini drew audiences—including a number of star-struck young ladies who would mob the stage door seeking autographs—and he really cared about singing at the Met: while Lauri-Volpi had received a fee of $1,500 per performance of the Duke the year before, Martini sang for $250. Having learned the trick of projection at the Met, he remained with the company for twelve seasons.

On January 11 a more significant artist came to the Met for the first time: Lotte Lehmann, who sang Sieglinde to Melchior's Siegmund and Emanuel List's Hunding. She sang only three times at the Met this year, in three different roles (Elisabeth in *Tannhäuser* and Eva in *Meistersinger* were the others). Indeed, though everyone's recollections of the Met in the 1930s and 1940s include Lehmann, she sang rarely, preferring the concert hall and the lieder repertory. Not until 1934–35 did a Met audience have the chance to cherish her first Marschallin, the role with which she was most frequently and intimately and triumphantly associated in New York, where people still remember that special intensity she brought to the aging 32-year-old's encounter with the hand mirror. And she never sang at the Met her own favorite role, Beethoven's Leonore (the occasion of her greatest triumph, in Vienna in 1926, when Henderson in the *Sun* chastised Gatti for failure to engage her), because by the time *Fidelio* re-entered the repertory Flagstad was at hand, and Lehmann refused to be second cast to anyone.

Perhaps because the process of public fund-raising had emancipated the new Association from Morgan and the pruderies of the boxholders—perhaps because all the parties were now driven by the need to sell tickets—the Met returned after 26 years to the presentation of *Salome*. The wicked princess was sung by Göta Ljungberg, who attempted the dance herself but resolutely and wisely failed to unveil. Olive Fremstad came to the performance as Gatti's guest to give good wishes to Ljungberg (who needed more than good wishes) and to the theater. All *Salome* performances sold out. Bodanzky, who had triumphed with the Strauss orchestra in *Elektra*, did so again in *Salome*, but the particular star of the evening was Donald Oenslager, a Broadway designer who gave the Met a new kind of setting for this kind of opera. It was, Downes explained, "a single set to be used throughout the opera. It is a 'built' set—that is, architectural and three-dimensional . . . Gone are the quaint confusions of Oriental decorations which characterized [*Salome*'s] one performance at the Met in 1907. The new setting . . . is as free from gewgaws and extraneous bedizening as the Empire State Building." Twenty-one years later, the Oenslager sets and costumes were still in use.

This was the only season ever when three American operas were on the Met boards—*Ibbetson*, *The Emperor Jones*, and Howard Hanson's *Merry Mount*, which Kahn had commissioned from the eminent pedagogue and Gatti had accepted for production before a note was written. Serafin conducted all three, and Tibbett

---

Lily Pons as Lakmé in Delibes' opera, revived for her in 1932 with new sets by Joseph Urban. Pons made the 1930s "a glamour time at the Met."

starred in all of them, making almost as much of a splash as Wrestling Bradford in Hawthorne's Puritan fable as he had as the Caribbean tyrant. The General Society of Mayflower Descendants helped publicize *Merry Mount* by attacking it as a libel on the pilgrims.

The two important American operas that had their premieres this season, however, were not at the Met. One was George Gershwin's *Porgy and Bess*, performed on commercial rather than operatic Broadway. The other was Virgil Thomson's and Gertrude Stein's *Four Saints in Three Acts*, with its all-black cast and John Houseman's original production, all flammable cellophane until a horrified fire department found out. *Four Saints*, which had its premiere in Hartford, would come into the annals of the Met only in 1972–73, when a version for reduced orchestra was done at Lincoln Center's tiny Forum theater by the experimental "Mini-Met."

Vocally, this was a distinguished season. *Lakmé* and *Linda di Chamounix* were staged for the sparkling Pons, who contributed to her own publicity by donating her pet jaguar to the Bronx Zoo, where the curator immediately annoyed the diva by telling the press it was really an ocelot. The *Mignon* that opened the broadcast season had as strong a cast as the Met had ever offered: Bori, Schipa, Pons, and Swarthout. Emanuel List immensely strengthened the bass line of the Wagner and Strauss repertory, and Schorr was still at his best. Toward the end of the year the fine American baritone John Charles Thomas made his first Met appearance as Germont in a broadcast *Traviata* that also presented Bori and Schipa. Pinza was perfecting his Don Giovanni, with Ponselle as his Donna Anna. Lotte Lehmann, Maria Müller, Frida Leider, and Elisabeth Rethberg were as strong a group of German sopranos as the world could then offer, with Maria Olszewska and Karin Branzell as their mezzo companions, and Melchior as their almost invariable tenor.

Lawrence Gilman in the *Herald Tribune* chided those who sighed for the Golden Age: "Those of us who can say, I heard De Reszke's Tristan and Lilli's Brünnhilde and Maurel's Don Giovanni and Fremstad's Isolde and Van Rooy's Kurwenal and Mary's Mélisande and Dufranne's Golaud and Renaud's Scarpia and Gilibert's Father in *Louise* can also say—as their daughters and sons will say in the future—I heard Lotte Lehmann's Marschallin and Olszewska's Fricka, and Bohnen's Gurnemanz, and Schorr's Wanderer, and Bori's Violetta, and Tibbett's Simon Boccanegra."

But it was not at all a happy time for Gatti. "The last three years in New York," he wrote in fall 1935 to Bruno Zirato, who shared the management of the New York Philharmonic with Arthur Judson and had been Caruso's secretary, "have been a Calvary such as no one can imagine . . ." It was one thing to deal with an Otto Kahn, who could be overbearing and had retained a rather brusque manner from the days when he did his military service as the only Jew in a regiment of Hussars; but Kahn was a banker and a continental, a man of large views—and, besides, a great

Singers of the Depression years: Frederick Jagel as Pollione in *Norma* (*above left*), John Charles Thomas as Germont *père* in *Traviata* (*above right*), Rose Bampton as Amneris in *Aida* (*below right*), Richard Crooks as Faust (*below left*), and Gladys Swarthout as Stéphano in Gounod's *Roméo* (*center*). All were Americans engaged by Gatti.

contributor of funds when needed. It was something else to deal with the very large Cravath, who was taller and fatter than Gatti and had a deeper voice and a commanding manner and the habits of a lawyer—picky, picky, picky, always after detail—and not a major source of subsidy although very rich.

When Kahn wanted Gatti to hire a singer, he dropped a mention that he had heard someone interesting. Cravath, by contrast, wrote (in this case to Ziegler) that "I am tired of being asked why Dusolina Giannini, considered by many the foremost American soprano, has never had an opportunity of singing at the Metropolitan . . . Unless there is some objection that I do not see, I think it would be wise to give her an opportunity of singing at the Metropolitan a couple of times this winter in two of her best roles, one of which, I presume, is Aida." (Giannini did indeed make her debut as Aida, but only the year after Gatti's departure.) Returning from Salzburg in 1933, Cravath let the *Times* know that he had taken "advantage of the festival to arrange for continental stars to appear at the Metropolitan this winter . . ."

Negotiating with artists who had an exaggerated sense of their own worth—or could get more money from Hammerstein or, later, from Mary Garden in Chicago—was hard enough; now Gatti (who had taken a 35 per cent pay cut himself, but was still richly rewarded at $43,000) had to haggle a Ponselle down from $1,900 a performance in 1932–33 to $1,500 in '33–34; and a Martinelli from $1,500 to $1,000. Even nastier work might be necessary, to chisel a Karin Branzell down from $650 to $625, or a Schorr from $562.50 to $535, a Melchior from $1,080 to $1,000. Sometimes cruelty was involved, as when a young Rose Bampton was cut from $120 to $70 a week, and for fewer weeks to boot. And not everyone *could* be cut, which Cravath did not always understand. Pinza, for example, who had signed for 1932–33 at $17,000 for the season, had to be paid $17,500 the next year, though the season was shorter; Maria Müller had to be raised from $750 to $800 per performance; Pons, who had become an immense box-office draw, from $550 to $700.

From 1928–29 to 1933–34, Gatti had had to cut the cost of his female soloists from $407,000 to $147,000; his male soloists, from $608,000 to $258,000; his chorus from $232,000 to $132,000; his orchestra, from $405,000 to $225,000; his ballet, from $101,000 to $49,000. About half the cuts were attributable to the shortened season; the rest Gatti had imposed. Only the conductors—Serafin and Bodanzky—were able to improve their fees on a per performance basis.

And it didn't help: the 50th anniversary season, for all its considerable artistic success, lost $317,000. ("Through my experience of New York," Gatti wrote bitterly to Zirato three years later, "it is not the quality of the spectacle and of the singers that counts, but the condition of the Stock Exchange. If the stocks go up, then everything is all right; if they go down, good night!") Cravath had said in early 1934 that there would be no need for another public fund-raising drive—which would be hard to carry off, anyway, because the Philharmonic (of which Cravath was also a trustee) was launching its own $500,000 campaign. More money would have to be raised this time from within the family, and the leadership of what *Time* Magazine unkindly called "tin-cup drives" passed to Cornelius Bliss of the boxholders' board, whose father's textile mills had left him rich enough to devote all his time to philanthropy and who joined Cravath's board as well. Along with Bliss came John Erskine of the Juilliard School, littérateur (specialist in the works of Lafcadio Hearn), educator, and pianist.

Erskine really did not like Gatti-Casazza. He had written the libretti for two operas the Met had not performed, and his school had turned out a number of singers the Met had not engaged. He complained about "the neglect of American singers and [this was astonishingly unfair] American composers." Gatti, he added, "had evolved a star system which eliminated the training of inexperienced talent, and even the artistic responsibility of making new productions." The house had been biased toward "Italian artists and Italian operas." The price of Juilliard support, it seemed—and Juilliard support was indispensable if there was to be an adequate guarantee fund—would be Metropolitan employment of a number of young singers: "artist pupils," as a joint announcement of the Met and Juilliard would call them.

In March 1934, Otto Kahn died of a heart attack suffered at a luncheon meeting in his office. Serafin informed Gatti that he was accepting an offer to become music director at the Rome Opera. Frida Leider, the world's leading Wagnerian soprano, announced after the season ended that she would not return to the Met. Gatti turned 65. Enough was enough: as the 50th anniversary season closed, Gatti told Cravath that he would not accept another term as general manager after his contract expired in June 1935.

Nothing in the file supports the universal belief that Gatti was pushed out. Cravath, in fact, refused to show Gatti's letter of resignation to his board, and asked him to take the summer and think it over. After all, Gatti—and of living men Gatti alone—had demonstrated that a grand opera house could be run profitably. When Gatti came under attack in 1933, Cravath told a meeting of the executive committee "that in all his dealings with a man of affairs he had never encountered anyone more logical in his decisions than Mr. Gatti-Casazza; that Mr. Gatti-Casazza never made an impulsive move and that his every decision was based upon a careful survey of the matter at hand." Cravath may have considered Gatti old-fashioned, but Cravath considered opera itself old-fashioned: "the last of our Victorian expressions," he once said. Quaintance Eaton and John Briggs have written that the Association had chosen Herbert Witherspoon as Gatti's successor, and Edward Johnson as his assistant, even before Gatti sent his final letter of resignation on November 1, 1934, and that the new team was already at work planning the next season—but this could not possibly have happened without somebody knowing it, and rumors were rife in

Overleaf: Comings and goings. Lawrence Tibbett congratulates Antonio Scotti backstage on January 20, 1933, following his last Met appearance, in *L'Oracolo* (*left*); oldtimer Ernestine Schumann-Heink, costumed as Erda, greets newcomer Marion Talley in February 1926 (*inset*). Floral tributes—to Grace Moore (*right, above*) at her debut in *Bohème*, February 1928; and to Claudia Muzio (*below*) backstage in January 1934, five months before her untimely death.

town about the leaders in the race for the general manager's job (*Time* printed a list of names with the odds on each) until the announcement in March 1935. Still, there was no doubt that the time had now come for Gatti to leave, and for an American to take over.

The 50th anniversary season had begun with a spate of rumors that the Met was about to leave 39th Street and Broadway for the new, smaller theater being built at the corner of 48th Street and Sixth Avenue as part of Rockefeller Center. This had been part of Downes's worry about commercializing the broadcasts: "Will it pave the way toward Radio City? It is to be hoped that if Radio City so desires it may go its own operatic way in peace, and sandwich in acts of *Faust* and *Lohengrin* with vaudeville or motion pictures, but that the Metropolitan will continue to maintain its prestige as a great operatic institution, which stands on its own feet and sustains its own traditions."

In fact, the notion of placing a new Metropolitan Opera House in what became Rockefeller Center, which the real estate company had been toying with since the veto of Kahn's 57th Street property, was enjoying its last gasps through the 1933–34 season. The first proposal, involving the site that eventually held the RCA building, had come to the board in June 1928. The Rockefellers were offering $6 million for the land, but would make it available to the Met for $3.5 million, on the assumption that a public square (where the skating rink now stands) would take much of the site; the entire project would have the name Metropolitan Square. Wallace Harrison, the eventual architect of the Lincoln Center opera house, was a young assistant at another firm in those days. He kept to the end of his life his initial drawings for an opera house on that site, featuring the sweeping arches that (somewhat constricted) became a feature of the façade when the Lincoln Center project matured a generation later.

By October 1929, the cost of an opera house in Rockefeller Center had risen to $13.3 million, and the board backed off. Then, in 1931, Rockefeller returned with a new proposal, reflecting in part the extreme difficulty he was having in renting the properties of the new Center. This was for a dual-purpose hall that would include the Philharmonic—and that could also be used in the off-season "for movies or other special entertainments." The rent suggested by Rockefeller's real estate agents was $600,000 a year. "It seems a most unusual opportunity from our point of view," Myron C. Taylor, chairman of the buildings committee, reported to the board, "that a new Opera House can be furnished by an individual, leaving our present property in the hands of the stockholders to sell . . . The alternative to going into Radio City seems to be that we should embark upon a building project involving enormous financing and resulting in a duplication of Opera facilities. Competitive Opera would probably be ruinous to both."

The next year Rockefeller made a firm offer, for the site later occupied by the parking garage, and plans were filed with the city showing an opera house on that land. The architect had assured all concerned that a dual-purpose auditorium was practical. What Rockefeller needed to make the project viable was a lease that would cover:

a) a pro rata share of Columbia University's ground rent;
b) 6 per cent on the cost of construction, then estimated at $5–$6 million;
c) the taxes applicable on this part of the property;
d) a 21-year amortization of the construction cost.

The total annual rent would be about $1 million a year, but Rockefeller was prepared to pick up some of it, leaving the Met with an annual charge of $875,000. If the Philharmonic put up $100,000 a year, and the 35 boxholders paid $10,000 each, maybe, just maybe . . .

But by now the board was totally uninterested in increasing its expenses. Chairman Cutting pointed out that the length of the season was about to be reduced. Taylor "felt that if the Opera Company and the Opera Association, even with the assistance they are receiving, have no present outlook for profit, and the Company has no assets to contribute, it would be very bad business on our part to undertake a partnership which would perhaps consume all our assets to carry out."

In fall 1933, as the anniversary season was about to begin, Rockefeller came back with the suggestion that the new Center Theater could be used at least on a temporary basis until things turned up and a real opera house could be built on the site of the garage. In the stories on the opening of the season, this plan was taken as a probability, but in fact it was always a non-starter, because the theater was hopeless backstage (in the front of the house, too: some years later, Herman Krawitz of the Met staff used as one of his arguments that he must be given supervisory power over the architects of the new house at Lincoln Center the fact that the same people had designed the Center Theater and had forgotten to build a box office).

In spring 1934, the real estate company learned that the decision *not* to build a new house also involved extraordinary costs. The fire department did an inspection of the Met, and returned with news of serious violations in the wiring. Hunter College, which had scheduled a benefit evening at the Opera House, canceled on the grounds that the facilities were unsafe, and the city suggested gently that if nothing were done, the license to operate the property as a theater might have to be revoked. David Sarnoff, chairman of RCA, who had joined the board of the Opera Association, had sent his own engineers to double-check the city's report of violations—and they had heartily agreed with the city (NBC had been supplying its own portable power source for the broadcast equipment, because the Met's electric

supply was inadequate). "No doubt," the minutes of the real estate board concluded gloomily, "conditions are equally bad in the Apartment building."

The opera company lease provided that expenses associated with "performance of violation recommendations made by City Departments" were to be shared 50-50 by the producing company and the real estate company, but "Mr. Bliss said it was hopeless to expect the Opera Company to share in the expense, as they had no surplus funds available . . . Mr. Brewster suggested that if this work were going to run between $100,000 and $200,000, as seems probable, it will be necessary to borrow, very likely on mortgage; if so, would it not be better to raise, say, $500,000, and proceed with additional improvements, particularly backstage, where a considerable amount of modernizing would be advantageous." Having cleared the property of debt in 1919, the real estate company had an asset to pledge—and it did. In the event, $600,000 was borrowed and various improvements were made backstage—most significantly, lighting bridges and switchboards, a new stage and new elevators, and improved sanitary facilities associated with the dressing rooms. A real broadcasting control room and studio were installed, and the auditorium was cleaned and painted. Gatti's last season began in clean surroundings—one last time with *Aida*, and a cast of Rethberg, Olszewska, Martinelli, Tibbett, and Pinza, Ettore Panizza, an Argentine from La Scala, making a surprisingly satisfactory substitute for the departed Serafin.

But more important innovations were now in the works. Eleanor Belmont had launched a Women's Metropolitan Opera Club whose members would have the use of the Grand Tier boxes and the Metropolitan Opera Club on Saturday nights (Saturday night had been chosen, the brochure explained, "for while the performances are identical with those of other nights it is possible to wear informal dress"). The Club "fills a need for the women who enjoy and love opera but who do not feel they can afford the regular subscription and who heretofore have not cared to attend alone." Two classes of membership were offered, at $30 for twelve performances or at $15 for six; it was, the Committee suggested, "a great opportunity to become closely associated with the institution which has contributed steadily and inspiringly to the artistic life of our city for over 50 years."

Mrs. Belmont had come onto the Metropolitan Opera Association board with a mission, which she described in an interview with the New York *American*: "What is of primary importance is that the people of New York should look upon the opera as theirs, that the people should look upon it as an integral essential part of the life of the city." The next year she would launch the Metropolitan Opera Guild with herself as Chairman. In a real if not entirely plausible way—for the Metropolitan Opera Guild was itself an expression of Society—what Mrs. Belmont liked to call "the democratization of opera" had begun.

Fun for funds: a surprise party on stage to raise money for the beleaguered Met. Beatrice Lillie and Paul Althouse spoof a Carmen-Siegfried duet (*above left*) while Lily Pons and Lauritz Melchior do a circus act (*above right*). The Gay '90s cyclists (*below*) are Virgilio Lazzari, Gladys Swarthout, Rosa Ponselle, and Frederick Jagel.

SIX

KIRSTEN FLAGSTAD AND THE AMERICAN YEARS

A date can be given for the event that saved the Metropolitan Opera: January 15, 1935. On that afternoon, Kirsten Flagstad made her first appearance on the Metropolitan Opera stage, dressed in costume as the *Götterdämmerung* Brünnhilde, surrounded by colleagues in street clothes. She had never sung the role before, and was not in fact scheduled to sing it until late February: the rehearsal was for a performance that would be sung by Gertrude Kappel. But nobody at the Met had ever seen Flagstad in costume or on stage. Bodanzky wanted to get a firmer grip on the singer he and Gatti had hired to take over what had been Frida Leider's roles for the second half of the 1934–35 season. At the end of the first act duet with Siegfried, Bodanzky—the hard man, bored with opera and its discontents—put down his baton and asked his assistant Karl Riedel to conduct a reprise. A messenger was sent to Gatti, but Bodanzky himself ran to Ziegler's door: "My God, Ned!" he called. "My God, come hear this woman sing!" Then he returned to the podium and with Gatti and Ziegler in the audience—and others of the house who had heard the rumors sweeping the corridors—he took her and Paul Althouse through the duet one more time. Flagstad always sang out in rehearsals, and "at that time," she later wrote, "I took the high C's regularly. The orchestra stood up and cheered me."

Flagstad had never been a major artist in Europe. She had made much of her early career in musical comedy (an odd thought, for so grave and innocent an artist), and nearly all of it in Norwegian or Swedish. Kahn had heard her sing Tosca in Norwegian on a business trip in 1929, and had come back to New York raving about her; but Gatti had been unable to find anybody south of the Skaggerak who had ever heard of her at all, and she didn't answer letters from the Met's European agent, Eric Simon. In 1932, Oscar Thompson, editor of *Musical America*, had heard her Isolde in Oslo and had written an enthusiastic review.

Simon went to Bayreuth at the close of the 1934 festival at which Flagstad had made a little-remarked entry into the operatic big time, singing a Sieglinde and a Gutrune, and asked her to come to St. Moritz to audition for Gatti and Bodanzky in an overstuffed hotel room with heavy hangings and draperies. From her

Kirsten Flagstad, photographed by Edward Steichen in 1935, the year of her Met debut.

description, it must have been quite an occasion, for there was a competitor—Elisabeth Delius, a far more experienced artist—and the judges ran both of them through a grueling program. After accepting Flagstad, Bodanzky said, "Don't you go and get fat now. Learn those roles. Find yourself a good coach . . ." On further consideration, he suggested a coach: George Szell, then conducting in Prague. Flagstad went for ten days to Prague, where Szell "was very severe with me. Not a single complimentary word until the very last day. Then he remarked, 'I'm going to write to Mr. Bodanzky and say that he doesn't have to worry about your not knowing the roles in time'."

At the age of 39, in other words, Flagstad was being treated as a tyro—which, in a sense, she was: she had never sung any of the Brünnhildes on any stage, or Isolde in a large house. As she worked on the heavier repertory that fall, mysteriously the voice grew. What astonished Flagstad herself was that her back muscles seemed to swell; though she was not gaining weight as Bodanzky had feared, she was splitting her dresses at the seams. Certainly nothing in her previous career had given anyone the impression that she would produce in the cavernous Metropolitan so dark and rich and large and seamless and musical a sound, totally without strain at top or bottom.

Bodanzky had told Flagstad that they would not want her Sieglinde, but it was in that role that she made her debut on February 2, 1935 (without a rehearsal), in a broadcast matinee. The voice proved not only a staggering experience in the house but also an astonishment through microphones and loudspeakers. The following Thursday, to a packed house (there was rarely thereafter an empty seat at the Met when Flagstad appeared), she sang her first Isolde, with Melchior, Olszewska, Schorr, and Ludwig Hofmann. Gilman in the *Herald Tribune* compared her to Olive Fremstad; Henderson in the *Sun*, to Lillian Nordica; and Downes in the *Times* simply exulted. She was lithe and youthful and in her own way beautiful, dramatically convincing as a woman in all three acts, and the source of sounds such as the house had rarely if ever heard before. Ten days later she sang the *Walküre* Brünnhilde for the first time in her life, again without a rehearsal. At the end of the season, on eleven days' notice (during a period when she was already traveling on recital engagements), she sang Kundry in *Parsifal*, a role she had never so much as read through before.

Appearance and a natural shyness (she feared celebrity too much to admit she enjoyed it) combined to give Flagstad a reputation as a goody two-shoes, but she was in fact a complex and often demanding personality. She had a confusing emotional triangle with her second husband, a much older man, and her teen-age daughter from her first marriage. She was remarkably dependent on and protective of her accompanist Edwin McArthur. She drank like a Norwegian (though not on the day of a performance), and she refused to play the game of social graces after performances or during intermissions, even when the request came from the

Edward Ziegler, Earle R. Lewis, and Edward Johnson (*above*). Johnson succeeded to the general manager's post on the sudden death in May 1935 of Herbert Witherspoon (*inset, right*), who had originally been chosen to follow Gatti-Casazza. Later that year the Metropolitan Opera Guild was founded at the behest of Eleanor Robson Belmont (*inset, left*), the first woman elected to the Met's board.

Norwegian embassy. And she quickly became a true prima donna, fighting with Melchior over solo curtain calls and relative prominence in the press, and demanding that McArthur be given conducting assignments when she sang.

The campaign on behalf of McArthur eventually became rather rough. The afternoon of the day Artur Bodanzky died, in 1939, Flagstad called NBC Artists (her managers) from Chicago, to tell them to propose McArthur to the Met as a substitute, and sent a telegram to Gatti's successor as general manager, Edward Johnson:

AM DISTRESSED WITH SAD NEWS OF BODANZKY'S PASSING. THE METROPOLITAN WILL NOT SEEM THE SAME WITHOUT HIM BUT LIFE GOES ON AND WE MUST ALL KEEP UP WITH THE MUSICAL TRADITION SO FINELY ESTABLISHED BY HIM. I KNOW THAT MELCHIOR WILL JOIN ME IN REQUESTING THAT YOU GIVE EDWIN MCARTHUR THE OPPORTUNITY TO CONDUCT OUR TRISTAN PERFORMANCES WHICH HE DID SO BRILLIANTLY IN CALIFORNIA AND IN WHICH OPERA WE BOTH FEEL SO PERFECTLY AT EASE WITH HIM IN THE PIT. I KNOW THAT OUR DEAR DEPARTED FRIEND HIMSELF WOULD HAVE APPROVED SUCH A CHOICE IF HE COULD HAVE HEARD HIM AND I WOULD FEEL PRIVILEGED TO HAVE BEEN INSTRUMENTAL IN THUS ESTABLISHING A GIFTED YOUNG AMERICAN MUSICIAN.

"I did not reply at once to this telegram," reads a memo prepared by Ziegler for Johnson to send to his board, "and impatient because a reply was not immediately forthcoming, she telegraphed from Chicago to Montreal where Melchior was singing a concert, and asked him if he would not come in to see me and lay the case of McArthur before me. She also asked him to get an immediate answer . . ."

Johnson stalled by telling Flagstad that the matter was one for the Association's Executive Committee, which wasn't going to meet for a while. Flagstad replied, "I have done the Metropolitan so many favors and this is the first time that I have ever asked a favor of the Metropolitan and if you wanted to you could of course grant it." Johnson's memo to the board ended philosophically with the comment that: "Her case is not unique in our experience as several years ago when we were doing the Russian opera *Le Coq d'or* in which Lily Pons was singing, she asked if we could not engage her husband, Mr. Kostelenetz [*sic*], who had coached her in this opera and who had conducted the opera in Russia several times. We explained that it would be impossible to do that as it would be a fling at our own conductors and that it would then open the door to other artists who wanted us to employ their husbands or relatives."

On the McArthur matter, however, Flagstad had the last laugh. Johnson had neglected to tie her down contractually for the Holy Week Wagner performances and the tour in spring of 1940, and on February 5 of that year she notified Johnson that she would not be available to the Met for those dates. "I am at a loss to understand your decision," Johnson wailed in a letter . . . and then, undermining what bargaining position he might have hoped to achieve, he had to mention that "you were today to give me a decision, so far as the Metropolitan is concerned, about your next season's plans. The Executive Committee has asked me to request such a decision from you . . ." The upshot was that McArthur conducted a *Tristan* in Boston, on tour, and the next season he was on the conductor's roster and on the podium for *Tristan* on February 17. When it was done, however, it was done right, for the performance was Flagstad's 100th Isolde and marked also the fifteenth anniversary of Melchior's debut at the Met.

Having signed originally for $550 a week, Flagstad had accepted $750 per performance in her second season, and thereafter she lived with the Met's announced ceiling price of $1,000 per performance (her contract did provide that if anyone else were paid more, she would receive at least as much). She was, therefore, whether or not Ziegler and Johnson wished to recognize it, doing the Met some favors. But the coin had another side, for in effect she was requiring the Met to build its schedule for her appearances around the engagements that NBC Artists arranged for her with symphony orchestras and on its nationwide network of Civic Concerts recital series.

Still, the fact is that every year she sang more performances than her contract guaranteed, and every time she stepped on stage she gave the best she had. Her audiences were profoundly grateful. "Give my love to Kirsten Flagstad," Fiorello La Guardia, a strong Wagnerian (he was the son of a bandmaster), wrote to Ziegler in 1938, "and again express to her my great admiration. I suppose the period of my administration will be known in years to come as the time that Flagstad sang in New York." Flagstad, like Caruso, was also immensely popular with and generous to the stagehands and the little people of the opera. In December 1938, she gave a party to celebrate the 25th anniversary of her debut as a singer, with champagne and the best cigars for all, and personally carried trays out to serve the watchmen, the only employees of the Met who were not packed into Sherry's restaurant for the occasion.

The presence of Flagstad—supplemented by Lotte Lehmann, presently by the majestic, brilliant Australian Marjorie Lawrence—made the Metropolitan a Wagner house again. In 1938–39 the regular season saw 41 performances of Wagner in a total New York subscription season of 124 presentations, the highest proportion since 1890–91; then the company, as its special presentation to the New York World's Fair, gave a week of nothing but Wagner in May. It was the popularity of the Wagnerian repertory that kept the box-office receipts rising from their low of $1.09 million in 1934–35 to $1.78 million in 1938–39, and this rising tide lifted all the Met's boats.

Overleaf: A new Golden Age of Wagner. Flagstad, Melchior, Branzell (*left*) posing on stage after Act I of *Tristan*, with (*inset*) conductor Artur Bodanzky. Helen Traubel as the *Walküre* Brünnhilde (*right*), with Marjorie Lawrence as the *Siegfried* Brünnhilde (*inset, left*), and Astrid Varnay as Elsa (*inset, right*).

Herbert Witherspoon had been angling for the job of general manager of the Metropolitan at least since early 1933, when his friend Percy Rector Stephen, president of the New York Singing Teachers Association (and chairman of the Committee on the Defense of Teachers and Other Professional People Against the Interpretation of the New York City Zoning Law), entered into a correspondence with Paul Cravath about the need to put the administration of the opera house into American hands. Witherspoon had sung bass roles at the Met for Gatti from 1908 to 1916, achieving his greatest prominence, perhaps, in his first season, when he called out "Salva me, fons pietatis" in Toscanini's performance of the Verdi Requiem. Later he rose in the German repertory to King Henry in *Lohengrin* and King Marke (again for Toscanini) in *Tristan*. But there were too many basses better than Witherspoon in New York, and after 1916 he went off to Chicago, where Mary Garden gave him administrative functions as well as roles. In 1931–32 he was manager of the Chicago Civic Opera, where he slashed the budget savagely, but not savagely enough to keep the institution afloat. The next year he was at the Cincinnati Conservatory of Music, running an opera performance workshop, and it was from Cincinnati that he set his friend Stephen to sounding out his prospects in New York.

When he began this effort, Witherspoon did not know that Gatti's contract had been extended to 1935, and he seems to have been nonplussed when a letter to his friend Ziegler asking in general about things at the Met produced a reply inquiring after any interesting inexpensive young singers in Cincinnati. Witherspoon did not wish to appear to be seeking Gatti's job—he considered himself on good terms with Gatti—but he knew he was not in competition with Ziegler, who had said he did not wish to become general manager when the position opened. The word in Cincinnati and Chicago was that Gatti was on his way out, and that Edward Johnson was the favorite to succeed him; and Witherspoon considered Johnson, who had no administrative experience at all, to be totally unqualified. The involvement of Juilliard in the Metropolitan's future had been in the newspapers as part of the story of the 1933 fund-raising drive, and Witherspoon wrote a long letter to John Erskine, full of suggestions of what should be done with the Met, not mentioning that he might like to carry them out himself.

Cravath replied to Stephen that it was indeed a good idea to have an American at the helm of the Met, but the time was not yet. Erskine was more interested, and brought Witherspoon east to teach singers and prepare operatic performances at Juilliard. No doubt they discussed the affairs of the Metropolitan, which Erskine was reluctantly supporting, having added a $40,000 gift in spring 1934 to the Foundation's $50,000 contribution to the Save the Met Campaign in 1933. According to Erskine's unreliable memoirs, he was invited to the Century Club around Christmas 1934 by Allen Wardwell, a Wall Street lawyer who was chairman of the Juilliard School Board and a member of the real estate company board, and was told that Cravath's board had thrown in the towel. Unable to pick a replacement for Gatti because there was no assurance the funds could be raised for another season, Cravath was declining to renew the lease on the theater for the next season. Erskine quotes Wardwell as saying, "They want to leave their baby on the Juilliard doorstep," and says that he went home that night and typed out the plan that was eventually adopted for the reorganization of the Met.

Juilliard's demands in return for a $150,000 three-year guarantee included a promise that subscription sales would be raised by 10 per cent, that the company produce a budget that promised operation without a deficit, and that a "supplementary season" of opera in English be given in the spring at popular prices, offering young Americans a chance to appear on the Met stage. It seems quite certain that an unspoken part of the deal was the choice of Witherspoon as Gatti's successor. Johnson, who had been talking of starting a touring company of young Americans to give opera in the hinterlands, would be hired as Witherspoon's assistant with special responsibility for the spring season. To police all of this, Erskine, his dean Ernest Hutcheson, and Juilliard board members Felix Warburg and John M. Perry would be added to the Metropolitan Opera Association board; and there would be an Administration Committee of Erskine, Cornelius Bliss (from the boxholders' board), Lucrezia Bori, and Wardwell to supervise the operations of the Association.

Witherspoon tore into the problem, and began planning extensive changes. His tentative budget, assuming 85 per cent attendance for a fourteen-week season, showed $10,000 per performance as the maximum the Met could spend and come out ahead. The Met's actual expenditures were running almost $12,000 per performance. Witherspoon's first cut at savings involved the sacrifice of some of the Met's best known and most highly paid singers, most notably Pons, Ponselle, Rethberg, Olszewska, Müller, Martinelli, Schipa, and De Luca. The chorus would be reduced to 90 voices by trimming deadwood; the money-losing Brooklyn Academy of Music performances would be abandoned in favor of a Tuesday night series in the main house; $2,000 would be saved by reducing the staff in the wardrobe department, $17,500 by substituting American for European artists, which eliminated the need to pay steamship fares. The only place where Witherspoon was prepared to spend more money was for stage directors. His own thoughts were Caspar Neher and Carl Ebert ("the best in the world"), to which Ziegler added Tietjens of Berlin and Wallerstein of Vienna.

"The more I study the situation," Witherspoon wrote in a memo, "the more I am convinced that the entire picture must be changed. Let artists wait until May. If some leave, replace them with new ones who will come cheap and help in establishing a new era in the Met. This is very important as a means of reducing the budget and providing new interest. A few should have letters now holding them for the future . . ."

Witherspoon did intend to add Europeans as well as Americans, especially artists who would come by the week and could sing several different styles and languages, insuring their steady use. The name that appears at or near the top of all his lists is that of the giant Belgian tenor René Maison. But he also wanted to sign the mezzo Ebe Stignani, who never sang at the Met, and Salvatore Baccaloni ("Best buffo in the world"), and Marjorie Lawrence, and a large number of young Americans who were in fact engaged: Charles Kullmann, Joseph Bentonelli, Julius Huehn, Hilda Burke, Ruby Mercer, Suzanne Fisher, Chase Baromeo, Rosa Tentoni, Josephine Antoine, and the bass Hubert Raidich, whose contract (at $50 a week) was the only one involving a singer that Witherspoon actually signed and gave to the artist.

By far the most interesting of the deals Witherspoon made was with a conductor. "Szell of Vienna," his memo reads, "accepts by cable $400 per week, 14 weeks, option for tour." It is fascinating to speculate on what might have happened at the Met if that ferociously intelligent musician had come on the scene in 1935 rather than in 1942.

Cravath was consulted throughout, and did not seem to feel constrained by Witherspoon's status as Erskine's man. In letters sent not to the Met but to Witherspoon's Park Avenue home, he urged the future general manager to make sure he signed Margaret Halstead, warned against the plan to drop Pons (citing her great success in Boston—"twenty-seven curtain calls"—exceeding even Flagstad's), and suggested that Witherspoon might be letting extraneous matters influence him in looking at the Italian artists: "You have spoken of opposition to the re-engagement of De Luca and Martinelli. I wonder if this does not grow out of their Fascist affiliations. I hear that Martinelli is an outspoken Fascist, which means that the Anti-Fascists oppose him. I do not know whether De Luca is Fascist or Anti-Fascist, but whichever he is, those of the contrary view would oppose him . . ."

That Cravath still considered himself very much the president and chairman of the Metropolitan Opera Association is shown by a letter he wrote Witherspoon recommending a dancer:

The greatest living classic ballet dancer has turned up in New York quite unheralded. She is Mme. Olga Spessitseva. She sent for me because we have a mutual friend in Mr. Maynard Keynes of London, who is much interested in her. I have had a talk with her, and while she is not entirely clear, I have the impression that she came over in the hope of establishing some connection with the Metropolitan for next year . . . When I saw her in London two years ago I thought she was the most delightful dancer I had ever seen. You will enjoy meeting her, and she will not be satisfied to leave New York without having had a talk with you. I would be very much obliged if you would send her word at the Waldorf-Astoria, making an appointment . . .

As a still-active member of the company, Edward Johnson could not be made privy to many of Witherspoon's plans. It is by no means clear that he was even consulted on Witherspoon's budget for his supplementary season, which Witherspoon projected at 15 weeks (!), with "artists to receive not more than $50 per performance, except in a few cases where special engagements are arranged. These should be limited to $100." Ruby Mercer reports that Johnson was discouraged by the apparently subordinate role he was to play, and was contemplating an early resignation—when Witherspoon, standing in the doorway of Ziegler's office and joking with Ziegler and Earle Lewis, fell dead from a massive heart attack. It was May 10, 1935. Johnson was with the company on tour, in Indianapolis; he rushed back to New York to be invested with the dignity of the general manager's job, which he would retain for fifteen years.

A Canadian by birth, Johnson had made his early career as a tenor in Italy under the name Edoardo di Giovanni, and had married into the Portuguese nobility. His wife died young, leaving him with a daughter whose upbringing was a major concern and considerable success (she married the man who became leader of the Conservative Party in Canada). A handsome man who acted intelligently and almost always got out of his voice all that was there, Johnson became a significant figure in Mary Garden's Chicago Opera Company, and came to the Met in 1922 as a leading man, accomplished enough to be given Des Grieux, Cavaradossi, Faust, Roméo, Don José, and Canio in a season that also boasted the services of Gigli, Martinelli, and Lauri-Volpi. He was especially welcome, however, in specialty roles that required the projection of atmospherics—Avito in *L'Amore dei tre re* and Pelléas, both of which put him in partnership with Bori and endeared him to Gatti, who was particularly fond of these operas.

What Johnson brought to the general manager's job were looks (he became even more handsome when he stopped dyeing his hair on retirement from the stage), elegance, a deep respect for social distinction that allowed him to tell the Metropolitan Opera Club (which had elected him to membership) that he had always "approached these sacred precincts with a certain diffidence," generous instincts, the support of colleagues who had grown increasingly and justifiably nervous about what Witherspoon was doing, and the willingness to rely on Edward Ziegler for day-to-day decisions. Basically, Johnson tried to follow through on Witherspoon's plans. Though he retained Pons, Ponselle, Rethberg, and Martinelli from Witherspoon's first hit list, he did let Olszewska, Müller, Schipa, and De Luca go. Ponselle was permitted, in effect, to abandon her struggle to maintain her capacity above the staff, and to begin what proved to be an abbreviated and unhappy career in the lower repertory, singing only Carmen (for $1,000 a night, down from the previous season's $1,400) and the next year Santuzza (for $500). Johnson signed most of the artists Witherspoon had wanted to add, including Witherspoon's friend the composer Richard Hageman (whose *Caponsacchi* was performed the next season) as a conductor. Herbert Graf, who had been number two in Vienna, then young,

---

Overleaf: Backstage in the 1940s. Joseph Novak paints a set for *Aida* (*left, above*) and costumes are ironed before being packed in trunks for the spring tour (*left, below*). Hoisting lights or scenery still required muscle power (*right, above*). The singers being fitted for a wig and a costume are Ezio Pinza and Zinka Milanov (*right, below*).

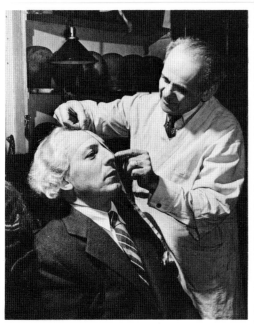

always solid and conscientious, was brought in to establish the stage discipline Witherspoon was planning to seek from the more drastic and imaginative Tietjens or Ebert. Well regarded by the critics, Graf was not a hit with everyone. The publisher Alfred Knopf sent a letter to Johnson: "I heard ELEKTRA last night. The singing, the acting, the playing, the conducting—well, you know I am sure what a high standard they set. But the stage direction—dear Mr. Johnson, why don't you take Herbert Graf out and shoot or drown him? Something very painful would be appropriate."

In one respect Johnson improved on Witherspoon's plans, for instead of Ruth Page he brought in George Balanchine to be ballet master, and Balanchine brought his own company. (The ballet continued, however, to be a fifth wheel at the Met. It is hard to imagine what could have been on Johnson's or Balanchine's mind when *Serenade*, a ballet to music by Schubert, was sandwiched between *Pagliacci* and *Gianni Schicchi*.) The most striking change Johnson made in Witherspoon's plans was the abandonment of the arrangement with Szell (which had never been announced); instead, Johnson rehired Gennaro Papi, whom Gatti had dropped in 1928. The board minutes note Johnson's smug announcement that "the savings he had made in the actual contract with [John Charles] Thomas (in comparison to the offer which had originally been made to Thomas by Mr. Witherspoon) more than covered Papi's salary for the entire season."

The newcomers were heavily employed. René Maison sang Lohengrin, Walther in *Die Meistersinger*, Loge in *Das Rheingold*, Florestan, and Don José (the next season he would add Hoffmann, Erik in *Holländer*, and Des Grieux, oddly, opposite Bidu Sayão's diminutive Manon). Charles Kullmann was the season's first Faust, and moved on to Alfredo, the Duke in *Rigoletto*, Don José, and Rodolfo in *La Bohème*. Marjorie Lawrence sang Rachel in *La Juive* as well as the three Brünnhildes in the first month of the season. In *Götterdämmerung*, Lawrence electrified the audience by swinging herself in one sweeping jump onto the back of Grane to ride to her Immolation, an athletic feat that left the saddest of memories six years later, when she was stricken with polio and permanently crippled. She would return to sing an emotionally received Venus, immobile on her couch, in *Tannhäuser*, and then a carefully staged seated Isolde.

The four-week spring season, from May 11 to June 6, 1936, was a disappointment in Erskine's terms, for it provided work for the second string of the regular season's casts rather than for new Americans. Most of the singers being Europeans, and most opera translations being what they are, the in-English aspect of the season could not be carried through, though Smetana's *Die verkaufte Braut* (also a translation, of course) did become *The Bartered Bride*, and the hit of the season. Gluck's *Orpheus* was mimed on stage and sung in the pit, which turned out to be a rather unhappy idea. And the auditorium grew uncomfortably muggy in late May and early June, the "air circulating" system installed as part of the real estate company's $500,000 modernization project being something considerably less than air-conditioning. Because regular season artists had to be used—there just weren't enough plausible "artist pupils" for that size theater—Witherspoon's $50 maximum was impossible, and he had grossly underestimated what he would have to pay stagehands and musicians. The house had to be scaled to a $3 top (Witherspoon had hoped for $2), and instead of making $2,000 a week, as Witherspoon had planned, the supplementary season lost about $4,000 a week.

The second year of the spring season did a little better artistically, with major roles for Hilda Burke, Rosa Tentoni, and Ruby Mercer, as well as for Lucy Monroe, who would later become the singer of "The Star Spangled Banner" on so many sporting occasions. During this low-priced season, Jennie Tourel made her Metropolitan debut; but she was not re-engaged until 1943. This was also the occasion for the debut of a soprano from St. Louis who would become one of the great stars of the house—the only "find" of the supplementary seasons: Helen Traubel, who first sang on the Met stage as the heroine in the world premiere of Walter Damrosch's not very interesting *The Man Without a Country*. Though scheduled a week earlier than the previous season, the second supplement suffered even more from mugginess; receipts dropped from $74,000 to $57,000, and the losses ran $50,000, which was too much. The experiment was not tried again.

By 1937, the Met had found a much more profitable, and arguably better way to locate and promote new American artists: the Metropolitan Opera Auditions of the Air, sponsored by the Sherwin-Williams Paint Company. It was among the first series of programs to tap the broadcast audiences' love for a real, live contest, and probably did more for the popularity of opera than the broadcast performances themselves. The first winner, Thomas L. Thomas, turned out to have strictly vocal rather than operatic value. But 1938–39 brought Leonard Warren, and two years later there was the admirable Mack Harrell. Later arrivals by the auditions-of-the-air route included Eleanor Steber, Robert Merrill, Patrice Munsel (at age 17!), Clifford Harvuot, Margaret Harshaw, Frank Guarrera, and Regina Resnik (then a soprano, who made her Metropolitan debut as Leonora in *Il Trovatore* without a rehearsal). In the Johnson days the auditions were to some extent rigged (that is, Johnson would insert into the broadcast contest artists he already knew he wished to engage, most notably Martial Singher, an established artist in France, to whom he had offered a contract several years before). Still, the number of winners who became ornaments of the house was significant.

What was most apparent to contemporaries was the flood of Americans. What is most remarkable half a century later is how many of the newcomers proved valuable to the house over time. The list includes not only the audition winners, but also Norman Cordon; Risë Stevens, whose gift for Octavian in *Rosenkavalier*, coupled with the presence of Lehmann and Emanuel List, made that opera a specialty of the house; Traubel; Jan Peerce; Astrid Varnay (Swedish by birth, but brought up in the United States); Richard Tucker; Dorothy Kirsten; Robert Weede; Blanche Thebom and Martha Lipton and Jean Madeira in the mezzo/alto repertory.

Not all the important newcomers were American, and not all the significant excitement was Wagnerian. Jussi Bjoerling arrived from Sweden in Johnson's prewar seasons, offering nothing but voice—but one of the most beautiful lyric voices ever heard at the Met. Zinka Milanov came from Yugoslavia, not the overwhelming soprano she later became but clearly a major artist. Rose Pauly came from Hungary to sing what everyone considered the finest Elektra New York had ever heard. Bruna Castagna made the mistake of entering New York in low-priced productions at the cavernous Hippodrome, and then had to work triply hard to get the Met management to take her seriously; she got her chance as Carmen in the first spring season, and moved on from there. Vina Bovy came from Belgium and sang all three roles in *Les Contes d'Hoffmann*, quite successfully, with Maison as Hoffmann and Tibbett as all the villains.

In 1940 came Licia Albanese, whose Violetta would win from Virgil Thomson "a royal crown" in what he called "the coronation of stardom"—and also the beautiful Jarmila Novotna, who sang a range from Violetta to Cherubino in her first year, placing a personal stamp on every role; and (at last) Alexander Kipnis, a great bass voice and an incomparable artist in the use of it who also happened to be an actor of immense force and power. (In whatever role, Kolodin wrote, "Kipnis left the listener with at least one valid reason for spending an evening in the Metropolitan.") As in Chaliapin's time, *Boris Godunov* was performed with a Russian czar and an Italian court.

John Brownlee came from Australia with the blessings of musicianship and stage savvy. Perhaps most fortunate of all, Bidu Sayão arrived from Brazil the year after Bori's triumphant retirement (she felt the growing strain in her voice before the audience heard it), and through mastery of projection became a great Susanna and Mélisande and Manon and Juliette and much else. Jan Kiepura, a favorite tenor in Vienna and master of upstaging, carried off the Rodolfo-Don José-Des Grieux repertory through sheer self-confidence. Gigli returned for five performances. "Nothing," he wrote Johnson, "would give me more pleasure than to be given the opportunity to collaborate with you in the renaissance of Italian art in America, an art of which you were a worthy follower and which I know is dear to you because Italian was the dear mother of your daughter, and in Italy you molded your soul and your mind." The executive committee of the board with some distaste agreed "to engage Mr. Gigli for a few performances if it could be done at terms no more advantageous than those of any other artist." Gigli's views of Johnson changed once he began singing in New York, and he denounced the Met on his return home.

Lotte Lehmann's Marschallin in *Der Rosenkavalier* was paired with the Octavian of Risë Stevens (*inset*), who made her first appearance with the company opposite the legendary German soprano.

Also added to the company in those years were the foundations of what was to be the world's best *comprimario* roster. George Cehanovsky was already there. Thelma Votipka arrived in 1935, Alessio de Paolis (whom Witherspoon had wanted, with a note that it was worth paying him well), in 1938–39. Paul Franke joined this select company in 1946, Charles Anthony in 1954, Andreas Velis in 1961, Shirley Love in 1963, Nico Castel in 1970. Coupled with the stream of young singers getting their training in small roles rather than small houses, they gave the Met a base of excellence that New Yorkers take for granted until they travel and find that other opera companies seldom have it.

Two young conductors with significant careers ahead of them were added in Johnson's early seasons: in 1936, Maurice Abravanel, a pupil of Kurt Weill, who would later create a fine orchestra in Salt Lake City, but who lasted only two seasons at the Metropolitan; and, in 1937, Erich Leinsdorf, who had been Toscanini's assistant in Salzburg, and who was still conducting at the Met 46 years later, having taken time off in the interim to lead the orchestras in Cleveland, Rochester, and Boston and to make guest appearances all over the world. Bodanzky was wearing down; it had indeed become his custom to conduct only the first and last acts of operas, turning over the baton to one of the assistants in the middle. When Bodanzky died in fall 1939, shortly before the opening of the season, Leinsdorf was in place. This was a year of 44 Wagner performances (out of 123 all told). Leinsdorf conducted every one of them, plus Gluck's *Orfeo* and Strauss's *Rosenkavalier*, for a total of 55 (plus the tour). The next year he added *Pelléas*. That was also the year Bruno Walter came to the Met, but he conducted no Wagner, only *Fidelio*, *The Bartered Bride*, and *Don Giovanni* (for which, finally, Johnson got Salvatore Baccaloni to pair his unforgettably intelligent and plummy and proletarian Leporello with Pinza's type-cast Don).

One of the problems of Johnson's regime is illustrated by his fruitless efforts to persuade Flagstad to sing Norma, and his acquiescence in 1935 to Ponselle's disastrous demand for Carmen. Brownlee was given a debut as Rigoletto, for which neither his voice nor his acting talents fitted him, then further abused as Iago; Warren was pushed into *Lohengrin* as the Herald; Stevens was used for Fricka and Erda; Varnay, at the age of 23, totally without experience, was thrown on stage as Sieglinde in *Die Walküre* on December 6 and then as Brünnhilde in the same opera on December 12; Rose Bampton sang both Amneris and Aida, a week apart. Rethberg's final season was made painful by a *Siegfried* Brünnhilde she could not have sung at any point in her career. Performances were disfigured, and voices damaged, by resolute miscasting.

Cast changes were commonplace, not just from week to week, but from performance to performance. Rehearsals were scarce, and very often ignored by the stars. "I was . . . the understudy for Pons, since we were the same size," the French-Canadian coloratura Pierrette Alarie told Ruby Mercer. "It was a big opportunity for me, because she never came to rehearsals." Leinsdorf's attempt to force the presence of principals at rehearsals led to his denunciation by Melchior and by Flagstad, who was also, of course, seeking employment opportunities for McArthur; in the process of this spat, it is conceivable (though unlikely) that Flagstad referred to Leinsdorf as a "damned Jew." In any event, the belief that she had done so would have reverberations later.

Johnson found it hard to say No to an artist—"He was," says Jerome Hines, "the nice guy who never soiled his hands"—with the result that he came to nurse grievances against people whom he thought had pushed him around. "He enjoyed keeping people down," the conductor Max Rudolf recalls. "He would give Tucker a lot of performances but when the broadcast came he'd give it to one of his old cronies." Johnson cared about the role of general manager, and played it with considerable panache: he was always backstage before performances and during intermissions, encouraging his cohorts, and Alfred Hubay, later the Met's box-office manager, remembered gratefully from his days as an usher that Johnson—in full fig of white tie, opera cape, and top hat—would even visit the Family Circle a few times a year before a performance to encourage "the lowest of the low" among his employees.

But the fact was that Johnson knew little about running an opera house, and he never learned. Strong artists and (eventually) strong conductors pulled the company through, and offered highlight performances long remembered, but there was throughout the Johnson period a catch-as-catch-can quality about the Met that lowered the average level far below what should have been possible. Symbolic, too, of the general manager's lack of grip on the house was his toleration of high-jinks on the audience side, especially on the disgraceful opening nights, when rich exhibitionists did outrageous things before the grateful paparazzi in hopes of seeing their picture in the paper beside that of Mrs. Vanderbilt.

The guilty secret of the early Johnson years was that they were profitable. (The secret was well-kept, because whoever spied for Irving Kolodin in the Met's ledgers when he was preparing the later editions of his history misread the figures, leading Kolodin to present profits as losses.) The wolf had been so visibly at the door that nobody who worked for the Met was making demands on management: the singers remained under $1,000 (Martinelli, for example, who had received $1,500 per performance as late as 1932–33, sang for $800), the orchestra played for $128 a week, the chorus sang for $65 a week (raised to $75 in 1938–39, when the ballet still worked for $35 a week). There were never more than two new productions a season,

and touching up was held to a minimum in the old ones (Novak, who had overseen a staff of five painters in the 1920s, was down to one in 1938). As the box-office receipts rose, the increased revenues dropped straight down to the bottom line, producing profits of $113,000 in 1936–37 and $107,000 in 1937–38 (a prudent $20,000 a year for later renewal of productions was taken off these totals on the books, but the money was not spent). In 1939–40, the Met made $171,000, which broke Gatti's record.

Meanwhile, the affairs of the real estate company had come to crisis. In retrospect, the doom of the old system had been sealed in 1935, for it was quite impossible that assessments could be increased by the necessary $1,000 per box to pay the debt service on the new mortgage. Toward the end of the 1938–39 season, the board of the real estate company formally notified the Metropolitan Opera Association that the lease on the opera house could not be renewed when it expired on May 31, 1940; the real estate company was going to have to sell its property and liquidate.

Cornelius Bliss, who had replaced the 78-year-old Cravath as chairman of the Association in November 1938, had known all about this for some time and was ready. A boxholder by inheritance and a former treasurer of the Republican National Committee, he knew everyone worth knowing, and he had been the guiding spirit of the 1933 fund drive. Eleanor Belmont later wrote that it was Bliss "to whom opera owes, more than to any other individual, the fact of its survival." A profit-making Metropolitan Opera Association *could* afford to own and operate the opera house, provided the price for the house were kept at a level that could be raised by a public fund drive for the purpose.

This was not going to be easy. The opera house was assessed for tax purposes at $5.4 million. Of the assessment, $5.3 million was for land and only $100,000 for "building." When Rockefeller had come around with his ideas for an opera house in his Center, the boxholders had suggested that $14 million might be a nice price for their old theater, and even in the Kahn days a $7 million price had been seriously proposed. That kind of money was far beyond the resources of the Metropolitan Opera Association. Counting the special assessment that had paid off the bonds in 1919, the boxholders had a capital investment of $90,000 each in the house (and recent purchasers had put up as much as $200,000), which meant a price of $3.15 million just to return what had been paid in. On the other hand, there had been all those years of opera for an assessment that could easily be recouped by renting the box a couple of nights a week. And most of the boxholders did want to help.

Bliss and Robert S. Brewster, a Morgan partner who had become chairman of the real estate company, negotiated a price of $1.97 million ($56,857.77 per box), of which $500,000 would be cash, $470,000 the assumption of the remains of the 1935 mortgage, and $1 million in 25-year, 4 per cent bonds secured by a second mortgage. Trustees for the estates that owned the boxes had to swallow hard to accept $2

The 1940 revival of *Figaro*, with Elisabeth Rethberg (the Countess), John Brownlee (the Count), and Ezio Pinza (Figaro) in the Act II finale.

million for a property assessed for tax purposes at $5.4 million, and a two-thirds vote of the boxholders' shares was necessary to sell the property. It would be, and was, a damned close thing: the proposal needed 7,000 shares and got 7,200. Bliss probably spent more time lobbying his fellow boxholders to accept the deal than he did raising the money from the public to make the sale possible: a campaign plan shows two, three, and even four people assigned to the task of persuading each boxholder.

The fund drive was set at a million dollars as a round sum that could be raised. Because only $500,000 in cash was needed, it would leave a fund of half a million to make some necessary or desired alterations to the theater, provide a few new productions, and form a reserve against future losses. Reporting to the board of the Association, Bliss, Wardwell, and Wardwell's very musical law partner Charles M. Spofford found that purchasing the house would increase annual expenses by $253,000 ($160,000 in real estate taxes, $61,000 in interest payments on the old mortgage and the new bonds, additional payroll, insurance, and heat) while increasing annual revenues by only $118,000 ($48,000 from the bank and apartment rentals, $70,000 from the rental of boxes formerly occupied by the boxholders). The net additional cost of $135,000 was then reduced by the average annual profit of the previous three years ($79,000) to show a projected annual deficit of $56,000.

"It is, of course, understood," the committee reported, "that the foregoing figures are estimates and may prove to be wide of the mark . . . A substantial item in producing revenue ($52,000 a year) is the Radio Auditions of the Air, sponsored by the Sherwin-Williams Company. This contract is on a year-to-year basis . . . It is also, of course, obvious that war conditions may make some of the leading artists unavailable for next year and may in other respects affect the box-office receipts."

On the other hand, "there is possibility of tax relief either by a reduction of assessment or exemption of part of the building on the grounds that the Association is an educational corporation and holds the property . . . exclusively for educational purposes." Taking one thing with another, the committee thought a $56,000 deficit was a "conservative" estimate, and that the suggested $250,000 reserve would "provide for annual deficits for several years before working capital is depleted. While present conditions make it impossible to forecast with any certainty, particularly in the case of an organization depending in great measure upon general prosperity, it is thought that a reserve of this amount will be adequate to insure the continuation of opera for a reasonable period in the future."

The fund drive raised $1,057,679.06 net of expenses—$372,000 from the radio audience, $145,000 from foundations (half of that the cancellation of a 1936 loan from Juilliard), $144,000 from boxholders who donated the sale price of their holdings, $143,000 from business groups, $86,000 from subscribers, $70,000 from directors of the Association, $61,000 from sponsoring groups in the tour cities. A little money would be left over to pay for new productions.

Dressing-room reflections: Giovanni Martinelli as the Moor in Verdi's *Otello*, and Jarmila Novotna as Cherubino in Mozart's *Figaro*.

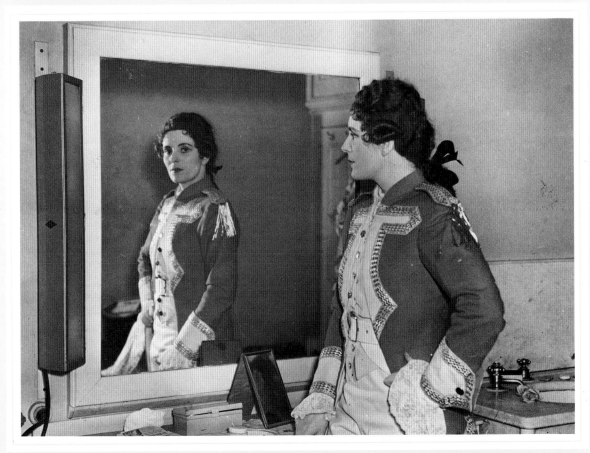

On May 31, 1940, title to the opera house passed to the Metropolitan Opera Association. When the season opened in autumn 1940, Box 35, no longer the personal property of J. P. Morgan *fils*, was occupied by Thomas J. Watson of IBM—but Box 3 still displayed Mrs. Cornelius Vanderbilt III, who had rented it, indeed, for every performance. A dissident group of boxholders brought suit to force a higher payment for their stock, and lost.

The 1940–41 financial results, with earned income up to $2,116,000, were on target with the committee estimates (the loss was under $51,000), but then the war cut into the receipts and deficits rose. Hopes for a real estate tax exemption were dashed in 1941, when Governor Herbert Lehman vetoed a bill that would have given the Met the same benefit as the city's colleges, hospitals, and churches—La Guardia, who blew hot and cold on and at the opera, had refused to send the usual "home rule" request that tradition required for a bill which would reduce a locality's revenues. By 1943, after two seasons had lost more than $200,000 each, Governor Thomas E. Dewey (once an aspiring tenor, and an inveterate operagoer) signed the bill despite La Guardia's disapproval. In fact, it took several years before the exemption phased in. The 1943–44 season lost another $110,000, the operating profit more than wiped out by taxes and interest. The reserve fund had to be replenished with a public appeal, led this time formally by the Metropolitan Opera Guild and drawing heavily, again, from the radio audience. The broadcasts themselves, meanwhile, had come onto a firm footing, with the arrival of Texaco as their sponsor, establishing a relationship between the opera company and the oil company that has extended to the underwriting of the telecasts that greatly widened the constituency for opera in the 1970s and 1980s.

☆ ☆ ☆

The impact of World War II on the Metropolitan was very different from that of World War I. The German artists at the Met now were mostly not German: Flagstad was Norwegian; Melchior, Danish; Lawrence, Australian; Branzell and Kerstin Thorborg, Swedish. And those who were German were often refugees, like List and Leinsdorf and Schorr, who were Jewish, or Lehmann, who was strongly anti-Nazi. Singers and conductors who could stomach Hitler had not been coming to the United States. When Schorr made his farewell appearance in 1933, he built his curtain speech on both the Deutsche Kunst celebrated in *Die Meistersinger* and Sharpless's "America forever" from *Butterfly*.

To be sure, Pinza got into trouble by boasting of the prowess of the Italian army (in which he had once served); in the jittery days of early 1942, his left-over Latin patriotism cost him two months' internment on Ellis Island. (Erich Leinsdorf recalls that after the radio audience had objected to the very fast tempo taken by Sir Thomas

Beecham when playing "The Star Spangled Banner," Frank St. Leger—Johnson's assistant—suggested that the Met offer to swap Beecham for Pinza.) But even the Fascist sympathizers found Mussolini's alliance with Hitler distasteful; there was no political dissension within the company. And when America entered the war, the visible presence in New York of so many anti-Nazi Germans meant the absence of pressure to follow the precedent of 1917 and drop the German operas. Only one work vanished—*Madama Butterfly*, on the reasonable ground that the audience might not feel the requisite sympathy for the Japanese heroine.

Still, the Met lost several stars, some of them because they could not safely get from their homes to New York, notably Bjoerling. And Flagstad was unwilling to try to get to New York: she had rejoined her husband in German-occupied Norway, where he was making himself useful to the Quisling government. The absence of such box-office draws began to be felt in ticket sales, and for 1942–43 prices were reduced to a $6.05 top on single sales ($5.50 plus the 10 per cent federal tax) from the previous $7.70. Reduced prices worked: two weeks were added to the company's time in New York and total box-office receipts were a few tens of thousands of dollars higher, producing a slightly smaller deficit. The house was made to seem even more full by a policy of patriotic papering, making seats available to servicemen and women when the tickets were unsold. Uniforms were common at the Met this year, a greater badge of honor than tails.

Artistically, the war brought the Met a superb conducting staff, and the sense of being on its own. The general manager's "function is undergoing an inevitable transition," Johnson wrote in the second of the annual reports that the Met began to publish following the purchase of the house, "from the purveyance of established foreign successes to the discovery and development of native talent."

Lothar Wallerstein, who had been chief *régisseur* in Vienna, set up a pre-season acting class for young artists Johnson had engaged, with Paul Breisach, who had been on Ziegler's list of possible replacements for Bodanzky a dozen years earlier, supplying the musical element. As young singers were assigned specific roles, Wallerstein gave them specific coaching, hour after hour ("like in the grammar school," Erich Leinsdorf said; "without Wallerstein, I don't think some of these new and untried singers could have gone on stage at the Metropolitan to do these great parts."). In 1944, Kathryn Turney Long gave funds to make such a program a permanent feature of the Metropolitan organization. To meet the needs of the younger and less experienced casts, Johnson and Ziegler steadily cut back on the number of different productions, which had remained virtually at Gatti levels in their early years (37 in the fifteen-week season of 1938–39), to only 24 in the seventeen weeks of 1949–50.

What the young American artists most benefited from, however, was the presence at the Met of a new class of conductors—Bruno Walter came in 1940, Sir Thomas

Beecham in 1941, George Szell in 1942. These three, with Leinsdorf, Breisach, and the excellent Italo-American Cesare Sodero, split up nine-tenths of the 1942–43 productions, and the odds that the audience would hear a finely led performance were greater than they had ever been in the history of the house. To the extent that there seemed to be an outpouring of native operatic talent in America in the years right after the war, credit must go first to the extraordinary quality of musical and artistic direction youngsters at the Met received in the early 1940s—not only from the masters, who were of the school that supervised details (the famous story was of Bruno Walter, asked to conduct *Fidelio*, inquiring immediately, "Who will sing First Prisoner?"), but also from the refugee assistant conductors, Max Rudolf, Hermann Weigert, Tibor Kozma, all of whom had been significant maestri in their home countries. Toward the end of these glory days, Szell was even given authority to wield a broom in the pit, replacing two dozen men to the continuing benefit of music at the Met.

The relative isolation of the war years meant that casts could be kept together not only during the season (when Johnson got organized enough to do it), but even from year to year. The team of Melchior, Traubel, Kipnis, and Thorborg sang *Tristan und Isolde* for Leinsdorf, Beecham, Leinsdorf again, and then Fritz Busch. Lehmann, Stevens, Steber, and List sang *Rosenkavalier* for Leinsdorf and Szell (with Irene Jessner spelling Lehmann occasionally, and Jarmila Novotna undertaking Octavian). Pinza, Steber, Sayão, Novotna (or Stevens), Brownlee, and Baccaloni sang *Le Nozze di Figaro* for Walter in 1942–43, for Leinsdorf in 1944–45, and then (the auditions winner Frances Greer substituting for Sayão) for Fritz Busch in 1946–47. With such artists working for such conductors, performances were strengthened and refined. There were Pinza-Baccaloni pairings in *Don Giovanni*, *Barbiere*, *Forza del destino*. Kipnis sang Boris; Grace Moore sang Tosca; Beecham delivered a rousing *Louise*, ending with what Thomson called "a triumphant rendition dramatically, vocally, and musically by Miss Moore, Miss Doe, Mr. Pinza, Sir Thomas and the orchestra of one of the most shocking family brawls I have ever witnessed." Szell demanded and got 21 hours of orchestral rehearsal for *Salome* (unprecedented in the Johnson regime); and everyone agreed, including the men, that the results in the pit were more than worth the time and money. A team of Singher and Sayão gave *Pelléas et Mélisande* at a level the general manager was willing to admit challenged that of himself and Bori.

Falstaff and *Magic Flute* were given in English. The former benefited from Beecham's light-fingered conducting and (once Tibbett's obligatory but hoarse first night was out of the way) from Warren's resonance and his capacity to absorb Beecham's direction (but he had forgotten it when Fritz Reiner revived the opera a few years later); the latter was blessed with Bruno Walter's absorbing love for the piece ("He paced the work so rightly," Thomson wrote, "speeded it so justly, and

Recruits from abroad: Licia Albanese (*above left*, as Violetta in *Traviata*), Jussi Bjoerling (*above right*, as Riccardo in *Ballo in maschera*), Ljuba Welitsch (*center*, as Richard Strauss's Salome), Giuseppe di Stefano (*below left*, as Gounod's Faust), and Bidu Sayão (*below right*, as Norina in *Don Pasquale*).

balanced its sonorities so clearly, that one was unaware there was any conductor at all"), and by Brownlee's long-lived Papageno.

Johnson's commitment to contemporary operas was, as might be expected from a singer, no more than skin deep. After the disasters of *The Man Without a Country* and *Caponsacchi*, he brought to the Met in 1937–38 the Curtis Institute staging of Gian Carlo Menotti's smart student opera *Amelia Goes to the Ball*, and three years later the same composer's static *The Island God*. In 1941–42, Johnson or Erskine arranged with the Carnegie Corporation to give a fellowship to a librettist-composer team who would spend time at the Met to help them develop a stageable opera. The first recipients were Christopher LaFarge and William Schuman, an admirably intelligent choice, but nothing came of it. Erskine was publicly critical about the reduction in opportunities for American composers.

In 1946–47, the Met attempted Bernard Rogers' *The Warrior*, a new setting of the Samson and Delilah story with Mack Harrell and Regina Resnik (and projected scenery by Bernard Lev, a first at the Met), as a one-act curtain raiser to *Hansel and Gretel* (sung in English). *The Warrior* appeared once more, on a Friday matinee, as an add-on to *La Traviata*, and then sank like a stone. The next year, a considerably more successful contemporary opera was offered—*Peter Grimes*, by the English composer Benjamin Britten, which had an ill-cast and ill-staged start but sold tickets anyway, and returned in the 1960s to become one of the few mid-20th-century operas to take a place in the Met's standard repertory.

In the first years after the house was purchased, the board authorized considerable expenditure for refurbishing old productions, and some money for new ones ($225,000 in 1940–41, $65,000 for 1941–42; this was much more than it seems to modern eyes, for Johnson's technical staff estimated that they could produce an opera as large as *Eugene Onegin* for $18,000, or as tricky as *Die Frau ohne Schatten* for $25,000). David Sarnoff, seconded by Allen Wardwell, said in a board meeting that he would rather see the company go down the financial drain proudly than linger in tatters. But Johnson did not, in fact, care deeply about settings or about direction (Wallerstein, having labored over a *Ring* cycle, was so discouraged by the results possible in the time and sets available that he demanded his name be taken off the program); and as time went on, Johnson proved increasingly amenable to the view of the board's silent majority that the easiest way to save money was to let the physical surroundings run down.

Backstage continued all but intolerable. In his unpublished memoir of that time, Max Rudolf remembered the burdens placed on the Metropolitan's corps of assistant conductors:

We were responsible for coaching, playing the piano for ensemble and stage rehearsals, performing on keyboard instruments in the pit, or on the organ backstage, and for literally everything behind the scene that needed synchronization with the music.

Recruits from home: Jan Peerce (*above left*, as Rodolfo in *Bohème*), Dorothy Kirsten (*above center*, as Marguerite in *Faust*), Robert Merrill (*above right*, as Enrico Ashton in *Lucia*), and Richard Tucker (*below*, after his debut in 1945 as Enzo in *Gioconda*, with general manager Edward Johnson offering congratulations).

Video equipment to transmit the beat by means of small monitors mounted backstage, did not exist. Coordination with the orchestra had to be achieved by ear—which could be precarious because of delayed sound in the big house—or by watching the conductor in the pit through small holes in the scenery. Some of these holes were "official," that is they had been provided by the stage crew. To cover the hole, a piece of material was fastened to the back of the canvas and could be lifted for looking. Unhappily, this device could fail. Perhaps the stage director, without telling us, had changed the location of a high chair, or a super had placed himself in front of the hole so that we were unable to see the conductor. Quick action was of the essence, because the music "didn't wait," so we took a knife, and cut a new hole, much to the chagrin of the stage people . . .

When the house had been rewired a few years back, no one had thought to put a public-address system backstage, which would permit the singers in their dressing rooms to follow the course of the opera, and the stage manager to request their presence on stage through a microphone. Instead, the callboy system of time immemorial was still in use. Worse, nobody had thought to rig up a system of small speakers backstage to permit the singers on stage (who often could not hear the orchestra) to keep to the pitch. Instead, the assistant conductors, in Rudolf's words,

used special instruments looking like miniature harmoniums with straps, which we had hanging around our necks. They had been imported from Italy and were played by blowing air through a curved metal tube. This had to be done softly, so that the sound wouldn't carry into the house, particularly when we gave the pitch from the wings to a singer on stage. People in the audience are ignorant of the ordeal which singers may go through when the orchestral accompaniment is inaudible on stage . . .

During the war, of course, the acquisition of scarce building materials for entertainment use would have been unthinkable, and right after the war the company had no funds for any substantial work in the house. By dint of rigorous cheeseparing, heavy ticket sales (97 per cent of capacity in the New York season), an extended and profitable tour (nine weeks, out as far as Los Angeles, booked and managed by the Sol Hurok agency rather than the Met itself, Ziegler having become too ill to carry this load in 1946 and no replacement for him being known)—and with surprising continued sympathy from the unions (plus, at last, the arrival of the real estate tax relief), the Met managed to break even in the period 1944–47.

Mrs. Belmont's Metropolitan Opera Guild launched an independent fund drive in 1946–47 to finance Lee Simonson's new settings of the *Ring* the next year. Budgeted at $100,000, that production actually cost $166,000 ($12,000 went to Simonson for the design, $3,000 to Graf for directing, $40,000 for painting, $36,000 for labor and materials in the built pieces, and $16,000 for extra lighting rehearsals). Unfortunately, it wasn't much liked when completed, and was subject to ridicule when the word leaked out that Simonson, never having seen the Rhine, based his designs on the appearance of the Hudson (including the Columbia-Presbyterian

Medical Center as an image of Valhalla). Neither the conductor (Fritz Stiedry) nor the casts greatly attracted the public (Melchior had grown fat and ungainly, and Traubel, equally fat, was never for all her excellence a draw at the box office); *Rheingold* did not reappear in 1948–49, and only *Die Walküre* of the *Ring* operas was offered in 1949–50.

Still, the full houses were well deserved. With the European economies in awful shape and the dollar astride the world like a colossus, the Met had both its American singers, full-time, and its pick of foreign artists. The tenor roster in 1947–48 included Bjoerling, Giuseppe di Stefano, Raoul Jobin, Max Lorenz, Melchior, Peerce, Set Svanholm, Ferruccio Tagliavini, Tucker, and Ramon Vinay. The next year saw one of the most spectacular debuts the Met had ever known, with Fritz Reiner and the red-headed Ljuba Welitsch, powerful of voice and temperament, joining forces for a *Salome* of enormous force that kept the house on its feet for fifteen minutes after the final curtain (which was by no means early, for in those days the Met offered a curtain-raiser, the ill-matched *Gianni Schicchi*—this evening with Italo Tajo, Cloe Elmo, and Di Stefano—to go with the one-act Strauss work). In the 1949–50 season, which would be Johnson's last, Reiner was conductor for a televised opening-night *Rosenkavalier*, with Steber graduating from Sophie to the Marschallin, Stevens and List still superbly in place, Di Stefano as the Italian singer, and the great German coloratura Erna Berger, getting on in years but still an artist of wondrous innocence with a remarkably pure voice, taking over as Sophie.

With the illness that forced the retirement of Ziegler in 1946–47 (and led to his death at the end of that year), Johnson was increasingly on his own in casting the company. His musical assistant Frank St. Leger, who had been Melba's accompanist for five years and an assistant conductor at Chicago while Johnson was there, seems to have been of the coaching school that believes anyone can sing any role if the notes are in the voice. The youth of the artists often gave them flexibility enough to keep miscasting from destroying performances, but the frequency with which light-voiced people sang heavy roles—and heavy-voiced people lumbered through light ones—became distressing, quite apart from more subtle questions of whether artists and roles fitted together in temperament or style.

Johnson could be generous to young singers, with everything from well-timed words of encouragement (and little coaching sessions during intermissions) to small but important gifts of money, but he could be brutal in personal matters, too, when he felt that he or the Met had been in some way slighted. Paul Breisach had been conducting performances at the San Francisco Opera before the Met season began, and wrote asking permission to delay for two weeks his arrival in New York (which would still get him there two weeks before the orchestra reported). It had been Johnson's habit (acquired during the years when the Met was not sure in the spring that it could open in the fall) not to offer contracts to any but the most important

artists until after the summer, so that Breisach had still not signed for the renewal of his job as music secretary and occasional conductor. Johnson called in Max Rudolf, who had come on George Szell's recommendation in 1945, and asked him to take a promotion to what Rudolf considered Breisach's duties. When Rudolf asked what Breisach would be doing—Breisach was a friend—Johnson waved off the question with the comment that he had plans for Breisach. When Breisach returned from San Francisco he found that he could not get in to see Johnson to ask why the Met was not going to offer him a contract.

Similarly, Rudolf remembered a visit one season shortly after Christmas from Kerstin Thorborg, the Swedish mezzo, an artist of many years' seniority in the house, to whom the Met was indebted for a number of courtesies over the years. Thorborg was not on Rudolf's roster, and he consulted with Johnson, who was furious: "Who would have thought it!" Johnson said. "Who would have thought it! I sent her a contract with only three performances in six weeks, and she's accepted!" More damagingly, Johnson refused to give Milanov a single performance at the Met during the season when his successor, Rudolf Bing, was looking over the company—he just didn't want her around, because she had left the Met for personal reasons two years earlier to return to Europe to live. Max Rudolf, informed by Milanov's agent that she was singing "better than ever," took Bing up to Hartford to hear her with a minor-league local company, and the results were enjoyed by Met audiences for fifteen years to come.

The *authenticity*, as it were, of the management had been damaged when Ziegler died. "You know," Erich Leinsdorf said, "he had a reputation as a terrible man, because he was the one who always had to say No. But I think he was an inspiring figure. It was not so much that he ran the house . . . Look. Ziegler once said to me of La Guardia, with whom he had had many fights, 'In the future when all the files are open, you will look in the La Guardia file and you will not find a single dishonest act.' It takes one to know one: I am sure the same statement can be made for Ziegler." It can be.

Real harm was done once by Johnson's tendency to think of himself before he thought of the artist or the opera company. Kirsten Flagstad's husband had been imprisoned at the end of the war and held for trial as a collaborator with the Nazis, and rumors were common to the effect that Flagstad had sung for German soldiers, appeared in Berlin, made pro-Nazi statements, etc. In fact, Flagstad had spent the war years after her return to occupied Norway as a secluded wife. She sang in Zurich (traveling through Germany to get there, of course) and in Stockholm, but never in Norway. So far as is known, she had no political views (though her husband's position must have precluded her from sharing the hatred for German occupation that suffused Norwegian society). Nevertheless, there was considerable and vocal opposition in the United States to her return.

❧

Alajalov's cover for the *New Yorker* evokes the glamour of opening night in 1937; press photographers and society reporters are at the ready as fur-jacketed women and top-hatted men emerge from their limousines. Mrs. Cornelius Vanderbilt III (*inset, right*) was a regular first-nighter from the 1890s until her death in 1953. Some first-nighters played up shamelessly to the newspapers' appetite for extravagant behavior.

Some of this opposition was eased when her husband died in custody in June 1946. Even before then, Mrs. Belmont had said in a speech at the Women's National Republican Club that if the State Department would issue Flagstad a visa, the Metropolitan "would welcome back her glorious voice." The Norwegian singers' union gave Flagstad a clean bill of health, and she sang in London without objection at the Queen's invitation, and at two benefits for Jewish orphans. On the other hand, the Norwegian embassy could not vouch for her prewar attitudes in the United States: the "damned Jew" epithet at Leinsdorf, whether apocryphal or not, rose to haunt her.

When Flagstad did get her visa, and did return to America for a concert tour in spring 1947, she saw no one from the Met. The tour was marked by picketing and demonstrations (including stink bombs set off in the Academy of Music during her recital in Philadelphia). That November, Flagstad sang in a staged opera in the United States for the first time since the war, when Artur Rodzinski and the Chicago Symphony did *Tristan* at the Civic Opera House, with Set Svanholm and Karin Branzell, both Metropolitan artists, as her companions.

In late spring 1948, Johnson attended a Flagstad performance in Zurich and came backstage, bearing flowers; but he said nothing about re-engaging her for the Met. Early in 1949, when Flagstad was in New York, Mrs. Belmont held a dinner party to which the soprano and Johnson were both invited, and Johnson delivered a toast to Flagstad in champagne. Even then—after the failure of the *Ring* cycle into which so much of the Guild's blood and sweat had been poured—Johnson did not speak to Flagstad about singing at the Met.

On March 2, 1949, after Johnson had agreed to remain as general manager for 1949–50, and before Rudolf Bing had been asked to take over in 1950–51, there was a meeting of the executive committee of the Met board, at which "Mr. Johnson raised the question of policy having to do with the employment of certain artists during the coming season, including the question of the engagement of Mme. Flagstad. After full discussion, it was the sense of the Committee that there was no objection from the standpoint of policy of the Association to the engagement of Mme. Flagstad for the next season." But that was the end of it. As a last contribution to the future of the Metropolitan, Johnson decided to let his successor take the heat on Flagstad.

Wartime sympathy for dismembered Czechoslovakia added poignancy to the Met's English-language production of Smetana's *Bartered Bride*, revived in 1941 under Bruno Walter's baton. In this stage photo of the final scene, Jarmila Novotna (Marie) and Charles Kullmann (Jenik) are standing in the horsecart; Thelma Votipka (Kathinka) is at the far left.

SEVEN

Milestones III: The Seventy-Fifth Anniversary Season. Mr. Bing in Charge

It was surely fitting, though unremarked at the time, that two native New Yorkers—Leonard Warren and Maria Callas—were to head the cast for the centerpiece of the 75th anniversary season in 1958–59: the production of a significant older opera never before done at the Met, Verdi's *Macbeth*. The conductor was to be Dimitri Mitropoulos, former music director of the New York Philharmonic; the direction was to be by Carl Ebert, who had been Rudolf Bing's boss in Darmstadt and Berlin and Glyndebourne before the war but had never before worked at the Metropolitan; and the sets were in the hands of Caspar Neher, whose work with Ebert in the late 1920s and early 1930s, on this opera among others, had greatly enhanced the reputations of both.

A prewar winner of the Auditions of the Air, Warren was the first great success of the policy of recruiting Americans that Erskine, Witherspoon, and Johnson had launched in the mid-1930s. Son of an immigrant Russian furrier, by no means destined for an operatic career (he went to work on leaving high school and began to study singing seriously only after an engagement in the chorus of the Radio City Music Hall gave him financial reason to do so), Warren was sent for a year's training in Italy at the expense of George A. Martin, president of the Sherwin-Williams Paint Company, which sponsored the auditions. In Europe, he acquired an intelligent American wife, a Juilliard graduate, who would later serve him and the Met inestimably by her ability to act as intermediary between conductors or directors and her husband (he found it difficult to accept instruction in rehearsals before his colleagues but could come to rehearsals with the conductor's or director's own ideas about what he should do if they were first communicated to Agathe Warren).

Vain, hearty, barrel-chested and barrel-bellied over legs which seemed too slight to carry him, thoroughly unneurotic (his hobby was electric trains), always willing to work, Warren after a while limited himself mostly to the Verdi roles, which the composer seemed to have written for precisely his superb head voice; and his characterizations, rarely better than embarrassing the first time around, invariably

Nothing in Rudolf Bing's 22-year tenure as general manager had more long-lasting repercussions than his invitation to Marian Anderson to become the company's first black singer. He welcomed her to the house in January 1955.

improved each time he came on stage. The seamless voice was a rich organ totally without strain at the top; he liked to say that every voice *really* had only nine notes in it (a maxim which protected him from operas like *Contes d'Hoffmann* that he didn't want to do), but in fact his own was loud and clear over two and a half octaves. At parties, Warren would sing tenor arias to show how they should sound. And he belonged to New York. Warren spent only one brief season in Italy after his career was established (the Italians were astonished that there *was* such a voice), and he came back from it grumbling about the weather: "The same gray cloud hangs over the Duomo the whole month of January, right at the top of the spires. When the cloud lifts and you can see the top of the spires, watch out—snow." From the mid-1940s until he died on stage on March 4, 1960, Warren's loyalty to the Met guaranteed the house several dozen nights each year when the audience would be happy they had gone to the opera: however awful the rest of a *Trovatore* might be, Warren singing "Il balen" made the night worth while.

Callas, of course, was different in every way but one—for she too had been born in poverty to immigrant parents in New York. The name was Kalogeropoulos, which proved unmanageable in New York, and her father changed it to Callas. Her mother was ambitious for her, and had her sing in churches and on radio "amateur hours" and children's shows. Later Callas would remember (or claim to remember) incidents when as a pubescent girl she was harassed by men at the stage doors to the radio stations. Her parents' marriage was a disaster, and she grew up obsessed by sex and by the evanescence of emotional ties. This Elektra found her Agamemnon *redivivus* in the person of Giovanni Battista Meneghini—one could not visit their apartment in Verona or even take a drive with them in an automobile and not sense the flux of sexual energy between them. But even after she had found a man with whom she could be both solicitous and obedient, Callas was forever on the edge of mental trouble, prone to call friends at three in the morning because her demons were upon her. She commanded attention in tragic roles because she put so much of her despairing self into them. Coupled with her extraordinary intelligence, the grace and intensity of her musicality, and her luminous curiosity about how the characters she played would act and feel (she worked for years, for example, on the threads of tone in the fourth act of *Traviata* that would be both beautiful to hear and expressive of terminal tuberculosis—and the critics then said she had seemed short of breath), Callas's neuroticism created performances that dominated audiences, even when the critical ear heard wolfs in the metallic voice.

At the age of thirteen, Callas was taken to Greece by her mother. Her teacher in Athens was Elvira de Hidalgo, who had first sung at the Met in 1909–10, and then in 1924–26 as second cast to Galli-Curci as Rosina, Gilda, and Lucia. Though it is hard to believe that De Hidalgo saw the bel canto possibilities in a voice that for the next half dozen years was used almost exclusively in very heavy repertory (Leonore in

Fidelio, Leonora in *Trovatore*, Turandot, Aida, Leonora in *Forza*, up to and including Isolde and Brünnhilde), the exercises and attitudes De Hidalgo taught must have been very useful when Tullio Serafin early in 1949 needed an Elvira for *I Puritani* in Venice and promised Callas she would be a success.

It was as Norma that Callas made her American debut—in Chicago, not at the Met—in October 1954. By then she had moved mostly into a lighter repertory and also into a lighter persona, the fat soprano of her first dozen years on stage having become . . . well, Maria Callas. She told people she had had a tapeworm; she also pulled herself together and dieted. Whatever the cost to the voice in this process—and comparison of recordings made before and after summer 1953 argues that there was some—the gain in dramatic projection and the birth of her self-confidence as a woman more than made up for it.

Bing had made contact with Callas in autumn 1950, shortly before the opening of his own first season as general manager, and he went to Florence to hear her in spring 1951. He was concentrating on getting Met productions to look better, and the extremely fat Miss Callas was not what he had in mind. Still, he offered her a *Traviata* in 1952–53, and thought he had a signed contract. When Meneghini was denied a U.S. visa on political grounds—he had been a member of the Fascisti—Callas canceled; and when the rules against former Fascists were relaxed enough to let her spouse come with her, Carol Fox of the new Chicago Lyric Theater outbid the Met for Callas's services.

But it must be said that Bing did little for Callas once he got her for opening night of the 1956–57 season. Her debut opera was *Norma*, followed by *Tosca*, followed by *Lucia*, all of them old and battered productions. For the first and last of these her conductor was Fausto Cleva. His touch was heavier than the light framework Callas liked; she had specifically asked Bing not to assign him to her operas. For the second and third of her three operas, Callas's tenor was the adequate but woolly Giuseppe Campora. Only Mario del Monaco, her Pollione in four of her six *Normas*, Dimitri Mitropoulos as conductor of *Tosca*, and George London as Scarpia were out of the Met's top drawer.

The Met did not get Callas's best, either: her tone was wiry and her pitch uncertain. Later that season, she wrote to Bing: "I am still trying to discover what happened in New York. I am only sorry I couldn't give you personally what other theaters have had." But Bing and Callas got on splendidly together because of their shared devotion to dogs: at the first stage rehearsal of *Norma*, Callas's little poodle peed on the stage tree, and she was grateful to Bing (who told her his dachshund might have done the same) for being sympathetic. And though she did not sing her best, the force of her interpretations carried the Met audience to frenzied excitement. When she sang *Traviata*, *Tosca*, and *Lucia* the next season, every place in the house was sold out as soon as the tickets became available.

Macbeth would be the Met's first new production for Callas. And this 75th anniversary season would also be the first one in which she was to appear in the spring tour—something the committees that sponsored the tour in the various cities were demanding. She was to be paid, in effect, $2,000 per performance ($1,500 as a fee, which put her on a parity with Milanov, Renata Tebaldi, Del Monaco, and Tucker, plus $500 "living allowance" for each performance). Because of the heavy crowd scenes and the variety of necessary costumes—witches, soldiers, courtiers, refugees—*Macbeth* would be the most expensive production in Met history to that point ($109,626, of which $63,329 went to Karinska for costumes, $5,000 to Neher for designs). Of the five new productions with which the house was celebrating its anniversary—*Wozzeck*, *Trovatore*, *Figaro*, and *Gypsy Baron* were the others—*Macbeth* was the hot ticket.

Then it all collapsed, in perhaps the most publicized incident in the history of the house. MARIA CALLAS BOOTED BY MET, read the front-page heading of the *Daily News*, on November 7, 1958. Callas was in Dallas, where impresario Larry Kelly had mounted two new and lavish productions for her (a *Traviata* directed by Franco Zeffirelli and a *Medea* directed by Alexis Minotis, with Jon Vickers as Jason and Teresa Berganza as Neris). From Dallas she was to go off on a busy two-week concert tour of Cleveland, Detroit, Washington, San Francisco, and Los Angeles, all at fees that were at least double what the Met was offering her. According to his own memoirs, Meneghini decided that his wife could make much more money during those seven weeks she was to be at the Met, and sought a way to force Bing to break her contract. (She did not dare break it herself: she had canceled out of San Francisco the previous fall, and had been brought up on charges before what Meneghini calls "the terrible American Guild of Musical Artists," which could deny her access to American stages.)

Callas in fact had not signed a contract with the Met for 1958–59. Nevertheless, there was a binding "letter of intent," which the artist and her husband now decided they could evade by demanding a change in the Met's schedule to free the soprano from the need to alternate the heavy role of Lady Macbeth with the lighter role of Violetta. But the letter of intent had dealt with this problem, stipulating a rest of three days between the two roles—and Bing's schedule actually gave rests varying between four and eight days.

The Met administration smelled a rat. There were some who thought Callas was afraid of Lady Macbeth, a notoriously difficult role she had sung only once in her life (in Milan in 1952; it had been *Macbeth* that Callas escaped when she canceled San Francisco). Bing felt that "the basic dissatisfaction was the tour, where she would have to sing in many cities off the international publicity circuit, under conditions she knew would be undesirable." At all events, Bing telegraphed an ultimatum that the contract would have to be signed by a certain hour of a certain day, and when the

Maria Callas on stage as Norma in her Met debut, October 29, 1956 (*above left*). There were public plaudits from an enthusiastic opening-night audience (*below*) and a private backstage hug from Giovanni Battista Meneghini, her husband and manager (*above right*).

time passed he issued an unwise statement to the press: "Let us all be grateful that we had the experience of her artistry for two seasons; for reasons, however, which the musical press and public can well understand, the Met is nevertheless grateful that the association is ended."

Though Callas had incited the breach, the manner of its imposition infuriated her. She was not merely seeking publicity when she told her friend Elsa Maxwell (for publication in the Hearst press, at a good price) that "I will do no more stinking performances . . . I'm not supposed to make money for Mr. Bing, I'm supposed to do art. My heart can't do otherwise. I don't do routine." Or when she commented for Harriett Johnson of the New York *Post* on "those lousy *Traviatas* he wanted to make me do—and they're lousy, really they're lousy, everybody knows it."

Rather to his surprise—because Callas's record of cancellation and abandonments was already so lurid (she had recently walked out of a performance in Rome that was graced by the President of the Republic)—Bing found himself the villain of the piece. He saved his *Macbeth* by engaging Leonie Rysanek, who was to become one of the most adventurous and admirable and durable sopranos in the house, to make her debut as the Lady (and he gathered sympathy for her at her entrance, he thought, by having an assistant shout "Brava, Callas!" as the substitute stepped on stage). But the general conclusion of the New York press was Irving Kolodin's, that "the 'star' in this instance was Bing himself, who wanted things *his* own way regardless of consequences."

The name of Rudolf Bing first appears in the Metropolitan archives in autumn 1935, when as the newly appointed general manager of the Glyndebourne Opera (a title that meant much less at Glyndebourne than it did in New York) he asked the Met for the loan of its list of subscribers to the high-priced seats, so that Glyndebourne could call to their attention the existence of its summer festival in the Sussex Downs. The Met was not parting with lists; but Johnson offered to distribute 5,000 brochures for Glyndebourne if Bing would supply them and pay the mailing and handling expense. Glyndebourne was soon well known in New York among that not inconsiderable fraction of the Met's patrons who spent "the season" in London. In 1936, one of the early luncheon meetings of the Metropolitan Opera Guild was the occasion for a talk by John Brownlee on Glyndebourne, where he had sung the summer before.

In January 1939, Bing and Carl Ebert visited New York to discuss a proposal that Glyndebourne give a season at the World's Fair, and Bing attended performances at the Met, admiring Melchior and listening with astonishment to the recitatives Bodanzky had written for *Fidelio*. When he returned ten years later, to discuss a suggestion by an obscure foundation that Glyndebourne set up a summer season in Princeton, N.J., he looked up his old friend Fritz Stiedry, who was conducting at the house, and Stiedry introduced him to Mrs. August Belmont and to Johnson. Bing had by then gathered deserved prominence internationally by organizing the Edinburgh Festival, originally as a showcase and financial prop for Glyndebourne but ultimately—thanks almost entirely to his own flair and his Central European contacts—as much more than that.

Johnson had recently received conclusive evidence that the next season at the Met would be his last. In 1945 and 1947, his suggested intention to retire at the end of the year had been greeted with two-year extensions of his contract, but this time the offer had been for only one year, and a public announcement had been made that the general manager would be leaving at the end of 1949–50. Very large losses in 1947–48 had soured the board, which was also unhappy at the increasing evidence of artistic mismanagement in the house and annoyed at Johnson's incompetent handling of the previous summer's labor disputes. These had produced the first of what would be many announcements, later reversed, that a season was being canceled. "The position of the management in connection with the discussion," Cornelius Bliss wrote Mrs. Belmont after the penultimate meeting before that announcement, "was not helpful. Johnson made an impassioned speech; pounded the table, shouted, etc. He said we were giving opera now just as we gave it in 1883; that we are in an impossible situation and that we should not have granted the Unions even another week—because it would be impossible for him to hold his artists and arrange a Season. In his talks with the officers and his talk yesterday he has changed his point of view several times . . ."

Johnson and Bing, meeting for the first time, chatted about the difficulty of producing operas under modern conditions to the standards one wished to achieve. Suddenly, almost certainly as a joke (for he had hopes and plans to turn the house over to his assistant, Frank St. Leger), Johnson asked Bing how he would like "*my* job." (This prefers Max Rudolf's more idiomatic version to Bing's "my successor.") The answer, diplomatically phrased, was that Bing, who was 48 years old and ambitious, would like it very much indeed.

Exactly how, and by whom, Bing was chosen became a subject of public dispute between Mrs. Belmont and John Erskine, still a member of the executive committee though in bad health, and still with the energy to grow furious at the decision to take a European non-musician. The facts appear to be that Bing, following his talk with Johnson, was introduced by Johnson to George Sloan, the Nashville philanthropist and fund-raiser who had become chairman of the Met board, and Sloan introduced him to Charles Spofford and David Sarnoff. He seemed socially acceptable to Sloan, sufficiently art-minded for Spofford, and enough of a businessman for Sarnoff. Mrs. Belmont was taking a trip to England that spring, and offered to check with her

British friends. Bing got a rave report from Lady Violet Bonham-Carter, who was chairing the board for Sadler's Wells, and whom Mrs. Belmont knew well. She communicated her information back to Spofford, who read aloud from her letter at a May meeting of the executive committee. Bing had by then returned to New York at Sloan's invitation, expressly for the purpose of meeting the executive committee's members.

From this sequence Erskine deduced that Bing had "been selected for us by Mrs. Belmont, who made a special trip to Europe for that purpose, and by Mrs. Otto Kahn, who immediately before her death conferred with Mrs. Belmont in London; also by an English lady of title, better known to music circles in London than to us, who assisted Mrs. Belmont in making her choice." Erskine's narrative was refuted in an irritated but carefully composed review of his book, which Mrs. Belmont published in the Guild's magazine *Opera News*. Erskine was certainly wrong in his statement that "the general manager has now been chosen not by the men of the Opera Board but by the ladies of the Opera Guild." But Mrs. Belmont's voice was probably the most important raised in Bing's behalf, which was entirely legitimate, for Eleanor Robson Belmont—quite apart from her dignity, beauty, force of personality, excellence of judgment, and devotion to the opera—shared with her friend Lucrezia Bori the distinction of being the only members of the board to have appeared on stage as dramatic professionals. And the fact was that Stiedry had introduced Bing to her on the same day he met with Johnson.

In the years to come, Mrs. Belmont and her friends would be a great source of strength for Bing. His opening-night *Don Carlo* was paid for by Mrs. John Barry Ryan (Otto Kahn's daughter; she and her brother sold a Rembrandt to raise the money), and over the years Mrs. Martha Baird Rockefeller, Mrs. Albert Lasker, Mrs. DeWitt Wallace, Mrs. Lewis W. Douglas and Mrs. Frederick K. Weyerhaeuser would provide Bing with the resources for many of the company's most splendid presentations. And it would be the "Annual Giving" program launched by Mrs. Belmont that would enable Bing to budget an operating deficit year after year without having to face more than occasional wrath on his board.

Bing was formally announced as the choice in June 1949. He was little known in New York, and the appointment got off on the wrong foot when the press release, based on the information distributed to the directors (Bing, Erskine noted wickedly, "had furnished the facts to Mr. Spofford"), considerably exaggerated his roles in Darmstadt, Berlin, and Glyndebourne, where his early duties had been entirely administrative in support of the artistic direction of Fritz Busch and Carl Ebert. More significantly, he knew virtually nothing of the Met. At his own suggestion, he was invited to spend the entire season of 1949–50 in residence at the house, learning what he would inherit and planning the following years. It was still possible in those days for a manager to plan a 1950–51 season in 1949–50, and by the time Bing had

Bing opened his first season with a trend-setting production of Verdi's *Don Carlo* directed by Margaret Webster, shown in rehearsal with (*l. to r.*) Delia Rigal, Cesare Siepi, Jussi Bjoerling (back to camera), and Robert Merrill. The on-stage photo (*inset*) is of the Grand Inquisitor scene, with Jerome Hines as the seated prelate and Siepi as Philip.

been in New York for three months he had created a future company very different from the one in being.

The major change was a new emphasis on stage presentation. At the close of Johnson's last season, Virgil Thomson had written that the Met was "not much fun, except for the music." Bing was going to change that. His goal, he wrote in the annual report following his first season, was "the improvement of the visual aspect of opera so that the sights would be more harmonious with the sounds." There would be major use of theater (even "Broadway") directors to put the Met's productions on stage. The opening-night *Don Carlo*, the first Met performance of this work since 1923, would be staged by the Shakespearean specialist Margaret Webster; and a revival of *Fledermaus* (which Bing planned for twenty performances, to allow more preparation time for other operas) would be done by Garson Kanin, in an English translation by Kanin himself and the songwriter Howard Dietz, to draw a new audience to the theater. Soon Bing would bring to the Met a galaxy of theatrical and movie directors: Alfred Lunt, Cyril Ritchard, Tyrone Guthrie, Jean-Louis Barrault, José Quintero, Joseph L. Mankiewicz, Peter Brook, Franco Zeffirelli, and others.

Another major change, though not much remarked at the time, was in the conducting staff. Antonicelli, Cimara, Cooper, Pelletier, and Perlea would all go. In their place, Bing regained the services of Bruno Walter, whom he had known since his Viennese childhood, brought back Fausto Cleva (whom Johnson had dropped), added Alberto Erede (a mainstay at Glyndebourne), promoted Tibor Kozma from the ranks of the assistants, and increased the opportunities for Fritz Stiedry, who in Bing's first season would do a full *Ring*, Mozart's *Magic Flute* (with an excellent cast including Jerome Hines as Sarastro, Tucker as Tamino, Steber as Pamina, Erna Berger as Queen of the Night, and Brownlee as Papageno)—and the opening-night *Don Carlo*, in which he displayed that special sense of Verdian architectonics that had been created in the German Verdi revival of the 1920s, a formative influence on Bing's taste.

The *Don Carlo* was to provide a debut for four new artists—Delia Rigal as Elisabetta, Fedora Barbieri as Eboli, Lucine Amara as the Celestial Voice, and Boris Christoff as Philip II. And it turned out there *were* four debuts, even though Christoff was unable to qualify for entrance to the United States under the terms of the McCarran Act, designed to keep "subversives" (in this case, a citizen of Communist Bulgaria) out of the United States. At the last minute, Bing was able to engage Cesare Siepi ("a replacement, rather than merely a substitute," in Kolodin's nice phrase), whose immense, rich bass and attractive figure would fill and ornament the house for a quarter of a century. Also new to the Met that first season would be the assured and lovely artistry of Victoria de los Angeles, whose Marguerite in *Faust*, however, was paired (it was the kind of problem Johnson always had and

Bing seemed unable to escape) not with Bjoerling or Giuseppe di Stefano, who had sung Faust earlier in the season, but with the lesser talent of Eugene Conley.

The splendid bass-baritone Hans Hotter came to sing in a new production of *Der fliegende Holländer*, directed by Herbert Graf and conducted by Fritz Reiner. For the first *Fledermaus*, Bing had the superb cast of Ljuba Welitsch, the Wagnerian tenor Set Svanholm (revealing previously unsuspected comic talents), Tucker, Brownlee as master of ceremonies, and Stevens—elegantly camp in yet another trouser role. Milanov returned to sing—better than she had ever sung before—Santuzza in *Cavalleria*, Leonora in *Trovatore*, and the top line of the Verdi Requiem for Bruno Walter.

Among the other newcomers were two unadvertised arrivals. One was the very young Roberta Peters, who was thrown on stage as a substitute for Nadine Conner to sing Zerlina in *Don Giovanni*, and then achieved front-page prominence with an excellently sung Queen of the Night in *The Magic Flute*. The other was the tenor Mario del Monaco, whom Bing had engaged for the next season and who stopped off on his way back from an engagement in San Francisco to sing a loud and unrehearsed Des Grieux as a "guest artist."

The great flap of Bing's first press conference was his announcement that Flagstad would return to sing Isolde, Leonore in a *Fidelio* conducted by Bruno Walter, and the three Brünnhildes, one each in a pair of *Ring* cycles (the others of the pair being sung by Traubel). Melchior would not be back. He had demanded that he be re-engaged before other artists or he would quit, and Bing had let him quit: Melchior would be no more likely to come to rehearsals for the new management than he had been for the old, and Bing wanted integrated performances. Traubel threatened to leave the Met because Flagstad was signed before she was, but Bing properly soft-soaped her with the chance to sing the Marschallin in *Der Rosenkavalier*, which she had always wanted.

The board had specifically approved Flagstad's re-engagement with a single dissenting vote from Morton Baum, a brilliant pianist and superb lawyer (but not a Wall Street lawyer), who had come on the board originally to help with the politics of the real estate tax exemption and would soon leave to become the guiding genius of the New York City Opera and the most nagging single thorn in Bing's side. The fact that Bing was "German" (Austrian, really) and the return of Flagstad created an explosion of ill-will, and Bing carried it entirely on his own shoulders, not soliciting help from the board. "I intend to run this house," he said, "unmoved by promises or threats, on the principle of quality only."

Bing was surprised by the violence of the reaction to the Flagstad announcement, though he had been warned. He was, after all, a refugee himself, with strong feelings about Nazi sympathizers—for years he refused to engage Elisabeth Schwarzkopf or Herbert von Karajan. And he had carefully arranged to have Walter, another

NEXT DOOR

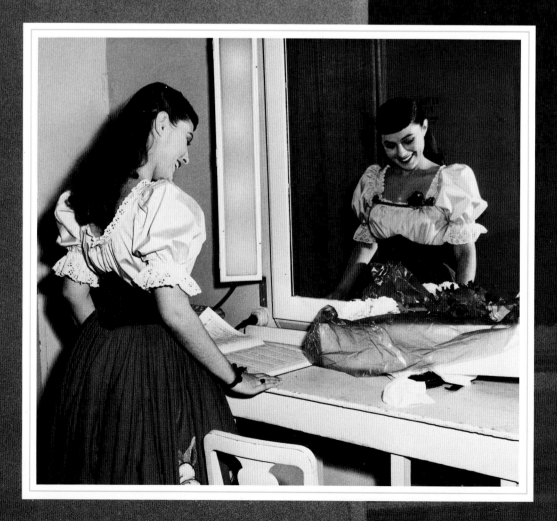

refugee, honor Flagstad's return by conducting her *Fidelio*. (This was not easy to do, incidentally, not because Walter had any political objections to anybody—he had been quite willing to continue working for the Nazis before the war if they would have had him—but because he had felt Flagstad too placid for the role when he had conducted her in 1940. Max Rudolf recalls that Bing ended this surprising conversation by inquiring whether "*im Notfall*"—as a last resort—Walter might not accept Flagstad, which provoked a laugh even from the very serious conductor.) In the end, Flagstad's return was triumphant, and deservedly so. "Vocally vast and impeccable," wrote Virgil Thomson. Those who wanted to hear her were much more numerous than the diehards who resented her return.

Organizationally, Bing cut a swath through the top level. Earle R. Lewis, who handled box office and subscription, had been with the company almost half a century and was older than Johnson; he had always said he would retire when Johnson did. Bing replaced him with Francis Robinson, a former theatrical press agent who had come to the Met originally with the Hurok office to handle the publicity for the tour when Hurok booked it. A Southerner of expansive charm, Robinson would remain throughout the Bing era and beyond, moving on to the job of press representative and becoming probably the most effective spokesman for the glamour of opera that America has ever known.

Frank St. Leger had been Johnson's own candidate for the top job; a nervous man, quick on the trigger, he was likely to keep for his own uses his extensive knowledge of relations backstage. Bing released him, and promoted to the leadership of the artistic administration the conductor Max Rudolf, an old acquaintance, who had been St. Leger's assistant. It may be worth noting that there was an element of continuity in Rudolf's appointment, for he would have been given this job if St. Leger had been made general manager. Rudolf made a strange demand: if he was going to be artistic administrator, he would have to stop conducting, because it would take all his time to do that job right. Later, he relented, taking over much of Fritz Reiner's work when Reiner left to take charge of the Chicago Symphony, and became a distinguished if little publicized member of the permanent roster until he himself departed to become conductor of the Cincinnati Symphony.

Following Ziegler's death, Johnson had tried several business managers: Eric Clarke, who left to work in Allied Military Government in Germany; then Julius Seebach, a broadcasting executive who returned to broadcasting; finally Reginald Allen, former manager of the Philadelphia Orchestra, a man whose sober mien and bland manner concealed not only a passion for Gilbert and Sullivan but also a strong competitive instinct (he had been a national collegiate doubles champion in tennis). During Bing's year as visitor, Allen had been working his way through a mare's nest of bad bookkeeping and had begun developing a system by which the company

---

Roberta Peters made an unscheduled debut in *Don Giovanni* as a last-minute replacement for Nadine Conner—her first appearance on any stage. Patrons who saw the announcement in the lobby had no reason to fret. She performed like a veteran and became an invaluable member of the company for over three decades.

would be able to keep track of both its expenses as incurred and its receipts as collected. Bing kept him; he would eventually become the prime conduit in the company's labor relations and in managing the liaison between the new Met and its new landlord, Lincoln Center.

For the vital post of stage director, Bing hung on to Désiré Defrère, a former singer who had been Johnson's all-purpose *régisseur*, because he knew he would need someone who could put a performance on stage, fast, without spending too much of the board's money. Defrère had skills without talent; but he successfully moved people from here to there. Bing remembered that in later years, "whenever news of a financial crisis would run round the house, Defrère would come to me earnestly to urge that I abandon at least some of those time-consuming and expensive stage rehearsals we had whenever we were putting on a new production or mounting an older one for its first appearance of the season."

Bing needed a new stage manager to get his new productions on the boards and do something, somehow, about the old ones. With some help from acquaintances on Broadway, he chose Horace Armistead, who was a babe in the woods in the intricacies of the Met's union contracts. After three years of costs suspiciously higher than they should have been, the board with Bing's reluctant consent asked for a report on backstage operations from a very young summer-theater technical consultant named Herman Krawitz, a tough dese-dem-'n'dose New Yorker who related more easily to the crew than to the general manager. He had been recommended by Broadway's experienced Richard Aldrich through Anthony Bliss, son of the late chairman of the Association and a Wall Street lawyer. Bliss had come onto the board on his father's death and had been slotted into the labor relations committee, which was considered a good place for a young man who had never taken much interest in opera and who thought he should learn something about how the place operated if he was to serve as a director.

Krawitz brought back a number of critical reports that Bing resented until he realized that the diagnoses were coming with suggested cures, at which point he took Krawitz into management. Thereafter Krawitz was the great facilitator of the house, managing relations between the technical crews and the designers of the theater's physical productions, supervising the planning for the new house when that time came, utterly loyal and hugely useful to Bing. He also developed (but never insisted on) his own aesthetic judgments. Because he knew more than anyone else about the subjects of direct concern to the board, he later became assistant secretary, present at meetings of the executive committee and the board whether Bing himself was there or not.

After the opening weeks' *Don Carlo* and *Fledermaus* had made their success, Bing decided another new production could be added to the season—*Cav* and *Pag*, which in their existing form traced back to 1924; the former had been presented 138 times in its battered sets, the later 180 times. Neither had been given in the previous three seasons, in large part because all those trips to and from the warehouse had left the fabric tattered. Armistead said he could do new productions cheap, and indeed he did—for only $22,041, including directors' fees. The results were universally disliked, opening another facet of Bing's personality: both privately and publicly he blasted the press for its negative attitude toward the "modern" approach to opera production.

The aftermath of this brief squall would plague Bing through the entire 22 years of his administration, for the violent defense of the new *Cav* and *Pag* cast doubt both on his taste and on his judgment. The real source of the problem was never recognized on either side. Bing knew perfectly well that the *Cav-Pag* was what he later called "a bargain-basement, inadequate production," and in his memoirs he revealed that Bruno Walter had sent him a "Dear Friend" letter warning him that such low-grade stuff would not go in New York. But what had been touched was Bing's need to give (and receive) loyalty.

Bing simply did not respect the critics, sometimes with reason (criticizing the version of *Don Carlo* used on opening night, for example, Olin Downes in the *New York Times* complained about the absence of the "bright and joyous" first act, which is in fact devoted mostly to the miseries of the French peasantry suffering the devastations of war and which expresses musically from the start the doomed nature of the love between Elisabetta and Don Carlo). But Bing's feeling of cultural superiority to the press was shallowly rooted in his own personality and in traditional European attitudes toward America, not in reality. He must always have been like George Orwell's friend who knew he was a genius long before he knew what he was a genius *at*. Bing had no university training—indeed, no academic or scholarly background of any kind. In those early years at the Met, he relied heavily for musical opinion on Max Rudolf, and for general culture on his old friend John Gutman, formerly a music critic in Berlin, who left a commercial job in New York to become his assistant and intellectual conscience, preparing each year lists of books Bing should—but did not—read on his summer vacation.

The press sensed more than it knew of Bing's buried insecurities. There is always a clash between the man preaching from a newspaper column (who must struggle to remember that he has an opinion because he is paid to have an opinion, not because he is always right), and the producer whose presentation the critic is paid to evaluate (who knows how desperately hard it was to get the results as good as they are). In Bing's case, the conflict was heightened by his supercilious manner, his deeply felt need to defend not himself but those who worked for him, and his refusal to participate in the life of the city any more than his job required.

In much of this he was like Gatti, who also lived in New York all but exclusively at the opera house (defended by his inability to speak English). He was like Gatti

Overleaf: Two other admirable productions from the early Bing years. *Carmen* (*left*) was directed by Tyrone Guthrie, with the title role sung by Risë Stevens, pictured (*inset*) with Guthrie (kneeling) and designer Rolf Gérard. *Così fan tutte* (*right*) benefited from the deft staging of actor-director Alfred Lunt, seen (*inset*) conferring with Blanche Thebom and Eleanor Steber, as the two sisters. Patrice Munsel sang the maid Despina.

too—and to its credit the press never failed to recognize the fact—in that he knew how to run an opera house. From the beginning, he brought a new standard of planning to the work of the company. Every year, he was earlier in completing his work of organizing the following season, until toward the end he was operating two and three years ahead of the actual productions of the house. Much of what he wished to accomplish turned out to be impossible—his early insistence on negotiating artists' contracts by the week rather than by the performance, for example, which would have greatly increased his casting flexibility, was soon frustrated by the economic conditions of the market for vocal talent (and in the end his record in keeping casts together proved little better than Johnson's). Except for Reiner in the first years and Mitropoulos in the brief period between his retirement from the Philharmonic and his illness, Bing was never able to persuade great conductors to take the entire season in his opera house, but he tried and tried and tried.

Something else should be said by someone who spent as much time with Rudolf Bing as I did (as his collaborator on the first volume of his memoirs, *5000 Nights at the Opera*). He was a decent and straightforward and by his own lights utterly honest man. And he had a first-rate sense of humor. He got into trouble in part because he could not keep from saying what he thought (and his gift of repartee gave his comments wide publicity), in part because a faulty sensitivity to others led him to compose wrong-headed scenarios of how they would react to actions or statements on his part. I used to say that when you stripped the mask off Rudolf Bing, you found an identical Bing underneath. The loyalties he gave were often reciprocated—certainly by Herman Krawitz, John Gutman, Reginald Allen, Francis Robinson, Max Rudolf and Rudolf's successor, Robert Herman, as also by Guthrie, Barrault, the designer Rolf Gérard, and many others. His belief that he ran a happy ship—and his distress when the press and to some degree the board failed to share that belief—derived from the fact that the people he saw most often *were* happy. And in the years after his retirement, many artists who had thought they hated his guts found that they missed him.

As early as the first weeks, Bing received conclusive evidence that his attempt to mix theatrical and operatic direction would not always work smoothly. Garson Kanin and Fritz Reiner came into nasty disagreement about how Johann Strauss's *Die Fledermaus* should go. Worse, Reiner had recorded highlights of the opera for RCA Victor even though the Met had a contract to record "original casts" for Columbia Records, which was advancing the house each year more than the royalties earned on the albums—and which had agreed to lend $50,000 to start a young touring company of *Fledermaus*, the loan to be repaid only out of the profits of the tour (which in the end lost money). Obviously, the original-cast recording of *Fledermaus* would lose much of its value if the original conductor was not in charge, and Columbia was upset. Bing made the first of what would be many demonstrations of how quick on his feet he could be if necessary: he went secretly to Eugene Ormandy and the board of the Philadelphia Orchestra, which was also under contract to Columbia, and arranged to have Ormandy take over the *Fledermaus* in the last week of rehearsals. This was a considerable gamble: Ormandy had never before conducted a staged opera, and somehow (it was hard to believe) had never even seen a performance of *Die Fledermaus*—and Reiner might quit the house altogether. Like so many (if not all) of Bing's subsequent gambles, this one paid off splendidly. Ormandy conducted a finely gauged *Fledermaus*, and Reiner—who was going to have a chance to conduct Flagstad in *Tristan*—remained. Ormandy enjoyed himself: he came back the next season to do *Fledermaus* again.

The first years of the Bing regime were devoted mostly to replacing or repairing the badly beat-up physical circumstances of Met productions. Rolf Gérard, who had done *Don Carlo* and *Fledermaus* the first season, became virtually a house designer in the second, creating sets for *Aida* (directed by Margaret Webster; an opening night for Zinka Milanov, and a debut night for George London as a savage yet regal Amonasro, dark of voice and dominating); *Così fan tutte* (a near relation to Gérard's production at Glyndebourne, elegantly directed by Alfred Lunt); and *Carmen* (for Risë Stevens, the company's biggest box-office draw, especially on tour; directed by Tyrone Guthrie, an old friend of Bing's from wartime London). A very distinguished scenic artist came to the Met for the first time this season, when Eugene Berman created sets and costumes for *Rigoletto*, setting it in the century of the Victor Hugo story rather than in the earlier period the censors had required of Verdi. Herbert Graf directed, and the handsome Viennese soprano Hilde Gueden made her American debut as Gilda; Warren repeated what was already the world's best Rigoletto, Tucker sang sumptuously as the Duke, Bing's friend Erede conducted convincingly, and Olin Downes proclaimed the result "one of the most interesting and exciting interpretations of the work that we have seen, . . . a freshly conceived and highly dramatic presentation of the music."

Berman returned as the designer for the next season's opening-night *Forza del destino* in an edition drastically cut by Fritz Stiedry; Milanov, Tucker, and Warren again, with Siepi assuming the dignity of Padre Guardiano as a truly magnificent partner to Milanov in the "Vergine degli Angeli" scene. Gérard very successfully set a new production of *La Bohème*, done in a rather unfortunate English translation that was quickly dropped. The third new production of the season was Bing's first American premiere, Stravinsky's *The Rake's Progress*, conducted (not entirely to Stravinsky's satisfaction) by the composer's old friend Fritz Reiner, directed (not entirely to the critics' satisfaction) by the choreographer George Balanchine. Horace Armistead did the sets, librettist W. H. Auden being on the outs with Berman.

This was the season Charles Elson began what became almost a career of stripping down and refreshing the old sets Joseph Urban had done for Gatti; the first opera "elsonized," as Bing liked to say, was *Lohengrin*. A little money was also found to refurbish a *Boris Godunov* production that went back before World War I and had been hard used (Gatti loved the opera). George London, who would later sing the role at the Bolshoi, was the first Boris. But London's great triumph of this season was as Don Giovanni, Reiner conducting, a characterization that combined physical attraction and an unusual degree of menace (heightened by a sly and bullied Leporello from the Viennese Erich Kunz), stimulating an enthusiastic but rather embarrassing review from Virgil Thomson, who hailed what he considered "the best pair of male legs on Broadway."

In the 1953–54 season Bing attained the watershed of his ambitions for the Met's physical productions: more than half of what the company offered was in settings created in the four years of his administration. The season opened with a new *Faust* designed by Gérard, with Peter Brook directing a rather nutty conception set in the 19th century, but with a cast of De los Angeles, Bjoerling, Merrill, and Nicola Rossi-Lemeni (a debut) to sing the leading roles grandly. The conductor was Pierre Monteux—Bing's accomplishment: he had read in the paper that Monteux was retiring from the San Francisco Symphony and had simply written him a letter to his summer home inquiring whether he might be lured back to the Met after a generation away.

Tannhäuser in the Dresden version was the season's other new production, again with Gérard sets, a cast that looked all right on paper but did not blend to the satisfaction of George Szell or the critics. It was kept together for three performances, then gutted in a fourth, after which Szell announced he was leaving the Met for reasons he would be glad to tell the Met's board but no one else. Someone said sorrowfully that George Szell was his own worst enemy. To which Bing retorted, "Not while I am alive."

Through these four seasons there were other debuts of considerable importance to the future of the house: Mildred Miller, a wonderfully boyish and lyrical Cherubino; Theodor Uppman, a specialty baritone whose light voice and stage presence meant much for Pelléas (his debut role), Papageno, Masetto, and Paquillo in Cyril Ritchard's later staging of Offenbach's *La Périchole*; Lisa della Casa, who started as the Countess in *Figaro* and brought unusual beauty and a handsome voice to a mostly Viennese repertory; Charles Anthony (né Caruso), who made his debut as the Simpleton in *Boris* in 1954 and was still singing at the Met 30 seasons later; and James McCracken, a product of Indiana University's opera workshop, who began in the *comprimario* roster and was instantly spotted by Noel Straus of the *New York*

Times for his "big, firm tones" in the virtually invisible and inaudible role of Parpignol in *La Bohème*. Bing was not so perceptive as Straus: McCracken had to make a career abroad before he was offered leading roles at the Met.

The next four seasons would see debuts of capital importance to the house—Dimitri Mitropoulos on the podium (first for *Salome*, with Christel Goltz making a debut in the title role); Renata Tebaldi as Desdemona (in a blonde wig that Bing personally begged her not to wear, beginning a pattern of two decades in which a lovely and beloved artist would maintain an image of not being a prima donna at all against a reality of absolutely always getting her own way); Maria Callas as Norma. Carlo Bergonzi would arrive miscast in his first season as Radames and Manrico, roles that his essentially lyric voice (despite its baritone beginnings) would grow to encompass only later. Never a box-office celebrity, Bergonzi nonetheless received the ultimate tribute from management: he was in the early 1960s the most highly paid male singer in the company, second only to Nilsson in the pay book.

Rudolf Kempe came and—alas!—went, after giving Bing and the Metropolitan a superbly felt American premiere of Richard Strauss's *Arabella*. Wolfgang Windgassen, the era's prime *heldentenor* already a little past his prime, came with Martha Mödl, a Wagnerian soprano who could act, for a *Ring* cycle planned for Kempe, necessarily left in the hands of an increasingly deaf Stiedry when Kempe called in sick. Thomas Schippers at age 25 conducted *Don Pasquale* and would remain with the company, taking occasional seasons off to work at La Scala, until his premature death. Tito Gobbi made the first of a number of brief visits. Ettore Bastianini came as Germont, and returned annually until his career was cut off by throat cancer. Antonietta Stella made a debut as, in Howard Taubman's words, "an Aida well above the average," a ranking she maintained for many seasons. Irene Dalis was given a gambling chance with a debut as Eboli in *Don Carlo*, and won. Nicolai Gedda began his more-than-quarter-century contribution of the most intelligent vocal artistry in the company.

An all-American cast made an English translation comprehensible when Bruno Walter returned to conduct a *Magic Flute* in the Mozart bicentennial year, in a new production designed by Harry Horner. Karl Böhm made his debut conducting a new *Don Giovanni*, with baroque Berman designs and a cast of Siepi, Fernando Corena, Cesare Valletti, Uppman, Giorgio Tozzi, Steber, Della Casa, and Peters—material for a universally acclaimed performance. There was a world premiere—Bing's first—of Samuel Barber's *Vanessa*, to a libretto by Gian Carlo Menotti (who also directed), in a visual setting by Cecil Beaton and a musical realization by Dimitri Mitropoulos. The Russian-Swedish Gedda gave a lesson in how to pronounce and sing English, and Rosalind Elias and Steber and Tozzi sang handsomely, but Barber's lyricism was wasted on a story that could never work up anyone's interest. That same year (1957–58), *Butterfly* was restaged with fine panache by the Japanese

Overleaf: Stars of the 1950s. Renata Tebaldi and a prostrate George London at the climax of *Tosca* Act II (*left, above*); Lisa della Casa at the Coachmen's Ball in *Arabella* (*left, below*); Mario del Monaco in *Pagliacci* (*opposite page, top*); Victoria de los Angeles in *Martha* (*above right*); Fernando Corena in *Barbiere* (*below right*); Hermann Uhde ministering to Paul Franke's Captain in *Wozzeck* (*below left*).

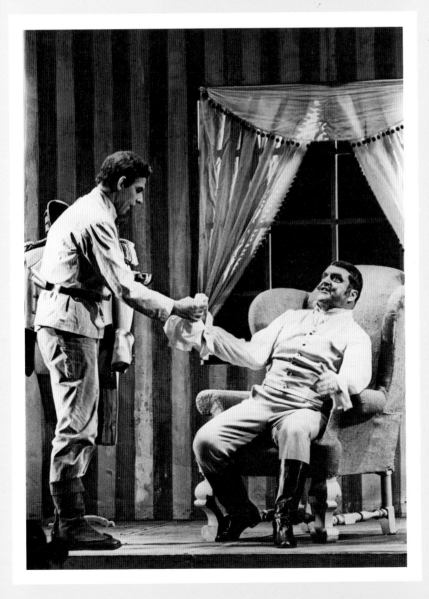

director Yoshio Aoyama and designer Motohiro Nagasaka, giving authenticity to Belasco's very American fantasy.

The most publicized of the debuts in Bing's early seasons was none of these, however. That distinction was reserved for the first appearance at the Met, in 1955, of Marian Anderson, the company's first black singer—fourteen years after Cravath wrote Ziegler he "would think" she was "vocally worthy of a hearing at the Metropolitan." Bing's brilliant choice for her was Ulrica in Verdi's *Ballo in maschera*, one of few true contralto roles in Italian opera, requiring presence and dignity in one large dimension rather than any developed acting skill. It was too late for Anderson to do more than contribute a symbolic presence to the quality of a Met performance, but she carried that off with complete professionalism, despite a foul-up in the communications system between stage and pit that had Mitropoulos starting the prelude to her scene before the stage was ready. George Sloan, in his last year as chairman of the Met board, was not Cravath; he offered no congratulations to Bing on his decision to bring a black artist to the Met.

In general, Bing's relations with his board during his first half-dozen years were far from close. Spofford, who was a musician as well as a lawyer and whom Bing had most liked of those he met in spring 1949, had been appointed by President Truman as American delegate to the NATO Council before Bing took over, and had disappeared from New York. Sloan served in Bing's first year as both chairman and president, contributing to the annual statement a warning that unless the Federal government relieved the Met from admissions tax (then running $550,000 a year) "the prospects for the continuance of the Metropolitan Opera beyond the coming season are extremely doubtful." Though Bing's first season had witnessed a gain of $400,000 in box-office receipts (and almost $200,000 in contributions), he was running an "expensive" opera house: his losses that year were $462,000 after contributions. The next year, the Met got its tax relief, sold the house to 97 per cent of capacity for the New York season (adding another $400,000 to box-office receipts)—and lost $369,000 anyway.

Sloan had come to the Met as a fund-raiser; he was a believer in the opera house as a social institution. He had raised $750,000 for Bing in his first season, and was appalled at the notion that he would have to go back for more after only two years. He did it, though, and raised $1.5 million—almost half of it for continuing improvements in the house (including the removal of the ring of Orchestra Circle seats and their replacement by an extension of the normal orchestra rows, which added 164 seats, increasing potential revenues by more than $200,00 a year). The $850,000 left from the drive to pay Bing's annual deficits then withered away— $220,000 (after $205,000 in annual contributions) in 1952–53, $218,000 (after $136,000 in contributions) in 1953–54, $337,000 (after $198,000 in contributions) in 1954–55.

Bing had struggled to increase the Met's income through the sale of its services. From the beginning, he had removed opening night from the subscription package, offering it at advanced prices as part of a "three firsts" series (the others being the premiere of *Fledermaus* and the Walter-Flagstad *Fidelio*). He cut the money-losing day trips to Philadelphia down to five a year, and began a Tuesday night series in New York. He worked out deals to present Met performances in closed-circuit theater television; arranged contracts with Ed Sullivan's "Toast of the Town" show and, when that failed, with the Ford Foundation for its "Omnibus" series. He changed comptrollers three times in four years until he found the man who could give him adequate control of his figures (Robert Stringer, who joined in 1953–54). He got directors and designers to work for ridiculously low prices—Lunt did *Così* for $2,000; Ritchard as late as 1956–57 did *Périchole* for $3,500, including expenses on trips from London; Berman designed the sets and costumes for *Barbiere* for $2,600. He held the line on a $1,000 top for singers by manipulating the Met's access to other, more lucrative engagements for them. He took the blame for the avoidance of contemporary scores. But he would not give up new productions or the rehearsal time for them. He budgeted for losses, and expected the board to find the money.

There is little question that Sloan wanted Bing gone, but he could not carry his board. Bing had made the Met exciting again, and newsworthy. Mrs. Belmont approved, and so did the members of her Guild, and she was prepared to shoulder more weight, forming a National Council to improve annual giving. The faction that said the money could be raised if necessary was triumphant on the board. In spring 1955, Bing's contract was renewed through 1959. Sloan resigned (and died shortly thereafter). With support from Spofford, who had returned, and from Mrs. Belmont, the relatively youthful Anthony Bliss ("I was fourteen years younger than any other member of the board") was elected president, and Lauder Greenway, who had been chairman of the Guild, became chairman of the board. In 1955–56, Bing hit on the device that would assure his freedom to plan new productions, when Mrs. John D. Rockefeller, Jr., made a special grant to the Met for Harry Horner's *Magic Flute*, the first of many productions she (especially) and others would give to the Metropolitan.

And the figures turned around in Bing's honeymoon years with Bliss. Contributions rose to $510,000 in 1956–57, $553,000 in 1957–58, $531,000 in the 75th anniversary year. The loss after contributions dropped to $95,000 in 1956–57, and in 1957–58 to a virtual break-even (the loss was $268). In the anniversary season, the Metropolitan would make money for the first time since 1946–47—only $3,149, but that was reason enough for celebration.

☆ ☆ ☆

Overleaf: The ubiquitous Mr. Bing—serving coffee to operagoers waiting on line for opening night (*left*), discussing a vital contractual clause with Renata Tebaldi's poodle (*right, above*), and sharing a good story with his genial assistant manager Francis Robinson (*right, below*).

Two typical Bing gestures opened the anniversary season of 1958–59. He told his annual pre-season press conference that he had to look for new artists (including American artists) in European opera houses because in the United States "there is no opera worth speaking of, outside New York . . . unrehearsed, shoddy performances with no production and bad scenery." This was particularly ungracious at the start of a season that was to feature Tebaldi (who had sung in both San Francisco and Chicago before coming to New York) and Callas (whom Bing had wooed away from Chicago with a widely photographed contract-signing in her Chicago dressing room, and who was currently starring in Dallas productions more lavish than anything on Bing's calendar). Irving Kolodin in his syndicated newspaper column thought Bing's comment a deliberate performance, "fanning the fires of interest, if nothing else"; but in fact he had spoken from the hip as well as from the heart. Kurt Adler in San Francisco, who had local political problems enough without this slap from New York, complained bitterly and invited Bing to come sample his wares. In collaboration with Francis Robinson and others, Bing crafted the following telegram of reply:

THANK YOU KIND INVITATION GREATLY REGRET UNABLE COME SANFRANCISCO THIS YEAR BUT AM OF COURSE FULLY AWARE OF YOUR COMPANY'S EXCELLENCE. WHILE I BELIEVE MUCH OF WHAT I SAID IS CORRECT I HAVE PARTICULARLY MENTIONED SANFRANCISCO AND CHICAGO AS EXCEPTIONS BUT TOTALLY IGNORANT INTERVIEWER AS USUAL MISQUOTED MOST OF IT. REGARDS.

The other gesture was equally spontaneous. From his first season, Bing had honored the enthusiasts of the Met audience by personally serving coffee to those waiting on line to buy standing-room tickets for opening-night. This year, arriving on a cold and rainy Saturday afternoon for the dress rehearsal of the opening-night *Tosca*, Bing noted twenty drenched young opera lovers on line 56 hours before curtain time, and took more effective pity. He had them admitted to the rehearsal and seated in the Opera Club box—after which, being opera lovers, they resumed their places on line. It was also typical of Bing that he would not take the time to meet his beneficiaries when they asked if they could somehow say a quick thankyou.

This *Tosca* marked Tebaldi's return to the Met after a year away mourning the sudden death of her mother, who had been a constant companion on all her travels. Del Monaco was her very assertive Cavaradossi, clearly the wrong choice to be part of a conspiracy; George London was her heavy and evil Scarpia. Mitropoulos conducted, whipping up climaxes but permitting Tebaldi her own tempo and her extraordinarily musical phrasing in "Vissi d'arte." *Time* Magazine gave the Met's anniversary a cover, and put Tebaldi's picture on it (probably worsening Callas's mood in Dallas, for the dislike between the two of them was real). For her opening night performance, Tebaldi wore real diamonds, some her own, some borrowed.

Leonard Warren was a virtually exclusive Met artist from the day of his debut as Paolo in *Simon Boccanegra*, January 13, 1939, to his death on stage, March 4, 1960. He had sung the title role of Boccanegra in Margaret Webster's new production, pictured here, just three days before that final appearance in another Verdi work, *La Forza del destino*.

The first new production of the season was a *Cav* and *Pag* with Gérard sets, José Quintero taking the works more seriously than most directors do, persuading Del Monaco to try some new tricks as Canio, and giving Amara a new self-image as an actress: "Some magic on Mr. Quintero's part," Winthrop Sargeant wrote in the *New Yorker*, "had overcome Lucine Amara's customary placidity of temperament and turned her into a wild and passionate Nedda." On December 22, concertmaster Raymond Gniewek earned a place in Met history by taking the baton from a suddenly ill Fausto Cleva and continuing Act III of Puccini's *Manon Lescaut* (Tebaldi was singing the lady) until assistant conductor George Schick could make his way to the pit.

Then came the controversy-ridden *Macbeth*, with Rysanek very well received (deservedly) and the production not very well received (also deservedly). What Ebert and Neher had given Bing, Irving Kolodin remarked in the *Saturday Review*, was "a revival of a revival," its crowd scenes and somewhat timid social comment not well suited to the attitudes of the 1950s, though they might have done somewhat better ten years later. Mitropoulos had suffered a heart attack less than two weeks before the premiere, with the work already in rehearsal, and Leinsdorf jumped into the breach, as he had when Bodanzky died nineteen years before, with musical results that were effective in the first performance and grew in value as the cast was kept together virtually unchanged for five more performances (Barry Morell, in his Met debut year, replaced Bergonzi as Macduff the last time).

The event of the anniversary year turned out to be the Metropolitan's first performance of Alban Berg's *Wozzeck*, which Bing had in effect promised before his first season, when he listed the opera as one of his ten favorites. It was a truly celebratory occasion for that fraction of the Met audience whose interest in opera transcended an interest in voices. Karl Böhm was a master of the score, knowing in his bones that it was a juicy post-Romantic work rather than something starkly "modern," and the orchestra played with opulence and fire. Hermann Uhde, who had been singing the Wagner repertory and the Grand Inquisitor in *Don Carlo* since his debut in 1955, had the voice, the crew-cut appearance, the acting skills, and thanks to his heritage (he was the son of a German father and an American mother) the linguistic and cultural resources to sing an English translation and make the German "little man" fully comprehensible to an American audience. Eleanor Steber contributed an affecting Marie; Karl Dönch, who made his debut that season as Beckmesser, was a superbly slimy Doctor; Paul Franke, an expressively self-important Captain (whose acclaim for Wozzeck as "a worthy man" rang in the ears for days afterward); Kurt Baum, the company's utility tenor through many of these years, was an aggressive and in Marie's terms glamorous Drum Major. Caspar Neher's sets, again drawn from the German 1920s, were a splendidly suitable doll's house on a platform, expanding to a projected background in the sinister place of reeds, easily changeable during Berg's powerful interludes. Herbert Graf put it all together: the glory was his too.

That the production did not make money seems irrelevant—it came back several times in later years, retaining its strength in Colin Davis's matter-of-fact musical presentation and James Levine's expressionist emphasis. In fact, the Guild benefit opening night, while far from sold out (those in attendance, making a stir, included Marilyn Monroe with her husband Arthur Miller), did return a profit of $16,000 for the production fund; and the other four performances were well attended.

Vocally, this was a season that looked ahead. There were announcements in the newspaper that the Met had signed the Canadian tenor Jon Vickers and the Swedish soprano Birgit Nilsson, who would make their debuts the next season. Teresa Stratas won the Metropolitan Opera auditions, now off the air and a responsibility of the volunteers of Mrs. Belmont's National Council. In the anniversary season itself, there were two debuts of artists who still were with the company in the centenary season: Mignon Dunn, who started in the *comprimario* cast as the Nurse in *Boris*; and Cornell MacNeil, who started on top in more ways than one, displaying his splendid upper register as a substitute for Robert Merrill in *Rigoletto*.

This anniversary season was the year that Edward Johnson died, the obituaries in the New York papers crediting him with bringing American singers to the Met. And it was the year the commitment was firmly, definitely, irrevocably made to the construction of a new opera house in Lincoln Center. On May 14, 1959, President Dwight D. Eisenhower came to New York and before an audience of 20,000—the Philharmonic playing, Leonard Bernstein conducting, the 200-voice Juilliard School choir singing—the President himself turned a shovel of earth and acclaimed the planned Center as "a mighty influence for peace and understanding throughout the world."

EIGHT

Vale atque Ave:
The Move to Lincoln Center

The man who got a new home for the Metropolitan was Charles M. Spofford. A musician as well as a lawyer, he had come to the Met board in the mid-1930s and was put in charge of liaison with Fiorello H. La Guardia on the mayor's recurring dream of a music center. "La Guardia," Spofford said some years later, "wanted to leave New York two legacies, an airfield and a music center, a home for the opera. We had talks with him about a new Met and a hall for an associated orchestra, hopefully the Philharmonic. In 1939 we had several meetings in the summer City Hall out at the World's Fair."

What Spofford wanted was a Metropolitan Opera *inside* Central Park (as the Metropolitan Museum is), at Columbus Circle. La Guardia was tempted, but Robert Moses, the state and city parks commissioner, talked him out of it. "I think the Mayor buried the plan," Moses said a quarter of a century later, "because of some comments I made about the boxholders." At La Guardia's urging, the Cornelius Bliss-Wardwell-Spofford committee, which was reporting to the Opera Association on the feasibility of acquiring the old Met from the boxholders, looked also at an auditorium then known as Mecca Temple on West 55th Street, which La Guardia thought might be convertible to multi-purpose year-round performing use—as indeed it was, rechristened "City Center," after falling into the city's hands for nonpayment of taxes a few years later. But the stage and the facilities here were even worse than they were at 39th Street.

When Spofford returned from the war and became president of the Association (Anthony Bliss recalls that his father insisted on stepping down to make way for Spofford, fearing that otherwise the Met might lose him), he made the quest for a new theater a continuing item of business. He began a permanent "New House Committee," chaired by C. D. Jackson, a vice-president of Time, Inc., who had been in the construction business as a young man. Spofford was still pushing for the Central Park site, and had access to La Guardia's successor, Mayor William O'Dwyer, with whom he had served in Italy, but again Moses put up the barriers. Then Congress passed the Federal Housing Act of 1949, with its "Title I" program to promote "urban renewal," permitting local authorities to mix cultural and

---

Saturday, April 16, 1966: the famous gold curtain in the old Met descends for the last time as artists and audience wave farewell.

Overleaf: Passing pedestrians on Broadway examine cast listings for the week of December 5, 1960. The old house was by then a relic from another era.

OPERA ASSOCIATION, Inc.

METROPOLITAN
OPERA
WEDNESDAY EVENING DECEMBER 7 AT 8 P.M
SUBSCRIPTION PERFORMANCE
NEW PRODUCTION
GIUSEPPE VERDI
NABUCCO

METROPOLITAN
OPERA
MONDAY EVENING DECEMBER 5 AT 8 P.M
SUBSCRIPTION PERFORMANCE
WOLFGANG AMADEUS MOZART
LE NOZZE DI FIGARO

METROPOLITAN
OPERA
THURSDAY EVENING. DECEMBER 8 AT 8 P.M
SUBSCRIPTION PERFORMANCE
NEW PRODUCTION
GAETANO DONIZETTI
L'ELISIR
D'AMORE
CONDUCTOR FAUSTO CLEVA
STAGED BY NATHANIEL MERRILL
SETS AND COSTUMES DESIGNED BY ROBERT O'HEARN
ADINA   ELISABE
NEMORINO   DINO F
SERGEANT BELCORE FRANK
DOCTOR DULCAMARA FER
GIANNETTA   M
CHOREOGRAPHY BY
CHORUS MAST

educational facilities with their housing programs and still qualify for federal subsidy of land costs. Moses became head of the city's redevelopment corporation. Obviously, the presence of the Metropolitan Opera House in a neighborhood would change people's perceptions of a site that might otherwise be hard to sell to an upper-middle-income public as a nice place to live. There was now something the Met could do for Moses; as Spofford put it, "we got on Moses's Title I mailing list."

Meanwhile, Spofford commissioned a study by Ebasco Services on the feasibility of a new house. The assumption of the study was that the demand for opera had outrun the supply of tickets at the Metropolitan Opera House: "Between the 1942–43 and 1946–47 seasons . . . the percentage of seating capacity represented by subscriptions increased from $27\frac{1}{2}$ per cent to 60 per cent. The proportion of total capacity placed by window-ticket sales declined from 55 per cent to $37\frac{1}{2}$ . . . In view of the fact that the house has played to virtually [*sic*] capacity . . . and that there have been long lines of box office ticket-seekers for many popular performances, the Opera management recognizes an active need of providing additional seating capacity." The figures thus were calculated on the basis of a 4,500-seat house with an average sale at 90 per cent of capacity. An air-conditioned house could be rented for summer performances . . . All in all, the consultants concluded, as consultants usually do, the thing was feasible—provided the site was inexpensive. "When you began seeing where the plots of land were," Spofford said, "you knew the only way you could do it was Title I."

Moses first suggested a large block south of Washington Square, but Jackson decided—after distributing questionnaires to Met audiences—that the location wouldn't work. "Too tricky," he said, "too expensive, too remote." Moses next came up with the right spot—Columbus Circle again, but across from the park—and then suddenly withdrew it (telling the newspapers before he told the Met), because he wanted the site for his trade-show Coliseum.

"There was never any chance of an opera house at the Coliseum," Moses said airily some years later. "Nobody really took it seriously." Jackson disagreed: "I took it seriously enough to get half a million dollars out of John D. Rockefeller, Jr., as a pledge to buy the land." Lamely, the Met explained that the problem was the size of the structure needed for an opera house, which would not leave enough space on the site for the housing that had to be part of the plan to qualify under Title I. But the Coliseum and its associated office building were, in fact, larger than the opera house would have been. It was Moses. At that stage in his astonishing career, he gaveth and he tooketh away, and nobody could explain why.

The majority of the board, Jackson recalled, was against a new house anyway: "a combination of nostalgia and conservatism," he said. The 1952–53 fund-raising drive was premised on continuation in the old house, with $650,000 of the receipts budgeted to make it more habitable.

Then, late in 1953, Moses gave again—this time, a piece of the largest slum-clearance program he ever planned, running for half a mile just north and west of the Coliseum site, where Columbus Avenue and Broadway crossed at Lincoln Square. It was the original Puerto Rican arrival site in New York, decayed, depressed, and overcrowded. Moses offered it by telephone to Joseph Hartfield, an extraordinary little man (four and a half feet tall) who had risen on a combination of brains, judgment, and charm to be senior partner of the Wall Street law firm of White & Case and chairman of the executive committee of the Met in the Spofford days. Hartfield and Spofford rode the subway together to 66th Street with the architect Max Abramowitz to look at the land. "Somebody," Abramowitz recalled, "said, 'What a hell of a neighborhood!' But here was all that land, for virtually nothing."

Moving to Columbus Circle was one thing; moving to this god-forsaken slum, however close to Columbus Circle, was something else. The Met board wrangled for more than a year over Moses' offer, until finally, in April 1955, he threatened to withdraw it and to take the Met off the list of potential Title I recipients. At this point, Hartfield pressed into service his partner Irving Olds, chairman of the board of U.S. Steel and a member of the Met board. Olds and Spofford undertook to raise the money, and they alerted Wallace K. Harrison, who had been designing a new house for the Met since the Rockefeller Center days, to give them a design they could use for fund-raising.

This project might have got no farther than all the others except for an extraneous event: a New York real estate developer named Louis Glickman bought Carnegie Hall and announced that he planned to tear it down and put an office building on the corner of 57th Street and Seventh Avenue. In three years, the Philharmonic was told, the orchestra would have to find a new place to play its concerts. Philharmonic chairman Arthur Houghton (of Corning Glass) and president David Keiser (of Cuban-American Sugar) began looking at possible sites for a new concert hall. They too approached Wallace Harrison, and he brought the Met and the Philharmonic together. Spofford and Houghton dined at the Knickerbocker Club in early summer 1955 and reached two conclusions: first, that they could go farther together than either could separately; and second, that they needed a Rockefeller. Both were members of the Council on Foreign Relations, as were most of the Rockefellers. They went down to a conference on world problems at the Inn at Buck Hill Falls in Pennsylvania, where John D. Rockefeller III was in attendance, and laid their suggestions before him.

The Rockefeller family had already made a corporate decision that its foundation should take an interest in the performing arts, and that John III should be the family representative. Rockefeller, who was nothing if not thorough, now sounded out some of the people with whom he had already been in contact on their views of the desirability of a new music center. One of the most enthusiastic was Lincoln

Overleaf: The Golden Age of Bing. Leontyne Price and Franco Corelli in *Trovatore* (*left*), with (*above*) Nicolai Gedda and Anna Moffo in *Manon*. Birgit Nilsson pulling out all the stops as Isolde (*right*), with (*inset*) Leonie Rysanek as Senta in *Der fliegende Holländer*.

Kirstein, who played financial, managerial, and artistic roles at the New York City Ballet, and who was appalled at the concrete-base floor on which his company had to dance at the City Center. At his suggestion, Rockefeller added a ballet theater to the plans—and there followed a repertory theater, a library-museum, and an educational facility (originally offered to Columbia University, which did not want it, now occupied by the Juilliard School). Following the reorganization of spring 1955 that had saved Bing's job and put Lauder Greenway and Anthony Bliss in charge of the Met (with Spofford returning to office as chairman of the executive committee), the Met was ready and willing to go along. That autumn, the board contributed Spofford and Jackson and Olds to an "exploratory committee" formed with John D. Rockefeller III in the chair; and Bing began to make an input.

In November 1955, Bing detailed in an internal office memorandum what would be necessary in a new house—the side stages and elevators, fly gallery, stage equipment, electrical equipment, workshops, storage facilities, rehearsal rooms, dressing rooms, lavatories and showers ("Good washing and shower facilities are important for the ballet as quite frequently they have to use heavy body-make-up"); loading and unloading docks (the peculiar horror of the old building having been the need to stack scenery and costumes on the street in all weathers as the trucks navigated Seventh Avenue); offices for stage departments and administration; entrances ("The present stage door arrangements can be taken as an example of what should not be"); p.a. systems; details of the orchestra pit ("easy plugging-in arrangements for the many lightweight music stands should be considered . . . Another important question concerning the pit is the organ console which should be installed in the pit"); first-aid rooms; box-office accommodations; press office ("a kind of green room for the reporters where they can leave their hats and coats as they are usually too stingy to check them").

Bing also tried to put an end to the 4,500-seat hypothesis: "I feel that, with very rare exceptions, our saturation point is about 4,000 seats . . . I don't think that an increased number of seats automatically means sale of those seats and nothing succeeds like success: a full house and the occasional turning away of people is the best publicity—empty seats are the worst publicity." In the end, what would keep the size of the house down was Rockefeller's commitment to expert advice: both the acoustical consultants and the theater technologists insisted that first-class results could not be got above 4,000 seats; even the 3,750 provided would be perilous.

In spring 1956, the Exploratory Committee formed itself into Lincoln Center, Inc., and the show was on the road. Thanks to the extensive work Harrison had already done on an opera house project—and to input from Bing, the recently arrived Krawitz, and the various Met department heads—the Philadelphia consulting firm called in to create a budget for construction brought forth what was in 1956 an almost realistic figure for building the new Met—$23.6 million. The rest of the estimates were remarkably—indeed, ludicrously—low: Philharmonic Hall, for example, the first to be completed (in 1962) was budgeted at $4 million, and came in at $15.4 million; and then another $10 million had to be spent in later years to make it work right and sound right. The consultants' estimate for all of Lincoln Center was $55 million in land and construction costs, with a fund-raising target of $75 million to allow for contingencies and to leave the Center with $10 million as an education fund. In the end, the Met alone cost more than $50 million, and the Center cost almost $190 million. Rockefeller, with help from other foundations and from the business community (for Lincoln Center shared with the old Met an origin in the city's commercial rather than its social leadership), uncomplainingly raised enough money to get the thing built.

The problems of 1880–83 paled beside those of 1955–66. The Board of Estimate of the City had to vote its okay, and then there were lawsuits related to the use of part of the Title I site by Fordham University, a Jesuit institution. Instead of buying the land from a single owner, as the promoters of the original Met had done, Lincoln Center had to negotiate with scores of owners and manage the condemnation proceedings authorized by Title I. The largest single building on the site was a warehouse leased to General Motors' Cadillac division. Its owner was Joseph P. Kennedy, the future President's father, who hated the Rockefellers and had no interest in the arts; he fought the condemnation award through the courts, twice, delaying demolition on a key part of the site for almost two years.

Rising costs for the project as a whole made it imperative to get some contribution from the state government. This took the form of replacing the ballet theater with a multi-purpose "State Theater" to which would come the constituent institutions of the City Center—the New York City Ballet, the Richard Rodgers Music Theater for summer operetta and musical comedy (reducing the attractiveness of the Met for summer rentals), and the New York City Opera, which Bing especially did not want on the same plaza with his opera house. He wrote a memo to Bliss in the middle of the 1958–59 season:

My first reaction is one of dismay at the inevitable lowering of artistic standards . . . The story that the City Center fills the gap that the Metropolitan cannot fill: i.e., provide good opera at cheap prices for the less affluent public, is simply not true. (a) They do not provide good opera, but this is of course an arguable point, but (b) the Metropolitan has more cheap seats available than the City Center only they are at less advantageous locations . . . I would like to see the official box office statements of the City Center supporting the story of the enormous demand for their season particularly after the Metropolitan has opened, that is to say during the weeks when their season and ours overlap . . . I understood from the earliest days of the Lincoln Center planning that the basic concept was no other opera company should be permitted at Lincoln Center without the Metropolitan's approval. The question of the City Center was even then discussed. Does it seem fair that a gun should now be pointed at the Metropolitan's head just because new political developments may put some money at the disposal of Lincoln Center for the building of a house which in fact is not wanted? . . .

But this decision was beyond the control of Bing and even of the Met board—who were, after all, receiving their new theater as a gift from Lincoln Center. Because the New York State Theater had to be ready for the 1964–65 World's Fair, and the Met's plans were falling farther behind schedule as specifications proliferated from Krawitz and Bing's senior consultant Walter Unruh (who had been involved in the building or rebuilding of opera houses throughout postwar Germany), Lincoln Center added rage to Bing's fury by deciding that the building of the new opera house would have to wait upon completion of the State Theater. For two infuriating years, the hole dug for the foundation of the new Met remained a great pond—"Lake Bing"—on the construction site.

The new Metropolitan was an entirely different proposition from the other halls. They would be places where attractions could be presented; the Met would be a factory for the production of opera. Costume manufacturing, which had always been farmed out, would now be under the Met roof; the construction of sets, which had been done in part at the warehouse and in part by outside contractors, would now occur entirely in the Met's own backstage. Lighting facilities, electronic gadgetry, and stage machinery were to be at the state of the art (which meant the German 1950s). And, of course, there was the auditorium itself—sight lines, acoustics, comfort, conformity with the fire and safety laws (which prohibited, for example, the space-saving steep slope of the old building's Family Circle, and dictated greater space between the back of one seat and the chair of the seat behind)—not to mention the public areas, including special rooms for the Metropolitan Opera Guild and the Club, restaurants, bars, assembly spaces, etc. The number of things that had to be considered was mind-boggling. This observer ran into a shaking Krawitz one day: he had just discovered, quite by accident, that the air-conditioning specifications had been written for the building as a whole, which meant that if people were to use their offices the entire auditorium would have to be cooled all summer long. By zoning the air-conditioning with a quick call to the architect, Krawitz had just saved the Met tens of thousands of dollars a year in operating expenses—but the notion that this sort of thing could simply sneak by, because people were paying attention to apparently more important matters, haunted the dreams of everyone involved in the project, year after year after year.

Opposite: Inside the new opera house at Lincoln Center. The lowered chandeliers rise just before performances begin.

Pages 274, 275: Eugene Berman was one of the distinguished artists recruited by Bing in the 1950s to design new productions for the Met. Illustrated here are some of Berman's sketches for his 1957 *Don Giovanni*, including costume designs for Donna Elvira (*above left*), Donna Anna (*above right*), and the Don (*below*); sets and costumes were still in use a quarter of a century later.

Pages 276, 277: The Robert O'Hearn-Nathaniel Merrill production of *Die Meistersinger*, first seen in 1962, moved from the old house to Lincoln Center, where this photograph of the final scene was taken. Eva (Jean Fenn) is seen crowning Hans Sachs (Giorgio Tozzi), while Walther (Sandor Konya) looks on approvingly.

To   Francis Robinson Litchik

Riccordo di "Don Giovanni"
("My Fair Don Giovanni")

with the friendship
of
E. B.
1957

New York.   Nov. 20. 1957.

When the 75th anniversary season opened in October 1958, Howard Taubman in the *Times* made reference to the new opera house to which the Met would be moving "three years hence." In fact, there would be seven more seasons on 39th Street before Bing could lead his troupe uptown. One of these, 1960–61, would be a season of tragedy, when the company was struck with the deaths of three of its most important active artists: Mitropoulos, Bjoerling, and Warren. But as a group they were the years of vocal glory in the Bing regime, the time the critics mean when they speak—as they do, these days—of the Golden Age of Bing.

Vickers and Nilsson (whose arrival earned a front-page story in the *Times*: great Isoldes are still news) were not the only debut artists of 1959–60: the list also included Giulietta Simionato, Elisabeth Söderström, Anna Moffo, Christa Ludwig, and Anselmo Colzani. The following season saw the debuts of Leontyne Price and Franco Corelli (together) in *Il Trovatore*, the former the first great American soprano since Steber and the first to sing the major Italian roles since Ponselle, the latter the man Bing (and his chosen successor Goeran Gentele, incidentally) considered the greatest tenor in the world, with the voice of a Richard Tucker and the looks of a movie star. Also Gabriella Tucci, who would later give the house so beautiful an Alice in *Falstaff*; and Anneliese Rothenberger, who started as Zdenka in a revived *Arabella* and would later grace productions of *Rosenkavalier* and *Figaro*, among others; and Eileen Farrell, the policeman's wife from Staten Island who could have been a great dramatic soprano had she cared about acting, but an immensely welcome voice whenever she chose to sing opera.

There were important debuts too in the pit and behind the scenes. Leopold Stokowski (*vice* Mitropoulos) came to conduct Cecil Beaton's glamorous setting of Puccini's *Turandot*, making orchestra sounds to match, with Nilsson, Corelli, and Anna Moffo as the refulgent principals. One of Bing's gambles paid off big, when he assigned a new production of Donizetti's *L'Elisir d'amore* to a young American team of Nathaniel Merrill and Robert O'Hearn, whose idea of having Dr. Dulcamara arrive in a balloon tickled the fancy of the operatic professionals as well as the audience. As director and designer, working together, they would over the next decade provide Bing with durable productions of *Die Meistersinger*, *Aida*, *Samson et Dalila*, *Die Frau ohne Schatten*, *Hänsel und Gretel*, *Der Rosenkavalier,* and *Parsifal*. The first *Elisir* itself, however, was the occasion for an egregious error in Bing's

---

Pages 278, 279: Three Shakespearean operas designed and staged by Franco Zeffirelli. The first, Verdi's *Falstaff*, was produced in 1964 and revived eight years later with (*left, above*) Geraint Evans as Falstaff and Renata Tebaldi as Alice Ford. Next came the world premiere of Samuel Barber's *Antony and Cleopatra*, which inaugurated the new house at Lincoln Center, on September 16, 1966. The photo (*right*) shows Cleopatra (Leontyne Price) lamenting the death of Antony (Justino Diaz). Verdi's *Otello*, the last of Rudolf Bing's new productions, dates from 1972. In the finale of Act III (*left, below*) Desdemona (Teresa Zylis-Gara) at center stage is being comforted by Emilia (Shirley Love) while Ludovico (Paul Plishka, the kneeling figure in red) looks on. Otello (James McCracken), overcome with emotion, slumps on his throne.

Opposite: Cav and *Pag*. Grace Bumbry was the Santuzza in *Cavalleria* (*above*), Richard Tucker the Canio in *Pagliacci* (*below*, with Lucine Amara as Nedda) for a new production—another Zeffirelli spectacular—of the enduring double-bill in 1970.

judgment, when he humiliated Cesare Valletti by replacing him after the last rehearsal, thereby losing the Met the services of its best *tenore leggiero*—permanently.

This same season of 1960–61 began with an ambitious attempt to make a Met opening night out of Verdi's very early and very coarse (if sometimes exciting) *Nabucco*, never before done at the house. It foundered on Günther Rennert's ultra-German direction and Rysanek's difficulties in climbing the vocal Matterhorn of Abigaille. When she got a bad press, she and Bing blamed it on the fact that her dress rehearsal had been disastrous (so had her dress rehearsal for *Macbeth*, after which she had an excellent press), and he instituted a rule against critics at rehearsals.

Price's great success at her debut gave Bing the hope that he could use her to salvage his *Nabucco*. She had never looked at the score, and he suggested she save time and go to a performance, which she did. The next day, a bright and cheerful Bing said, "Miss Price, *will* you be my Abigaille?" Miss Price looked at him in amazement. "Man," she asked, "are you *crazy?*" *Nabucco* went off the boards and did not return. Price, unfortunately, did accept Bing's equally reckless invitation to open the next season as Minnie in *Girl of the Golden West*, a voice-killer of a role she had to drop like a hot potato, disrupting her and Bing's schedule considerably. Luckily for Bing and the audience, the indestructible Dorothy Kirsten was available to play Minnie, and very well too.

Joan Sutherland came in 1961–62. She had auditioned three years before, on the recommendation of George London, who had been dazzled by the Donna Anna she sang opposite his Don Giovanni in a summer festival performance in Vancouver. To the astonishment of John Gutman and Leinsdorf, what she offered as her audition piece was "Caro nome"—in English—and she was sent off, not unreasonably, to learn her trade. By the time Sutherland came back to New York for a concert performance of Bellini's *Beatrice di Tenda* at Town Hall, early in 1961, she was world-famous: nobody living had heard before such a combination of vocal power and flexibility. Her debut at the Met (indeed, her entire season in 1961–62) was as Lucia, thrice with Tucker and twice with Peerce as Edgardo, the Swiss conductor Silvio Varviso making his debut in the pit. Kolodin observes shrewdly that her Mad Scene was dramatically more convincing than the rest of her performance, because she had worked on it—hard—with Franco Zeffirelli in London.

This was a season of debuts by some who would make their mark elsewhere—notably Phyllis Curtin and Galina Vishnevskaya—and those who would stay at the Met a long time, especially George Shirley, Sandor Konya, John Alexander, Morley Meredith, Lili Chookasian, and Judith Raskin. The first *Ring* cycle in five years, Leinsdorf conducting, provided debuts for Paul Kuen as a universally admired Mime and Gottlob Frick as the giant Fafner—and also the first revelation of Birgit Nilsson's three Brünnhildes, warrior, maid, and wife, an accomplishment of voice, musicianship, and acting that established this intelligent artist not only in the history of the Met but in the history of opera.

The next year, 1962–63, Bing concentrated on the conducting staff, which badly needed new blood after the departure of Leinsdorf to the Boston Symphony. He introduced Lorin Maazel (who unwisely tried to conduct opera performances from memory, with confusing results), and Ernest Ansermet for a *Pelléas*. Schippers and Böhm returned—Schippers in an *Ernani* that was the best work he had done in the theater, with Leontyne Price triumphant as Elvira; Böhm in the Met's first production of Strauss's *Ariadne auf Naxos* in settings by Oliver Messel, Carl Ebert directing. Georg Solti, who had come in 1960–61 for four performances of *Tannhäuser*, returned to take a more substantial piece of the season, two months of *Tristan*, *Boris*, and *Otello*, the last of them celebrating the return of James McCracken, who had become the world's leading specialist in its title role, his explosive tenor and menacing manner dominating Robert Merrill's sly Iago and Tucci's gracious Desdemona in Eugene Berman's last Met production.

The significant debuts were of Régine Crespin, a French soprano effective in three repertoires, who opened as the Marschallin in *Rosenkavalier*, and Jess Thomas, an American who had been singing in Germany. In addition to Bacchus in *Ariadne* and Walther in *Die Meistersinger*, Thomas sang Radames in an emergency, all of it but "Celeste Aida" in German, provoking some appreciative mail from German-émigré subscribers who had started their operagoing in the old country and were happy to hear this role sung again in the language of their childhood.

This was also the season of Bing's most bitterly felt fiasco. A few years before, he had met Rosa Ponselle at a dinner for the company on its Baltimore tour, and had asked her to tell him the real reason why she had left the Met while still in her early forties. "And I said," Ponselle told Ruby Mercer, "'You want to know the truth? Because they wouldn't revive *Adriana*.' He told me, 'I don't blame them. I loathe it. I wouldn't give it if I had to close the opera house.'" Nevertheless, a revival of *Adriana Lecouvreur*, previously done (twice) at the Met in 1907, was the price that had to be paid before Renata Tebaldi would return to the house; and Bing decided that he had no choice. Tebaldi returned as Cilèa's implausible classic actress and ran into the vocal troubles that would keep her off all stages for the next year—and Bing was stuck with *Adriana*, both at the Met and on tour.

The triumph of that year was a *Meistersinger* of which the heroes were the director-designer team of Merrill and O'Hearn. Most remarkable was a second act with the curving streets of hilly Nuremberg leading down to Sachs's workbench, from which Otto Wiener in his debut observed the world and repaired shoes, trapped Beckmesser, and resisted the considerable appeal of Ingrid Bjoner's beauteous Eva. Dönch's Beckmesser impressed again, Konya was an admirable Walther, and Murray Dickie made an agile debut as David.

For this observer, who attended the rehearsals and wrote an article about the preparation of the performance, 1963–64 was the year of the marvelous *Falstaff* that brought together Leonard Bernstein and Franco Zeffirelli in their Met debuts. The women were the stars: Regina Resnik as a Quickly who kept amazing and delighting Zeffirelli with gestures and bits of business; Gabriella Tucci as a grave and beautiful Alice trapped by circumstance and anger into participation in a game that got out of hand, singing gloriously throughout; Rosalind Elias as a perfect Meg; Judith Raskin as a Nannetta whose floated A in the second scene rang in the ears for days after the performance. Luigi Alva in his debut was a boyish and musical Fenton. Colzani in the title role and Mario Sereni as Ford were inspired by the ensemble; and the *comprimario* singers (whose participation in the concerted numbers is crucial) were nothing short of wonderful—Paul Franke as the outraged Caius, Norman Scott as the stupid Pistol, and Andrea Velis (especially) as a simian Bardolph. Later, Geraint Evans would fly in from London, at Zeffirelli's insistence, to sing a pair of Falstaffs and nothing else. Zeffirelli's sets, the largest built at the Met to that time, were evocations of Elizabethan color; and Bernstein's temperament, theatrical mastery, and musical gift created an ensemble of unique grace—and accuracy.

Most of the debut artists this season were Americans—Donald Gramm and William Dooley, Justino Diaz (starting out as Monterone), plus the stunning Mary Costa, David Ward, and the Canadian Leopold Simoneau. Another interesting debut was made by Beni Montresor as the designer of Gian Carlo Menotti's *The Last Savage* in its American premiere. Montresor set the interior platform stage in view of the audience to start the first scene, and generally delivered a delightful ambience for a work which offered no other reasons for delight whatsoever.

The war was nineteen years past in 1964, and Bing finally relented on Elisabeth Schwarzkopf, permitting her a Metropolitan *Rosenkavalier*. Her memorable Marschallin, with Lisa della Casa's Octavian, was heard at the Met only this one season (and she herself returned only once, for Donna Elvira in *Don Giovanni*, after which she became ill and had to cancel everything else).

It was a year that opened with Sutherland singing gloriously in a dreadful new production of *Lucia*, in lieu of the *Norma* she had decided she was not ready to do. There followed a more satisfactory O'Hearn and Merrill staging of *Samson et Dalila*, with Georges Prêtre conducting Rita Gorr as the temptress, Jess Thomas as the tempted, and Gabriel Bacquier, a singing actor of superb quality who would make his mark at the Met in dozens of roles, in his debut as the High Priest. Then the season had its triumph in a new *Salome*, Birgit Nilsson, fresh from new conquests as Lady Macbeth, making herself convincing as well as brilliant in yet another characterization (there were 26 curtain calls), Böhm conducting one of his specialties, the German designer Rudolf Heinrich giving the Met a setting of truly rotten decadence that framed the action remarkably.

A triumphant new production in the old house: Verdi's *Falstaff*, designed and staged by Franco Zeffirelli, conducted by Leonard Bernstein. During rehearsals the camera caught Bernstein (*above*) in earnest discussion with Anselmo Colzani (Falstaff) and Rosalind Elias (Meg), while Zeffirelli is seen (*below*) working out a piece of stage business with Regina Resnik (Quickly).

William Steinberg conducted at the Metropolitan Opera for the first time this season, beginning at his own insistence with what turned out not surprisingly to be a very Germanic *Aida*, following with what turned out unexpectedly to be a rather low-key *Die Walküre*. His accomplishment was the revival of *Vanessa*, revealing a score of much greater lyrical depth and complexity than had previously been realized. And this was the season of Callas's return, for a pair of Toscas—Cleva again with Gobbi as her extraordinary Scarpia in both, Tucker and Corelli splitting the Cavaradossis. She came on without a rehearsal, and the voice was strained to the breaking point even at unexpected places—but it was still the Tosca to remember.

Bing began 1965–66, the last season in the old house, with the work that had opened it—Gounod's *Faust*, rehearsed in a heat wave that reconciled everyone to leaving these non-air-conditioned surroundings, for a September 27 opening—the earliest ever. Though Gedda, Tucci, Siepi, and Merrill were all in the scale of good-to-excellent, the stars of the occasion were in the pit and in the wings—Prêtre, the French actor-director Jean-Louis Barrault, and the designer Jacques Dupont. Siepi's ultra-sophisticated but very human Mephistopheles was a special favorite. The very next night, equally a victim of sweat, Tchaikovsky's *Queen of Spades* returned to the Met for the first time since Mahler conducted it in 1910; Schippers this time, with Vickers as a splendidly obsessed and brutal Gherman, Teresa Stratas as a believably fragile Lisa, and Regina Resnik overpowering as the Countess whose knowledge of the three cards could be wrested from her only with death. It was the last new production in the old house, giving the shops a whole year for the nine—count 'em, nine—new productions the Met would bring to its first season in Lincoln Center.

It was a year of debuts to rival 1959–60: Mirella Freni as Mimi (Francis Robinson told of Zinka Milanov running back to the press room during the first intermission to say, "She's so wonderful, this girl—she sounds like a young me"); Grace Bumbry as Eboli in *Don Carlo* (her mascot role: she had got her start singing "O don fatale" on the Arthur Godfrey show); Renata Scotto as Butterfly; Montserrat Caballé (a one-performance guest); Sherrill Milnes and Nicolai Ghiaurov in *Faust*; James King as Florestan; Pilar Lorengar as Donna Elvira; Alfredo Kraus as the Duke in *Rigoletto*; Reri Grist as Rosina; Thomas Stewart as Ford to Gobbi's Falstaff. Zubin Mehta conducted at the Met for the first time (*Aida*), still very much learning his trade; and so did Francesco Molinari-Pradelli, who knew his trade backwards and forwards, but it was not as interesting a trade as Mehta's.

What keeps this list from being the most important collection of newcomers the Met ever introduced in a single year is the fact that most of them would be only sporadically available in the seasons to come. The jet plane and the growing prosperity of Europe had caught up with the Metropolitan Opera. A dozen years had passed since Risë Stevens made news by singing Thursday night at La Scala and flying to New York for a Saturday matinee *Carmen* at the Met. Now it would be commonplace—and not only in New York. Leinsdorf describes the Saturday morning scene of the 1980s at Vienna airport, where the Staatsoper's lofty Kammersänger—released by house rules from weekend rehearsals in Vienna—were waiting to board planes for engagements all over Central Europe.

Gatti had engaged artists by the season, then for the half-season, keeping control of their time while they were under contract to the Met. Johnson had been forced by economic circumstance and the organization of AGMA [the American Guild of Musical Artists] to loosen considerably the Met's hold on its artists, but it was still generally true that the specific dates on which artists would sing were not known until a few weeks before a performance, and singers had to hold sizable chunks of time open for the opera. Bing's organizational ability had, from early on, enabled him to tell artists well in advance of the season not only which evenings they would sing, but which afternoons they would rehearse—and with whom, and where in the building, and at precisely what times. By holding fees below world scale through the 1950s, the Met invited situations where singers would offer the house just exactly what the schedule proclaimed, demanding extra fees to "cover"—keep themselves available as possible substitutes—for scheduled artists.

The new system worked against the Metropolitan's long-established "repertory" scheme of presenting operas—six or even seven different operas a week, each production running for a large fraction of the season, presumably employing members of a regular company as needed. Instead, it worked to the advantage of the "stagione" plan, by which artists were hired for a relatively short period, to perform just one opera, which would be done twice a week for three or four weeks and then disappear. As the name indicates, "stagione" had been the Italian way of presenting operas; now it spread to Covent Garden, Paris, the Swiss theaters, and even "festival months" at the German houses. Bad enough when the departure of singers forced undesirable cast changes, the new pattern of running around the world was ruinous to the cohesion of the Met when conductors too became stars, conducting at the Met on off nights during engagements with the New York Philharmonic, taking weekends away from the opera house for guest appearances with other orchestras, or simply dividing their time among five or six opera houses for the season.

Many singers who became stars at the Met did not make their American debuts for Bing—San Francisco and Chicago were more adventurous, and in any event opened their seasons earlier in the year. But once he got them, they usually made

Overleaf: Until the very end, Monday nights at the old Met were full-dress occasions (*right*). Between the acts, patrons gathered in the foyers (*left page, top right*), in Sherry's restaurant (*below*), or—if they were members—in the Metropolitan Opera Club bar (*top left*).

sizable commitments of time to the Met. Bing was especially shrewd at getting the not-quite-great to sign for full seasons in New York—the Stellas and Konyas, who guaranteed the quality of the performances that were not sung by the box-office celebrities. A good fraction of Bing's casts, of course, were or had become resident New Yorkers with families to hold them near; even the peripatetic artists, the Nilssons and Corellis and Prices, had settled down near what had become their home base. But by the late 1960s, those days were gone. Major artists no longer had a home house. And given the requirements of the spring tour, which the board compelled a reluctant Bing to take very seriously, there was no way to move the Met very far toward "stagione" principles. The publicized productions of the early months of the season had to be made ready for travel toward the end. And there were the broadcasts, which of necessity began only after the end of the college football season. It was a riddle Bing would leave to all his successors.

Not wishing to become possessors of a pot of money that the organizers of Lincoln Center might then claim as a contribution to the costs of the new theater, the Met had leased rather than sold the land under the old house, on which a real estate developer planned an office building. The receipts from the rental—on a sliding scale rising from $200,000 the first year to $600,000 annually—would help defray operating costs in the new house, and take some of the burden off the annual fund-raising drive. As the end neared, however, Sol Hurok organized a rather inchoate movement to "Save the Met," as Carnegie Hall had finally been saved, by a combination of state legislation and private contributions. Rentals would pay the running expenses—Hurok himself would take the house for four or five months or more to present touring opera and ballet companies.

Bing's management team and the Met board were appalled by the idea—first, because they knew how badly they had allowed the building to run down (and thus the kind of money that would be necessary to put it into even minimally usable shape); second, because they felt threatened by the possible loss of the revenue from the ground rents (and the long-term asset of continued ownership of the land when the lease expired); third, because the last thing they wanted was another competing opera house in New York. Nevertheless, a bill was passed by the state legislature which determined that the fair value of the site was $8 million, and delayed demolition for 180 days while a newly organized Old Met Corporation, with a board appointed by the Mayor, could look around for the estimated $15 million needed for purchase and rehabilitation. The Save-the-Met drive did raise the $200,000 the law required as a payment to the Met in lieu of the first year's rent, but it soon became clear that in the absence of support from the people who were behind Lincoln

The Met's much-loved Zinka Milanov coming off stage at her 25th anniversary performance as Maddalena in *Andrea Chénier*, December 17, 1962.

Center—and who were not greatly tempted to make gifts to a rival—the money could not be found; and eventually the law was declared unconstitutional anyway.

Bing had planned to say farewell to the old house with a final performance of *Faust*, perhaps adding a concert on Sunday night (the tour, as usual, would begin on Monday in Boston). Like every manager of the Met since Gatti, Bing had little love for the theater in which he had to labor, with its antiquated backstage, inadequate rehearsal space, nonexistent storage, and makeshift technical facilities. Rootless himself, he did not understand the emotional attachment so many people felt to Cady's yellow-brick brewery, which was a part of their youth, an enduring symbol and reminder of so many hours of excitement and artistic satisfaction. For Bing, focused on the new theater, leaving the old Met was all triumph, no tragedy; he looked ahead. The Save-the-Met drive was for him a romantic, and stupid, exercise; any special celebration of departure would be fuel for that fire.

The leaders of the Metropolitan Opera Guild—Mrs. Belmont, Langdon van Norden, Mrs. William Francis Gibbs, Harriet Gilpatric—were irritated by Bing's insensitivity and his impracticality, for a Gala celebrating 83 years at the Met could be rewarding not only as an experience but as a money-raising venture. Sets and costumes for the operas going on tour would be unavailable, already en route, but there were other operas from which pieces could be staged—and much of the evening could be done in concert form. Artists who were actually engaged elsewhere for that evening could not come, but much of the company would be in New York and others would—some did—fly in for the occasion. For all their complaining, artists as well as audiences felt the pull of that glorious past: they would donate their services or work for AGMA minimums (and they did). Meanwhile, the Guild could sell the tickets at very high prices: in fact, the house sold out, with thousands of unsatisfied requests for tickets, at a $200 top. In the final accounting, the Met took in $318,688, and the costs of presenting the gala were only $25,176—and Texaco contributed more than enough to cover that.

It was an evening of great nostalgic power, opening with the Entrance of the Guests from *Tannhäuser* and the seating on stage of 31 stars from the Met's past, who would form the background for the first half of the evening. Leopold Stokowski conducted (calling out from the podium an appeal to the audience to "save this beautiful house"); the baritone Osie Hawkins, who had become the Met's stage manager, called out in stentorian tones the names of the artists as they took their places, in alphabetic order: Lawrence, Lehmann, Pons, Rethberg, and Stevens; followed by Brownlee, Crooks, Kipnes, and Martinelli. Kolodin pointed out that many of the performers that night were singing not merely for the audience, but for their old heroes and their teachers.

There followed a potpourri program in which there was not, to tell the truth, much great singing. A Triumphal Scene from *Aida* with John Macurdy, Madeira,

---

The Gala Farewell at 39th Street and Broadway was an evening of stars and sentiment. Leopold Stokowski (*above*) opened the show, and Birgit Nilsson appeared (*below right*) wearing the same golden sash that had been presented to Christine Nilsson on opening night in 1883. At a pre-performance dinner party (*below left*), Mrs. August Belmont shared a table with Giovanni Martinelli and Risë Stevens.

Curtis-Verna, Baum, and Sereni did not really put one in mind of Didur, Homer, Destinn, Caruso, and Scotti. Still, Price sang a glorious "D'amor sull'ali rosee" from her debut role in *Trovatore*; Birgit Nilsson, wearing the laurel sash presented to Christine Nilsson on opening night 83 years earlier, gave the theater as overpowering an Immolation Scene from *Götterdämmerung* as it had ever heard; Dorothy Kirsten sang a "Depuis le jour" from *Louise* that reminded everyone of how excellent as well as useful an artist she had been through a long career; Tucker and Milanov (who had formally retired in an almost equally emotional episode the previous Wednesday) sang "Vicino a te" from *Andrea Chénier*; Merrill sang "Eri tu," and Siepi "Ella giammai m'amò," while Vickers flung an exquisite "Winterstürme" at an audience that did not have time to adjust itself to such brief glory.

There were tears in many eyes at 1:17 the next morning, when the curtain came down on an "Auld lang syne" sung by soloists, chorus, stagehands, and audience. Then the place began to be picked apart for souvenirs; and much glorious dust returned to dust.

Time for the wreckers—"glorious dust returned to dust."

NINE

New House, New Era

When a new management took over the Met in 1972, an extraordinary statement appeared in the annual report from the board: "For the first time since 1958, the Metropolitan Opera Season opened with labor peace." It was the closest anyone ever came to criticizing Bing in public after his departure, and the implied boast that in his absence the board could keep its labor relations happy turned out to be premature. But from the very beginning, there had been an uneasy feeling about Bing among the labor unions: "There is no question," Bing wrote later, "that my style and personality are not right for the American labor movement. They don't feel comfortable with me, and to tell the truth I don't feel comfortable with them." Anthony Bliss remembers that soon after he came on the board, during Bing's observation year, he was assigned to a committee "to negotiate with the labor unions—a committee of one, plus Reggie Allen. The rumor had spread in the unions that Bing had been brought in from Germany to break unions."

The Met had been dealing with unions on a formal basis since before World War I. In 1904, the American Federation of Musicians had approached Theodore Roosevelt to keep Heinrich Conried from destroying the New York local by importing a new orchestra for the Met. It was an election year. President Roosevelt received Maurice Smith, head of the New York local, in his home at Oyster Bay. As a later president of the AFM reported the conversation, Roosevelt said that "as he was not quite sure whether the law was in our favor, he had instructed the immigration authorities that if European musicians appeared from Europe to hold them at the port of entry until the courts had passed upon the validity of their admittance under contract . . . Mr. Conried did not import an orchestra."

In the 1920s, Ziegler dealt with a union of choristers as well as Local 802 of the musicians' union and Local 1 of the International Association of Theatrical Stage Employees. In the mid-1930s, repeatedly pushed to the wall, singing for reduced fees but still required to pay commission to the Met on their outside engagements (Lawrence Tibbett complained that the commissions received by the Met on his radio and movie contracts totaled more than the house paid him for singing), the

The new house at Lincoln Center.

soloists organized. Cravath and the senior Bliss were dead set against recognizing a soloists' union, and Ziegler needed advice from labor law specialists to convince them that New York State's "little Wagner Act" gave the soloists the right to organize whether or not they were covered by the federal Wagner Act. The first contract between the Met and the singers' American Guild of Musical Artists was signed July 26, 1938, and laconically announced in a press release clearly written by Ziegler, proclaiming that the Met and AGMA "are happy to announce that after many interesting conferences both sides have reached an agreement . . ." The union representatives present at the conference had been Tibbett, Melchior, Pinza, and Bonelli.

In 1941, the board appointed its first Labor Relations Committee, chaired by George Sloan. This committee, the minutes read,

had no powers, and wanted none; and . . . would at all times be at the disposal of the Management for advice on any and every kind of labor problem with which the Association might have to deal. Mr. Sloan suggested, and the Committee agreed, that in future negotiations, it would be well for the Management to state its position and make its requests, before reviewing those that the labor organizations might present; that the size of the deficit should be stressed, together with the argument that demands adverse to the Association might actually prevent its reopening.

With this sort of advice before him—and the steadying hand of Ziegler removed—it is perhaps not surprising that Johnson got in trouble in 1948, when the needs of employees stricken by postwar inflation clashed with the re-emergence of a large deficit on the Met's books. The announced cancellation of the season shocked AGMA—which had a continuing contract—and led that union to act as mediator between the Met and the musicians and stagehands. It was agreed that, given the deficit, wage increases were not possible, and the unions even accepted an indefinite delay on their most important and reasonable demand—that the Met waive the exemption its educational status gave from state unemployment insurance taxes, and thus make it possible for employees to receive payments from the state fund during the more than five months a year the opera did not employ them.

When Bing arrived, then, one of the first items on his plate was the decision on unemployment insurance, which would cost the Met $60,000 a year and yield perhaps eight times as much to the workers. Amazed that it had not been done before, he told Reginald Allen to work that additional expense into the budget, and his relations with the unions started cheerfully. Having been brought up in German houses with their long-established pension plans (and desperately needing a way to get superannuated chorus members out of the company without creating unbearable hardship), Bing supported the idea of a fund for retirement purposes, first formally proposed to the board by Lucrezia Bori in 1940; and the Met established first a severance pay plan and finally (in the 1960s) a minimal pension plan, later improved.

The first big flap with organized labor occurred in 1953–54, when Anthony Bliss brought in Herman Krawitz to explore the organization of backstage, and to investigate the charges of nepotism, featherbedding, and kickbacks that had been brought by knowledgeable observers. In protest, the stagehands began a wildcat strike that threatened that evening's *Tannhäuser*. Management and Bliss donned work clothes in expectation that they would have to do the backstage work (in the end, the crew worked *Tannhäuser*, though not the next afternoon's dress rehearsal of *Norma*, for which Bing operated the curtain, nearly killing Zinka Milanov when he let it down too soon and too fast). This was Bliss's problem, and Bliss handled it: "I was told," he remembers, "that the key to the stagehands was Dick Walsh [president of Local 1]. I called a friend, said, 'How do I meet Dick Walsh?' He called back and said, 'Go to the 21 Club and ask Mac Kreindler, he'll introduce you.' Walsh said, 'They can't strike without my permission . . .'"

Bliss also attempted to handle the negotiations for a new AGMA contract in 1956. The musicians and the stagehands had agreed in 1955 to a three-year extension without wage increases, as part of the board's commitment to continue with Bing's expansion program (which meant more work weeks) rather than shrink to Sloan's recommendation. AGMA would have to do the same. In July 1956, with no agreement in sight, a letter was sent to John Brownlee, president of AGMA, with a copy to all members, threatening cancellation of the season unless AGMA accepted similar terms: "The Metropolitan Opera Association cannot countenance further increases in basic labor costs which would threaten the very existence of this organization, now facing the future with no working capital."

The cancellation threat betokened a key misalignment of perception between management and labor in all the Met's negotiations. It seemed reasonable to the board that labor negotiations could not go to the wire as they normally do in industrial disputes. The Met's resources between seasons were essentially the advance receipts from subscriptions, which had to be held in escrow until the performances to which they applied were given. To pay for rehearsals, the Met borrowed against the security of that escrow account, and could not see its way clear to do so without assurance that the performance would take place. To the members of the unions, all this was folderol, and they saw no great urgency in coming to terms, at least until rehearsals started and they were expected to report for work. Thus the board kept setting what seemed to the unions arbitrary deadlines—a belief reinforced when the deadlines were forever moved back (in 1956, Bliss and Greenway insisted that by June 1 they must have "reasonable assurance that the present stalemate can be resolved," but cancellation was not announced until July 17, after which a contract was quickly negotiated, and the season restored).

Bliss, Greenway, and Allen having had little luck in 1956, Bing himself took a hand in April 1958, when the next batch of contract renewals was on the table.

Overleaf: Floor plan of the new Met (*left, above*) and the construction in an early phase (*below*). The inset photos are of architect Wallace K. Harrison (*left*) and acoustician Cyril Harris. With the steelwork in place (*right*), the new house begins to take on its now familiar aspect.

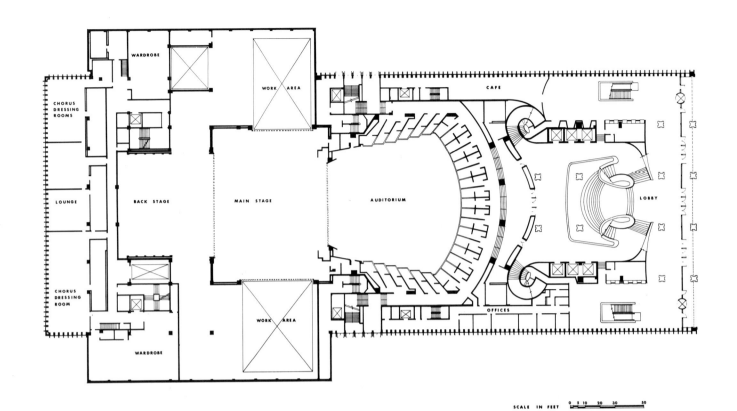

SCALE IN FEET   0 5 10   20   30   50

Writing to Hy Faine, the working head of AGMA, he unconsciously defined the reasons why these problems would always be beyond him:

I am sure you will realize that our negotiators have now for weeks negotiated with you with every good will and in good faith . . . Also, I feel the time has arrived when some of your members should come down to earth and recognize the fact that they are jeopardizing the continuance of the Metropolitan Opera and their employment. In the face of a deficit for this season in the neighborhood of one-half million dollars (in spite of excellent box-office receipts), our Board has agreed to certain increases which we have offered . . . Our deficit, largely as a result of such increases, will be increased to an amount greatly exceeding the annual contributions received by the Association heretofore . . . It is clear . . . that the economic limit of these negotiations has, with possible minor adjustments, been reached . . . We had all hoped that for once these negotiations could reach their satisfactory conclusion without having to go through the by now nauseating spectacle of mutual threats, of cancellation of the season, and crises which in the end have to be carried to the public. We still sincerely hope to avoid this, and, as far as we are concerned, will make every effort to avoid it. But those of you who seem to feel that a contract cannot be signed without having reached a crisis are about to have their way . . .

Virtually everyone engaged in a dispute tends to feel that *he* is being reasonable and his opponents are being outrageous. Bing had this normal human characteristic to an extraordinarily exaggerated degree. Moreover, the general manager of an opera house, because he is under incessant pressure from his board to cut expenses and reduce the deficit, necessarily sees the financial picture as darker than it really is. In the end, the unions did accept something very close to the Met's offer, and the reason for their acceptance may well have been related to Bing's forcefulness and obvious if impolite sincerity. And then the 1958–59 season, with contributions down slightly from the year before ($531,000 against $553,000), wound up with black ink on the books for the first time since 1947.

Because the Met now published an annual report, the unions and their members knew about this "profit," and they came into the 1961–62 negotiations with a feeling that they had been cheated. By then, moreover, the site was being cleared for the new opera house at Lincoln Center. Tens of millions of dollars were being raised for a new building, and it seemed cruel and perverse of the board to insist that it could not find even a few hundred thousand for the people whose work, after all, provided the opera.

In 1961, the unions arrived at the bargaining table with a laundry list of demands, which were compromised and settled by all but one of them: the orchestral musicians. They were asking a 60 per cent salary increase over three years, a guarantee of year-long employment, and a reduction of their work load to a maximum of six performances a week. There was in addition the case of a horn player who had outraged Karl Böhm not only by breaking on an exposed note in *Fidelio* but by disrespectful conduct at rehearsals, related to his often expressed belief that Böhm had been a Nazi during the war and should not be permitted to conduct at the Met. Any discussion of his dismissal was made all but impossible by his position on the union's negotiating committee.

Probably in anticipation of increased labor costs following a year in which contributions of $828,000 fell $41,000 short of meeting the deficit, only one new production had been scheduled for 1961–62. The season was to open with Price in a revival of Puccini's *Girl of the Golden West*, a production borrowed from Chicago; it was indeed hung on stage, as the most convenient place to store it, when the company adjourned for summer vacation. On August 1, with negotiations still on dead center with the musicians, the Met summoned forth the unthinkable prospect of those sets simply hanging on that stage all year, illuminated by a single bulb. Singers were released from their contracts, and a week later there was a formal announcement that the season had been canceled.

In the end, only the intervention of the President of the United States saved the opera season. Responding to a telegram from Risë Stevens, who had just sung her last season at the Met (a single Carmen), and perhaps motivated by a desire to save Price's opening night (which was important to part of the civil rights movement his administration was seeking to placate), John F. Kennedy ordered Secretary of Labor Arthur Goldberg to arbitrate the dispute. Neither the Met nor the musicians' union was in a position to resist such pressure—and the musicians in any event liked the idea of arbitration by the former counsel to the United Steel Workers. Three weeks after the cancellation had been announced and proclaimed irrevocable, the season was reinstated, on schedule. The award Goldberg brought in paralleled what the other unions had settled for (not surprisingly, though the musicians were surprised)—a roughly 14 per cent increase, including fringe benefits, over a three-year contract. Goldberg had refused to have anything to do with the case of the horn player, Böhm's nemesis, which was left up to Theodore Kheel, New York's premier labor arbitrator, generally considered friendly to the union side. He approved the dismissal. The ex-horn player thereupon became editor of the Local 802 newspaper, which helped keep the pot boiling in the pit.

Such events necessarily cast shadows forward. When the 1961 contracts ran out in 1964, the Met asked its unions to sign for five years, to cover the first three seasons in Lincoln Center. The sweetener was the long-sought guarantee of year-round employment starting with the final year of the new contract. Again, everyone signed but the musicians, who played for two years without a contract—and then announced that while they would be on hand for the opening night of the new opera house, they would not accept overtime work to prepare the subsequent performances, and would strike the day after the opening if their demands were not met.

The weeks before the new Met opened at Lincoln Center were thus at best a bittersweet experience for the Met management and board. The old house still stood, vandalized but temporarily protected by act of legislature, capable of rehabilitation and thus, the Met believed, a threat to the economic viability of the company in its new home. And there was no assurance that there would be a season, given the impasse at the bargaining table and the uncertainty over what the other unions might do if the musicians won (as they did win) a contract much superior to anything the other workers at the house had accepted.

It was a great comedown from the feelings of the previous spring, when the new theater had first been tried and found lovely. The occasion was a student performance of *The Girl of the Golden West* and, as there was no hope of keeping such an event secret, the press was invited, swearing on its collective mothers' graves not to speak a word in print on the matter. When it was over, the critics were released from their vows: by any measurement (and there were instruments making measurements all over the house), the new theater's acoustics exceeded anyone's expectations, considerably surpassing those in the old Met. Sight lines, while not quite perfect, did permit a view of nearly all the stage from nearly all the seats. (Tradition had dictated that the new house had to look a little horseshoe-shaped, which left inescapable sight-line problems for a few seats near the stage. Actually, the auditorium is rectangular, acoustical consultant Cyril Harris having absolutely forbidden any concave surfaces that might make focal points for reflected sound.) If the building was not architecturally elegant—nobody would ever gasp walking into this auditorium as everyone did on entering Cady's masterpiece—there were elegant touches, especially the glass chandeliers that rose to signal the dimming of the house lights, a gift from the Austrian government. It would be a grand enough home for opera in a time that did not cherish (or even understand) the aristocratic virtues; and—what counted—it worked in many ways that the old Met simply did not.

But as the union crisis deepened, the euphoria dimmed. Moreover, management had to face the fact that its plans for the opening season had been impossibly ambitious: nine new productions, four of them in the first week. Among the first decisions that had to be made was the stretching out of this schedule, to give something more than two weeks between the first night and the fourth new production.

Opening night was a world premiere, of Samuel Barber's *Antony and Cleopatra*, set to a text drawn with minimal alteration from the Shakespeare play by Franco Zeffirelli, who also designed and directed. The production almost foundered on Zeffirelli's need to think through the details of his staging during rehearsals. Literally hundreds of people could be seen standing around the stage well into the evening while Zeffirelli stroked his chin and pondered. Then a key part of the stage machinery, the turntable, broke down under the accumulation of passengers. (Later investigation revealed that a zero had been left off the specifications for the weight it would have to carry.)

Nevertheless, the show went on, and it was a great first night. An all-American cast headed by Leontyne Price, Justino Diaz, and Jess Thomas, with Schippers conducting, presented lavishly an opera that at the worst deserved Irving Kolodin's accolade: "an occasional work of more than occasional quality." And Bing came on stage at the end of the first intermission to announce that the Met had settled with the musicians, and the season would proceed; he got the greatest applause of the evening.

Next came a new *Gioconda*, Beni Montresor as designer revealing that his dramatico-visual gifts were effective in dark repertory as well as bright, Tebaldi delighting a devoted audience with evidence that her new vocal technique had given her a brass so highly burnished it was almost the equal of her lost gold. Corelli illustrated the acoustics of the house by beginning "Cielo e mar" with his back to the audience . . . Then a new *Traviata*, Cecil Beaton dressing it to the nines, Alfred Lunt's lack of operatic background betraying him into permitting (or suggesting) a second act set on a porch and in a garden rather than the luxurious interior demanded by the libretto . . . Finally, delayed ten days, the triumph of the season and of the new theater—Richard Strauss's fairy-tale *Die Frau ohne Schatten* in its first Met production, Merrill and O'Hearn using all the magic of the stage equipment to match miracles in the pit by Karl Böhm and an inspired orchestra, strong singing by James King and Leonie Rysanek as the fairy-tale personages, exquisite vocalism and acting from Walter Berry and his wife Christa Ludwig (it was Berry's debut) as the very human Dyer and his even more human Wife.

All the other new productions were either successful or interesting, sometimes both. The most astonishing of them was a new *Magic Flute* with sets and costumes by Marc Chagall. Chagall's wife and Nina Bing had been schoolgirl friends, and the two families were close. The artist had done a rather coy new ceiling for the Opéra in Paris, and Bing had persuaded him to design the two giant panels that flank the atrium of the Met's entrance area, rescuing what might otherwise be a rather disturbingly confused architecture; the *Magic Flute* in a sense came with the package.

It was (and is) an extraordinary tribute from one art to another, all canvas, really, toning from brilliant yellow at the beginning to dark blue toward the end as the cardboard central characters of Schikaneder's farce achieve Mozart's humanity. Josef Krips's woeful technique was a problem in the pit, but he did nothing that was not Mozartean, and on the stage he had happy collaborators. Nicolai Gedda was a grave and euphonious Prince; Hermann Prey, an ebullient but not clownish Papageno. The Pamina was Pilar Lorengar, lovely as always (though straining a little to fill the house, as always); the Sarastro, the always imposing Jerome Hines. Queen of the Night was Lucia Popp, making her debut, not really a coloratura in the

most coloratura of roles but always a musically graceful artist (she would later sing Pamina in this production, just wonderfully). Andrea Velis was a menacingly ratty Monostatos; Patricia Welting (also a debut), an entrancing Papagena. And Günther Rennert directed them all with a matter-of-fact sleight of hand that somehow made everybody and everything believable, leaving the fantasy to Chagall.

Also triumphant was the return of *Peter Grimes*, in finely calculated not-quite-realistic sets by Tanya Moiseiwitsch, Jon Vickers totally convincing and vocally overwhelming in the title role, Colin Davis the conductor in a debut that was one of Bing's most daring gambles. (Solti had been planned, but had backed out in a dispute over casting; Davis had never even seen a performance of *Peter Grimes* before he conducted it.) Tyrone Guthrie won characterizations not only from Vickers and Geraint Evans as Balstrode, but also from Lucine Amara as Ellen and Lili Chookasian as Auntie.

Almost in this class was a new *Elektra* in Rudolf Heinrich's dark and ruined hillside setting, Birgit Nilsson pouring voice into a rapt auditorium, Regina Resnik adding depth with a remarkably dignified, warm, ultimately terrified conception of Klytämnestra. But Schippers had little feeling for this score; Herbert Graf, who had been staging the opera at the Met for thirty years, seemed to have lost interest; and Leonie Rysanek, perhaps inevitably, saw Chrysothemis as a rival rather than a foil for Elektra.

And there were (even in retrospect, the thought of the burden the management had assumed rouses pity and terror) two others: a new *Lohengrin* that Wieland Wagner planned but did not live to execute, a Bayreuth export mismatched to the ethos of the Met; and a second world premiere, Marvin David Levy's *Mourning Becomes Elektra*, a debut vehicle for sopranos Evelyn Lear and Marie Collier, designer Boris Aronson, and director Michael Cacoyannis, Zubin Mehta in the pit, the entirety demonstrating that for operatic purposes Eugene O'Neill was no Hofmannsthal, and composer Marvin David Levy definitely no Strauss.

This was also a season when Sutherland and Price alternated as Donna Anna in *Don Giovanni*; Caballé and Martina Arroyo as Leonora in *Trovatore*; Sutherland and Scotto as Lucia. Teresa Stratas established herself as a star in the house with a touching Mimi in *Bohème*. And there was a major debut nobody could possibly have recognized as such when the young bass Paul Plishka sang an Uncle-Priest in *Butterfly* through the microphones at a concert performance during the company's new venture of free opera in the city's parks.

Meanwhile, the pressure grew rather than diminished in the administrative offices of the new building. This was a season with as much anguish as triumph. For the Lincoln Center house proved expensive to operate, not just beyond Bing's planning but beyond his imagining. What with the extravagance of the first productions, the added costs of the musicians' union contract, and the unprecedented levels of

Bing and Marc Chagall at the unveiling of the painter's giant panels that hang just behind the front arches of the new house. Chagall also designed the sets and costumes for a new *Magic Flute* (*inset*); the singers shown are George Shirley, Jerome Hines, and Judith Raskin.

maintenance expenses ("When you move from a hovel to a mansion," said John W. Drye, Jr., the lawyer who chaired the Lincoln Center building committee, "your housekeeping costs go up"), the Met in the first months hemorrhaged money. And it was six weeks into the season before Bing or the board even realized what was happening to them. "We didn't have controls enough to know we were going broke," said Frank Taplin, looking back fifteen years later from the vantage point of president of the Association.

Bing had budgeted the season for a deficit of $3.05 million, and the board had estimated contributions of $3,197,000. By November, the operating loss was projected at $5,489,000: the new productions would cost $856,000 more than expected; "building problems" would add $307,000; new house operating costs would be $796,000 more than planned; and artistic salaries (the musicians' contract) would be $280,000 over budget. The problem was entirely on the expense side: income was better than budget, and for the full season the new house would sell over 99 per cent of capacity. Nevertheless, a new line of credit had to be negotiated with the banks to keep the company going through this glamorous year and to assure that the doors could be opened in 1967–68. An emergency fund drive would be necessary; meanwhile, ticket prices (which had been kept as they were in the old house) were raised 20 per cent in mid-season and subscribers were asked to send the Met a tax-deductible contribution of 20 per cent of their subscription. (Most did.) The management consulting firm of Booz, Allen & Hamilton was brought in to examine all the "non-artistic and administrative" operations of the Association. A new Director of Finance, William H. Hadley, was installed at the expenditure controls, and an Administrative Committee headed by Spofford was appointed to oversee "the affairs of the Opera on a day to day basis."

And while all this was going on, the board had to make a decision on the relationship that should exist between the Met and the "cause" of opera throughout the United States—the geographical spread of performances, training for young artists, tickets at prices young audiences could afford, etc. For it was by serving that cause, not by presenting performances to its established New York audiences, that the Met could make a case for government support, and in the populist 1960s it was not easy to see how the company could survive over time without government support.

This discussion had been going on for a generation, ever since John Erskine had demanded the spring season as the price of Juilliard assistance in 1935. Educational activities—particularly the provision of student matinee performances—were central to the work of the Opera Guild. Shortly after the war ended, Herman Adler had proposed to the Met the creation of an "Opera Comique" in New York, and Mrs. Belmont had secured him an attentive consideration, complete to sample budgets, from the Met management. In 1956, when the New York City Opera seemed likely to go under, Anthony Bliss, newly installed as president, persuaded a reluctant Bing to explore the possibility that the Met might run both companies, a proposition that foundered instantly on the rocky fact that Morton Baum, chairman of the City Center, wanted the Met around even less than Bing wanted the chore of operating the City Opera.

The City Opera had been started in 1944 by Laszlo Halasz, a conductor who had been running a failed opera company in St. Louis and thus had access to sets and costumes. Fiorello La Guardia, finding himself in possession of the Mecca Temple and with a little extra money in the New York City treasury thanks to wartime prosperity, at last had the chance to realize his long-cherished municipal music center. Halasz got the assignment to start an opera company in the Mecca Temple, now renamed the City Center. (Among those who read a newspaper story about this announcement was a nineteen-year-old refugee music student named Julius Rudel, who came to the stage door and applied for the job of rehearsal pianist, beginning a career with the City Opera that would last 36 years.) The result was not exactly Adler's Opera Comique, for the City Opera offered a number of works that were standard in the Met's repertory. But by producing modern opera, the new company took some of the pressure for such unprofitable activity off the shoulders of the Met management, and it was obviously an ideal place for future Met artists to get their basic training.

In the Johnson days, relations between the Met and the City Opera were cordial. Baum was on the Met board, providing an automatic liaison. Met seasons ran twenty weeks or less in New York, and the short spring and fall City Opera seasons overlapped little, if at all. Met artists were permitted to take engagements on 55th Street, and youngsters could consider the City Opera a showcase allowing them to display their wares to the Met. Bing decided early on that he did not like the City Opera, probably because the press, sometimes fatuously but sometimes not, was in the habit of comparing City Opera and Met productions to the detriment of the senior house.

The fact was that at its best the City Opera provided real competition for the Met. Julius Rudel in Mozart and Richard Strauss, in French opera, and in specialty pieces like Boito's *Mefistofele* and Handel's *Julius Caesar*, was a far better conductor than most of those Bing offered. Especially after the company moved into its new theater and its budgets rose, City Opera usually gave value for money. Alberto Ginastera's *Don Rodrigo*, which opened the first season at the New York State Theater in Lincoln Center (Placido Domingo in the title role), was superior as an overall experience to any U.S. premiere attempted by the Met under Bing, excepting only *The Rake's Progress*; and the Handel *Julius Caesar* of the next fall (which infuriated Bing, who thought it was planned to upstage his *Antony and Cleopatra*) was opera at a level not often achieved at the Met. Poulenc's *Dialogues des Carmélites*, Janáček's *Makropoulos*

Affair, Prokofiev's *Flaming Angel*, Shostakovich's *Katerina Ismailova*, Dallapiccola's *The Prisoner*—all these and others were staged at Rudel's City Opera and not at Bing's Met. Beverly Sills's Cleopatra in *Julius Caesar* made her a major figure among the world's sopranos. For at least half the Bing years, *Figaro* was a better bet at the City Opera than at the Met; and when the Alfred Lunt staging of *Traviata* at the Met competed with the Frank Corsaro staging across the plaza (especially when Maralin Niska was singing), the true aficionado was happier in the less expensive house.

Through the Bing years, the City Opera was a more important source of new American artists for the Met than all the European houses and the auditions put together. Any list would have to include Dorothy Kirsten, Judith Raskin, Tatiana Troyanos, Shirley Verrett, Ruth Welting, Maralin Niska, John Alexander, Kenneth Riegel, John Reardon, Placido Domingo, José Carreras, Cornell MacNeil, Sherrill Milnes, Richard Cassilly; and there were many others. But an appearance on 55th Street (and, later, in the Lincoln Center State Theater) was a minus rather than a plus for aspirants to the Met; many of those who came to the Met did so only via detours to German houses. The idea of sharing artists in the same season was anathema to Bing. He believed that people would not pay Met prices to hear singers who had been available to them for one-third as much a few weeks earlier. This was fine for the City Opera, which was able to keep some of its major box-office attractions, notably Sills and Norman Treigle, as exclusive artists. But it was a little hard on the talent—and a source of some annoyance on Bing's board.

Training for the Met was done during the Bing years in part by other opera companies, in part by the formal classes paid for by the Kathryn Long estate, and in part by a Metropolitan Opera Studio formed by assistant manager John Gutman, with the enthusiastic support of Anthony Bliss and Mrs. Belmont, to present scenes and arias in schools and hospitals around the New York area. Both Bliss and Mrs. Belmont felt that something more elaborate was needed—and also that the Met, which was receiving nationwide contributions through the Guild and the National Council, owed the country more than the radio broadcasts and the seven-week tour. If there was not to be an Opera Comique in New York—and the need for such a house was clearly in doubt with the success of the City Opera—they wanted a "Metropolitan Opera National Company" that would tour extensively every year, bringing the message and the reality of opera to cities that knew it not, giving young singers—and designers and directors and conductors—the baptism of fire that would help them assume their proper place, eventually, in New York.

Bing never liked the National Company, said so, and grudgingly assented to its creation only upon the assurance that the involvement of his management would be minimal (an assurance gladly given) and that funds be raised to meet the deficits separately from (and not competitively with) the Met's own contribution drives. It was agreed that the new company would be not only young, but dashing and

Across the Plaza at Lincoln Center, the New York City Opera was reaching new artistic levels under the musical direction of Julius Rudel (*below*) with such stars as Beverly Sills (*above left*, as Handel's Cleopatra) and Norman Treigle (*above right*, as Boito's Mefistofele).

innovative, with a large leaven of new or unfamiliar works and of old operas done in new ways. A deal was struck to bring over Walter Felsenstein, the wizard of East Berlin's Komische Oper, as the company's guru—and then, once again, the State Department refused to give a visa to some subversive who said he was going to work at the Metropolitan Opera. Risë Stevens was made director of the new company, with Michael Manuel, a Met stage director, to serve as her administrator and as liaison with the Met. It was understood that Stevens would report *to* the board *through* Bing.

An entire year was taken for planning, choosing artists and repertory, auditioning, booking, etc., and in late summer 1965 the company settled in for two months of rehearsals in a new opera house in Indianapolis, to which the national press trekked for a generally successful opening week. The company offered *Carmen*, *Butterfly*, Rossini's *Cenerentola*, and Carlisle Floyd's *Susannah*, perhaps the most successful of the City Opera's foundation-sponsored American premieres. When the National Company came to New York that season, it played the State Theater, to the great annoyance of both the Met and the City Opera, which had not yet moved in—and eventually also to the annoyance of Stevens and Manuel, for their young artists could not master the acoustical problems of this difficult house, which were remedied only in 1982. In all, the company played for nine months, visited 72 cities, gave 249 performances—and lost $700,000 ($500,000 after earmarked contributions).

The National Company's second season began shortly after the new Met opened, with *Traviata*, *Bohème*, *Figaro*, and Benjamin Britten's *The Rape of Lucretia*, reducing from 50 per cent to 25 per cent the fraction of its repertory not shared with the senior company. Bleeding cash from every pore in Lincoln Center, the Met had to advance funds to the National Company; by mid-October the total "loaned" to the new venture was a million dollars. The question of whether the Met should continue its sponsorship of the National Company divided the board. Bliss and Royall Victor, Jr., chairman of the board's National Company Committee, felt strongly that the new operation was a credit to the Met, a public relations plus, a contribution to the national culture, and an important first step toward federal subsidy. Treasurer George Moore, chairman of the First National City Bank of New York, felt that the burden could not be carried and that, in any event, "The Met is not in business to produce opera in East Lansing." Bing could not have agreed more.

On October 22, while the new Director of Finance was trying to get a fix on the first month's cost overruns in the new building and to prepare a revised budget for the season, opposing recommendations were formally presented to the board. A firm commitment to continue for three additional years was urged by the National Company Committee of Royall Victor, Frank E. Taplin (a Cleveland lawyer and businessman, chamber music player, and former assistant to the president of

Princeton), Howard Hook (director of the National Council's regional audition program), and Roger Stevens (real estate developer, Broadway producer, and chairman of Washington's oncoming Kennedy Center). The operas suggested for the following year were *Tosca*, *Rigoletto*, and *Barbiere*, all Met staples. Abandonment at the earliest possible moment was urged by Bing, for every possible reason—that the company wasn't good enough to represent the Met ("I do question whether it is wise and, indeed, advisable to perform *The Barber of Seville* with no first-rate singers in Orlando, Florida and/or East Lansing"), that it earned as much ill will as good will around the country because it seemed to supplant efforts to produce opera locally, that it took time from Met management and money from Met coffers. On December 6, the executive committee—Bliss and Victor dissenting and asking to have their negative votes recorded—voted to disband the National Company at the close of the 1966–67 season.

When this news got out, Mrs. De Witt Wallace of the *Reader's Digest* offered a gift of $1 million to keep the National Company going. Another $350,000 would be available from the National Council for the Arts, predecessor of the National Endowment; and Roger Stevens, who saw uses for the company in Kennedy Center, was prepared to find guarantors for another $250,000. The board's National Company Committee had estimated that $1.9 million would be necessary to carry on for three more years, and here was almost all of it. "I was beside myself," Taplin said recently, "when Mr. Moore turned down the million dollars. The failure of the National Company set us back a number of years in gaining national support."

In fact, there were sound arguments both ways—especially as the poor box-office receipts of the National Company's second season kept pushing up the deficits. Moore was the man who had to find the loans that would keep the Met going, and to plan the fund drives that would pay off the loans. (The troops in the trenches who raised the money were led by Mrs. Lewis W. Douglas, Mrs. John Barry Ryan, and Wallace Buckner.) Given the disagreement between them, either the President or the Treasurer had to go; and Moore, as chairman Lauder Greenway told the Annual Meeting, "was the engineer who got the train back on the tracks."

In the cycle of attitudes that had always vied for supremacy on the board of the Met, the wheel had come around once again to the group that wished to limit the deficit as a first priority. Bliss resigned from the presidency (though not from the board), and Moore took over. Bing had won his political battle, but in a sense he and his successor had lost a war. In trading away Bliss for Moore, the Met management was losing a lawyer solicitous of a client's views and familiar with opera, gaining a banker accustomed to telling people what to do, for whom opera was a recent and exotic entertainment.

☆ ☆ ☆

Those problems still lay some years ahead. For the time being, Mrs. Douglas raised not only the $3 million extra needed to cover the 1966–67 losses, but $500,000 on top of that to reduce the working capital deficit—and in 1967–68 Bing put on a season that kept the town talking. Its feature attraction was the debut of Herbert von Karajan, who came with *Die Walküre*, the first installment of his Salzburg conception of the *Ring*, to be financed by a $500,000 grant from Eastern Air Lines (which took a further interest in the Met by supplying chartered aircraft for the spring tour—the first time the company had traveled by a means of transportation other than rail). The result was an extraordinary imposition of one man's will on an institution.

This observer was at Karajan's first rehearsal with the orchestra, whose members came in a mood that combined awe and belligerence. Maestro began with the second act, and from the beginning he was holding everybody down, shortening the dynamics, lightening the textures. The orchestra played extremely well (everybody, it seemed, had been practicing at home to show this s.o.b. what he could do), but the men were puzzled by the approach until Karajan told them that for this *Walküre* the movable pit would be raised to its highest level in the new theater's two-year history. Then everyone understood, and there was a round of applause (opera orchestras like the idea that maybe somebody will get a chance to watch them at work). At the performance, the press noted that the conductor seemed more visible than usual, and thought Karajan had brought an especially high podium.

Karajan directed, moving his cast around the elliptical platform that was Günther Schneider-Siemssen's brilliant contribution. (This was Schneider-Siemssen's Met debut; he would later give Bing a miraculous, largely abstract *Tristan*, and give Bliss and Levine in 1981–82 an equally but differently miraculous, "realistic" *Contes d'Hoffmann*.) Karajan also supervised the lighting, for which the Met had to purchase more powerful lamps than it had ever used before (which Karajan then covered with dark lenses because he liked a dark stage). The Met contributed Birgit Nilsson, who had not been part of Karajan's previous Salzburg cast. (They didn't get on, because Nilsson, however hard she tried, was unable to accord Karajan the reverence he considered his due. This was the season Bing had himself alerted to her first arrival in the theater to begin rehearsals, and went to greet her at the stage door by falling to his knees in tribute. She smiled graciously at him and said, "Nu? Where's Herbie?") Karajan contributed the Hunding of Karl Ridderbusch and the Sieglinde of Gundula Janowitz, who had never before sung at the Met. The Siegmund was the impeccable Jon Vickers; Thomas Stewart was an imposing if occasionally strained Wotan, Christa Ludwig a dominating Fricka.

In the next season's *Rheingold*, with its astonishingly fluid first scene and its terrifying ride through the Nibelungens' workshop—with dramatically vivid portrayals of Alberich by Zoltan Kelemen and Loge by Gerhard Stolze (Salzburgers

Günther Schneider-Siemssen's fluid settings for *Das Rheingold* gave full rein to the sophisticated stage equipment in the new house. The production was masterminded by Herbert von Karajan, seen (*inset, left*) rehearsing the orchestra and (*right*) demonstrating a gesture to Thomas Stewart.

making Met debuts), and with real giants from Martti Talvela and Ridderbusch—Karajan built a foundation for his *Walküre* conception. It must be taken as more than possible that everything would have fitted together in an unforgettable totality had he completed his *Ring*—but he dropped out after a strike in 1969 postponed the *Siegfried*, and he never returned. When *Siegfried* came, the conductor was Leinsdorf; when *Götterdämmerung* arrived, the conductor was Rafael Kubelik; and when the Met offered the complete *Ring* in Karajan's conception, four years behind schedule, the conductor was Sixten Ehrling.

The year of Karajan's *Walküre* also featured a generally admired new production of Gounod's *Roméo et Juliette*, with sets and costumes by Rolf Gérard, direction by Paul-Emile Deiber, who would become the *régisseur* of choice in the French repertory in the coming years; Corelli and Freni as the lovers, Molinari-Pradelli in the pit. Then came a universally panned new production of *Carmen*, all four acts set in a Roman amphitheater supposed to connote a bull-ring, balletically conceived (which is cockeyed for this opera) by Jean-Louis Barrault, burying the effective Carmen of Grace Bumbry.

Among this season's debuts were those of Tom Krause as the Count and Teresa Berganza as Cherubino in a leisurely *Figaro* conducted by Joseph Rosenstock; Christina Deutekom as Queen of the Night; Jeannette Pilou as Juliette; and Fiorenza Cossotto, a mezzo of remarkable power, temperament, and temper, as Amneris. And there were two other new productions: a gingerbread *Hänsel und Gretel* by Merrill and O'Hearn, and Verdi's *Luisa Miller* in its first performance since 1930–31, with sets apparently derived from Piranesi prison scenes by the heavy-handed Attilio Colonnello, with fine singing from Caballé, Tucker, and Milnes. It is probably worth noting that the five new productions together cost only $900,000—less than the two operas, *Antony and Cleopatra* and *Gioconda*, that had opened the house the year before. The Met this season sold 97 per cent of its tickets, but the loss was $3.5 million. Bing's contract was extended one last time, to include the 1971–72 season.

The debuts in 1968–69 included Placido Domingo (who had appeared in a summer engagement in 1966 but first stepped on the Met stage in a revival of *Adriana Lecouvreur* this year); Luciano Pavarotti (as Rodolfo: it has been a matter of policy for him, wherever he sings, to make his debut in *La Bohème*); Martti Talvela; Shirley Verrett; Teresa Zylis-Gara; Renato Bruson; and Theo Adam.

It was the year of Karajan's *Rheingold*; of a new *Rosenkavalier* in which Christa Ludwig would display first her youthful Octavian and then her aging Marschallin, equally beautiful; of a *Tosca* designed by Rudolf Heinrich, rather frantically directed by Otto Schenk in his Met debut, Nilsson a surprisingly persuasive Floria Tosca (for fun, she duplicated the Jeritza feat of singing "Vissi d'arte" in a prone position), Bacquier a clearly dangerous Scarpia, Corelli a Cavaradossi no conspirator in his

---

Two spectacular productions from the opening season at Lincoln Center: Benjamin Britten's *Peter Grimes* (*above*, with Jon Vickers and Lucine Amara) and Richard Strauss's *Die Frau ohne Schatten* (*below*, with James King and Leonie Rysanek towering over Walter Berry and Christa Ludwig).

right mind could possibly trust; and of a hideous *Trovatore* by Colonnello, borne bravely by the superb cast of Price, Bumbry, Domingo, and Milnes.

This was also the year when the Met first experimented with the televising in color of a performance in the house, accepting an offer by the Japanese government network NHK to tape a *Barbiere*. There was some hope on the board that a U.S. network would pick up the show when it was in the can, but in fact the results were not good enough to tempt purchasers.

The failure of the *Barbiere* television tape, hampered by a less than all-star cast and by the television technology of the time (for which operatic lighting was inadequate), deeply depressed a Met board that had been hoping to develop a major new source of revenue from electronics. The 1968–69 season had shown a loss of $567,000 after contributions of more than $4 million. Bing was sent into the labor negotiations of that summer with a mandate to give the unions as little as possible, preferably nothing.

These were impossible instructions. The success of the musicians in the opening year of the house had embittered the members of the other performing unions, who saw themselves falling behind. In 1963–64, the orchestra, chorus, and ballet had averaged $9,600, $6,200, and $4,800 a year, respectively; in 1968–69, orchestra salaries had jumped to $16,400 (up 71 per cent), while the chorus salaries rose only to $10,200 (up 65 per cent), and the ballet only to $6,700 (up 39 per cent). Meanwhile, the musicians felt that they had learned the benefits that could be won by being tough. Very tough.

So this time there really was a strike, by all the performing unions, postponing the opening of the season from September 15 to December 29, 1969. Having been subjected to severe criticism for canceling a season in midsummer in 1961, the Met now locked out its employees by canceling rehearsals, but kept in being its contracts with (and obligations to) fourteen leading artists whose services would be necessary to sell tickets for the forthcoming season if it could be rescued. The conventional wisdom now was that the Met *could* not cancel a season: press, public, and political pressure would be too great. To put economic pressure on the strikers, the company withheld summer vacation payments (traditionally given in advance of the season, because the fiscal year and the contracts ran from July 1 to June 30), and also informed the New York State Unemployment Insurance Fund that its employees were out of work because of a labor dispute, which under state law delayed for seven weeks their eligibility to collect compensation. (The courts later ruled that in fact the Met workers *were* entitled to unemployment compensation, because their unemployment had begun before the lockout was declared.)

The attempt to impose economic hardship—which seemed reasonable enough to the management team and a board composed mostly of non-unionized lawyers and bankers—greatly increased the bitterness of the strike, especially among the choristers and dancers, many of whom had sought a paternalistic relationship from their employer. The decision to pay the stars to hold them through the strike was even more deeply resented by people who were being denied not only their normal income but the chance of unemployment compensation. (The Met stopped paying the soloists on November 15—when it was, after all, as some of them reflected, quite late in the game for them to secure other engagements.)

One must remember, of course, the atmosphere of the time. The year before, the teachers' union had closed the New York City schools for almost three months. Student strikers littered the campuses, nurses were picketing. Among people who worked for nonprofit or tax-supported institutions, and had accepted lower pay than their skills might warrant because their employers couldn't afford any more, there was a growing sense that nobody knew what the employers could really afford: there was no telling how much was there if you *really* demanded it. And there was considerable feeling among the artists at the Met that their concerns were peripheral to the national federations that were supposed to represent them, for most of the members of those federations were people who worked for broadcasting companies and record companies and theaters and movie producers and night clubs. They could not understand the problems or prospects of serious musicians. Only the unions of performers went on strike: the stagehands, the technicians, the box office and the press department all settled. At bottom, as Jane Boutwell put it in an article in *Opera News*, the strike at the opera house was "a revolt by 350 performing artists against their own unions."

What settled it finally was the dispersal of the fog that shrouded for the performers the relationship between management and the board. Partly because the web of loyalties Bing had woven at the top of his cadre gave management a monolithic appearance, the performers were convinced that what was preventing agreement was the evil, still-dapper spirit of Rudolf Bing. A meeting between the leaders of the striking performers and the officers of the board, with management excluded, led the unions to the discovery that management had been operating under instructions: following the meeting, the board communicated its absolutely final position direct to the membership rather than to the people with whom the officers had met. After the burst of outrage at this procedure, cooler heads accepted the proposition that what was on the table now was in truth all that would be there, and the contracts were signed.

The ballet held out longest, until its leader said reflectively that what the dancers had wanted was not so much the money as the feeling that they were being considered, and they had that now. At the party after the signing, with champagne

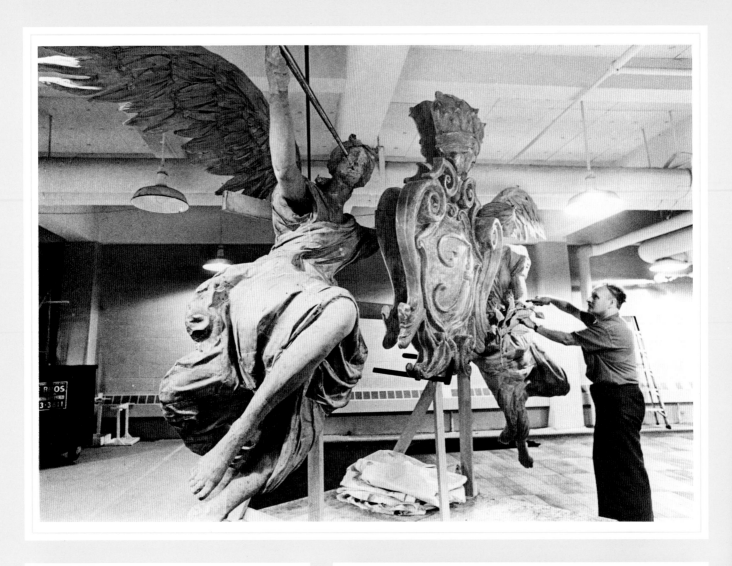

all round, it was the leaders of the ballet who started a spontaneous salute to Bing with a ragged and not entirely sincere rendition of "For he's a jolly good fellow."

For the Met, the 1969 strike was a disaster. Of the $2.85 million of subscription tickets to canceled performances, almost $2.3 million had to be refunded despite the drive to get subscribers to contribute their refunds. Simply processing the refund application forms and the returns for 20,000 subscribers in twenty different series took 18,000 man-hours of work and cost the company $160,000. Though some performances were made up in a month-long June season, box-office receipts dropped from $11.2 million to $7.5 million, and while contributions rose from $4 million to $4.5 million, the company had to add $1.4 million to its working capital deficit. Ticket sales, which had been at 96 per cent of capacity in 1968–69, plunged to 89 per cent the year after the strike, and would not return to their pre-strike level until 1977–78.

A perfectly adequate truncated season was put together for 1969–70, though only two of the six new productions planned for the year could be staged: Franco Zeffirelli's conventional yet spectacular presentation of *Cav* and *Pag*, Leonard Bernstein conducting the Mascagni, and a *Norma* that saw the Met debut of Marilyn Horne; she and Joan Sutherland sang eighteen performances of the work in the single season, including the tour, not missing a night. Frederica von Stade and Gail Robinson made debuts together as Genies in the *Magic Flute*; the Mexican soprano Gilda Cruz-Romo was a debut Maddalena in *Chénier* on tour. "I do not want to bore readers," Bing wrote in the company's annual report, "with accounts of the daily crises that plagued us as we tried to save a season which had been planned down to the last *comprimario* role." He looked forward with confidence: "Anyone who could live through the 1969–70 season and is still here to tell the tale, need not be afraid of anything."

But it was closing time for the Bing regime: the board blamed him for the strike, even if the unions did not. In any event, he would be 70 years old in June 1972, when the current extension of his contract (and all the new union contracts) ran out. In December 1970, it was announced that Goeran Gentele of the Stockholm Opera would succeed Bing as general manager. Greatly assisted by the strong feelings of Never Again on both sides of the bargaining table, Gentele got agreements with nearly all the unions in the first week of his incumbency, before he went off on his ill-fated vacation. There followed the boast about labor peace in the Met's 1972 annual report—and then, in 1980, came another devastating strike.

Bing's penultimate season, 1970–71, continued his effort to make amends for past neglect offering new productions of Gluck's *Orfeo* (in the Berlioz edition) and

Backstage at Lincoln Center: putting the finishing touches on a prop, wig, and piece of scenery

Massenet's *Werther*, the former yet another effort to keep Gluck going by dancing, the latter a new revelation of the talents of Rudolf Heinrich as a designer and of the new theater's lighting resources, as well as of the artistry of Christa Ludwig, the production's Charlotte. Beethoven's 200th birthday was celebrated with a new production of *Fidelio*, essentially an import from Vienna, Otto Schenk directing in the context of a Boris Aronson setting, Böhm on the podium, Vickers improving what was already the most powerful and arresting Florestan in anyone's memory. O'Hearn and Merrill contributed a splendidly straightforward *Parsifal* as a setting for Helge Brilioth's debut in the title role, Leopold Ludwig in the pit.

The debut list was strong: Caterina Ligendza, Adriana Maliponte, Stuart Burrows, Matteo Manuguerra, James Morris, and Ruggiero Raimondi. But the most significant of the debuts came after the main season was over and more or less by accident, when the conductor James Levine, signed for 1971–72, led a *Tosca* in the June supplement. By the time the next season began, Fausto Cleva was dead, and Levine took over *Luisa Miller*. Gentele was in the house as an observer and was dazzled, as were many merely in the audience for pleasure, by the *liveliest* early Verdi the theater had recently experienced. A foreigner himself, who planned to ask another foreigner (Rafael Kubelik) to be his music director, Gentele felt the need for an American musician in his artistic leadership. He asked Levine, who was all of 28 years old, to take the title and invent the job of "Principal Conductor." It was the most important decision the general-manager-elect made in the eighteen months he was at the Met.

Meanwhile, the Bing administration wound down, its work mostly completed (for seasons now had to be laid out at least two years in advance, and the future was Gentele's). Herman Krawitz and Robert Herman, who would leave with their boss, devotedly sought Gentele's intentions and served them. (The dozens of planning memos Herman wrote to Gentele in this year are a definition of noblesse oblige: it was Bing's last vanity that the transition to new management should be made without any of the petty nastiness that had accompanied the changeover from Johnson to himself.) It was a year to look backwards not forwards—the only major debut was that of a shooting star, Anja Silja. Having opened the last season of the old house with the opera that had launched it, Bing began his own last year with his own beginning, a *Don Carlo* in which (as he noted with "particular pleasure") three of the artists of 21 years earlier resumed their original roles—Siepi, Merrill, and Amara.

The new productions illustrated the full palette of the Bing years, ranging from awful (a *Freischütz* that was Deutsche Kunst at its dullest and most routine, Rudolf Heinrich's only failure at the house) to magical (a *Tristan* by August Everding and Schneider-Siemssen that wrapped the lovers in their own world as no other production anyone had ever seen, Nilsson in her glory bringing Jess Thomas with her). In between there was a splendidly atmospheric *Pelléas et Mélisande*, designed by

Desmond Heeley and directed by Deiber, Barry McDaniel in his debut as a very youthful Pelléas, Judith Blegen as an even younger, touching, deeply musical Mélisande. The conductor was Colin Davis (again trying out a work for the first time on the Met stage); he produced a strikingly delineated Debussy, none of the usual haze and pedal points, very convincing—and the orchestra played beautifully for him.

There was a borrowed production—*La Fille du régiment* from Covent Garden, Sutherland enjoying herself, Pavarotti a graceful fat man with a beautiful light spinto voice pushing the button for the nine high C's of "Ah, mes amis," Richard Bonynge conducting. And there was one last tribute to the later Verdi that meant so much to Bing, a massive setting and highly charged staging of *Otello* by Zeffirelli, with Teresa Zylis-Gara a carefully composed, vocally elegant Desdemona, McCracken and Milnes in the male leads, the chorus on its super-best behavior both dramatically and vocally in the overwhelming first act. Böhm conducted. In his final contribution to a Met annual report, Bing pointed up the fact that for this final *Otello*, as for his first *Don Carlo*, he had gone to his roots for a conductor of the German school.

TEN

The Tenth Decade,
the Second Century

A theatrical and film director, Goeran Gentele had run the Royal Opera in Stockholm with great success, staging operas while administering a relatively small national theater. His special triumph had been Verdi's *Un Ballo in maschera*, a story based on the murder of the Swedish King Gustav III (in the opera house), which was sung in a Swedish translation by the poet laureate—except that the King, brilliantly played by the tenor Ragnar Ulfung, often sang in French. In descriptions by people who did not see this production, it is solemnly said that the King was played—historically accurately—as a homosexual, but a better word would be "swish." As an explanation of why members of the court wished to kill this apparently admirable hero, the Frenchified effeminate manner worked perfectly—and though Birgit Nilsson once complained of the difficulties of singing the role of Amelia opposite that characterization, the fact is that one was not conscious of the problem in the opera house. An equally imaginative Gentele production had made a hit of a contemporary opera, Blomdahl's *Aniara*, a space-age fantasy using *musique concrète* for special effects; and Gentele had also been successful as a manager in bringing other major directors to stage operas in his theater, notably Ingmar Bergman, who had created a production of Stravinsky's *Rake's Progress* much admired by the composer.

Several people working in New York knew Gentele, notably Schuyler Chapin, who had been vice-president for programming at Lincoln Center. George Moore, who as chairman of First National City Bank had information resources all over the world, checked out the Swede's credentials and reputation, and made the choice. Bing was disappointed: he had hoped to have his tenure ratified, as it were, by the appointment of his assistants Robert Herman and Herman Krawitz as a duumvirate, and his sense of loyalty was violated. But the Gentele appointment was generally acclaimed.

Before formally accepting the job, Gentele approached Rafael Kubelik, formerly music director of the Chicago Symphony and Covent Garden (and thus completely adept in English), to become music director at his Met; and he engaged Chapin as his

"The story of the Metropolitan as it moves into its second century will likely be in large part the story of the mid-life of James Levine," Music Director since 1976.

assistant manager. Chapin had worked in radio, concert management, and recordings before his Lincoln Center job; and after the collapse of the Lincoln Center festival program, he had signed on with Leonard Bernstein to handle the maestro's multifarious special projects. Chapin came on board almost immediately—he spent much of the 1971–72 season at the Met familiarizing himself with the operation—but Kubelik, who was in charge of the musical end of Bavarian Radio, would not be available even to conduct a performance until 1973–74, and could not begin to assume the duties of music director until a year after that.

By the same token, much of the 1972–73 season had been set in concrete before Gentele was appointed. Bing had already signed Marilyn Horne and James McCracken for opening night. Major American artists, they had never before sung an opening, and Bing planned to heighten the interest of the occasion by introducing them to Wagnerian roles in *Tannhäuser*. Gentele did not want this old production, and looked around for another opera that could employ the rather special talents of Horne and McCracken. He found it in *Carmen*, which had recently been restored to Bizet's original (more or less) in a new edition. Gentele would direct *Carmen* himself, and Bernstein, who was interested in working with him and wanted to do a favor for Chapin, would conduct. Josef Svoboda, an imaginative Czech artist who had done distinguished work for a number of European houses, would make his Met debut as designer. The only other new production of the year would be the *Siegfried*, third installment of Karajan's *Ring*, which had nothing to do with the new management.

When Gentele, Kubelik, and Chapin met in July 1971 to plan the future of the company, they perforce started with 1973–74. Kubelik would bring Berlioz's *Les Troyens*, which he had led at Covent Garden and La Scala; Gentele would do his *Ballo*; the Karajan-conceived *Ring* would be completed with *Götterdämmerung*, Kubelik conducting; Bonynge and Sutherland would bring a Seattle Opera production of *Les Contes d'Hoffmann*, in a new performing edition; Jean-Pierre Ponnelle would come to the Met for the first time as designer and director of a Rossini *Italiana in Algeri* for Marilyn Horne. As a gesture of continuity in the house, Karl Böhm, who had conducted the Berman-designed *Don Giovanni* when it was new, would also conduct its replacement, which was to be designed by Jo Mielziner, his first assignment for the Met since *The Emperor Jones*.

It is impossible even to speculate on what would have happened to these productions—or to the Met—had Gentele lived. He put almost nothing on paper. The planning documents that survive are the carbons of Robert Herman's memos *to* Gentele, on which Herman noted in the margins the decisions the new manager passed back to him, *viva voce*. "Gentele," Chapin later wrote, "had one bothersome habit: he hated making final decisions."

The financial crisis that was descending upon the Met would have handicapped Gentele as badly as it did Chapin, and it is by no means clear that Gentele would have been more effective in fighting off George Moore's demands: that money be saved at every turn; that one of the new productions be killed (Chapin chose the *Don Giovanni*); that donors who wished to subsidize special projects be pushed to contribute to the general fund; that efficiency experts trained at a big bank be authorized to reorganize the opera house.

When Gentele's death in an automobile accident in July 1972 elevated Chapin to the job of acting general manager, the leadership of the opera company passed into hands that would never in other circumstances have been given such responsibilities. By temperament as well as training, Chapin at age 48 was someone's assistant: he had never in fact been the decision-maker in any organization. Neither Moore nor chairman Lowell Wadmond was prepared to let Chapin exercise the full authority of a general manager, and some members of the company, administrators as well as artists, took the attitude that the cat was away and the mice were at liberty.

Some of the projects Gentele had suggested could not be carried out properly—the "mini-Met," for example, an attempt to use the resources of the big company for early opera and experimental work in the manner of Milan's Piccola Scala, was projected by Gentele for the 900-seat jewel of the Juilliard Theater. By union rules, however, once that theater was used by a professional company selling tickets to the public it would become a union house: student productions using student carpenters, painters, stagehands, electricians would no longer be permitted. The mini-Met therefore had to play the tiny (280-seat) Forum in the basement of Lincoln Center's repertory theater building, with the orchestra in a balcony rather than in a pit and the singers out amongst the audience on a thrust stage. Two productions were mounted there (one being Virgil Thomson's *Four Saints in Three Acts*, the choreographer Alvin Ailey directing). Everyone wanted to be kind, but most observers felt like the French general at Balaklava: *C'est magnifique, mais ce n'est pas la guerre.*

On the higher time-horizon, Chapin found himself trapped. His own tenure in office being uncertain, he was poorly placed in negotiations for seasons three and four years off. And because Kubelik as music director and Levine as principal conductor would command so high a fraction of the best assignments in the years Chapin had to plan, he was unable to offer attractive opportunities to first-class conductors. When Kubelik quit in early 1974, running out on his engagements for a 1974 75 season in which he was to conduct the American premiere of Britten's *Death in Venice*, the first *Jenufa* since 1924–25, and the first complete *Ring* in a decade, Chapin was left with a hole he could not fill at the center of the company's artistic enterprise.

The most important of Chapin's decisions was the replacement of Gentele as the company's premier stage director and production supervisor. His choice fell on John Dexter. A British director from the National Theatre in London, he had

worked at Lincoln Center on a Peter Ustinov play while Chapin was vice president for programming, and had produced Janáček's *From the House of the Dead* with Kubelik as conductor at the Hamburg Opera, where he had also staged a number of other operas for that company's adventurous general manager, Rolf Liebermann. Dexter came to the Met to stage Verdi's *I Vespri Siciliani*, which Chapin, Kubelik, and Levine (who conducted it) decided to substitute for the *Ballo* that Gentele had planned for himself. A year later, Dexter would join the management team as "director of production," re-establishing the tripartite administration Gentele had planned—with Chapin now at the apex, Levine (as functional music director) and Dexter both reporting to him.

By then, Moore had resigned as president of the Association, defeated by deficits that rose to $7.8 million in 1972–73 and $9 million in 1973–74, with cumulative losses after contributions of $3.9 million for the two seasons. He was replaced by William Rockefeller, who was also connected with First National City Bank as a partner in the bank's law firm, Shearman & Sterling. Once again, the remedy for the Met's fiscal problems was sought in the appointment of a board "administration committee" to supervise the day-to-day affairs of the company, as Erskine and Cornelius Bliss had done in the 1930s, Spofford and Wadmond in the crisis attendant on the opening of the new house in 1966–67. This time, however, there would be a difference: the head of the administration committee, Anthony Bliss, would give the matter full-time attention, retiring from his law practice and moving into the Met with the new title of Executive Director.

Artistically, the results of the Chapin years were much like those of the later Bing years—not surprisingly, as much of the planning had of necessity been done by Bing before Gentele was chosen. Of the new productions in those years, one was a total success: an astonishing *Boris Godunov*, in an edition close to Mussorgsky's original. Martti Talvela's commanding Boris was splendidly framed dramatically and visually by August Everding's imaginative direction and Ming Cho Lee's inventive sets, rough-hewn for exteriors, iconographic inside, all joined to bring a unique confluence (rather than the usual conflict) of the public and personal aspects of the tragedy. Schippers conducted.

Of the others, Berlioz's *Les Troyens* was a personal triumph for Shirley Verrett, who doubled the role of Dido in the second part with her scheduled Cassandra in the first part when illness forced Christa Ludwig to cancel her participation in the premiere; Britten's *Death in Venice* was atmospheric but eventually wearisome, though it introduced two fine singing actors in Peter Pears (making a Met debut at the age of 64) and John Shirley-Quirk; and Rossini's *L'Assedio di Corinto*, in an edition originally mangled for La Scala, made a bang-up introduction for Beverly Sills, finally welcomed at the Met with several seasons of superb voicecraft and stagecraft still left to her.

Goeran Gentele (*left*), Bing's successor as general manager, died in July 1972 before his first season got under way. Schuyler G. Chapin (*right*), his assistant, took over the reins until 1975. The responsibility for running the Met then passed to Anthony A. Bliss (*below*), the present general manager, who first joined the board in 1949.

The *Vespri Siciliani* that introduced Dexter to the Met in 1973–74 was, like the first-night *Carmen* of the previous season, designed by Svoboda in black-and-white, and it was set on an enormous staircase that most observers found insufficiently evocative of Palermo. And nobody much liked the new productions of Janáček's *Jenufa* and of Bartók's *Bluebeard's Castle*.

Dramatically, a change of policy more important than any individual production: prior stagings were no longer sacrosanct when operas were revived. In every operatic production, the director is followed around by an assistant stage director who keeps a detailed prompt book of everything expected from the performer of each role. Robert Herman had first come to Bing's attention as the most precise and perfect of these assistants, who could convey, say, Tyrone Guthrie's instructions exactly as Guthrie had uttered them, even after the passage of years. Those prompt books were now to play a lesser role. Chapin and Dexter (and, perhaps most firmly, Levine) felt that a revival should be an opportunity to improve on rather than reproduce the original.

In *La Forza del destino* (where the edition was changed), in *Macbeth*, in *Don Giovanni*, in *Wozzeck*, Dexter & Co. opened up old productions for changes in emphasis and characterization. (A warehouse fire in November 1973, which destroyed the costumes for half the Met's productions, doubtless helped the drive to restage old ventures rather than merely resurrect them.) The *Don Giovanni* and *Wozzeck* productions were especially important because they gave Levine his first opportunities to expand his Met repertory beyond the Italian category, and began the revelation of how major a conductor the house had acquired.

The first of Chapin's three years had been rich in conducting debuts, some prearranged by Bing, some initiated by the new management. There were no fewer than six new conductors: Peter Herman Adler, who had been director of the NBC Opera; Carlo Felice Cillario, a veteran of the Chicago Lyric Opera; Sixten Ehrling from Stockholm; Kazimierz Kord from Poland; Henry Lewis, Marilyn Horne's husband and the Met's first black conductor; Peter Maag from Switzerland; and Charles Mackerras from Australia. Of these, Mackerras, who found the right scale for Gluck's *Orfeo* (and had the right Orfeo in Marilyn Horne), made the strongest impression. By 1975–76, the conducting staff was a shambles: Kubelik, Leinsdorf, Max Rudolf, and William Steinberg, who had all worked at the house in 1973–74, were gone; except for Schippers, who was dying, the only conductor of world stature on the Met roster was Levine, and his qualities were not yet widely recognized. One aspect of the musical performance, however, had vastly improved: the new chorus master, David Stivender, had brought to life a body that had been moribund for years.

The Chapin years also saw a number of significant new singers at the Met. The most spectacular debut was that of Kiri Te Kanawa in 1974, as Desdemona in a

Stars of the Eighties, I. José Van Dam (*above left*, as Golaud in *Pelléas*), Marilyn Horne (*above right*, as Isabella in Rossini's *L'Italiana in Algeri*), Ileana Cotrubas and Frederica von Stade (*center*, as Ilia and Idamante in Mozart's *Idomeneo*), Hildegard Behrens (*below left*, as Leonore in Beethoven's *Fidelio*), and Martti Talvela (*below right*, as Mussorgsky's Boris Godunov).

Saturday matinee performance of *Otello* for which she had not been scheduled. Allen Hughes reported in the *Times* that the audience was still in the theater after six o'clock, cheering an artist who—like Ponselle, Tibbett, Flagstad, and Nilsson—had leaped in one bound to a leading position in the company. Among the others introduced in the Chapin years were Rita Hunter as an awkwardly large but powerful Brünnhilde; Yvonne Minton as a stylish Octavian; Gwyneth Jones as a gorgeous Sieglinde; Hans Sotin as Sarastro; two splendid Swedes, Ingvar Wixell as Rigoletto and Ragnar Ulfung as Mime in *Siegfried*; Brigitte Fassbaender, a mezzo of unique timbre, as Octavian; Benita Valente as Pamina and Rita Shane as Queen of the Night on the same evening; Magda Olivero at the end of a long career, as Tosca; Katia Ricciarelli as Mimi; Richard Stilwell as Guglielmo in *Così*; José Carreras, who had first come to the United States for the City Opera, as Cavaradossi.

In short, the Met neither fell apart nor reached new heights under Chapin's administration. But it went broke. Revenues remained stagnant while costs were rising. Bing's last season had taken in $12.9 million at the box office; Chapin's third would take in only $13.5 million, selling only 86 per cent of capacity, though expenses had risen from $22.4 million in 1971–72 to $27.9 million in 1974–75. Backstage and in the board room, there remained a feeling that the general manager was not entirely in control of the house. Chapin had been effective in raising funds for new productions, and he had negotiated one of the Met's largest and most interesting ventures—a three-week tour of Japan in spring 1975, made possible by a $2.5 million subvention from a Japanese corporation. But few people on the board saw much reason to believe that Chapin's leadership could pull the company out of its financial quagmire, or yield sufficient artistic advance to make the Met exciting in the eyes of the big donors of funds, then defined by both Chapin and the board as the foundations and the government.

In early spring 1975, Chapin was informed that his contract as general manager would not be renewed. In the future, there would be no general manager: Bliss as executive director would run the opera company, with Levine and Dexter giving artistic guidance. Chapin was offered instead a contract as head of a fund-raising foundation for the Met, out of the chain of command of the opera company. It can scarcely have been expected that he would take it.

Chapin's memoirs, written after he became Dean of the School of the Arts at Columbia University, reveal a persisting bitterness at Moore, Bliss, Rockefeller—the leaders of the board. More recently, the fires have been banked. "Before I became general manager of the Met," Chapin said a half dozen years after his dismissal, "I had always been number-two to someone else. This was my first chance to be number-one, which is a very different thing from being number-two. It takes time to learn. I was learning; but they wouldn't give me time."

☆ ☆ ☆

Stars of the Eighties, II. Tatiana Troyanos (*above left*, as Eboli in *Don Carlo*), Montserrat Caballé (*above right*, as Cilèa's Adriana Lecouvreur), Katia Ricciarelli (*center*, as Verdi's Luisa Miller), Sherrill Milnes (*below left*, as Iago in *Otello*), and Cornell MacNeil (*below right*, as Rigoletto).

The opera company over which Anthony Bliss assumed control in summer 1975 was closer to bankruptcy than it had been at any time since the 1930s. The numbers were no worse than what had been left to Moore in 1967, but that disaster had been caused by a miscalculated single venture, the move to Lincoln Center, while the problems Bliss inherited were cumulative and continuing. A two-week reduction in the length of the 1975–76 season and the abandonment of the post-tour June performances at Lincoln Center held expenses level, year-to-year, but produced a $700,000 reduction in box-office income, despite an improvement from 86 per cent to 95 per cent in the percentage of the house sold in New York. That improvement was achieved in part with the help of the Met's first large-scale advertising campaign, which increased "other expenses" by $600,000. Fund-raising was more or less stuck at $9 million a year, and the net result was a loss of $2.1 million, which pushed the "working capital deficit" over $9 million.

Martha Baird Rockefeller had left the Met $5 million in her will, money that had come in during Bing's last season. The insurance company had paid $2.6 million for costumes lost in the warehouse fire; by not scheduling most of the affected operas, the Met had been able to hang onto most of that. In 1974–75, the sale of the land under the old house had produced $3.9 million. By spring 1976, nearly all the money from all these sources was gone. To pay its expenses in the summer of 1976, the Met was forced to borrow from the banks against the security of its subscription sales for the next year.

Many, perhaps most, members of the board thought the time had come to cut and run, to abandon year-round employment, abandon the tour (which was now losing more than a million dollars a year), reduce the New York season to the 24 weeks of the Gatti and early Bing years—in effect, to turn the Met into a "regional" opera company like San Francisco or Chicago. Bliss fought: expansion, not contraction, he argued, would save the Met. More advertising would permit higher ticket prices and boost income; electronic media could be exploited to make the house more national and produce additional earnings; profits could be gained from a diversification of activities, especially the presentation of ballet companies; government, corporations, and individuals could all be tapped for greater contributions if the fund-raising were fully professionalized.

Among Bliss's allies was Frank E. Taplin, who had been on the Met board since 1961 and had been part of the committee urging the continuance of the National Company a decade before. Taplin had retired young from commercial life, and had demonstrated considerable ability as a fund-raiser. At one time or another, he had been chairman of the board of Sarah Lawrence College, had reorganized the Marlboro Festival for Rudolf Serkin, organized the board for the Lincoln Center Chamber Music Society, and served as president of the Met's National Council. In effect, the Met board told Taplin that if he was so eager to see Bliss's program tried,

---

The artist David Hockney and stage director John Dexter (*above*) collaborated on two magical evenings of 20th-century works. *L'Enfant et les sortilèges* (*below left*, Hilda Harris on left as the naughty Child) formed part of an all-French program. Stravinsky's *Le Rossignol*, danced by Anthony Dowell and Natalia Makarova (*below right*), was given along with *Le Sacre du printemps* and *Oedipus Rex* to honor the composer's centenary.

he should take the responsibility himself. On consideration, he agreed, accepted the title of president of the Association, took a small office in the fund-raising section, where he would spend three days a week, and found another office for his volunteer Patron Program chairman, Katharine T. O'Neil (later president of the Metropolitan Opera Guild).

Taplin and Bliss like to give the credit for the 1976–77 fund drive, which raised more than $13.6 million, to Marilyn Shapiro, who had previously run campaigns for social and political causes and signed on with the Met in fall 1975 (she came from a job as administrative assistant to Congresswoman Elizabeth Holtzman). Her first assignment was "government and public affairs work," and she negotiated a challenge grant from the National Endowment for the Arts and a major contribution from the Rockefeller Foundation to make the challenge realistic. When Taplin became president, Shapiro was named director of development (she later became an assistant manager, coordinating all non-earned income).

At about this time, the Guild (then selling 30 per cent of the Met's unsubscribed tickets and conducting its own membership fund-raising program) began developing a computerized mailing list of all Met contributors and ticket buyers, a group it dubbed the "Met Family." Advised by board member Andrew Kershaw, president of the advertising agency Ogilvy & Mather, the Guild explored the wonders of sophisticated direct-mail appeals, which raised membership (and thus subscription to the Guild's magazine *Opera News*) from 60,000 in 1971 to 100,000 by 1977. Now Shapiro and the Met's marketing department extended the systems to radio and television promotions and advertising, telephone campaigns, ever more refined mailings and lists. By the Met's 100th season, Shapiro's full-time staff of two-dozen (enormously helped by board members and hundreds of volunteers) was raising $24 million a year—about $2 million of it from government grants, another $2 million from corporations, and an astonishing $20 million from individuals and foundations, in donations ranging fro $15 to $500,000.

Coming into its Centennial, the Met would have the support of no fewer than 200,000 contributors, only a minority of whom saw performances in the opera house. Of the 1,700 "Patrons" who give at least $1,000 a year, 500 live outside the New York metropolitan area; and of the 1,200 in and around New York, fewer than 800 are subscribers. "It's a big constituency and it's a wonderful institution," Shapiro says. "Most people support us because they love us. It's the best kind of support: they stay with you in hard times."

What has happened, obviously, is the development of a truly national constituency for the Met. The source of that constituency, equally obviously, is the broadcast audience, which runs three to five million on Saturday afternoons, and may have gone as high as seven million for the first, remarkably successful Public Broadcasting Service telecast of Puccini's *La Bohème*—with Renata Scotto and

Other 20th-century operas in the Met's recent repertory include Alban Berg's *Lulu* (*above*, Teresa Stratas as Lulu and Franz Mazura as Dr. Schoen), Benjamin Britten's *Billy Budd* (*below left*, James Morris as Claggart), and Francis Poulenc's *Dialogues des Carmélites* (*below right*, Régine Crespin as the Old Prioress).

Luciano Pavarotti—on March 15, 1977. An offer of a free sample copy of *Opera News* on that telecast drew more than 25,000 requests; public broadcasting stations that used the telecast as part of their own fund drive raised more than $1 million in response.

Each year since has seen three to five telecasts of Metropolitan Opera productions, with the costs paid by Texaco, the National Endowment for the Arts, and the Charles E. Culpeper Foundation. Whatever plans are eventually adopted to produce earnings for the Met through electronics, the PBS telecasts will be retained: along with the radio broadcasts, they are the primary return the Met gives for the $2 million a year of direct government contributions and the tax-deductions on $22 million given by corporations and the public.

As part of his program of expansion, Bliss permitted Levine and Dexter to devote to unfamiliar operas a far greater proportion of the Met's new-production budget than the house had ever before allocated to such purposes. In 1976–77, only one of the six new productions was an opera normally in the company's previous repertory (Wagner's *Lohengrin*, Levine conducting, Everding directing, René Kollo making his debut in the title role). Of the others, one was an opera not heard at the Met for forty years (Meyerbeer's enormous *Le Prophète*) and three were Met premieres— Massenet's *Esclarmonde* in a production borrowed from San Francisco, Alban Berg's *Lulu*, and Francis Poulenc's *Dialogues des Carmélites*. The last of these, done in English, was a management triumph: a critical and popular success (all performances after the first were sold out), it had been mounted at trivial cost. Dexter used costumes and pieces of sets from other productions with such splendid taste and imagination that no audience could have guessed it was in the presence of hand-me-downs.

Later the commitment to 20th-century repertory would take even more interesting forms. There was a conventional and excellent staging of Britten's conventional and excellent *Billy Budd* (old Peter Pears and young Richard Stilwell sharing the honors with Raymond Leppard in the pit, Dexter as director, and scenery by William Dudley, whose set of the poop deck of a sailing ship rose magnificently to five decks for the great condemnation scene). And then there was a successful production of Kurt Weill's and Bertolt Brecht's *The Rise and Fall of the City of Mahagonny*, an off-Broadway or even cabaret piece designed by Jocelyn Herbert to be big enough and powerful as well as entertaining in a 3,800-seat house (with considerable help, of course, from a huge cast highlighted by Stratas, Varnay, MacNeil, Cassilly, Plishka, and Ulfung).

Though there are in fact a number of 20th-century operas that have remained in repertory outside New York and have never been performed at the Met, history does argue that few modern pieces can take and hold that stage. To keep the house from resuming its decline into a 19th-century museum, Levine and Dexter decided to create 20th-century evenings of different works that could be combined into a single experience. The first of these was a visit to the first half of the century in France. Called *Parade* after the Satie ballet that opened it, the confection included Poulenc's naughty *Les Mamelles de Tirésias* and Ravel's nice *L'Enfant et les sortilèges*. Dexter staged, with sets and costumes by the splendidly original British artist David Hockney; the conductor was the venerable Manuel Rosenthal, making his Met debut, drawing from the Met orchestra performances (especially of the Ravel) that were the stuff people who love a work can dream of but rarely are blessed enough to hear. A heavily papered (and thus by definition rather supercilious) house erupted with gratitude when the evening was over, and the other six performances sold to the walls. The next year, Dexter and Hockney were at it again, this time with Levine in the pit (or, rather, on the podium, for the orchestra sat on a level with the parquet, separated from the audience by a low plexiglass screen), honoring Stravinsky on the centenary of his birth with *Le Sacre du printemps*, *Le Rossignol*, and *Oedipus Rex*.

For the rest, it is too soon after the event to try to identify the major debuts of the last few years or the most important new productions (except perhaps for the work of Schenk and Schneider-Siemssen on *Tannhäuser* and *Contes d'Hoffmann*, both *hors de combat*, and the stupendous Christmas Eve party on Montmartre that Franco Zeffirelli supplied for *La Bohème*). What cannot be skipped is the significance of James Levine, who assumed the title of Music Director and Principal Conductor in 1976, and whose steady, rapid growth through the decade was the source of the company's impressive artistic dignity as its first century came to a close.

Trained as a pianist by Rosina Lhevinne and Rudolf Serkin, as a conductor by Max Rudolf and George Szell, Levine had arrived at the Met in 1971 a technician of the first order, who could maintain rhythmic tension at any tempo, follow singers when they deserved that tribute, and lead them when the arch of a work required a conductor's architectonic discipline. Fat of face and figure (he has since slimmed down a bit), with a dark aureole of a curly Afro hair-do, he offered also that distinctiveness of appearance that accelerates the achievement of celebrity.

The striking aspect of Levine's work at the Met, however, was something else: his visible, fully communicated delight in making music. There was never a routine evening for performers or audience with Levine on the podium: he was always *up*. And there was not a glimmer of self-satisfaction in the *rayonnement* of his delight, for he took it as given that every performance could be better than it was—and should be better than the last time the same forces offered the same work. No conductor has ever given his first performance of so many operas at the Met, and inevitably Levine's initial conception of some of the scores he led provoked critical complaint. But it was the universal experience of the critical fraternity that Levine improved his performances with every repetition, refining, sometimes tightening (more commonly, relaxing), adjusting the balances between expression and narration.

Overleaf: Met performances are now filmed "live" for television by cameras positioned throughout the house. The monitor screen pictured here (*right*) shows a close-up from Act II of *Tannhäuser*. The Otto Schenk production featured Eva Marton in the role of Elisabeth (*left, above*) and Bernd Weikl as Wolfram (*left, below*).

With help from artistic administrator (later assistant manager) Joan Ingpen, who came to the Met from a career at Covent Garden and several years of helping Rolf Liebermann give Paris a major opera company, Levine has had command of both repertory and casting ("Joan comes and tells me what will work"). He believes in tailoring an opera company's work to the available talent—and to the evolving relationship between opera and its audience. "The wonderful thing about this period," Levine says,

is that we have an art form going through enormous change. As you get further and further away from the time when these works were created, we have to be *specifically* re-creative. And if you were to name the thirty greatest singers in the world today as against 1950 or 1940, you would be dealing with a different breed of singer. Thirty years ago, singers like Varnay and Mödl and Vinay, singers who were interested in a total performance of their roles, were rarities. It was the Flagstads and Melchiors and Tebaldis who dominated the stage, the great stand-up-and-sing singers. Today, people want a singer to be dramatically plausible; then, few people cared.

One of the most creative aspects of my job is to balance the repertoire and create what you can cast right, do the big operas at those moments when the casting can be seen to survive. We've scheduled a lot of *Parsifals* and *Tannhäusers* and *Lohengrins*, and a new *Dutchman*, waiting for the cycle to turn and give us the singers we need for the *Ring*.

What has mattered most is that Levine was *there*, all year long. "I approve of that period in history," he says, "when people stayed with an organization, didn't take the jet plane flying everywhere all the time. When Ormandy had the Philadelphia Orchestra before the jet plane, he conducted 85 per cent of the performances; Reiner conducted 85 per cent of the performances in Chicago." Toscanini in 1908–12 conducted between two-fifths and half of all the performances at the Met; Levine in the early 1980s was running at about one-third. There is an argument to be made that other major conductors shun a house where the music director appears to have first choice of artists, works, and rehearsal time—but a viable opposing argument holds that conductors and singers are drawn to work with companies disciplined by a resident leader. Szell had his pick of the world in choosing conductors for the Cleveland Orchestra in the weeks he programmed for guests.

"People don't digest what it means to do seven performances every bloody week," Levine says. "This is not like Covent Garden, where they do only two operas for six weeks, or Vienna, where the only thing that ever gets rehearsed at all is the new production. We don't have the relief of ballet evenings, or the relief of a small house." Levine has tried to concentrate each season's performances of an opera

Opposite: The final moments of Verdi's *Un Ballo in maschera* with Judith Blegen (Oscar) and Luciano Pavarotti (Riccardo). The 1980 production was staged by Elijah Moshinsky, with sets by Peter Wexler and costumes by Peter J. Hall.

Pages 346, 347: Leading ladies: Teresa Stratas (with José Carreras) in *Bohème* Act I (*left, above*), Renata Scotto as Puccini's Manon Lescaut (*left, below*), and Joan Sutherland as Lucia (*right*).

Pages 348, 349: David Hockney was commissioned to provide the designs for "Parade: An Evening of French Music Theater" in 1981. Illustrated here is his sketch for Francis Poulenc's *Les Mamelles de Tirésias*.

within a brief period, so that casts and conductors can be kept together. The seven weekly performances now involve no more than five, often only four, different operas. "Of the 22 to 24 operas we do," Levine claims, "20 are on a stagione basis." Where a work must be kept in repertory for a good part of the season, Levine has worked toward having two entirely separate casts, both stable—and on the things he conducts himself, of course, the leadership remains.

The result has been to make the Metropolitan more dependent on one man than it has been at any time since the days of Toscanini—and Levine as the century ended was enthusiastically hoping to increase that dependence. Willing to trust Dexter's judgment on stage—and with his own position not entirely established—Levine had accepted for a time the restriction of his own area of control to the musical preparation and performance. That held as long as Dexter remained in management. In autumn 1980, however, having reorganized the production staff as a permanent team and having installed Gil Wechsler as the Met's first fully qualified lighting designer, Dexter decided he had paid his dues as director of production, and resigned that post to work only on the operas he staged himself—a decision made easier by the fact that the technical operations backstage were firmly in the hands of assistant manager Joseph Volpe. Looking ahead, then, Levine envisioned productions in which he would exercise overall artistic control, either through contracts for individual operas or as artistic director of the company. "The separation of musical and dramatic," he said, echoing in another language what Toscanini must have said to Gatti, "has become for me intolerable."

Barring bad luck, which can come in so many guises, the story of the Metropolitan as it moves on into its second century will likely be in large part the story of the mid-life of James Levine, who turned forty on June 23, 1983.

Levine is unlikely to suffer Toscanini's disappointments in financial constraint or organizational rigidity. Taplin and Bliss and the board determined as early as spring 1978 that the fact of the Centennial should be exploited to assure the Met an endowment of major size. It was the absence of such an endowment, Taplin felt, that had created the crisis of 1975–76: "When I came, the endowment of the Metropolitan Opera was almost exactly the size of that of Sarah Lawrence College, or Marlboro, or the Lincoln Center Chamber Music Society—two million dollars."

The fund drive announced in spring 1980—to be concluded toward the end of the Centennial season in spring 1984—would be for no less than $100 million, of which 10 to 15 per cent would be available for improvements in the house. Some of these

Pages 350, 351: More leading ladies. Richard Strauss's *Elektra* was performed in 1980 by (*left*) Leonie Rysanek as Chrysothemis and Birgit Nilsson as Elektra. The 1982 season opened with the same composer's *Der Rosenkavalier*, featuring Kiri Te Kanawa (*right*) as the Marschallin.

Opposite: A resplendent 1982 production of *Les Contes d'Hoffmann*, designed by Günther Schneider-Siemssen and staged by Otto Schenk, had Ruth Welting as the mechanical doll Olympia and Placido Domingo as a bespectacled Hoffmann.

are technological ("the technology of this theater," Bliss observed, "is that of the German 1950s, which is now out of date"). Other improvements relate to space utilization and running expenses—moving set construction, storage, and other functions to a new production center in Weehauken and redesigning areas to provide homes for ancillary activities (notably the Metropolitan Opera Guild and National Council) occupying expensive space outside. Still others advance the creature comforts and "home" qualities of the house—especially a new cafeteria (for which Taplin's own half-million-dollar gift was earmarked), aimed to create a little more community in a theater where principals, orchestra, chorus and ballet, *comprimario* singers, stagehands and craftsmen, clerks and secretaries and mainten- ance staff all have their own areas, dressing facilities, and hours, and rarely mingle or find expressions of esprit de corps.

But most of the money will simply earn income for the Met, relieving what would otherwise be an intolerable strain on the company's fund-raising capacity as the costs of producing opera remorselessly advance more rapidly than the box-office receipts. In good years (it is hoped) the endowment fund will increase; in bad years, that accumulated increase can be drawn down. In any event, the days of negative working capital and bank loans will be gone forever, and the artistic direction will be able to budget some years ahead—as it must in this age when major artists are signed four and five years before the performances planned for them.

Organizationally, the Met settled down in the last years of its first century. The management consultants went back where they had come from. In 1981, Anthony Bliss was appointed to the restored post of general manager, and patterns of reporting by "directors" to "assistant managers" were established. The result, structured both hierarchically and through committee meetings, is something quite unlike what Bing left, far less personal and much more predictable. Erich Leinsdorf has observed that "the Metropolitan Opera today is a corporation, more like other corporations that make, say, refrigerators, than it is like any opera company of a generation ago. I am not criticizing," Leinsdorf added, "merely observing."

The disadvantages of the corporate organization are all on the surface. In theory, a corporation will be less willing to experiment and take risks; in fact, at the Met, the division of business and artistic responsibility leaves the creative departments with a budget specifically targeted for novelty: the Met at 95 was far friskier than it had been when younger. There have been losses of personality and of touches of emotional support—the presence of the general manager backstage before each performance and during intermissions, for example—that characterized previous regimes. Corporations are today-oriented organizations and may neglect anniver- saries of debuts, significant birthdays, echoes of past triumphs. But now the artists are corporations too. Patti's (and Meneghini's) insistence on cash on the barrelhead has been replaced by wire transfer of funds to Swiss bank accounts. In any event, at

$70 million a year and rising, the Met has become too big an operation to be run out of a general manager's hat.

Moreover, artists can now rely more on the organization than they could in the past, and there has been considerable reduction in the sort of competitive backbiting that was not uncommon in a more personal era. Fees, for example, really have been standardized—nobody in the 100th season got more than $8,000 per performance, and there was none of the jiggery-pokery of only a few years before, when artists would sign for a standard fee on an arrangement where they would be "guaranteed" performances they would not be asked to sing. Revivals have been more carefully staged, and in a number of instances their original directors have been not only recalled but encouraged to improve their work rather than merely duplicate it.

Rudolf Bing's opera house had been an attractive place for major artists to work, because they knew there more than anywhere else what would be asked from them, and when, and where. The new corporate Met, inheriting a house that had slid back pretty far from Bing's standards in that regard, has improved on Bing's system: there is a kind of security about the Met as it enters its second century that makes the place comforting for singers. Levine argues, with examples and statistics, that most major international artists spend more of their time in New York than at any other opera house, despite fees that can be several thousand dollars a performance less than the government-subsidized European theaters can pay, simply because they like working at the Met.

In August 1982, the Metropolitan concluded 29 years of negotiations with its unions and signed contracts that will permit a great expansion of its electronic services: broadcast television (worldwide), cable television, video cassette, video disc. The principle is a 50-50 split between the Association and its work forces of all revenues received from such sources, with the share to the work force allocated pro rata to their proportion of the costs of putting on the performance.

The conclusion of these contracts made it possible for the Met to enter into a long-term contract with Beta Film in Germany for the distribution of live-by-satellite performances of the Met on Saturday afternoons (Saturday evening in Europe), with the Europeans thereafter acting as agent for the Met in the sale of the material in the United States and around the world. The old optimism that pay-cable and video recordings would by themselves make opera financially viable has died as realistic revenue projections have emerged. Still, with the expenses of producing the broadcasts and the videotape largely met by Texaco and the foundations, the gain to the opera company will be substantial, with $5 million a year a plausible target for the end of the decade. Equally important, the availability of video recordings and the permanence of the PBS broadcasts, which the Europeans have been told are inviolable, should help maintain the Met's status as a "national" company even if the tour should have to be sharply cut back.

What has made the Met's prospects particularly cheerful as the company enters its second century is the great growth of interest in opera across the United States. Not since the burst of enthusiasm for Wagner in the late 19th century has opera as an art form stood so high in the assessments of the intellectual community. Sixty years ago, Otto Kahn complained that the press, by making a cult of personality around conductors, had glamorized the symphony orchestras to the point where they seemed more important than opera in the minds of the musical public. Today, the orchestras must program vocal soloists to meet their ticket-buyers' incessantly growing taste for singing and for opera. In the early 1980s, there were opera companies of international quality not only in San Francisco and Chicago and across the plaza at Lincoln Center, but also in Washington, Philadelphia, Dallas, Houston, San Diego, Miami, Newark, Seattle, and Boston. Though St. Louis, Kansas City, Minneapolis-St. Paul, Santa Fe, and Norfolk do not seek to draw singers from around the globe, what they do is often interesting enough to lure critics from around the country. Somebody out there is listening, looking, and paying.

Increased popularity has, oddly, exacted a price in reduced glamour. The Metropolitan opera season still opens with the spectacle of a swarm of photographers coming on stage before the curtain to point their cameras at the auditorium in order to register forever the opening-night audience—but now the pictures are more likely to be filed than printed. Once upon a time people went to the opera to see and be seen; now their attention is focused all but exclusively on the stage. When there were only 7,000 subscribers to the Met, at the start of the Bing era, a high fraction came in evening dress; with 28,000, that fraction would be smaller even in the absence of other changes. And there have, of course, been other changes—not least in the move from 39th Street to Lincoln Center, from a surpassingly elegant auditorium to a useful theater.

It is the middle class that makes the world turn these days, and opera—much for its own good—has become a middle-class rather than an aristocratic entertainment. In this new era of opera, as in the past, the Met is not just primus inter pares; it is primus, period. Sporadically, the Met gets challenged—by La Scala under Toscanini in the 1920s and again in the 1950s, by Covent Garden when Solti was music director, by Paris when Rolf Liebermann had easy access to the French exchequer. But the balance of nature seems to be that the Met is number-one. Not many institutions can show such certainty of purpose, financial security, continuing accomplishment, and visible confidence on their hundredth birthday. The Metropolitan Opera at 100 has reason to celebrate.

The posters listing casts of forthcoming Met performances have moved from Broadway (page 264) to Lincoln Center Plaza, but their hold on opera fans remains as potent as ever.

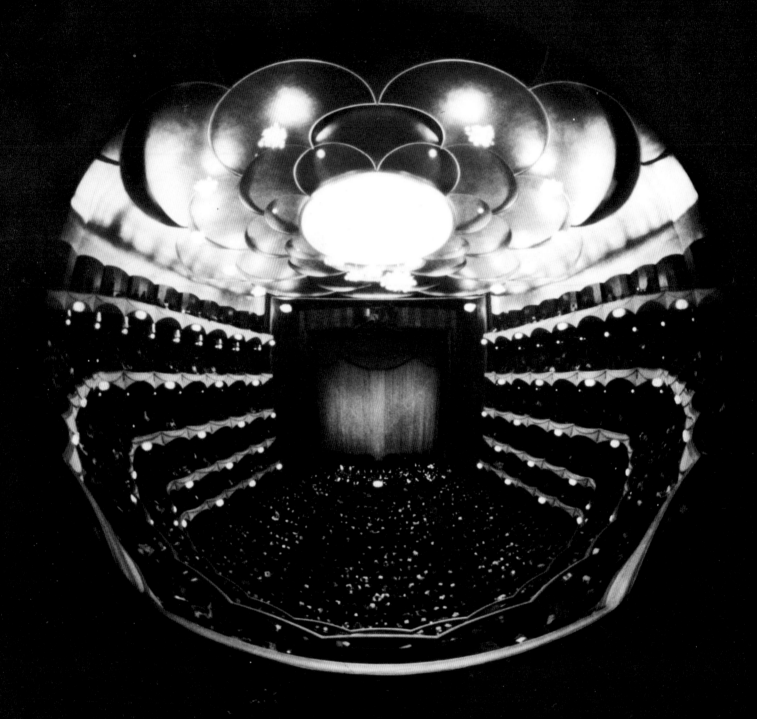

NOTES ON THE TEXT

Page numbers are shown in bold type;
individual documents in the Metropolitan Opera Archives are identified by an asterisk.

ONE

10 De Reszke: Irving Kolodin, *The Metropolitan Opera*, 4th ed., Alfred A. Knopf, New York, 1966, p. 121.
Odell quote: George C. A. Odell, *Annals of the New York Stage*, Columbia University Press, New York, 1927–38, vol. VI, p. 186.
Whitman on *Ernani*: Robert D. Faner, *Walt Whitman and Opera*, Southern Illinois University Press, Carbondale and Edwardsville, Ill., 1951 (paper ed., 1971), p. 80.
12 Mapleson's honor: New York *Dramatic Mirror*, 5/10/84, p. 6.
Belmont letter: August Belmont, Sr. to Levi P. Morton, 5/7/78.
13 Lehmann quote: Lilli Lehmann, *My Path Through Life*, G. P. Putnam's Sons, New York, 1914, p. 340.
16 Potter and Robinson, "Competitive Design Proposal for the Metropolitan Opera House," *American Architect and Building News*, vol. viii, no. 255, 11/30/80, pp. 234, 235.
18 J. Cleaveland Cady, "The Essential Features of a Large Opera House," *American Architect and Building News*, vol. xxii, no. 618, 10/29/87, p. 208.
24 Miller quote: Alice Duer Miller, "The Opera Box: The Sorrows of a New York Hostess," in George Marek, *A World Treasury of Grand Opera*, Harper & Bros., New York, 1957, pp. 121–2.
Food: "The Giddy Gusher," New York *Mirror*, 10/27/83.
25 Henry T. Finck, "German Opera in New York," *The Cosmopolitan*, vol. 5, no. 1, March 1888, pp. 3 and 19.
Belmont letter: Belmont to J. H. Mapleson, 7/18/77.
28 Lehmann on Stanton: Lehmann, op. cit., pp. 342–3.
Mapleson quote: in Harold Rosenthal (ed.), *The Mapleson Memoirs, 1858–1888*, Appleton-Century-Crofts, New York, 1966, p. 179.
Lehmann on *Tristan*: Lehmann, op. cit., pp. 366–7.
30 Aldrich quote: Richard Aldrich, "English Opera at the Met," *The Critic*, October 1900, p. 327.
31 Farrar quote: Geraldine Farrar, *American Singer*, Macmillan, New York, 1916, p. 88.
Alma Mahler: *Gustav Mahler, Memories and Letters*, by Alma Mahler, ed. by Donald Mitchell, John Murray, London, 1968, and Viking, New York, 1969, p. 127.

TWO

33 Krehbiel quote: Henry E. Krehbiel, *Chapters of Opera*, Henry Holt, New York, 1908, p. 93.
34 Appearance: "The Usher," New York *Dramatic Mirror*, 8/18/83; M. Schuyler, "The Metropolitan Opera House," *Harper's*, November 1883, pp. 878, 888.
36 Lehmann on backstage: Lehmann, op. cit., pp. 342, 343.
39 Pit: M. G. van Rensselaer, "The Metropolitan Opera House, New York—II," *American Architect and Building News*, vol. xv, no. 426, 2/3/84, pp. 86 and 88–9.
New York Times: 10/14/83, 10/23/83. The 8:23 starting time for opening night (see p. 33) is also taken from the *Times* of 10/23/83.
Decor: Van Rensselaer, op. cit., pp. 88, 87.
40 Acoustics: ibid., p. 86.
42 Scenery and costumes: "The Usher," New York *Dramatic Mirror*, 11/17/83.
Lehmann, op. cit., p. 349.
44 Henderson, *New York Times*, 12/25/83.
48 Krehbiel quote: in William H. Seltsam (compiler), *Metropolitan Opera Annals*, H. W. Wilson Co., New York, 1947, p. 12 (henceforth listed as *Annals*).
59 Krehbiel, *Chapters*, p. 170.
63 Nordica quote: in Ira Glackens, *Yankee Diva*, Coleride Press, New York, 1963, p. 180.
Finck, op. cit., p. 63.
Lehmann, op. cit., p. 385.
66 Club history: Eugene Bonner, *The Club in the Opera House*, Princeton University Press, Princeton, 1949, p. 61.
68 Krehbiel on Melba: *Annals*, p. 60.
Henderson on *Carmen*: ibid.
72 Krehbiel on De Reszke: *Annals*, p. 78; on Ophelia: ibid., p. 79.
79 Reamer quote: Lawrence Reamer, "A New Regime for American Opera," *The American Monthly Review of Reviews*, 1903, pp. 444, 445.

THREE

83 Shabby Met: Frances Alda, *Men, Women and Tenors*, Houghton Mifflin Co., Boston, 1937, p. 109.
Gatti quote: Giulio Gatti-Casazza, *Memories of the Opera* (trans., Howard Taubman), Scribner's, New York, 1941, p. 20.
86 Mahler to Dippel: in Alma Mahler, op. cit., p. 317.
87 "Harriman Extermination League": Otto H. Kahn, *Of Many Things*, Boni & Liveright, New York, 1927, p. 141.
88 Kahn on profit: Kahn to Hyde, 4/2/06.
90 Aldrich: *Annals*, p. 145.
92 Puccini quote: in Quaintance Eaton, *The Miracle of the Met*, Meredith Press, New York, 1968, p. 170.
Krehbiel quote: *Annals*, p. 172.
93 Aldrich quote: in John F. Cone, *The Manhattan Opera Company*, University of Oklahoma Press, 1966, p. 71.
Kahn to Hyde, 4/2/06.
Kahn to Conried, 5/21/08.*
94 Henderson quote: *Annals*, p. 144.
95 Conried description: Mahler, op. cit., p. 128.
Kahn to Conried, 5/21/08.*
99 Gatti's complaint: New York *Sun*, 1/8/09.
Toscanini quote: Gatti, op. cit., p. 148.
100 Musician quote: New York *Post*, 10/24/08.
Farrar quote: Geraldine Farrar, *Such Sweet Compulsion*, Greystone Press, New York, 1938, p. 121.
Meltzer quote: New York *American*, 10/12/08.
102 Eames and Mahler: New York *Press*, 1/14/09.
Eames and Toscanini: Emma Eames, *Reflections*, Appleton & Co., New York, 1917, p. 299.
Farrar-Toscanini: New York *American*, 12/7/08.
103 Smith quote: New York *Press*, 11/17/08.
Aldrich and Krehbiel quotes: *Annals*, p. 196.
Henderson quotes: New York *Sun*, 11/22/08.
104 New York *Post*, 11/19/08.

Met artists' letter: in Farrar, *Such Sweet Compulsion*, p. 118.
105 *Daily Telegraph*, 12/5/08.
Met management letter: Farrar, op. cit., p. 119.
Smith quote: New York *Press*, 12/06/08.
106 Farrar story: Farrar, op. cit., pp. 121–3; "friendly overtures": Farrar, *American Singer*, p. 109.
Sachs quote: Harvey Sachs, *Toscanini*, Lippincott, Philadelphia, 1978, p. 129.
108 Aldrich quote: *New York Times*, 1/14/09.
111 Henderson quote: New York *Sun*, 3/14/09.
The *Independent*, 4/29/09, p. 895.

FOUR

116 Krehbiel quote: *Annals*, p. 350.
117–18 Caruso on singers: Walter Slezak, *What Time is the Next Swan?*, Doubleday, Garden City, N.Y., 1962, p. 34.
Henderson: in Kolodin, op. cit., p. 175.
120 Caruso at Academy: Stanley Jackson, *Caruso*, Stein & Day, New York, 1972, p. 284.
123 Alda, op. cit., p. 219.
124 Fremstad: Mary Watkins Cushing, *The Rainbow Bridge*, G. P. Putnam's Sons, New York, 1954, p. 198.
127 Piano endorsement: Kolodin, op. cit., p. 15.
Gatti's fly: Helen Noble, *Life with the Met*, G. P. Putnam's Sons, New York, 1954, p. 56.
128 Diaghilev: The statement (Kolodin, op. cit., p. 17) that Kahn charged the losses on the Diaghilev company against the books of the Metropolitan Opera Company ("I know," Kolodin wrote. "I have seen the books") misrepresents a more complicated transaction. At the same time that the Met was picking up $326,000 of Diaghilev losses ($50,000 for 1915–16, $276,000 for the disastrous tour under Nijinsky's direction in fall 1916), Kahn was in effect writing off the $363,000 the Met owed him and Vanderbilt as the result of the first two Gatti seasons. If Kahn is to be deprived of credit for backing Diaghilev, he should be given credit for absorbing the losses of 1908–10. The stock he took in lieu of his bonds paid no dividends and could not be sold (and was, in the end, worthless), while the bonds had in fact yielded 4 per cent, and were backed by a $38,000-a-year sinking fund that had accumulated $228,000 when Kahn canceled the bonds and transferred the money to the Met's surplus account.
130 Kahn to Ziegler, 5/2/29.*
Alda, op. cit., pp. 206, 207.

133 Sachs, op. cit., p. 138; Dal Monte: ibid., p. 151; Martinelli: ibid., p. 127.
134 Krehbiel: ibid., p. 126; Gatti letter translation: ibid., p. 130.
Johnson invitation: Ruby Mercer, *The Tenor of His Time*, Clarke, Irwin & Co., Toronto, 1976, p. 202.
135 Gatti, op. cit., p. 196.
146 Briggs: John Briggs, *Requiem for a Yellow Brick Brewery*, Little, Brown & Co., Boston, 1969, p. 124.
148 Olin Downes quote: *Annals*, p. 651.
150 Farrar on Jeritza: *Such Sweet Compulsion*, p. 131.
151 Role for Tibbett: Ziegler to Cornelius W. Bliss, 5/17/34.*
Gilman on Schorr: *Annals*, p. 416; Olin Downes: ibid., p. 686.
154 Walter quote: Briggs, op. cit., p. 170.

FIVE

166 Judels and spaghetti: Talk of the Town, in *The New Yorker*, 2/10/34.
Mapleson on parts: Lionel Mapleson to Edward Ziegler, 5/7/31.*
168 Irving Weil: Otto Kahn to William Randolph Hearst, 12/26/29.*
169 Chorus demands: Edward Ziegler to Giulio Gatti-Casazza, 6/2/22,* and to Fortune Gallo, 5/9/22.*
174 "Some idiot": Briggs, op. cit., p. 217. "Yarborough": Paul Cravath to Edward Ziegler 1/4/34.*
176 "Harsh settlement": Paul Cravath to Edward Ziegler, 1/30/33.*
179 Cravath and Bori quotes: *New York Times*, 3/6/33; Bori on fund-raising: H. J. Brock, "Half a Century and the Opera Goes On," *New York Times Magazine*, 12/24/33, pp. 10, 11.
180 Downes on sponsor: Olin Downes, "Opera Season Begins," *New York Times*, Entertainment Section, 12/24/33, p. 6.
Downes review: "The Opera in Review," *New York Times*, 12/27/33, p. 22.
182 Downes quote: *New York Times*, 12/24/33.
185 Gilman: New York *Herald Tribune*, 1/21/34.
Gatti quote: Bruno Zirato, "Voice from the Past," *New York Times*, Sunday Music Section, 11/5/50.
186 Cravath on Giannini: Paul Cravath to Edward Ziegler, 11/16/34;* on Salzburg stars: *New York Times*, 9/10/33.
Gatti: in Zirato, loc. cit.
187 Tin-cup drive: *Time* Magazine, 3/18/35.
Erskine complaint: John Erskine, *The Memory of Certain Persons*, Lippincott, Philadelphia, 1947, p. 387.
190 Downes: *New York Times*, 12/24/33.
193 Belmont: New York *American*, 1/8/34.

SIX

195 "My God, Ned!": Noble, op. cit., p. 150.
High C's: Louis Biancolli, *The Flagstad Manuscripts*, G. P. Putnam's Sons, New York, 1952, p. 73; audition: ibid., pp. 66–7.
196 Bodanzky-Szell: Biancolli, op. cit., p. 70.
198 McArthur on telegram: Edwin McArthur, *Flagstad, A Personal Memoir*, Knopf, New York, 1965, p. 105.
199 La Guardia: Ziegler to Lawrence Gilman, 4/30/38.*
203 Erskine, op. cit., pp. 390–91.
204 Fascists: Cravath to Herbert Witherspoon, 4/9/35.*
Spessitseva: Cravath to Witherspoon, 4/10/35.*
208 Knopf: Alfred A. Knopf to Ziegler, 1/20/38.*
210 Thomson review: Virgil Thomson, *The Musical Scene*, Knopf, 1945, p. 141.
213 Alarie: Mercer, op. cit., p. 250.
215 Cornelius Bliss: Eleanor R. Belmont, "John Erskine and the Met," *Opera News*, 11/27/50, p. 26.
219 Johnson: Metropolitan Opera Association Annual Report 1942, p. 8.
220 Thomson: on *Louise*, op. cit., p. 161; on Walter: *Annals*, p. 674.
228 Belmont quote: McArthur, op. cit., p. 175.

SEVEN

233 Callas: Rudolf Bing, *5000 Nights at the Opera*, Doubleday, Garden City, 1972, p. 238.
234 Memoirs: Giovanni Battista Meneghini, *My Wife Maria Callas*, Farrar, Straus, Giroux, New York, 1982, and The Bodley Head, London, 1983.
Tour: Bing, op. cit., p. 243.
236 Kolodin, op. cit., p. 607.
237 Cornelius N. Bliss to Eleanor Belmont, 7/22/48.*
238 John Erskine, *My Life in Music*, William Morrow & Co., New York, 1950, p. 236.
Eleanor R. Belmont, loc. cit.
Erskine on choosing general manager: Erskine, op. cit., p. 234.
240 Virgil Thomson, *Music Left and Right*, Holt, New York, 1951, p. 82.
Kolodin, op. cit., p. 498.
241 "Quality only": Cecil Smith, *Worlds of Music*, Lippincott, Philadelphia, 1952, p. 181.
243 "Vocally vast": Virgil Thomson, *Music Reviewed, 1940–54*, Vintage Books, New York, 1967, p. 328.
244 Bing on Defrère: Bing, op. cit., p. 141.
245 Walter letter: ibid., p. 277.
"Bright and joyous": Olin Downes, "Met

Newcomers Nucleus of Cast," *New York Times*, 11/7/50, p. 33.
249 Downes, in *The Annals*, Supplement I, p. 49.
251 Stella: Taubman, in ibid., p. 103.
260 Sargeant: in ibid., Supplement II, p. 19.

EIGHT

263ff. Much of the material included on these pages is drawn from Martin Mayer, *All You Know Is Facts*, Harper & Row, New York, 1969, pp. 18ff. Also, see the author's "Report to the Task Force" in *Bricks, Mortar, and the Performing Arts*, Twentieth Century Fund, New York, 1969. A shorter version of the article appeared in *Horizon*, July 1962.

273 Taubman, *New York Times*, 10/26/58, Section II, p. 9.
283 Mercer, op. cit., p. 188.

NINE

297 Bing and unions: Bing, op. cit., p. 271. Importing an orchestra: "President's Report to the Baltimore Convention," *International Musician*, July 1927, p. 1.
302 Rudolf Bing to Hy Faine, 11/30/58.*
305 Kolodin, in *The Annals*, Supplement III, J. T. White & Co., Clifton, N.J., 1978, p. 9.
308 *Peter Grimes*: I reviewed this performance for *Musical America*, dutifully consulting a score I had borrowed from Boosey & Hawkes, and I criticized Lucine Amara

for "her failure even to attempt some of the ornaments" in her part. Colin Davis later informed me that, subsequent to the edition lent me by the publisher, the composer had expunged the ornaments. This footnote makes amends and also, I hope, raises in a somewhat different way the old question of how much expertise a critic must seek when reviewing a performance of a relatively unfamiliar piece.
321 Jane Boutwell, "A Matter of National Concern," *Opera News*, 6/13/70, p. 8.

TEN

328 Chapin: Schuyler G. Chapin, *A Life in the Arts*, G. P. Putnam's Sons, New York, 1977, p. 296.

SOURCES OF ILLUSTRATIONS

All numbers refer to pages on which illustrations appear; wherever necessary, a brief description is also given to aid identification. A separate list of photographers (other than those specifically named in the list of sources), graphic artists, and publications is appended.

© 1983 Beth Bergman: 253 (Corena), 313, 333, 334 (Caballé, Ricciarelli, MacNeil), 337 (*L'Enfant, Rossignol*), 338, 342
Eugene Berman: 274–75
The Bettmann Archive, Inc.: 27, 97 (Kahn), 109 (Mahler)
Michael Bronson, courtesy of: 26 (audience arriving)
George Cehanovsky, courtesy of: 167
Lowell Chereskin: 301
Columbia University, Avery Library: 84
Columbia University, Rare Book and Manuscript Library: 138–39
© 1983 Eugene Cook: 259, 293 (Martinelli/Stevens/Belmont)
Culver Pictures, Inc.: 11 (Belmont), 89 (audience departing), 91 (Morgan), 96 (Gatti/Dippel), 110 (Garden, Hammerstein), 129 (Matzenauer), 152 (Easton), 192 (Lille/Althouse), 197 (Belmont)
© 1983 Erika Davidson: 17, 295, 300 (Harris), 347 (Sutherland)
Rubén de Saavedra, courtesy of: 274 (Donna Anna)
Frank Dunand, Education Department, Metropolitan Opera Guild: 269 (Rysanek), 276–78, 280
Alfred Eisenstaedt, *Life* Magazine, © 1946 Time, Inc.: 206, 207 (stagehands, Pinza)
© 1983 Johan Elbers: 345, 346 (Stratas/Carreras), 351
Stan Fellerman: 330 (Bliss)

Joe Gaffney: 337 (Hockney/Dexter)
Barrett Gallaher: 257 (Bing/poodle)
Alexandre Georges: 54–55, 208
Burt Glinn: 247 (rehearsal)
Robert G. Goelet, courtesy of: 17 (Robert Goelet)
Henry Grossman: 317 (Karajan, Stewart/Karajan)
Harvard College Library, Theatre Collection: 11 (Academy), 38 (Fursch-Madi), 43 (Materna, Stanton), 71 (Journet, Melba)
James Heffernan: 296, 334 (Troyanos, Milnes), 346 (Scotto), 350, 352, 358
© 1982 David Hockney, courtesy of Petersburg Press, New York/London: 348–49
Terry Hourigan: 56
Tony Ray Jones: 252 (Della Casa)
The Library of Congress, Prints and Photographs Division: 14
Alan MacWeeney: 319 (*Frau*)
© Costa Manon, Magnum Photos, Inc.: 264–65
Ron Manville: 17 (Ogden Goelet)
William McCourt, courtesy of: 20 (40th Street façade), 21 (architectural design)
Metropolitan Opera Archives: 26 (diners), 32, 35 (program, Nilsson), 45, 50–51, 65, 89 (notice), 96–97 (chorus, playbill), 118–19 (playbill, Amato, Destinn, Caruso), 122 (*Amore, Francesca*), 125 (*Magic Flute, Rosenkavalier*), 126, 132 (telegram), 147 (*Zazà*) 152 (Martinelli/

Ponselle), 160 (Schorr), 172 (Fleischer/Mario), 183 (*Lakmé*), 184 (Jagel, Crooks, Bampton), 197 (Ziegler/Lewis/Johnson), 201 (Lawrence), 221 (Di Stefano), 226 (Vanderbilt), 239 (rehearsal), 246 (rehearsal), 269 (Nilsson), 317 (setting), 322 (wigs), 330 (Gentele)
Metropolitan Opera Guild/*Opera News*: 11 (Academy, Patti), 46, 49, 52–56, 60 (Brandt, Reichmann), 61 (Alvary, Niemann), 70 (Edouard de Reszke, Nordica), 71 (Calvé), 91 (program), 107 (Slezak, Scotti, Alda), 119 (Gatti/Belasco/Toscanini/Puccini), 140–41, 143 (*Don Giovanni* group, Steber), 144, 153 (De Luca), 184 (Thomas), 188, 197 (Witherspoon), 200, 201 (Traubel, Varnay), 207 (Milanov), 211 (Stevens), 217, 221 (Albanese, Bjoerling, Sayão), 222, 229, 230, 242, 247 (*Così* on stage), 253 (Del Monaco, De Los Angeles), 257 (Robinson/Bing), 269 (Rysanek), 288
Gjon Mili: 257 (Robinson/Bing), 269 (Nilsson)
Ralph Morse, *Life* Magazine, © 1958 Time, Inc.: 2
Museum of the City of New York, Theater Collection: 35 (Abbey), 43 (Leopold and Walter Damrosch), 77, 91 (Conried, Fremstad)
Steven Mark Needham: 306–307, 343, 357
New York Daily News: 226 (man standing on his head)

New Yorker: 226 (opening night)
New-York Historical Society: 8, 17 (Vanderbilt, three society ladies), 37, 38 (Trebelli), 62 (Brünnhilde), 137
The New York Times: 140–41, 184 (Bampton), 222 (Johnson/Tucker), 229, 256, 322 (prop shop)
Yoichi R. Okamoto, reprinted by courtesy of Stagebill Group Publications: 273
Gordon Parks, *Life* Magazine, © 1956 Time, Inc.: 235
The Rosa Ponselle Museum, Villa Pace: 192 (bicycle quartet)
Günter R. Reitz: 322 (wigmaking)
Gary Renaud: 309 (*Magic Flute*)
The Francis Robinson Collection: 60–61 (1890–91 roster portrait), 76, 80, 101, 109 (Farrar), 110 (Cavalieri), 114, 122 (*Oracolo*), 125 (*Königskinder*), 129 (Homer), 132 (Caruso), 147 (crowds), 153 (Chaliapin, Galli-Curci), 160 (Lauri-Volpi/Jeritza), 164, 172 (Falco/Ponselle/Petina), 173,

181, 214, 239 (*Don Carlo* on stage), 246 (*Carmen* on stage), 257 (Bing/poodle), 259, 268 (Price/Corelli), 275, 285, 289, 300 (architectural plan), 309 (Bing/Chagall)
Carl Roodman: 322 (painter)
Roosevelt Hospital, courtesy of: 17 (Roosevelt)
Arnold Rosenberg: 253 (Uhde/Franke)
John G. Ross: 252 (London/Tebaldi)
Michael Rougier, *Life* Magazine, © 1966 Time, Inc.: 279
Mrs. Richard Rychtarik, courtesy of: 142–43 (*Magic Flute*)
Salve Regina, the Newport College: 17 (Ogden Goelet)
© 1983 Paul Seligman: 289, 300 (construction), 330 (Chapin)
E. Fred Sher: 293 (Nilsson), 309 (Bing/Chagall)
Vernon L. Smith, Scope Associates: 262, 268 (Gedda/Moffo), 293 (Stokowski)

Edward Steichen, Condé Nast Publications, Inc.: 194
Christian Steiner: 326
Katrina Thomas: 300 (Harrison)
Robert L. B. Tobin, courtesy of: 274 (Don Giovanni)
Wally Toscanini, courtesy of: 119 (Gatti/Belasco/Toscanini/Puccini)
Trinity College, Watkinson Library: 21 (Cady)
Robert A. Tuggle, courtesy of: 29, 38 (Campanini, Stagno, Del Puente), 62 (Carmen), 70 (Jean de Reszke), 107 (Toscanini), 109 (Eames), 156, 161, 178, 183 (Pons), 184 (Swarthout), 189, 192 (Pons/Melchior), 211 (Lehmann), 274 (Donna Elvira)
Grey Villet, *Life* Magazine, © 1962 Time, Inc.: 290
Wide World Photos: 189 (Muzio), 192 (Pons/Melchior), 197 (Ziegler/Lewis/Johnson), 221 (Bjoerling)

LIST OF PHOTOGRAPHERS, ARTISTS AND PUBLICATIONS

Jas. Abresch: 201 (Traubel), 221 (Albanese)
Acme Photo: 207 (Milanov)
Constantin Alajalov: 226 (cover)
American Architect and Building News, The: 14
E. M. Ashe: 27
George G. Bain: 96 (Gatti/Dippel)
Byron Company: 76, 91 (Conried, Fremstad)
Century Magazine: 89 (audience departing)
Josiah Cleaveland Cady: 20–21, 65 (architectural drawings)
De Bellis: 222 (Kirsten)
Fernand de Guedre: 167
Aimé Dupont: 70, 71 (Journet), 107 (Alda), 109 (Mahler, Eames), 129 (Homer)
Carlo Edwards: 152 (Martinelli/Ponselle), 156, 160 (Schorr), 161, 164, 172 (Fleischer/Mario), 178, 183 (Pons), 184 (Swarthout), 188 (Scotti/Tibbett), 192 (bicycle quartet), 200 (*Tristan*), 211 (Lehmann)

B. J. Falk: 38 (Del Puente), 46, 62 (Brünnhilde)
John Filmer: 37
Gerlach: 101
Hanlen & Weller: 38 (Trebelli)
Harper's Weekly: 20 (Broadway façade), 26 (diners), 32
Illustrated American 9/10/82: 65 (fire, devastation)
International Newsreel: 188 (Schumann-Heink/Talley)
Ray Lee Jackson, NBC Studios: 173 (Cross/Farrar)
J. S. Johnston: 8
Arthur I. Keller: 89 (audience departing)
Sedge Leblang: 239 (*Don Carlo* on stage), 242, 246, 247 (*Così* on stage)
Lumière: 153 (Galli-Curci)
Louis Mélançon: 221 (Welitsch, Di Stefano), 253 (Del Monaco, De Los Angeles), 268 (Price, Corelli), 285, 317 (*Rheingold* setting), 319 (*Grimes*)

Herman Mishkin: 107 (Slezak/Scotti), 114, 126 (Galli), 129 (Matzenauer), 132 (Caruso), 152–53 (Easton, Chaliapin, De Luca), 160 (Lauri-Volpi/Jeritza)
José Maria Mora: 11 (Patti), 17 (three society ladies), 29, 35 (Nilsson), 38 (Campanini, Stagno)
Nadanz: 110 (Cavalieri)
Price Picture News: 147 (crowds)
Charles Hope Provest: 26 (audience arriving)
Puck Magazine: 50–51, 137
Reutlinger: 71 (Calvé), 109 (Farrar)
Renato Toppo: 197 (Witherspoon)
E. Prentice Treadwell: 49
Underwood & Underwood: 189 (Moore)
Joseph Urban: 138–39
A. B. Wenzell: 26 (diners)
White Studios: 80, 96–97 (chorus), 118–19 (Amato, Destinn, Caruso), 122, 125, 126 (*Boris*), 147 (*Zazà*)
Zanini: 107 (Toscanini)

INDEX

For references to individual operas, see under titles of works.
Page numbers in *italics* refer to illustrations.

Abbey, Henry E., 28, 31, 33, 36, 41, 42–7, 57, 63, 67, 68, 73; *35*
Academy of Music (New York), 10–13, 25, 33, 34, 41–4, 48, 58, 112
Abbey, Schoeffel and Grau, 64, 68–9, 72, 73–5
Abramowitz, Max, 267
Abravanel, Maurice, 212
Adam, Theo, 318
Adler, Herman, 310, 311
Adler, Kurt, 258
Adler, Peter Herman, 332
Adriana Lecouvreur (Cilèa), 283, 318
Aegyptische Helena, Die (R. Strauss), 150
Africaine, L' (Meyerbeer), 69, 174–5
Aida (Verdi), 73, 75, 93, 98, 100, 103, 112, 134, 146, 148, 151, 186, 193, 212, 233, 249, 251, 281, 283, 286, 292; *206*
Ailey, Alvin, 329
Alarie, Pierrette, 213
Albanese, Licia, 210; *221*
Albani, Emma, 47, 64, 67
Alboni, Marietta, 10
Alda, Frances, 83, 108, 116, 117, 123, 124, 130, 131, 136, 146; *107*
Aldrich, Richard, 30, 90, 93, 103, 108, 244
Alexander, John, 282, 312
Allen, Reginald, 243–4, 248, 297, 298, 299
Althouse, Paul, 195; *192*
Alva, Luigi, 284
Alvary, Lorenzo, *144*
Alvary, Max, 59; *60–1*
Amara, Lucine, 240, 260, 308, 324; *280, 319*
Amato, Pasquale, 104, 131, 146; *118–19, 122*
Amelia Goes to the Ball (Menotti), 223
American Architect and Building News, The, 15–16, 18
American Federation of Labor, 169
American Federation of Musicians, 297
American Grand Opera Alliance, 169
American Guild of Musical Artists (AGMA), 234, 287, 292, 298, 299–302
American Tobacco Company, 180
Amico Fritz, L' (Mascagni), 69
Amore dei tre re, L' (Montemezzi), 124, 134, 205; *122*
Amore medico, L' (Wolf-Ferrari), 124
Anderson, Marian, 254; *230*
Andrea Chénier (Giordano), 150, 294, 323

Aniara (Blomdahl), 327
Ansermet, Ernest, 283
Anthony, Charles, 212, 250
Antoine, Josephine, 204
Antonicelli, Giuseppe, 240
Antony and Cleopatra (Barber), 304–5, 311, 318; *278–9, 322*
Aoyama, Yoshio, 254
Arabella (R. Strauss), 251, 281
Arditi, Luigi, 42
Ariadne auf Naxos (R. Strauss), 283
Ariane et Barbe-Bleu (Dukas), 124
Armide (Gluck), 121, 124, 146
Armistead, Horace, 244, 245, 250
Arnoldson, Sigrid, 68
Aronson, Boris, 308, 324
Arroyo, Martina, 308
Assedio di Corinto, L' (Rossini), 331
Astor, Caroline, 23, 81, 100
Astor Place Theater, 10
Atlanta, Ga., 166, 171
Auden, W. H., 250
Aylesworth, Merlin, 174

Baccaloni, Salvatore, 148, 204, 212, 220; *142–3*
Bacquier, Gabriel, 284, 318
Bada, Angelo, 116; *122*
Baker, George F., 163
Balanchine, George, 208, 250
Ballets Russes, 128
Ballo in maschera, Un (Verdi), 25, 124, 131–3, 254, 327, 328, 331; *345*
Baltimore, Md., 44, 111
Bampton, Rose, 177, 186, 212; *184*
Barbiere di Siviglia, Il (Rossini), 25, 41, 75, 86, 148, 150, 151, 154, 220, 255, 286, 315, 320
Barbieri, Fedora, 240
Baromeo, Chase, 204
Barrault, Jean-Louis, 240, 248, 286, 318
Barrientos, Maris, 123
Bartered Bride, The (Smetana), 98, 99, 111, 208, 212; *229*
Bastianini, Ettore, 251
Batten, Barton, Durstine & Osborne, 170
Bauermeister, Mathilde, 69
Baum, Kurt, 260, 294
Baum, Morton, 241, 311
Bayreuth, 16, 39, 48, 63, 90
Beardine, Thomas, 169
Beaton, Cecil, 251, 281, 305
Beecham, Sir Thomas, 133, 218–20
Beethoven, Ludwig van, 83, 123, 136, 324
Behrens, Hilde, *333*
Belasco, David, 123, 145, 166, 254; *118–19*
Belmont, August, 177

Belmont, August H., 10–12, 13, 25; *11*
Belmont, Eleanor Robson, 177, 179, 193, 215, 224, 228, 237–8, 255, 261, 292, 310, 312; *197, 293*
Bentonelli, Joseph, 204
Berganza, Teresa, 234, 318
Berger, Erna, 225, 240
Bergman, Ingmar, 327
Bergonzi, Carlo, 251, 260
Berlioz, Hector, 10, 323
Berman, Eugene, 249, 250, 251, 255, 283, 328; *274–5*
Bernays, Edward L., 117
Bernstein, Leonard, 261, 284, 323, 328; *285*
Berry, Walter, 305; *319*
Billy Budd (Britten), 340; *338*
Bing, Nina, 305
Bing, (Sir) Rudolf, 30, 121, 123, 150, 227, 228, 233–61, 270–2, 281–91, 292, 297, 298–303, 312–15, 316, 320–3, 324–5, 327, 355; *230, 256–7, 309*
Bjoerling, Jussi, 31, 148, 210, 219, 225, 241, 250, 281; *221, 239*
Bjoner, Ingrid, 283
Blegen, Judith, 325; *345*
Bliss, Anthony A., 179, 244, 255, 263, 270, 297, 299, 310–16, 331, 335, 336–40, 353–4; *330*
Bliss, Cornelius, 179, 187, 193, 203, 215–16, 237, 263, 298, 331
Blois, Col. Eustace, 149
Bluebeard's Castle (Bartók), 332
Bodanzky, Artur, 63, 130, 135, 170, 177, 182, 186, 195–6, 198, 212, 219, 236, 260; *200*
Bohème, La (Puccini), 79, 85, 92, 103, 104, 116, 117, 148, 150, 208, 249, 251, 286, 308, 314, 318, 339–40, 341; *346*
Böhm, Karl, 251, 260, 283, 284, 302–3, 305, 324, 325, 328
Bohnen, Michael, 155, 185
Bonci, Alessandro, 93, 104, 115–16, 120, 177
Bonelli, Richard, 177, 298
Bonham-Carter, Lady Violet, 238
Bonynge, Richard, 325, 328
Booz, Allen & Hamilton, 310
Bori, Lucrezia, 146–8, 155, 177–9, 180, 185, 203, 205, 210, 220, 238, 298; *122, 156, 181*
Boris Godunov (Mussorgsky), 124, 134, 150, 154, 210, 220, 250, 261, 283, 331; *126*
Bosio, Angiolina, 10
Boston, Mass., 44, 128; — Opera Company, 108, 112
Boutwell, Jane, 321
Bovy, Vina, 210

Brandt, Marianne, 57, 59; *60–1*
Branzell, Karin, 155, 185, 186, 218, 228; *200*
Breisach, Paul, 130, 219, 220, 225, 227
Brema, Marie, 78
Brewster, Robert S., 193, 215
Briggs, John, 146, 187
Brilioth, Helge, 324
Brook, Peter, 240, 250
Brooklyn Academy of Music, 98, 102–3, 165–6, 203; *50–51*
Brownlee, John, 130, 210, 212, 220, 223, 236, 240, 241, 292, 299; *214*
Bruson, Renato, 318
Bryan, William Jennings, 67, 82
Buchter, Jacob, 165
Buckner, Wallace, 315
Buenos Aires: Teatro Colón, 100
Bull, Thomas, 169
Bumbry, Grace, 286, 318, 320; *280*
Burgstaller, Alois, 90
Burke, Hilda, 204, 209
Burnhall, Frederick T., 151
Burrows, Stuart, 324
Busch, Fritz, 130, 220, 238

Caballé, Montserrat, 286, 308, 318; *334*
Cacoyannis, Michael, 308
Cady, Josiah Cleaveland, 16–18, 19, 22, 24, 39, 40, 64, 292, 304; *20–1*
Caïd du tambour-major, Le (Thomas), 112
Callas, Maria, 231, 232–6, 251, 258, 286; *235*
Calvé, Emma, 68, 69, 72–3, 75, 78; *70–1*
Campanari, Giuseppe, 69
Campanini, Cleofonte, 34, 47, 85, 95, 112, 113
Campanini, Italo, 3–4, 57; *38*
Campora, Giuseppe, 233
Caponsacchi (Hageman), 205, 223
Capoul, Victor, 41
Carmen (Bizet), 41, 68–9, 72, 73, 104, 121, 131, 133, 145, 150, 205, 212, 249, 287, 303, 314, 318, 328, 332; *156, 246*
Carnegie Corporation, 223
Carreras, José, 312, 335; *346*
Carrère & Hastings, 15, 81, 83; *54–5*
Caruso, Enrico, 30, 31, 78, 79, 90, 92, 93, 94, 100, 102–3, 104–6, 115–21, 128, 131, 134, 136, 146, 148, 149, 169, 199, 294; *114, 118–9, 132*
Casals, Pablo, 123, 130
Case, Anna, *126*
Cassilly, Richard, 312, 340
Castagna, Bruna, 210

Castel, Nico, 212
Castelmary, Armand, 74
Cavalieri, Lina, 85, 90, 112; *110*
Cavalleria rusticana (Mascagni), 68, 112, 241, 244–5, 260, 323; *280*
Cehanovsky, George, 128, 151, 212; *144*
Cenerentola, La (Rossini), 314
Chagall, Marc, 305–8; *309*
Chaliapin, Feodor, 150, 210; *152*
Chapin, Schuyler G., 327–35; *330*
Chicago, 44, 98, 177; — Civic Opera, 202, 205; — Grand Opera Company, 112; — Lyric Opera, 233, 336; Chicago-Philadelphia Opera, 113; — Symphony Orchestra 228
Chookasian, Lili, 282, 308
Chopin, Frédéric, 47
Chotzinoff, Samuel, 180–2
Christoff, Boris, 240
Cid, Le (Massenet), 79
Cillario, Carlo Felice, 332
Cimara, Pietro, 240
Cincinnati, Ohio, 44; — Conservatory of Music, 202
Clarke, Eric, 243
Cleva, Fausto, 233, 240, 260, 286, 324
Cleveland, Ohio, 166; — Symphony Orchestra, 344
Collier, Marie, 308
Colonnello, Attilio, 318, 320
Columbia Records, 248–9
Columbia University, 81, 191
Colzani, Anselmo, 281, 284; *285*
Cone, John F., 112
Conley, Eugene, 241
Conner, Nadine, 241
Conried, Heinrich, 41, 79, 83, 87–98, 113, 115, 116, 117–20, 146, 297; *91*
Contes d'Hoffmann, Les (Offenbach), 85, 92, 112, 148, 208, 210, 232, 316, 328, 341; *139, 352*
Cooper, Emil, 240
Coq d'Or, Le (Rimsky-Korsakov), 121, 123, 150, 198; *140–1*
Cordon, Norman, 209; *140–1*
Corelli, Franco, 281, 286, 291, 305, 318–20; *268*
Corena, Fernando, 251; *253*
Corsaro, Frank, 312
Così fan tutte (Mozart), 149, 249, 255, 335; *139, 247*
Cossotto, Fiorenza, 318
Costa, Mary, 284
Cotrubas, Ileana, *333*
Cravath, Paul D., 108, 171, 174–9, 186–7, 202–3, 204, 215, 254, 298
Crespin, Régine, 283; *338*
Crispano, Philip, 165
Crooks, Richard, 177, 292; *184*
Cross, Milton, 174; *173*
Cruz-Romo, Gilda, 323
Curtin, Phyllis, 282
Curtis Institute, 223
Curtis-Verna, Mary, 294
Cutting, R. Fulton, 158, 191
Cyrano de Bergerac (Damrosch), 78

Dalis, Irene, 251
Dallas, Tex., 234
Dal Monte, Toti, 133

Dalmores, Charles, 93
Damnation de Faust, La (Berlioz), 73
Damrosch, Leopold, 28, 48, 57, 58–9; *43*
Damrosch, Walter, 59, 67, 72, 75, 78, 79, 105, 123, 179; *43, 60–1*
Damrosch-Ellis Grand Opera, 75
Davis, Colin, 261, 308, 325
Death in Venice (Britten), 329, 331
Debussy, Claude, 10, 28, 121
De Forest, Lee, 127–8
Defrère, Désiré, 244
De Hidalgo, Elvira, 252–3
Deiber, Paul-Emile, 318, 325
Delius, Elisabeth, 196
Della Casa, Lisa, 250, 251, 284; *252*
Del Monaco, Mario, 233, 234, 241, 258, 260; *253*
Del Puente, Giuseppe, *38*
De Luca, Giuseppe, 146, 148, 166, 203, 204, 205; *153*
De Paolis, Alessio, 212; *144*
De Reszke, Edouard, 64, 67, 68, 69, 72, 74, 75, 78, 79; *32, 70–1*
De Reszke, Jean 10, 64, 67, 68, 69, 72, 73, 74, 75, 79, 90, 185; *32, 70–1*
De Schauensee, Max, 115, 136, 149, 150, 151
Destinn, Emmy, 100, 103, 106, 111, 131, 294; *118–19, 125*
Deutekom, Christina, 318
Dewey, Thomas E., 218
Dexter, John, 329–31, 332, 335, 340–1, 353; *337*
Diaghilev, Sergei, 123, 127, 128
Dialogues des Carmélites (Poulenc), 311, 340; *338*
Diana von Solange (Duke of Saxe-Coburg-Gotha), 64
Diaz, Justino, 284, 305; *278–9*
Dickie, Murray, 283
Didur, Adamo, 103, 104, 108, 166, 294; *122, 126*
Dietz, Howard, 240
Dillingham, Charles C., 98
Dippel, Andreas, 86–8, 98, 103, 104–6, 111–13; *96–7*
Di Stefano, Giuseppe, 225, 241; *221*
Doe, Doris 220
Domingo, Placido, 311, 312, 318, 320; *352*
Don Carlo (Verdi), 124, 150, 169, 238, 240, 244, 245, 249, 251, 260, 286, 324, 325; *239*
Don Giovanni (Mozart), 25, 39, 41, 57, 58, 67, 69, 78, 92, 170, 185, 212, 220, 241, 250, 251, 284, 286, 308, 328, 329, 332; *142–3, 274–5*
Don Pasquale (Donizetti), 25, 78, 148, 251
Don Quichotte (Massenet), 150
Don Rodrigo (Ginastera), 311
Dönch, Karl, 260, 283
Donna Juanita (Suppé), 124
Donne curiose, Le (Wolf-Ferrari), 124
Dooley, William, 284
Dos Passos, John, 67
Douglas, Mrs. Lewis W., 238, 315, 316
Dowell, Anthony, *337*
Downes, Olin, 148, 151, 180, 182, 190, 196, 245, 249
Drye, John W., 310
Dudley, William, 340
Due Foscari, I (Verdi), 25

Dufranne, Hector, 185
Du Maurier, Daphne, 180
Dunn, Mignon, 261
Dupont, Jacques, 286

Eames, Emma, 64, 67, 68, 69, 75, 78, 93, 99, 100–2, 104, 105–6, 108; *56, 109*
Eastman, George, 159
Easton, Florence, 148–9, 150; *152*
Eaton, Quaintance, 187
Ebasco Services, 266
Ebert, Carl, 203, 208, 231, 236, 238, 260, 283
Eckstein, Louis, 179
Edinburgh Festival, 237
Ehrling, Sixten, 318, 332
Eisenhower, Dwight D., 261
Elektra (R. Strauss), 177, 182, 208, 308; *350*
Elias, Rosalind, 251, 284; *285*
Elisir d'amore, L' (Donizetti), 115, 120, 154, 177, 281–2
Ellis, Charles, 75
Elman, Mischa, 123
Elmo, Cloe, 225
Elson, Charles, 250
Emperor Jones, The (Gruenberg), 121, 123, 177, 182–5; *178*
Enfant et les sortilèges, L' (Ravel), 341; *337*
Erede, Alberto, 240, 249
Ernani (Verdi), 10, 124, 148, 150, 283
Erskine, John, 187, 202–3, 208, 223, 231, 237–8, 310, 331
Esclarmonde (Massenet), 340
Eugene Onegin (Tchaikovsky), 148, 223
Euryanthe (Weber), 134
Evans, Geraint, 284, 308; *278–9*
Everding, August, 324, 331, 340

Fabbri, Egisto P., 15, 22–3
Fahnestock, William, 163
Faine, Hy, 302
*Falco, Thiline, *173*
Falstaff (Verdi) 69, 111, 151, 220–3, 281, 284, 286; *278–9, 285*
Farrar, Geraldine, 31, 90, 92, 100, 102, 104–8, 123, 133, 134, 136–46, 150, 166, 174, 179; *80, 101, 109, 125, 147, 172–3*
Farrell, Eileen, 281
Fassbaender, Brigitte, 335
Faust (Gounod), 9, 28, 33–4, 63, 73, 75, 79, 86, 92, 103, 112, 145, 150, 151, 190, 208, 240–1, 250, 286, 292; *32, 52–3*
Favorita, La (Donizetti), 25
Feinhals, Fritz, 24, 103
Felsenstein, Walter, 314
Fenn, Jean, *276–7*
Fernandez Arbos, E., 130
Fidelio (Beethoven), 25, 57, 83, 99, 182, 208, 212, 220, 233, 236, 241, 255, 286, 302, 324
Field, Marshall, 159
Fille du régiment, La (Donizetti), 10, 325
Finck, Henry T., 25, 63
Fischer, Emil, 59, 155; *46*
Fisher, Suzanne, 204

Flagstad, Kirsten, 31, 130, 136, 151, 182, 195–9, 204, 212, 213, 218, 219, 227–8, 241–3, 249, 255, 344, 355; *194, 200*
Flaming Angel, The (Prokofiev), 312
Fledermaus, Die (J. Strauss), 90–2, 150, 240, 244, 248–9, 255
Fleischer, Editha, 155; *156, 172*
Fliegende Holländer, Der (Wagner), 67, 208, 241, 344
Fokine, Michel, 123
Ford, Henry, 82
Ford Foundation, 255
Fordham University, 271
Forza del destino, La (Verdi), 124, 149, 220, 233, 249, 332
Four Saints in Three Acts (Thomson), 185, 329
Fox, Carol, 233
Francesca da Rimini (Zandonai), *122*
Franke, Paul, 212, 260, 284; *253*
Frau ohne Schatten, Die (R. Strauss), 223, 281, 305; *319*
Freischütz, Der (Weber), 25, 57, 151, 324
Fremstad, Olive, 24, 31, 90, 92, 103, 124, 135, 146, 182, 185, 196; *91*
Freni, Mirella, 286, 318
Frick, Gottlob 282
From the House of the Dead (Janáček), 331
Fursch-Madi, Emma, 41; *38*

Gadski, Johanna, 78, 103, 135, 136
Galeffi, Carlo, 133
Galli, Rosina, 123, 127; *126*
Galli-Curci, Amelita, 149–50, 232; *152–3*
Gallo, Fortune, 169
Garden, Mary, 85, 93, 113, 185, 186, 202, 205; *110*
Garrison, Mabel 148
Gary, Emma, 108
Gatti-Casazza, Giulio, 25, 82–8, 98–113, 117, 120, 121–8, 131–4, 135–6, 145, 149–50, 151–4, 155 7, 165–8, 170, 171–4, 176, 180, 182, 185–6, 187–90, 195, 202–3, 205, 245–8, 250, 287; *80, 96–7, 118–19, 137, 164*
Gay, Maria, 104
Gedda, Nicolai, 251, 286, 305; *268–9*
Geltzer, Ekaterina, 123
Gentele, Goeran, 281, 323, 324, 327–9, 331; *330*
Gérard, Rolf, 248, 249, 250, 260, 318; *246*
Gerryflappers, 102, 145
Gerster, Etelka, 41
Ghiaurov, Nicolai, 286
Giannini, Dusolina, 186
Gianni Schicchi (Puccini), 124, 148, 208, 225; see also *Trittico, Il*
Gibbs, Mrs. William Francis, 292
Gigli, Beniamino, 148, 149, 176, 205, 210; *156*
Gilibert, Charles, 79, 185
Gilman, Lawrence, 151, 185, 196
Gilpatric, Harriet, 292
Gioconda, La (Ponchielli), 28, 41, 151, 305, 318
Giordano, Umberto, 124
Girl of the Golden West, The (Puccini), 102, 123, 146, 150, 166, 282, 303,

304; *118–19*
Glackens, Ira, 74
Glickman, Louis, 267
Gluck, Christoph Willibald, 10, 83
Glyndebourne, 236–7
Gniewek, Raymondo, 260
Gobbi, Tito, 251, 286
Godfrey, Arthur, 286
Goelet, Ogden, 13; *17*
Goelet, Mrs. Ogden, 163
Goelet, Robert, 13, 159, 163; *17*
Goldberg, Arthur, 303
Goldmark, Carl, 28
Goltz, Christel, 251
Gordon, Jeanne, 155
Gorr, Rita, 284
Götterdämmerung (Wagner), 99–100, 108, 195, 208, 294; see also *Ring des Nibelungen*
Gounod, Charles, 74, 83
Goyescas (Granados), 124
Graf, Herbert, 134, 205–8, 224, 241, 249, 261, 308
Graham, Martha, 170
Gramm, Donald, 284
Grau, Maurice, 41, 64, 68, 69–79, 83, 88, 94, 117; *77*
Greenway, Lauder, 255, 270, 299, 315
Greer, Frances, 220
Grenfell, Wilfrid, 180
Grist, Reri, 286
Guard, William J., 168
Guarrera, Frank, 209
Gueden, Hilde, 249
Guillaume Tell (Rossini), 25, 57, 58
Guthrie, Tyrone, 240, 248, 249, 308, 332; *246*
Gutman, John, 245, 248, 282, 312
Gye, Ernest, 47
Gypsy Baron, The (J. Strauss), 234

Hadley, William H., 310
Hageman, Richard, 205
Halasz, Laszlo, 311
Hall, Peter J., *345*
Halstead, Margaret, 204
Hamburg Opera, 331
Hamlet (Thomas), 72–3
Hammerstein, Oscar, 81, 85, 87, 93, 94, 95, 103, 111–13, 115–16, 121, 174, 177, 186; *110, 137*
Hänsel und Gretel (Humperdinck), 92, 155, 174, 180, 223, 281, 318; *172*
Harrell, Mack, 209, 223
Harriman, E. H., 87, 88, 95
Harris, Cyril, 304; *300–1*
Harris, Hilda, *337*
Harrison, Wallace K., 190, 267, 270; *300–1*
Harrold, Orville, 155
Harshaw, Margaret, 209; *140–1*
Hartfield, Joseph, 267
Hartford, Conn., 185
Harvuot, Clifford, 209
Hasselmans, Louis, *156*
Haven, George C., 158
Hawkins, Osie, 292
Hearst, William Randolph, 168–9
Hecht, Ben, 168
Heeley, Desmond, 325
Heinrich, Rudolf, 284, 308, 318, 324
Hempel, Frieda, 131, 148; *125*

Henderson, W. J., 10, 44, 68–9, 78, 79, 94, 103, 111, 120, 182, 196
Herbert, Jocelyn, 340
Herbert, Victor, *60–1*
Herman, Robert, 248, 324, 327, 328, 332
Hertz, Alfred, 79, 87, 103, 111, 135
Heure espagnole, L' (Ravel), 30
Hillary, Thomas, 166
Hines, Jerome, 78, 213, 240, 305; *239, 309*
Hock, Wilhelm, 57
Hockney, David, 341; *337, 348–9*
Hofmann, Ludwig, 196
Holtzman, Elizabeth, 339
Homer, Louise, 24, 79, 92, 103, 111, 294; *129*
Hook, Howard, 315
Horne, Marilyn, 323, 328, 332; *333*
Horner, Harry, 251, 255
Hosli, Fred, 165–6
Hotter, Hans, 241
Houghton, Arthur, 267
Houseman, John, 185
Hubay, Alfred, 213
Huehn, Julius, 204
Hughes, Allen, 335
Hugo, Victor, 249
Huguenots, Les (Meyerbeer), 42, 57, 58, 69, 73
Huneker, James, 127
Hunter, Rita, 335
Hurok, Sol, 224, 243, 291
Hutcheson, Ernest, 203
Hyde, James H., 88, 93

Idomeneo (Mozart), *333*
Ingpen, Joan, 344
Insull, Samuel, 177
International Association of Theatrical Stage Employees, 297
Iris (Mascagni), 134
Irving Place Theater, 79, 94
Island God, The (Menotti), 223
Italiana in Algeri, L' (Rossini), 121, 328

Jackson, C. D., 263, 266, 270
Jackson, Stanley, 120
Jagel, Frederick, *184, 192*
Janowitz, Gundula, 316
Jarboro, Caterina, 174–5
Jenufa (Janáček), 124, 150, 329, 332
Jeritza, Maria, 150, 176, 318; *156, 160*
Jessner, Irene, 220
Jobin, Raoul, 225
Jochum, Eugen, 130
Johnson, Edward, 127, 134, 154, 165, 177, 180, 187, 198–9, 202, 204–16, 219, 220, 223, 225–8, 231, 236, 237, 240, 243, 248, 261, 287, 298; *156, 197, 222*
Johnson, Harriett, 236
Jones, Gwyneth, 335
Jones, Robert Edmond, 170
Jongleur de Notre Dame, Le (Massenet), 112
Jonny spielt auf (Křenek), 30, 124; *161*
Journet, Marcel, 79; *70–1*
Judels, Jules, 166
Judson, Arthur, 185
Juilliard, Augustus D., 87, 175

Juilliard, Fred A., 159, 175, 202–3, 216
Juilliard Foundation, 179
Juilliard School, 175, 187, 202, 261, 270
Juilliard Theater, 329
Juive, La (Halévy), 57, 116, 120, 128, 208
Julius Caesar (Handel), 311, 312

Kahn, Otto, 82–95, 98, 102, 104–5, 108, 111–12, 116, 117, 120, 127, 128–31, 134, 136, 155–7, 158–63, 165, 168–9, 170, 171, 174, 179, 182, 185–6, 187, 195, 238, 356; *96–7*
Kahn, Mrs. Otto, 238
Kalisch, Paul, 64
Kane, Jasper Innis, 81
Kanin, Garson, 240, 248
Kappel, Gertrude, 155, 195
Karajan, Herbert von, 133, 241, 316–18, 328; *317*
Karinska (costume designer), 234
Katerina Ismailova (Shostakovich), 312
Katz, Emil, 170
Kautsky, Hans, 121
Keiser, David, 267
Kelemen, Zoltan, 316–18
Kellogg, Clara Louise, 9
Kelly, Larry, 234
Kempe, Rudolf, 251
Kennedy, John F., 303
Kennedy, Joseph P., 271
Kershaw, Andrew, 339
Keynes, Maynard, 204
Kheel, Theodore, 303
Kiepura, Jan, 210
Kierkegaard, Søren, 58
King, James, 286, 305; *319*
Kipnis, Alexander, 210, 220, 292
Kirstein, Lincoln, 267–70
Kirsten, Dorothy, 210, 282, 294, 312; *222*
Knopf, Alfred, 208
Kollo, René, 340
Kolodin, Irving, 47, 133, 210, 213, 236, 240, 258, 260, 282, 292, 305
Königskinder (Humperdinck), 123; *125*
Konya, Sandor, 282, 283, 291; *276–7*
Kord, Kazimierz, 332
Kountze, Mrs. Luther, *17*
Kozma, Tibor, 220, 240
Kraus, Alfredo, 286
Kraus, Auguste, see Seidl-Kraus, Auguste
Krause, Tom, 318
Krawitz, Herman, 191, 244, 248, 270, 272, 299, 324, 327
Krehbiel, Henry H., 33–4, 47, 48, 58, 59, 72–3, 74, 92, 103, 116, 134
Krips, Josef, 305
Kubelik, Rafael, 318, 324, 327–8, 329, 331, 332
Kuen, Paul, 282
Kuhn, Loeb & Co., 87, 171
Kullmann, Charles, 204, 208; *229*
Kunz, Erich, 250
Kurt, Melanie, 135

LaFarge, Christopher, 223

La Guardia, Fiorello, 176, 199, 218, 227, 263, 311
Lakmé (Delibes), 166, 185; *183*
Lanzilotti, Nicholas, 165
Larsen-Todsen, Nanny, 155
Lasker, Mrs. Albert, 238
Lassalle, Jean, 64, 67, 68, 69
Last Savage, The (Menotti), 284
Lauri-Volpi, Giacomo, 155, 168–9, 182, 205; *160*
Lawrence, Marjorie, 199, 204, 208, 218, 292; *200*
Lazzari, Virgilio, *192*
Lear, Evelyn, 308
Ledner, Emil, 99
Lee, Ming Cho, 331
Lehman, Herbert, 218
Lehmann, Lilli, 13, 28, 31, 36, 42, 59, 63, 64, 75–8, 149, 185; *62*
Lehmann, Lotte, 182, 185, 199, 210, 218, 220, 292; *211*
Leider, Frida, 177, 185, 187, 195
Leinsdorf, Erich, 212, 213, 218–19, 220, 227, 228, 260, 282, 283, 287, 318, 332, 354
Leoncavallo, Ruggiero, 124
Leppard, Raymond, 340
Lert, Ernst, 166
Lev, Bernard, 223
Levine, James, 261, 316, 324, 329, 331, 332, 335, 340–53, 355; *326*
Lewis, Earle R., 168, 177, 205, 243; *197*
Lewis, Henry, 332
Lhevinne, Rosina, 341
Liebermann, Rolf, 331, 344, 356
Ligendza, Caterina, 324
Lillie, Beatrice, *192*
Lincoln, Abraham, 12
Lincoln Center, 18, 185, 190, 244, 261, 263–72, 304–10, 336; *273, 296, 300–1, 306–7, 322*
Lind, Jenny, 10, 12
Linda di Chamounix (Donizetti), 185
Lipton, Martha, 210
List, Emanuel, 182, 185, 210, 218, 220, 225
Listerine, 180
Ljungberg, Göta, 182
Lohengrin (Wagner), 25, 34, 40, 41, 57, 58, 59, 79, 116, 135, 146, 190, 202, 208, 212, 220, 308, 340, 344
London, George, 39, 233, 249, 250, 258, 282; *252*
London: Covent Garden, 13, 47, 66, 68, 75, 136, 149, 287, 325, 344, 356
Long, Kathryn Turney, 219, 312
Lorengar, Pilar, 286, 305
Lorenz, Max, 225
356
Los Angeles, Victoria de, 240–1, 250; *253*
Los Angeles, Cal., 224
Louise (Charpentier), 85, 145, 185, 220, 294
Love, Shirley, 212; *278–9*
Lucia di Lammermoor (Donizetti), 25, 41, 68, 74, 150, 233, 282, 284, 308; *347*
Ludwig, Christa, 281, 305, 316, 318, 324, 331; *319*
Ludwig, Leopold, 324
Luisa Miller (Verdi), 124, 168, 318, 324

Lully, Jean Baptiste, 10
Lulu (Berg), 340; *338*
Lund, John, 59
Lunt, Alfred, 240, 249, 255, 305, 312; *247*

Maag, Peter, 332
Maazel, Lorin, 283
MacArthur, Charles 168
McArthur, Edwin, 196–9, 213
Macbeth (Verdi), 25, 231, 234–6, 260, 282, 332
McCormack, John, 113
McCracken, James, 250–1, 283, 325, 328; *278–9*
McDaniel, Barry 325
Mackay, Clarence H., 112, 113, 159
Mackerras, Charles, 332
McKim, Mead & White, 81
MacNeil, Cornell, 261, 312, 340; *334*
Macurdy, John, 292
Madama Butterfly (Puccini), 92, 102, 104, 106, 134, 145, 169, 174, 218, 219, 251–4, 286, 308, 314
Madame Sans-Gêne (Giordano), 134
Madeira, Jean, 210, 292
Magic Flute, The (Mozart), 25, 78, 121, 146, 148, 220–3, 240, 241, 251, 255, 305–8, 323, 335; *125, 142–3, 309*
Mahler, Alma, 31, 94–5
Mahler, Gustav, 24, 31, 82, 86–7, 95, 98, 99, 100–2, 108–11, 133, 135, 146, 286; *109*
Maison, René, 204, 208, 210
Makarova, Natalia, *337*
Makropoulos Affair, The (Janáček), 311–2
Maliponte, Adriana, 324
Mamelles de Tirésias, Les (Poulenc), 341; *348–9*
Mancinelli, Luigi, 68, 69, 72
Manhattan Opera, 81, 85, 93, 95, 111; *110*
Mankiewicz, Joseph L., 240
Manon (Massenet), 69, 73, 145, 148, 177, 208; *268–9*
Manon Lescaut (Puccini), 92, 116, 260; *346*
Manuel, Michael, 314
Manuguerra, Matteo, 324
Man Without a Country, The (Damrosch), 209, 223
Mapleson, Col. James Henry, 12, 25, 28, 33, 34, 41–4, 48, 57, 58, 112; *50–1*
Mapleson, Lionel, 63, 166
Mario, Queena, 155; *172*
Martha (Flotow), 115, 120
Martin, George A., 231
Martinelli, Giovanni, 31, 131, 133, 148, 166, 186, 193, 203, 204, 205, 213, 292; *152, 217, 293*
Martini, Nino, 180–2
Marton, Eva, *342*
Mascagni, Pietro, 124
Massenet, Jules, 74, 124
Materna, Amalia, 57; *43*
Matz, Mary Jane, 117
Matzenauer, Margarete, 131, 146; *129*
Maurel, Victor, 69, 73, 78, 185
Maxwell, Elsa, 236
Mazura, Franz, *338*

Medea (Cherubini), 234
Mefistofele (Boito), 73, 150, 311
Mehta, Zubin, 286, 308
Meistersinger von Nürnberg, Die (Wagner), 59, 64, 72, 79, 86, 111, 134, 146, 151, 155, 180, 208, 218, 281, 283; *46, 276–7*
Melba, Nellie, 68, 69, 73, 74, 75, 78–9, 93, 116, 117, 130, 225; *32, 56, 70–1*
Melchior, Lauritz, 151–4, 179, 182, 185, 186, 196, 198, 199, 213, 218, 220, 236, 241, 298, 344; *192, 200*
Melton, James, *142–3*
Meltzer, Charles Henry, 90, 100
Meneghini, Giovanni Battista, 232, 233, 234, 354; *235*
Menotti, Gian Carlo, 251
Mercer, Ruby, 204, 205, 209, 213, 283
Meredith, Morley, 282
Merrill, Nathaniel, 281, 283, 284, 305, 318, 324; *276–7*
Merrill, Robert, 209, 250, 261, 283, 286, 294, 324; *222, 329*
Merry Mount (Hanson), 182–5
Messel, Oliver, 283
Metropolitan Opera:
  architecture (old house), 15–18, 22, 34–40, *10, 20–21, 54–55, 84*;
  Auditions of the Air, 209, 216, 231; broadcasts from, 174, 180, 320, 339–40, 355, *172–3, 342–3*; Centennial, 353–4, 356; finances, 19, 22–3, 42–4, 47, 93, 121, 155, 157, 169–71, 175–9, 186, 209, 215–6, 254–5, 270–1, 310, 335–9, 353; fire and rebuilding, 64–7; German seasons, 48–64; labor relations, 94, 297–303, 320–3; move to Lincoln Center, 244, 261, 263–72, 304–10, 336, *273, 296, 300–1, 306–7, 322*; "Mini-Met", 185, 329; National Company, 312–5; National Council, 255, 261, 312, 354, at New Theater, 111; Sherry's restaurant, 34, *54, 288*; Vaudeville Club, 66; see also entries below
Metropolitan Opera and Real Estate Company, 68, 73, 75, 82–5, 92, 94, 105, 120, 158, 162, 175, 190–1, 215
Metropolitan Opera Association, 175–6, 179, 182, 187–90, 193, 203, 215–18, 263, 299
Metropolitan Opera Club, 34, 67, 193, 205; *288*
Metropolitan Opera Guild, 193, 218, 224, 236, 238, 255, 272, 292, 310, 312, 329, 354
Metropolitan Opera Studio, 312
Mielziner, Jo, 121, 177, 328; *178*
Mignon (Thomas), 41, 83, 112, 185
Milan: La Scala, 16, 86, 108, 117–20, 133, 134, 356; Teatro Lirico, 121
Milanov, Zinka, 78, 210, 227, 234, 241, 249, 286, 294, 299; *142–3, 207, 290*
Miller, Alice Duer, 24
Miller, Mildred, 250
Milnes, Sherrill, 286, 312, 318, 320, 325; *334*
Minotis, Alexis, 234

Minton, Yvonne, 335
Mishkin (photographer), 170
Mitropoulos, Dimitri, 231, 233, 248, 251, 254, 258, 260, 281
Mödl, Martha, 251, 344
Moffo, Anna, 281; *268–9*
Moiseiwitsch, Tanya, 308
Molinari-Pradelli, Francesco, 286, 318
Mona (Parker), 123
Monoghan, Roger, 19
Monroe, Lucy, 209
Montemezzi, Italo, 28
Monteux, Pierre, 121, 250
Monteverdi, Claudio, 10
Montreal, 112
Montresor, Beni, 284, 305
Moore, George, 314, 315, 327, 329, 331, 335, 336
Moore, Grace, 154, 220; *189*
Moranzoni, Roberto, 135
Mordkin, Mikhail, 123
Morell, Barry, 260
Morgan (family), 13
Morgan, J. Pierpont, 81, 85, 87–8, 92, 104–5, 162, 182; *91*
Morgan, J. P., Jr., 179, 218
Morris, Benjamin, 162
Morris, James, 324; *338*
Morton, Levi P., 12
Moses, Robert, 263–7
Moshinsky, Elijah, *345*
Mourning Becomes Elektra (Levy), 308
Mozart, Wolfgang Amadeus, 10, 83, 311
Muette de Portici, La (Auber), 57
Müller, Maria, 155, 185, 186, 203, 205
Mulrooney, Edward B., 180
Munsel, Patrice, 209; *247*
Muzio, Claudia, 148; *189*

Nabucco (Verdi), 282
Nagasaka, Motohiro, 254
National Broadcasting Company (NBC), 128, 170, 171–4, 179, 180, 191–3
National Endowment for the Arts, 315, 339, 340
Navarraise, La (Massenet), 72
Neher, Caspar, 203, 231, 234, 260–1
Newman, Ernest, 30
New York:
  American, 90, 100, 102, 193;
  City Ballet, 270, 271;
  City Opera, 241, 271, 310–12, *313*;
  Daily News, 234;
  Daily Telegraph, 88, 105, 180–2;
  Dramatic Mirror, 24, 34, 44;
  Evening Journal, 168;
  Evening Post, 25, 100, 104;
  Evening Sun, 88;
  Herald, 24, 127;
  Herald Tribune, 185, 196;
  Philharmonic Orchestra, 10, 72, 112, 186–7, 190, 191, 263, 267, 287;
  Post, 236;
  Press, 102, 103, 105;
  Radio City Music Hall, 190;
  Saturday Review, 260;
  Sun, 99, 103, 111, 120, 182, 196;
  Times, 30, 39–40, 79, 90, 93, 103,

108, 151, 179, 180, 186, 196, 245, 250–1, 281, 335;
  Tribune, 33, 47, 92, 103;
  World, 98;
  see also Brooklyn, Manhattan, and under names of institutions, etc.
New Yorker, The, 260; *226*
Niemann, Albert, 28, 59; *60–1*
Nilsson, Birgit, 33, 150, 251, 261, 281, 282–3, 284, 291, 294, 308, 316, 318, 324–5, 327, 335; *269, 293, 350*
Nilsson, Christine, 28, 31, 33–4, 41, 44, 47, 48, 294; *35*
Niska, Maralin, 312
Noble, Helen, 127
Nordica, Lillian, 63, 64, 67, 69, 72, 73, 74, 75, 78, 79, 85, 136, 196; *70–1*
Norma (Bellini), 149, 212, 233, 284, 299, 323; *138*
Notte di Zoraïma, La (Montemezzi), 124
Novak, Joseph, 165, 215; *206*
Novara, Franco, 63
Novotna, Jarmila, 210, 220; *142–3, 217, 229*
Nozze di Figaro, Le (Mozart), 25, 69, 98, 99, 100–2, 108–11, 135, 154, 220, 234, 250, 281, 312, 314, 318; *109, 142–3, 214*

Ober, Margarete, *125*
Oberon (Weber), 149
Odell, George, 10
O'Dwyer, William, 263
Oedipus Rex (Stravinsky), 341; *337*
Oenslager, Donald, 121, 182
O'Hearn, Robert, 281, 283, 284, 305, 318, 324; *276–7*
Olds, Irving, 267, 270
Olivero, Magda, 335
Olszewska, Maria, 177, 185, 193, 196, 203, 205
Onegin, Sigrid, 155
O'Neil, Katharine T., 339
O'Neill, Eugene, 177, 308
Opera News, 238, 321, 339, 340
Oracolo, L' (Leoni), 124; *122, 188*
Orfeo ed Euridice (Gluck), 121, 146, 208, 212, 323–4, 332
Ormandy, Eugene, 249, 344
Orwell, George, 245
Otello (Verdi), 25, 69, 83, 108, 146, 151, 212, 283, 325, 332–5; *107, 278–9*

Page, Ruth, 208
Pagliacci, I (Leoncavallo), 112, 116–17, 149, 208, 244–5, 260, 323; *280*
Panizza, Ettore, 193
Papi, Gennaro, 121, 150, 208
Parade (French works), 341; *348–9*
Paris: Opéra, 9, 66, 287, 305, 344, 356; Palais Garnier, 16
Parkhurst, Charles, 67, 68
Parravicini, Angelo, 98
Parsifal (Wagner), 90, 94, 104, 146, 196, 281, 324, 344; *91*
Patti, Adelina, 10, 12, 31, 41–2, 44, 48, 63, 67, 115, 354; *11*

366

Pauly, Rose, 210
Paur, Emil, 63
Pavarotti, Luciano, 318, 325, 340; 345
Pavlova, Anna, 121
Pears, Peter, 331, 340
Pêcheurs de perles, Les (Bizet), 72
Peerce, Jan 210, 225, 283; 222
Pelléas et Mélisande (Debussy), 85, 148, 205, 212, 220, 283, 325
Pelletier, Wilfred, 240
Périchole, La (Offenbach), 250, 255
Perlea, Jonel, 240
Perry, John M., 203
Perry, Commodore Matthew 10
Peter Grimes (Britten), 223, 308; 319
Peter Ibbetson (Taylor), 30, 123, 180, 182–5
Peters, Roberta, 241, 251; 242
Petina, Irra, 172
Philadelphia: 44, 72, 85, 103, 111, 165; — Academy of Music, 15, 112, 228; — Orchestra, 249, 344
Philémon et Baucis (Gounod), 68
Pilou, Jeannette, 318
Pini-Corsi, Antonio, 78
Pinza, Ezio, 31, 154, 170, 185, 186, 193, 212, 218–19, 220, 298; 142–3, 207, 214
Pipe of Desire, The (Converse), 123
Pique Dame (Tchaikovsky), 99, 146, 286
Plançon, Pol, 68, 69, 73, 75
Plishka, Paul, 308, 340; 278–9
Pogany, Willy, 121; 140–1
Polacco, Giorgio, 135
Ponnelle, Jean-Pierre, 328
Pons, Lily, 31, 171, 179, 185, 186, 198, 203, 204, 205, 213, 292; 183, 192
Ponselle, Rosa, 31, 149, 174, 185, 186, 203, 205, 212, 281, 283, 335; 152, 172, 192
Popp, Lucia, 305–8
Porgy and Bess (Gershwin), 185
Prêtre, Georges, 284, 286
Prey, Hermann, 305
Price, Leontyne, 31, 281, 282, 283, 291, 294, 303, 305, 308, 320; 268, 278–9
Prince Igor (Borodin), 124
Prisoner, The (Dallapiccola), 312
Prophète, Le (Meyerbeer), 57, 340
Public Broadcasting Service (PBS), 339–40, 355
Puccini, Giacomo, 28, 85, 92, 95, 102; 119
Puritani, I (Bellini), 233
Puvis de Chavannes, Pierre, 121

Queen of Sheba, The (Goldmark) 59
Queen of Spades, The, see Pique Dame
Quintero, José, 240, 260

Rachmaninoff, Sergei, 123
Raidich, Hubert, 204
Raimondi, Ruggiero, 324
Rake's Progress, The (Stravinsky), 249–50, 311, 327
Rape of Lucretia, The (Britten), 314
Raskin, Judith, 282, 284, 312; 309
Ravogli, Giulia, 64
RCA Victor, 248

Reader's Digest, 315
Reamer, Lawrence, 79
Reardon, John, 312
Reichmann, Theodor, 60–1
Reiner, Fritz, 220, 225, 241, 243, 248–9, 250, 344
Reinhardt, Max, 127
Renaud, Maurice, 93, 154, 185
Rennert, Günther, 282, 308
Resnik, Regina, 209, 223, 284, 286, 308; 285
Rethberg, Elisabeth, 151, 174, 185, 193, 203, 204, 212, 292; 167, 214
Rheingold, Das (Wagner), 86, 208, 225, 316–18; 317; see also Ring des Nibelungen
Ricciarelli, Katia, 335; 334
Richards, Harry, 169
Richmond, Va., 171
Ricordi, G., 85, 121
Ridderbusch, Karl, 316, 318
Riedel, Karl, 195
Riegel, Kenneth, 312
Rienzi (Wagner), 59
Rigal, Delia, 240; 239
Rigoletto (Verdi), 9, 25, 30, 41, 44, 57, 79, 108, 115, 128, 133, 150, 155, 180–2, 208, 212, 249, 261, 286, 315, 335
Riis, Jacob, 67
Ring des Nibelungen, Der (Wagner), 63, 75, 78, 79, 121, 154, 170, 223, 224–5, 228, 240, 241, 251, 282–3, 316–18, 328, 329, 344; see also Das Rheingold; Die Walküre; Siegfried; Götterdämmerung
Rise and Fall of the City of Mahagonny, The (Brecht/Weill), 340
Ritchard, Cyril, 240, 250, 255
Robert le Diable (Meyerbeer), 41
Robinson, Adolf, 57, 59
Robinson, Francis, 243, 248, 258, 286; 257
Robinson, Gail, 323
Rochester, N.Y., 166
Rockefeller, (family), 190, 267
Rockefeller, John D., Jr., 190–1, 215, 266
Rockefeller, John D. III, 267–71
Rockefeller, Martha Baird, 238, 255, 336
Rockefeller, William, 331, 335
Rockefeller Center, 190
Rockefeller Foundation, 339
Rodzinski, Artur, 228
Roller, Alfred, 83
Roméo et Juliette (Gounod), 47, 67, 79, 148, 318
Rondine, La (Puccini), 156
Roosevelt, James Alfred, 19, 64, 66; 17
Roosevelt, Theodore, 67, 82, 297
Rosa, Carl, 47–8
Rosenkavalier, Der (R. Strauss), 94, 121, 124, 148, 150, 182, 209–10, 212, 220, 225, 241, 281, 283, 284, 318; 125, 351
Rosenstock, Joseph, 318
Rosenthal, Manuel, 341
Rossi-Lemeni, Nicola, 250
Rossignol, Le (Stravinsky), 341; 337
Rossini, Gioacchino, 58
Rota, Vittorio, 98
Rothenberger, Anneliese, 281
Rothschild (family), 12

Rubinstein, Artur, 123
Rudel, Julius, 311, 312; 313
Rudolf, Max, 213, 220, 223–4, 227, 237, 243, 245, 248, 332, 341
Ruffo, Titta, 150–1
Russell, Henry, 112
Russell, Lillian, 73
Ryan, Mrs. John Barry, 238, 315
Rychtarik, Richard, 142–3
Rysanek, Leonie, 236, 260, 282, 305, 308; 268–9, 319, 350

Sachs, Harvey, 106–8, 133
Sacre du Printemps, Le (Stravinsky), 170, 341; 337
Sadko (Rimsky-Korsakov), 170
St. Elizabeth (Liszt), 149
St. Leger, Frank, 219, 225, 237, 243
St. Louis, Mo., 44
Sala, Mario, 98
Saléza, Albert, 78
Salome (R. Strauss), 9, 85, 92, 93, 121, 182, 220, 225, 251, 284; 91
Salvi, Luigi, 10
Samaroff-Stokowski, Olga, 174
Samson et Dalila (Saint-Saëns), 116, 128, 281, 284
San Francisco: earthquake, 93; — Opera, 225, 336, 340
Sanderson, Sybil, 69
Sargeant, Winthrop, 260
Sarnoff, David, 191, 223, 237
Sayão, Bidu, 208, 210, 220; 142–3, 221
Scalchi, Sofia, 63, 69, 73
Schalk, Franz, 63, 78, 130
Scheff, Fritzi, 79
Schenk, Otto, 318, 324, 341; 342–3, 352
Schertel, Anton, 166
Schick, George, 260
Schiff, Mortimer, 171
Schikaneder, Emanuel, 305
Schipa, Tito, 177, 185, 203, 205
Schippers, Thomas, 251, 283, 286, 305, 308, 331, 332
Schmedes, Erik, 24, 88, 103
Schneider-Siemssen, Günther, 316, 324, 341; 317, 352
Schoeffel, John B., 64
Schoen-René, Anna, 145–6
Schorr, Friedrich, 151, 185, 186, 196, 218; 160
Schott, Anton, 57, 59
Schröder-Hanfstängl, Marie, 57
Schubert, Franz, 208
Schuman, William, 223
Schumann, Elisabeth, 154
Schumann-Heink, Ernestine, 78; 188–9
Schwanda the Bagpiper (Weinberger), 124; 160
Schwarzkopf, Elisabeth, 241, 284
Scott, Norman, 284
Scotti, Antonio, 78, 92, 93, 102, 103, 104, 105–6, 108, 111, 117, 124, 146, 150, 151, 294; 107, 122, 188
Scotto, Renata, 286, 308, 339–40; 346
Seattle Opera, 328
Seebach, Julius, 243
Segurola, Andrés de, 117, 166
Seidl, Anton, 10, 28, 57, 59–64, 67, 72, 73, 78, 99, 133; 45, 60–1

Seidl-Kraus, Auguste, 57, 59; 46
Sembrich, Marcella, 28, 31, 41, 47, 48, 75–8, 92, 103, 104, 106, 108; 29, 56
Serafin, Tullio, 135, 151, 180, 182, 186, 187, 193, 233
Sereni, Mario, 284, 294
Serkin, Rudolf, 336, 341
Setti, Giulio, 98; 156
Shane, Rita, 335
Shapiro, Marilyn, 339
Shaw, George Bernard, 67, 90
Sherwin-Williams Paint Company, 209, 216, 231
Shirley, George, 282; 309
Shirley-Quirk, John, 331
Siegfried (Wagner), 74, 75, 146, 151, 328, 335; see also Ring des Nibelungen
Siepi, Cesare, 240, 249, 251, 286, 294, 324; 239
Signor Bruschino, Il (Rossini), 154
Silja, Anja, 324
Sills, Beverly, 312, 331; 313
Simionato, Giulietta, 281
Simon, Eric, 195
Simon Boccanegra (Verdi), 124; 259
Simoneau, Léopold, 284
Simonson, Lee, 224–5
Singher, Martial, 209, 220
Slezak, Leo, 31, 117–20, 146; 107, 125
Sloan, George, 237–8, 254, 255, 298, 299
Smith, Maurice, 297
Smith, Max, 103, 105
Snow Maiden, The (Rimsky-Korsakov), 124
Sodero, Cesare, 220
Söderström, Elisabeth, 281
Solti, Georg, 283, 308, 356
Sonnambula, La (Bellini), 10
Sontag, Henriette, 10
Sotin, Hans, 305
Sparkes, Leonora, 108–11; 126
Speck, Jules, 166
Spessitseva, Olga, 204
Spetrino, Francesco, 86, 103, 104
Spofford, Charles M., 216, 237–8, 254, 255, 263–70, 310, 331
Stagno, Roberto, 41; 38
Stanton, Edmund C., 28, 36, 59, 63; 43
Staudigl, Josef, 57
Steber, Eleanor, 209, 220, 225, 240, 251, 260, 281; 142–3, 247
Stein, Gertrude, 185
Steinberg, William, 286, 332
Steiner, Hans, 88, 98
Steinway, William, 73, 79
Stella, Antonietta, 251, 291
Stephen, Percy Rector, 202
Stevens, Risë, 145, 171, 209–10, 212, 220, 225, 241, 249, 287, 292, 303, 314; 211, 246, 293
Stevens, Roger, 315
Stewart, Thomas, 286, 316; 317
Stiedry, Fritz, 225, 237, 238, 240, 249, 251
Stignani, Ebe, 204
Stilwell, Richard, 335, 340
Stivender, David, 332
Stockholm Royal Opera, 327
Stokowski, Leopold, 170, 281, 292; 293

Stolze, Gerhard, 316–18
Stotesbury, Edward T., 159
Stratas, Teresa, 261, 286, 308, 340; *338, 346*
Straus, Noel, 250–1
Strauss, Richard, 28, 121, 130, 311
Stravinsky, Igor, 170
Stringer, Robert, 255
Sullivan, Ed, 255
Susannah (Floyd), 314
Sutherland, Joan, 282, 284, 308, 323, 325, 328; *347*
Svanholm, Set, 225, 228, 241
Svoboda, Josef, 328, 332
Swarthout, Gladys, 171, 185; *184, 192*
Szell, George, 130, 196, 204, 208, 220, 227, 250, 341, 344

Tabarro, Il (Puccini), 148; see also *Il Trittico*
Taft, William Howard, 82
Tagliavini, Ferruccio, 225
Tajo, Italo, 225
Talley, Marion, 155; *188–9*
Talvela, Martti, 318, 331; *333*
Tamagno, Francesco, 69
Tannhäuser (Wagner), 57, 58, 59, 135, 146, 151, 154, 182, 208, 250, 282, 292, 299, 328, 341, 344; *342–3*
Taplin, Frank E., 310, 314–15, 336–9, 353, 354
Taubman, Howard, 251, 281
Taylor, Joseph Deems, 174
Taylor, Myron C., 179, 190–1
Tebaldi, Renata, 234, 251, 258, 260, 283, 305, 344; *252, 257, 278–9*
Te Kanawa, Kiri, 332–5; *351*
Tentoni, Rosa, 204, 209
Ternina, Milka, 78
Tetrazzini, Luisa, 85, 95, 149, 154
Texaco, 218, 292, 340, 355
Thaïs (Massenet), 85, 150
Thebom, Blanche, 210; *247*
Thomas, Jess, 283, 284, 305, 324–5
Thomas, John Charles, 185, 208; *184*
Thomas, Thomas L., 209
Thompson, Oscar, 195
Thomson, Virgil, 210, 220–3, 240, 243, 250
Thorborg, Kerstin, 218, 220, 227
Tibbett, Lawrence, 31, 69, 123, 151, 177, 180, 182–5, 193, 210, 220, 297, 298, 335; *161, 178, 188*
Tiefland (D'Albert), 98, 104
Tietjens, Heinz, 203, 208

Time Magazine, 187, 190, 258
Tokatyan, Armand, *156*
Tosca (Puccini), 93, 94, 104, 112, 134, 150, 154, 220, 233, 258, 286, 315, 318–20, 324, 335; *252*
Toscanini, Arturo, 82–3, 85–8, 95, 98, 99–106, 108, 111, 117, 121, 123, 124, 131–4, 136, 146, 150, 202, 212, 344, 353, 356; *80, 107, 118–19*
Tote Stadt, Die (Korngold), 30, 124, 150
Tourel, Jennie, 209
Tozzi, Giorgio, 251; *276–7*
Traubel, Helen, 209, 210, 220, 225, 241; *200*
Traviata, La (Puccini), 9, 25, 41, 74, 75, 93, 104, 148, 150, 185, 208, 210, 223, 232, 233, 234, 236, 305, 312, 314; *144*
Trebelli, Zelia, 41, 47; *38*
Treigle, Norman, 312; *313*
Tristan und Isolde (Wagner), 10, 24, 28, 63, 72, 74, 75, 78, 79, 82, 86–7, 99, 108, 111, 135, 146, 154, 196, 199, 202, 208, 220, 228, 233, 241, 249, 283, 316; *222, 280*
Trittico, Il (Puccini), 148; see also *Gianni Schicchi; Il Tabarro*
Trovatore, Il (Verdi), 25, 41, 115, 133, 134, 146, 166, 209, 232, 233, 234, 241, 281, 294, 308, 320; *268*
Troyanos, Tatiana, 312; *324*
Troyens, Les (Berlioz), 328, 331
Truman, Harry S., 254
Tucci, Gabriella, 281, 283, 284, 286
Tucker, Richard, 210, 213, 225, 234, 240, 241, 249, 281, 282, 286, 294, 318; *222, 280*
Tuggle, Robert A., 150
Turandot (Puccini), 150, 233, 281; *160*

Uhde, Hermann, 260; *253*
Ulfung, Ragnar, 327, 335, 340
Unruh, Walter, 272
Uppman, Theodor, 250, 251
Urban, Joseph, 121, 162, 250; *138–9, 161, 183*

Valente, Benita, 335
Valletti, Cesare, 251, 282
Van Dam, José, *333*
Vanderbilt (family), 13, 65–6
Vanderbilt, Cornelius (III), 65–6

Vanderbilt, Mrs. Cornelius (II), *17*
Vanderbilt, Mrs. Cornelius (III), 163, 218; *226*
Vanderbilt, William H. 15, 18–19; *17*
Vanderbilt, William K., 13, 16, 93, 128
Vanderbilt, Mrs. William K., 81; *17*
Van Dyck, Ernest, 75, 78
Vanessa (Barber), 215, 286
Van Norden, Langdon, 292
Van Rensselaer, M. G. 39, 40
Van Rooy, Anton, 78, 185
Varnay, Astrid, 210, 212, 340, 344; *200*
Varviso, Silvio, 282
Vaudeville Club, 66–7
Velis, Andrea, 212, 284, 308
Verdi, Giuseppe, 69, 83, 131; Requiem, 111, 202, 241
Verrett, Shirley, 312, 318, 331
Vespri Siciliani, I (Verdi), 331, 332
Vianesi, Augusto, 34, 39, 40, 44, 67
Vickers, Jon, 234, 261, 281, 286, 294, 308, 316, 324; *319*
Victor, Royall, Jr., 314–15
Victor Talking Machine Company, 169–70
Vida Breve, La (Falla), 124; *138*
Vienna: Court Opera, 9; — State Opera, 78, 344
Villa, Luigi, 124–7
Villi, Le (Puccini), 98
Vinay, Ramon, 225, 344
Vishnevskaya, Galina, 282
Volpe, Joseph, 353
Von Stade, Frederica, 323; *333*
Von Wymetal, William, 166; *156*
Votipka, Thelma, 212; *144, 229*

Wadmond, Lowell, 329, 331
Wagner, Cosima, 90
Wagner, Richard, 10, 16, 28, 39, 48, 57–8, 59–63, 83, 90, 121, 136, 199, 356
Wagner, Wieland, 308
Walküre, Die (Wagner), 57, 59, 63, 103–4, 135, 151, 169, 182, 196, 212, 225, 286, 316–18; see also *Ring des Nibelungen*
Wallace, Mrs. DeWitt, 238, 315
Wallerstein, Lothar, 203, 219, 223
Wally, La (Catalani), 98
Walsh, Dick, 299
Walter, Bruno, 154, 212, 219, 220–3, 240, 241–3, 245, 251, 255; *142–3*
Warburg, Felix, 203

Ward, David, 284
Wardwell, Allen, 202–3, 216, 223, 263
Warren, Agathe, 231
Warren, George Henry, 13
Warren, Leonard, 209, 212, 220, 231–2, 249, 281; *259*
Warrior, The (Rogers), 223
Washington, D.C., 44
Watson, Thomas J., 218
Weber, Carl Maria von, 10
Webster, Margaret, 240, 249; *239, 259*
Wechsler, Gil, 353
Weede, Robert, 210
Weigert, Herman, 220
Weikl, Bernd, *342*
Weil, Irving, 168–9
Weill, Kurt, 212
Weingartner, Felix, 88
Welitsch, Ljuba, 225, 241; *221*
Welting, Patricia, 308
Welting, Ruth, 312; *352*
Werther (Massenet), 69, 324
Wexler, Peter, *345*
Weyerhaeuser, Mrs. Frederick K., 238
Wharton, Edith, 12–13
Whitehill, Clarence, 154–5
Whitman, Walt, 10, 58, 124
Whitney, Cornelius Vanderbilt, 159
Whitney, Harry Payne, 81, 159
Wiener, Otto, 283
Windgassen, Wolfgang, 251
Witherspoon, Herbert, 187, 202, 203–5, 208, 209, 212, 231; *197*
Wixell, Ingvar, 335
Women's National Republican Club, 228
Wozzeck (Berg), 170, 234, 260–1, 332; *253*

Ysaÿe, Eugene, 123

Zauberflöte, Die, see *Magic Flute*
Zaza (Leoncavallo), 145, 166; *147*
Zeffirelli, Franco, 234, 282, 284, 304, 323, 325, 341; *278–9, 280, 285*
Ziegler, Edward, 127–30, 145, 149, 151, 165, 166–8, 169, 174–5, 176, 179, 186, 195, 198, 199, 202, 205, 219, 224, 225, 227, 244, 254, 297, 298; *197*
Zirato, Bruno, 185, 186
Zylis-Gara, Teresa, 318, 325; *278–9*